Dirty Discourse

Dirty Discourse

Sex and Indecency in Broadcasting

Second edition
Robert L. Hilliard and Michael C. Keith

Blackwell
Publishing

BLACKWELL PUBLISHING

350 Main Street, Malden, MA 02148-5020, USA
9600 Garsington Road, Oxford OX4 2DQ, UK
550 Swanston Street, Carlton, Victoria 3053, Australia

The right of Robert L. Hilliard and Michael C. Keith to be identified as the Authors of this Work has been asserted in accordance with the UK Copyright, Designs, and Patents Act 1988.

First published 2003 by Iowa State University Press
Second edition published 2007 by Blackwell Publishing Ltd

1   2007

Library of Congress Cataloging-in-Publication Data

Hilliard, Robert L., 1925–
    Dirty discourse : sex and indecency in broadcasting / Robert L. Hilliard and Michael C. Keith.–2nd ed.
        p.   cm.
    Includes bibliographical references and index.
    ISBN-13: 978-1-4051-5053-8 (pbk. : alk. paper)
    ISBN-10: 1-4051-5053-X (pbk. : alk. paper)
    1. Sex on radio–United States.   I. Keith, Michael C., 1945–   II. Title.

PN1991.8.S44H55 2006
791.44′6538–dc22

                                                                2006006919

A catalogue record for this title is available from the British Library.

Set in 10.5 on 12.5 pt Dante
by SNP Best-set Typesetter Ltd, Hong Kong
Printed and bound in Singapore
by COS Printers Pte Ltd

The publisher's policy is to use permanent paper from mills that operate a sustainable forestry policy, and which has been manufactured from pulp processed using acid-free and elementary chlorine-free practices. Furthermore, the publisher ensures that the text paper and cover board used have met acceptable environmental accreditation standards.

For further information on
Blackwell Publishing, visit our website:
www.blackwellpublishing.com

There is what I call the American idea. . . . I will call it the idea of freedom.

—**Theodore Parker**

Because the touchstone of indecency determinations—contemporary standards—is subjective, the distinctions that arise from that standard are arbitrary and seem more arbitrary the more they are explained.

—**John Crigler**

CONTENTS

FOREWORD

This book examines a most important and complicated topic. One of the central questions it probes is whether or not the government should continue to expect broadcasters to operate in a manner that upholds community standards pertaining to moral conduct and behavior. My answer is an unequivocal yes because broadcasting is different than other media. I go back many years to what my law school friend Justice John Stevens wrote in a Supreme Court First Amendment opinion about why radio is different. When you are in a car with a child there is no way you can edit or censor what is coming out of the speaker. It comes at you without warning, so as long as we are concerned as a society about protecting and helping our young people, I don't think there will be an end to the limits pertaining to what can be said over the air. The Supreme Court has made it clear that with respect to the First Amendment broadcasting is a special case because it uses the public airwaves. Not everyone who wants to be a broadcaster can be one. It is a privilege to get a broadcast license, which under our law requires holders to serve the public and not the private interest. There will always be arguments about the First Amendment. They are healthy arguments, and they should continue, but I don't think that the First Amendment as applied to broadcasting is the same as it is when applied to other media, such as print. Debating significant issues is a good thing. It is what has made this country strong. Of course, to argue any point effectively, you must be well informed. Hilliard and Keith offer enough information on the subject of indecency and obscenity in radio to give the reader a solid appreciation and understanding of this ongoing and controversial issue.

Newton N. Minow
Northwestern University,
Annenberg Professor of Communication, Law and Policy;
former Chair, Federal Communications Commission

PREFACE

Freedom of speech is what differentiates democracies from most other forms of government. When a government—federal, state or local—imposes restrictions on what its citizens may say out of its belief that "big brother" knows best, then civil liberties are threatened.

When it is done for political purposes—sometimes under the guise of national emergencies as during America's era of McCarthyism when the public was brainwashed to believe that anyone who disagreed with McCarthy was a threat to the country's well-being—the democracy teeters on the edge of fascism.

In most countries criticism of the nation's leaders is tantamount to treason, based on the "if you don't support us, you're against us" dictum. With rare exceptions America's leaders have resisted this means of gaining or consolidating power. Most have agreed, albeit sometimes reluctantly, with Republican president Theodore Roosevelt that "to announce there must be no criticism of the president, or that we are to stand by the president right or wrong, is not only unpatriotic and servile, but is morally treasonable to the American public."

Is there not, then, any speech that is impermissible in a democracy? Over the years government control of political speech has fluctuated with the political attitudes of the country as a whole, most often resulting in post-facto mea culpas that are ignored and repeated from time to time. What most Americans have with some consistency generally agreed upon, however, since the European settlement of this part of the North American continent, is the unacceptability of speech that is obscene, profane, blasphemous or indecent. As historically presented in Chapter 1 of this book, the United States has long been a country that has reflected the legacy of the Puritanism and Victorianism brought by the earliest immigrants.

The problem is that changes in time and social attitudes, the pluralistic nature of the citizenry and the geographic breadth of the commonwealth preclude a common definition of what is indecent and even of what is profane or obscene. What may appear to be "dirty discourse" to some may be considered to be laudable satire to others.

Where at one time perceived dirty discourse was dealt with at the local level on which it was disseminated, the advent of the mass electronic media now makes such communication a national matter—and with the development of the Internet, an international concern.

We try in this book to present not only information on what constitutes alleged dirty discourse and the development and current status of statute, case and administrative law dealing with it, but also the beliefs, attitudes and actions of those who present such material, those who condemn such material and those who defend it. Needless to say, our principal concentration is on the means of greatest distribution—radio with the phenomenal growth of "shock jocks" and rap music lyrics at the end of the twentieth century and the beginning of the twenty-first. We give more moderate attention to television and the Internet.

Even as authors we are sometimes not sure what we would label obscene or profane or indecent. The language of sex and dirty words, as disturbing as it sometimes is to us, is not as disturbing as the language we discuss in our book *Waves of Rancor: Tuning in the Radical Right*, in which the language of hate groups advocating hatred and violence against designated minority and other groups appears to us to be the extreme of dirty discourse.

But, as you read this book, judge for yourself. Should Mae West have been penalized in the 1930s for sexual innuendo, without uttering a profane word, to a greater degree than Howard Stern has been for overt sexual descriptions and profane language in the past decade?

Many, if not most, Americans think that concern with indecency in the media began with the partial baring on television of one of Janet Jackson's breasts in the 2004 Super Bowl half-time show. Crackdowns on perceptions of indecency in America have been going on since even before the British colonies became the United States. Compared to shock-jock material, co-medians' late-night "blue" routines, and many prime-time sex-oriented sitcoms, the Jackson *cause célèbre* was, in the opinion of many media experts, rather mild. Yet, it set off the strongest nationwide protests, fueled by media exploitation, and resulted in the strongest government reaction and action in our history regarding indecency.

If, after you have finished this book, you can devise reasonable definitions of the obscene, profane and indecent that can be applied to the mass media today, please let us know, for it's something we believe Congress, the courts and the Federal Communications Commission have not yet been able to do.

Another kind of censorship that we believe to be more insidious than that related to material labeled as indecent is the censoring of ideas and information. This kind of censorship is endemic in governments that attempt to control their citizens' hearts and minds, given that radio and television, in today's world, are the most powerful forces for manipulating people's beliefs and feelings. Such media control is common practice in totalitarian governments and even in ostensibly democratic countries where the party in power wishes to convince the public to support its special interest agenda and its efforts to stay in power. In such situations alternative viewpoints and even objective information are labeled "right wing" or "left wing" (depending on the political orientation of the party in power) and condemned as being false and prejudicial. In the United States the alternative media system is what we call public broadcasting, the noncommercial radio and television stations and networks differentiated from the dominant privately owned broadcasting entities. Because it has generally offered information and ideas—both objective and alternative—not provided by the politically conservative owned and operated private media, public broadcasting has frequently been vilified by political parties and politicians who do not wish the public to see that, on occasion, the Emperor's clothes are indeed deceptive. In the United States, at this writing in 2006, the increasingly extremist right-wing government has taken unprecedented steps to censor and even to try to eliminate the alternative potentials of public broadcasting. Using the time-worn crying-wolf term of "liberal"—a pejorative term in a conservative political atmosphere— President George W. Bush, through his appointed head of the Corporation for Public Broadcasting, has attempted to remove any critical information about or discussion of his controversial policies by vilifying public broadcasting, demanding that it censor any material not supportive of his administration's beliefs and policies, and drastically cutting its appropriations. Should he succeed, America will no longer have free, alternative media discourse. We would consider such a situation the epitome of real indecency.

We wish to thank Elizabeth Swayze, Laura Stearns, Desiree Zicko, Tessa Hanford, and their colleagues at Blackwell Publishing, the media personalities and critics who provided comments for this book, and our friends and family members who lent their encouragement and support. And, lest we forget, our appreciation to the Tom Paines and William O. Douglases who have fought and continue to fight to protect America's freedom of speech, press and assembly and all of our personal civil liberties and rights against those who would usurp them, whether the usurpers are foreign, domestic or in our own government.

CHAPTER 1

I CAN'T DEFINE IT, BUT . . .

In 1937 Mae West, the Hollywood sex symbol of the 1930s, was blacklisted from radio for several decades. In a skit about the Garden of Eden on NBC's *Chase and Sanborn Hour*, written by famed radio writer Arch Oboler, she played the role of Eve seducing Adam. She wasn't blacklisted because of *what* she said. It was the *way* she said it—with the sultry, sexual innuendo in the *tone* of voice that was expected of her. By today's standards her performance and the skit would hardly raise an eyebrow. But then, the Federal Communications Commission (FCC), reflecting the standards of so-called morality at the time, reprimanded NBC, and NBC banished West from the principal mass medium of that era.[1]

In 1996 the FCC fined a station $10,000 for carrying a Howard Stern program that included the following dialogue:

> So, I start dancing with her . . . I'm rubbing . . . she doesn't have any panties on. I'm rubbing her legs . . . and I'm squeezing her ass . . . once in a while my arm slides into the wrong place, you know what I mean? . . . I'm manipulating her . . . spreading her cheeks . . . had her going, writhing with pleasure . . . then I got her down on the bed and then with the vibrators . . . and the vibrator disappeared . . . and my tongue was used.[2]

The degree of dirty discourse in Stern's performance was considerably more than that in the vocal quality of Mae West's. Yet West's punishment considerably exceeded that levied on Stern and the station carrying his program. Why the discrepancy?

Certainly, time—60 years in this instance—was a factor. Public attitudes change with time, and official implementation of those attitudes changes concomitantly. Place, however, is also a factor. What may be regarded as

1

indecent by most of the population in one geographic area or in one town or city may not be so considered in another. Supreme Court Justice Potter Stewart summed up the problem many years ago when he said that he couldn't define obscenity, but that "I know it when I see it."[3]

Since the establishment of the Federal Radio Commission in 1927, federal regulators have been trying to establish definitions of indecency and obscenity. Today, the Federal Communications Commission relies on a 1973 Supreme Court decision that may be the best effort possible, but that still leaves the meanings cloudy and confused.

The FCC has noted that obscene material has been defined by the Supreme Court as follows:[4]

(1) an average person, applying contemporary community standards, must find that the material, as a whole, appeals to the prurient interest;

(2) the material must depict or describe, in a patently offensive way as measured by contem porary community standards, sexual or excretory conduct;

(3) the material, taken as a whole, must lack serious literary, artistic, political, or scientific value.

While noting that obscene material is banned from the airwaves at all times, in a 1987 statement asserting its commitment to monitor indecency over the airwaves, the FCC used some of the Supreme Court's language above to define indecency for purposes of limiting the broadcast of such materials, with the exception of specified hours under the label of adult programming:

Language or material that depicts or describes, in terms patently offensive as measured by contemporary community standards for the broadcast medium, sexual or excretory activities or organs.[5]

Given the impossibility of defining who an "average" person is and the existence of a myriad of contemporary community standards, depending on what locality in the country one happens to be in at a given time, one falls back on the subjective "I know it when I see it." In other words, no one size fits all.

From Whence it Came

The roots of attempts to define obscenity and control it in the supposed public interest, as applied to the United States and, in particular, its mass media, go back long before the United States became a sovereign entity.

The concepts of indecency or obscenity, as we think of them today, developed primarily in the English common law of the seventeenth and eighteenth centuries. Prior to that, censorship of public utterances, verbally or in print, was principally oriented to political and religious speech. In the Middle Ages in Europe, the power of the Catholic Church included censorship and punishment for dissemination of material it disapproved of. But the church's concern was more with blasphemy and heresy than it was with sexual material. Still, Boccaccio's *Decameron*, a classic in its brothel language and licentious stories, was banned by the pope in the thirteenth century, not for its obscenity, however, but for its satire—satire of the clergy.

A couple of centuries later the first Catholic index of banned books was issued. Again, indecency or obscenity per se was not the issue—the books on the list were banned because of their "theological errors."

Pre-Victorian England was as hypocritically Victorian as its succeeding generations. In the early eighteenth century the controlling powers began to seek action against representations of sex in literature. The increasing literacy among populations no longer restricted the reading of bawdy writing to the elite, many of whom believed that they could not be corrupted by such material, but that the rest of the population could be. Not yet governed by precedents of common law, prosecutions took place in the church. In fact, the first case brought to the civil courts, in the early 1700s, was dismissed because the government had not yet enacted any laws pertaining to indecency or obscenity in writing, and the case was referred to the church courts.

In 1725 the first conviction for obscenity in the civil courts, that is, under English common law, was for the writing of a book entitled *Venus in the Cloister, or the Nun in the Smock*. The author, Richard Curl, was charged with disturbing society's civil order. From that time on, concerns about and prosecutions of the writing and distributing of alleged obscene materials increased, and catch-all laws were developed to cope with the increasingly common phenomenon through the remainder of the eighteenth century.

Administrators in the British colonies in North America not only reflected the attitudes in the mother country, but sometimes went beyond them in restricting material that disturbed their fancies. The colonial legislature of Massachusetts led the way in 1712 with a law that criminalized the publishing of "any filthy, obscene, or profane song, pamphlet, libel or mock sermon."[6] The censure of the church restricted the speech of lay and religious people alike.

Arguably one of the most important events regarding the suppression of alleged obscene speech was the founding in England in 1802, by Thomas Bowdler, of the Society for the Suppression of Vice. His effectiveness in censoring any material he and his followers considered immoral or improper gave us the term *bowdlerize*. In the decade following the founding of his society, dozens of writers and publishers were convicted of disseminating obscene materials.

New World Standards

Although no longer colonies of England, the United States did not extend its newfound political freedom, or its First Amendment guarantees of freedom of speech and press, to speech, literature or arts that might be considered an affront to the puritan sensibilities of its leading citizens. The first common law conviction for obscenity in the United States was of Jesse Sharpless in Philadelphia in 1815 for distributing allegedly obscene pictures. A few years later, in the same state, Peter Holmes was convicted of obscenity for attempting to distribute the book *Fanny Hill*. At the same time, the first state statute law dealing with obscenity was enacted in Vermont. The concern with obscenity grew. In 1842 America enacted a tariff act that prohibited the "importation of all indecent and obscene prints, paintings, lithographs, engravings and transparencies." In 1857 printed matter was added to the list.[7] Mailing any allegedly obscene materials was made a criminal act by Congress in 1865.

By midcentury the common law was well established, and in 1857 in Britain, Parliament codified the common law into a statute law called the Obscene Publications Act, or, more popularly, Lord Campbell's Act. Although this act was principally oriented toward the question of seditious libel and for the first time established truth as a defense in libel cases, it also put greater restrictions on speech that might be deemed to be obscene. The first prosecution under Lord Campbell's Act occurred in 1868 in a case that had a profound impact on American law as well. Benjamin Hicklin, the recorder of London at that time, voided the seizure of an anti-Catholic pamphlet written by a Henry Scott. Hicklin's decision was reversed by the chief justice of Britain in the case *Regina v. Hicklin*, which established what became known as the Hicklin rule. This rule stated, in effect, that obscenity may be judged by the degree to which it would appear to corrupt with immoral influence the most susceptible persons in society—presumably children. Specifically, the Hicklin rule, which became the basis for judging obscenity in the United States for the remainder of the nineteenth century and into the early twentieth century, was as follows:

The test of obscenity is whether the tendency of the matter charged as obscenity is to deprave and corrupt those whose minds are open to such immoral influences and into whose hands a publication of this sort may fall.[8]

This meant, of course, that any matter that was deemed to have a potential immoral influence on the youngest child would be banned as well from the eyes and minds of adults. It was well into the twentieth century before the United States revised that approach, and it was still another half century when a version of the Hicklin rule, applied by Congress to the Internet, was declared unconstitutional.

A name that became synonymous with the crusade against indecency, obscenity and profanity, under the rubric "vice," was that of Anthony Comstock. He founded citizens' groups throughout the United States to combat his version of vice. In 1873 his lobbying of Congress resulted in what became known as the Comstock Law, in which the Post Office was given authority to ban the mailing of any "obscene, lewd, lascivious, or filthy book, pamphlet, picture, paper, letter, writing, print, or other publication of an indecent character."[9] And who was designated by the Post Office to oversee this task? Why, Anthony Comstock, of course! The Comstock approach, finding virtually any reference to sex obscene, became paramount in the United States.

Prurient Ether

The first important reversal of the Hicklin rule and the Comstock influence in the United States occurred in 1933, when a federal judge, John Woolsey, allowed the importation of James Joyce's *Ulysses*. Instead of judging the book's immoral influence based on its impact on the most susceptible members of society, per the Hicklin rule, Woolsey judged it based on its effect on a person with average adult sexual instincts. The Hicklin rule was finally laid to rest in U.S. jurisprudence in 1957 in the case of *Roth v. United States,* in which Samuel Roth was found guilty of mailing obscene material, but in which the concept of obscenity was stated by the Supreme Court as

whether to the average person, applying contemporary community standards, the dominant theme of the material taken as whole appeals to the prurient interest.[10]

It was during this period of continuing court tests of obscenity cases that broadcasting grew and along with it problems relating to indecency and obscenity on the airwaves. Although for the present generation radio and television appear to have been around forever, millions of Americans still alive remember when radio began and millions more when television was introduced. As history goes, radio and television are still quite young. The first radio station with regularly scheduled programming, KDKA in Pittsburgh, went on the air in 1920; the first station to be licensed, in 1921, was WBZ in Springfield, Massachusetts. There were no rules and regulations for radio. Anyone who had the money to set up a transmitter and broadcast equipment merely went to the Department of Commerce in Washington, D.C., got a license and went on the air. Within a short time there was chaos on the air. Stations broadcast on the same frequencies, with those with more power and higher antennas drowning out the others. For years radio station owners literally begged the government to do something about it, to establish regulations that would facilitate the orderly development of radio services nationwide without signal interference. Finally, in 1927 Congress passed the Dill-White Act (named for its principal sponsors), more formally known as the Radio Act of 1927. The act established the Federal Radio Commission (FRC), which was given regulatory authority over radio. The principal duties of the FRC were to issue licenses; allocate frequency bands for use by different classes of stations, including ship and air communication; assign specific frequencies to individual stations; and assign permissible power for each station. It was also authorized to take actions that could prevent monopolies, require stations to be individually and solely responsible for whatever programming they aired, and develop other regulations that it deemed necessary. Perhaps the most significant aspect of the Act was the requirement that stations operate in the "public interest, convenience, or necessity."[11] Concomitant with this clause was one that stated that "no person within the jurisdiction of the United States shall utter any obscene, indecent, or profane language by means of radio communication."[12] Although the FRC did not issue any rules regarding indecency or obscenity at that time, the "indecency" clause was incorporated into the Communications Act of 1934 and provided the basis for later federal regulation regarding perceived "dirty discourse" on the air. It was subsequently made a part of the U.S. criminal code in 1948 and specified a fine of up to $10,000 and imprisonment of up to two years. It was three years after the passage of the Federal Radio Act of 1927 and the establishment of the FRC that the first action was taken against a station for violating the "indecency clause." Defeated in a congressional primary election, a man named Robert Duncan continued to attack his opponent on program time he purchased from radio station KVEP in Portland, Oregon. Not only did the station lose its license, but Duncan was tried and sentenced to six months in jail and a $500 fine for "knowingly, willfully and feloniously uttering obscene, indecent and profane language by means of radio communication."[13] In an appeal Duncan was found by the court not to have uttered indecent or obscene language in terms of criminal statutes; although his language was deemed to be "extremely abusive and objectionable," it did not arouse "libidinous" feelings or meet the Radio Act requirement of obscene or indecent. It had to do more than be "vulgar, abusive, insulting, and calculated to arouse angry passions and resentment." It had to "deprave and corrupt . . . morals" and stimulate "lewd or lascivious" thoughts or desires. Nevertheless, the court let his conviction stand because it decided that his use of the words *damn* and *by God* violated the Radio Act's prohibition against profane language.[14]

The FRC did crack down on program content that it determined was deceptive or exploitative of the listener. Self-regulation by the stations and by the two recently established networks resulted in programming consisting principally of music and variety shows; dramas, soap operas and comedy programs came later and were written carefully in regard to content. Very little could be considered even borderline indecency in respect to sex and language. This, despite the increased abandonment of conservative social mores during America's Roaring Twenties, a time of prohibition and bootlegging, of jazz and public dance contests, of avant-garde art and literature, of national machismo and more liberal attitudes toward sex, from the popularization of artist Salvador Dali, writers Gertrude Stein and Ernest Hemingway, composers George Gershwin and Cole Porter, movie idols Greta Garbo and Rudolph Valentino, to that of hoodlums like Al Capone. For those who were white and upper- or middle-class, it was a decade of "affluence, joy, daring, and abandon."[15] For others, radio brought into increasing numbers of American homes music and other forms of entertainment that heretofore had been available only to those with enough money to go to nightclubs and vaudeville and burlesque shows.

With the Wall Street crash of 1929, radio became even more important. For more and more millions of Americans it was the only entertainment they could afford. Ten cents for admission to a movie was a lot of money during the Great Depression. Most of America became a captive radio audience. Audiences, programming and, sweet to the ears of the industry, advertising and the radio business grew.

Broadcast Banned

As diverse programming on radio grew, so did the range and specialties of performers. Some of the leading nightclub and vaudeville and burlesque stars, not noted for a lack of indecent and obscene monologues and skits, gravitated to this booming national medium. The FRC, while eschewing any direct censorship, nevertheless exerted enough influence through threat of regulation that radio stayed away from program content that might be considered too sexually provocative or that might disturb any potential buyers of its advertisers' products. Because radio in the 1930s depended on network prime-time programming for its principal advertising income—just as broadcast television does today—the networks tried not to offend anyone. Broadcasters paid special attention to songs that might contain racy lyrics suggesting indecent and/or obscene thoughts. In 1933 NBC employed a "song censor" to clear all music.

By 1934 further communications legislation was needed and enacted. Because regulation of different aspects of communication, especially radio (used in the generic sense for all wireless communication), was in the hands of a number of different federal agencies depending on the distribution means being used, the Communications Act of 1934 put the regulation of all interstate and foreign communications by wire and radio in the hands of one agency, the Federal Communications Commission (FCC). This included broadcasting, telephone and telegraph, and included provisions for new media, some already developed, such as television, and others still unknown. The FCC assumed considerably more regulatory authority, including that over program content, than had its predecessor, the FRC.

Many people, including members of Congress, assumed that if they personally found a piece of aired material offensive, then all they would have to do is inform the FCC and the broadcaster of that material would be duly punished. They could not conceive that their interpretation of obscenity, indecency or profanity isn't everybody's. The most widely known case in history—that is, known by the lay public in general—was the Mae West skit in 1937. It was part of the *Chase and Sanborn* weekly variety program on NBC. Starring ventriloquist Edgar Bergen and his dummy Charlie McCarthy, it was

---

Charlie Weston
WRTA, Altoona, Pennsylvania

I must be old-fashioned, but I still cringe when I say "crap" on the air. I don't think our speech should be a matter of governmental oversight. I do think that we should be more discriminate in what we say and listen to. People push the envelope on the air because it gets ratings. It would be nice if we could all be intelligent, instead of always seeking the lowest level. Just when I think we've sunk as low as we can go, Howard Stern and others like him sink even lower under the bar. Government? No! Personal discretion? Yes!

one of the most popular shows in all of broadcast history. The religious right, not as powerful then as it is today in its influence on Congress and, depending upon who is president, on the White House, nevertheless wielded considerable power. Complaints poured in and speeches were made on the floor of Congress condemning the skit as "blasphemous, sensuous, indecent, obscene, profane."[16] Was it? Compared with program content in this first decade of the twenty-first century, it wouldn't even twitch an eyebrow. At that time it appeared to many people to be outrageous, especially Mae West's portrayal of Eve. The story was of such national importance that *Time* magazine even published part of the script.[17] Judge for yourself.

Snake: That's the forbidden fruit.
Eve: Oh, don't be technical. Answer me this—my palpitatin' python—would you like to have this whole Paradise to yourself?
Snake: Certainly.
Eve: O.K., then pick me a handful of fruit—Adam and I'll eat it—and the garden of Eden is all yours. What do ya say?
Snake: Sssounds all right . . . but it's a forbidden fruit.
Eve: Listen, what are you—my friend in the grass or a snake in the grass?
Snake: But forbidden fruit!
Eve: Are you a snake or are you a mouse?
Snake: I'll—I'll do it. (hissing laugh)
Eve: Now you're talking. Here—right in between those pickets.
Snake: I'm—I'm stuck.
Eve: Oh—shake your hips. There, there now, you're through.
Snake: I shouldn't be doing this.
Eve: Yeah, but you're doing all right now. Get me a big one . . . I feel like doin' a big apple.
Snake: Here you are, Missus Eve.
Eve: Mm—oh, I see—huh—nice goin', swivel hips.
Snake: Wait a minute. It won't work. Adam'll never eat that forbidden apple.
Eve: Oh yes he will—when I'm through with it.
Snake: Nonsense. He won't.
Eve: He will if I feed it to him like women are gonna feed men for the rest of time.
Snake: What's that?
Eve: Applesauce.

The sponsor, *Chase and Sanborn,* publicly apologized for allowing the skit to be aired, and NBC banned Mae West from its network and its owned-and-operated stations. It ordered that "no script utilized as a basis of broadcast programs over these stations shall contain any reference to Miss West, nor shall her name be mentioned by entertainers or others."[18]

The FCC took no action against the NBC stations that had carried the program (it did not have direct jurisdiction over the network itself), but it did send a letter of condemnation to NBC. The chair of the FCC, Frank McNinch, warned broadcasters to monitor closely the content of their programs:

> You know as well as the members of the Commission what is fair, what is vulgar, what is profane, what will probably give offense. It is your duty in the first instance to guard against these.
>
> It is the commission's duty in the last instance to determine fairly and equitably and reasonably whether you have lived up to the high duty that is yours. The tenure of your license is so long as you exercise it in the public interest, convenience and necessity.
>
> May I suggest for your own good that you scrutinize more carefully the sponsored advertising script and ask yourself, in each case, not how profitable this will be, not will the public tolerate this, not can we get by with this, but—will this be in the public interest?[19]

That was not the end of the Mae West incident. Not long afterwards, when the FCC began its inquiry on network monopoly practices, which eventually resulted in the breakup of NBC's two networks (the Red network remained as NBC, the Blue network became ABC), the Mae West skit became an important part of the Commission's deliberations.

Another NBC broadcast the following year, 1938, also became grist for the puritan mill. The culprit this time was the Pulitzer Prize–winning *Beyond the Horizon* by America's foremost playwright, Eugene O'Neill. The Commission at first granted temporary license renewals to the stations that carried the play, then reversed its decision. The offending material? The play contained the words *God* and *damn*.[20]

The First Amendment of the U.S. Constitution states that "Congress shall make no law respecting an establishment of religion, or prohibiting the free exercise thereof, or abridging the freedom of speech, or of the press; or the right of the people peaceably to assemble, to petition the Government for a redress of grievances."

The Communications Act of 1934 applied these principles to broadcasting:

> Nothing in this Act shall be understood or construed to give the Commission the power of censorship over the radio communications or signals transmitted by any radio station, and no regulation or condition shall be promulgated

or fixed by the Commission which shall interfere with the right of free speech by means of radio communication.[21]

However, the U.S. Criminal Code states that

Whosoever utters any obscene, indecent or profane language by means of radio communication shall be fined not more than $10,000 or imprisoned for not more than two years, or both.[22]

Perhaps it was because of what appear to be contrary decrees that the communications regulatory commission did not take consistently strong action until recently against any stations concerning what might appear to be indecent material. Concomitantly, the lack of clear definitions of what indecency and obscenity are has caused and continues to cause confusion and uncertainty on the part of station managers and program directors and has prompted the FCC to rely on court decisions regarding nonbroadcast material—with the exception of one key case—in its attempts to establish a base of judgment for determining whether any given piece of broadcast material is indecent or obscene.

Unprotected Speech

If there had been any legal doubt about the permissibility of obscenity, it was resolved in a landmark 1957 case, *Roth v. United States*. While affirming that the First Amendment did not apply to obscene speech, the Court also established a new concept for judging what was obscene. Roth was sentenced to five years in prison and a $5,000 fine for mailing pamphlets purportedly containing obscene material. His appeal was turned down by the U.S. Court of Appeals, despite the following dissent by Justice Jerome M. Frank, which later became a key basis for judging obscenity:[23]

The troublesome aspect of the federal obscenity statute . . . is that no one can show that with any reasonable probability obscene publications tend to have any effects on the behavior of normal, average adults, and that under the . . . statute . . . punishment is apparently inflicted for provoking, in such adults, undesirable sexual thoughts, feelings or desire—not overt dangerous or anti-social conduct, either actual or probable.[24]

When the case reached the Supreme Court, however, more conservative views prevailed. Even "liberal" Justice William J. Brennan, writing the Court's majority opinion, affirmed that obscene material had no constitutional protection. The Court's decision became the guide for obscenity cases for the foreseeable future. Brennan wrote,

> All ideas having even the slightest redeeming social importance—unorthodox ideas, controversial ideas, even ideas hateful to the prevailing climate of opinion—have the full protection of the guarantees [of free speech and press], unless excludable because they encroach upon the limited area of more important interests. But implicit in the history of the First Amendment is the rejection of obscenity as utterly without redeeming social value.[25]

Brennan added a definition that appeared to narrow the judgment of what was obscene, one still used today:

> whether to the average person, applying contemporary community standards, the dominant theme of the material taken as a whole appeals to prurient interest.[26]

For a number of years two Supreme Court justices, William O. Douglas and Hugo Black, maintained strong First Amendment positions on all speech and influenced a number of Court decisions on what constituted obscenity. Among these were decisions that reversed lower-court rulings holding that nudist magazines and nude studies in journals published by art students were obscene, that a magazine for homosexuals was obscene, and that the owner of a bookstore that sold books that might be considered obscene could be held responsible for distributing obscene materials.[27] In the *Roth* case, for example, Douglas wrote in his dissent that a

> test that suppresses a cheap tract today can suppress a literary gem tomorrow. All it need do is incite a lascivious thought or arouse a lustful desire. The list of books that judges or juries can place in that category is endless.[28]

Confusion still reigned, however, about what was impermissible on the air. One example: in 1959 the FCC threatened to revoke the license of radio station KIMN in Denver because of alleged offensive material. Some of the most offensive remarks that generated complaints from two listeners: "I wonder where she puts KIMN radio when she takes a bath—I may peek—watch yourself, Charlotte" in response to a postcard from "Charlotte" saying she took KIMN radio with her wherever she went. "Gee, I ain't never either, sure would like to sometime, wouldn't you?" followed the record *I Ain't Never.* And the on-air comment "Say, did you hear about the guy who goosed the ghost and got a handful of sheet?"[29]

Public attitudes clearly influenced the courts, Congress, the regulatory agencies and the media. A coauthor of this book was, about that time, television critic for a New York newspaper and had just written a review of a television adaptation of the play *Arsenic and Old Lace,* in which two elderly ladies poison lonely elderly men and bury their bodies in the cellar. Their nephew doesn't want to marry his fiancée because he thinks he may be as crazy as his aunts. Then he finds out he is illegitimate and not of their bloodline. The second-act curtain line has him shouting, "Hooray, I'm a bastard!" This was changed in the TV version. Shortly afterward, the same coauthor was interviewing a BBC television dramatist in London who had recently adapted and produced *Arsenic and Old Lace* and who was shocked to learn that the United States would allow such bowdlerization of a famous play.

A key case, liberalizing the definition—and judicial determinations—of obscenity, occurred in 1966. The Supreme Court reversed the State of Massachusetts' banning of an eighteenth-century novel about a prostitute, *Fanny Hill, Memoirs of a Woman of Pleasure.*[30] Justice William J. Brennan emphasized the need for a work to be utterly without redeeming social value and to be patently offensive to the average person in order to be considered obscene. Few works could meet that test—depending, of course, on what one's personal concept of obscenity was. For the FCC and the broadcasting industry, particularly, it remained a case of the "I know it when I see it" amorphous subjectivity.

Another key case in 1966 narrowed or, to some, skewed the field a bit. In *Ginzburg v. United States* the court found Ralph Ginzburg, who published magazines generally considered pornographic, guilty of distributing his magazines in ways that appealed to the prurient interests of subscribers, but the court did not make its judgment based on the content of the magazines.[31] (He attempted to mail the magazines from towns with names such as Intercourse and Blue Ball and finally chose Middlesex.) In 1968, another Ginsberg (different spelling) had his conviction in New York for selling allegedly obscene materials to minors upheld by the Supreme Court.[32] The reintroduction of children into the equation foreshadowed the key element in subsequent rules and regulations and FCC actions against broadcasters.

In 1970 the FCC struggled with another high-profile case, the fining of WUHY-FM, Philadelphia, for the broadcast of an interview with Jerry Garcia, a member of the Grateful Dead rock band. In the interview Garcia's language included the following: "shit, man," "I must answer the phone 900 fuckin' times a day, man," "it sucks it right fuckin' out of ya, man," "that kind of shit," "it's fuckin' rotten, man, every fuckin' year," "political change is so fuckin' slow." The FCC did not find the material obscene because it did not have prurient appeal, but the Commission said that it was indecent and "patently offensive by contemporary community standards and utterly without redeeming social value."[33] The significance of this case is that all previous Notices of Apparent Liability were for obscene or profane language.

This was the first time a station had been fined for indecent speech. In fact, the Commission had hoped to make this a test case, with the federal courts having to promulgate a definition of indecency applicable to broadcasting when making their decisions. That would not happen for another few years.

In 1972, in *United States v. Orito,* the Supreme Court stated that obscene material may not be carried across state lines, even by common carrier for private use. This directly went to the root of the principle behind FCC authority: regulation of interstate commerce (broadcast signals by their nature cross state lines) on behalf of the public. It was the following year, 1973, that the Supreme Court issued the definition of obscenity that still comprises the basis for judgment of broadcast as well as print materials. In *Miller v. California* it revised the *Roth* case definition to add the concept of patent offensiveness, it recognized the different standards in different parts of the country and defined community standards as being essentially local, and it changed the redeeming social standard criterion to what became known as the SLAPS test: to be judged obscene the material must be without serious literary, artistic, political or scientific value.[34]

Air is not Paper

But while regulations were developed for the electronic media, none were developed for the print media, including newspapers and magazines. This is still a bone of contention for broadcasters. Why the difference in regulation? Because of something later called the "scarcity" principle. The reasoning was that because there are a limited number of frequencies for radio communication, it was necessary to protect them on behalf of all of the people to prevent them from becoming the property of a limited number of wealthy private interests, which would limit the public to those few owners' viewpoints and program preferences. The scarcity principle was coupled with the principle of "diversity." The airwaves were deemed to belong to the people and therefore should be regulated on behalf of the people by the people's elected and appointed representatives. On the other hand, there was no limit on the number of newspapers or magazines that could be published; anyone with the money for a printing press could publish in the print medium. There was no theoretical scarcity of print, and given the number of papers and journals being published at the time, no literal scarcity, either.

In 1973 another Supreme Court decision added further legal standards to the *Roth* concept of obscenity and was subsequently incorporated into the FCC's judgment of indecency as well. Following a spate of obscenity cases, judged largely by the *Roth* test, the Supreme Court in 1973 heard *Miller v.*

California. In the previous cases the Court decisions were based on a plurality, not on a majority. In other words, there was still no clear agreement, despite the *Roth* decision, on what constituted obscenity. This was an opportunity for the Court to find a new definition that satisfied a consensus of the justices.

Chief Justice Warren A. Burger confirmed that Marvin Miller, in mailing graphic brochures regarding books and a film about sex, was subject to prosecution under the obscenity standards. He stated that the case dealt with "a situation in which sexually explicit materials have been thrust by aggressive sales action upon unwilling recipients or juveniles."[35] He affirmed that obscene materials had no First Amendment protection. Further, in an attempt to find a new consensual definition, he threw out the caveat established in the *Fanny Hill* case in 1966 that for material to be judged obscene, it had to be proved that it was "utterly without redeeming social importance."[36]

Five justices agreed on the following revised definition:

> We now confine the permissible scope of such regulation to works which depict or describe sexual conduct. That conduct must be specifically defined by the applicable state law, as written or authoritatively construed . . . The basic guidelines for the trier of fact must be: a) whether "the average person, applying contemporary community standards" would find that the work, taken as a whole, appeals to the prurient interest . . . b) whether the work depicts or describes, in a patently offensive way, sexual conduct specifically defined by the applicable state law, and c) whether the work, taken as a whole, lacks serious literary, artistic, political or scientific value. We do not adopt as a constitutional standard the "utterly without redeeming social value" test of Memoirs v. Massachusetts . . . that concept has never commanded the adherence of more than three justices at one time.[37]

This decision also introduced a new concept of community standards or, more accurately, nonstandards. Stating that one standard could clearly not be applied to every state in the Union, that citizens in Maine or Mississippi should not be forced to accept depictions of sexual conduct citizens in New York City or Las Vegas might tolerate, the Court stated that it would not try to issue a national uniform standard, but that material would have to be judged in terms of individual communities' standards.[38] But even the new clarification and the combination of both the *Roth* and *Miller* tests could not provide a workable base for determining whether any given piece of material was obscene. In the next decades many of the Supreme Court's decisions on obscenity cases were split 5–4. Justice Brennan's dissent in *Miller v. California* expressed the consistent minority view: "the outright suppression of obscenity cannot be reconciled with the fundamental principles of the First and Fourteenth Amendments . . . we have failed to formulate a standard that sharply distinguishes protected from unprotected speech."[39]

From Nation to Small Station

Relying on local community standards—the new concept that presumably would avoid imposing a national view on disparate and diverse communities—didn't quite work out as expected. In some instances more harm was done by considering local community standards than might have been done with the imposition of a national standard. For example, in Georgia a movie theater owner was convicted, under a state statute, of distributing obscene material because he showed the film *Carnal Knowledge*. The theater owner appealed, and the Supreme Court found the action as well as the contemporary community standards applied in this case to be ludicrous. The Court stated that the film contained no obscenity under the definition in *Miller v. California*. It had no

> representations or descriptions of ultimate sexual acts, normal or perverted, actual or simulated [or] representations or descriptions of masturbation, excretory functions, and lewd exhibitions of the genitals.[40]

Between the *Roth* and *Miller* cases, the FCC found itself attempting to deal with numerous complaints from listeners alleging programming was obscene or indecent. Among the stations whose programming was reviewed were several belonging to the Pacifica Foundation, whose licenses were up for renewal in 1964. As noted later in reference to the landmark "Seven Dirty Words" case, the Pacifica stations were dedicated to First Amendment freedoms and presented materials and viewpoints of concern to society, whether politically or socially popular or not. Among the complaints were objections to a program that presented one of Edward Albee's early and most brilliant plays, *The Zoo Story,* some poetry readings and a program in which eight homosexuals discussed their lifestyles and minority status in society. The FCC did not single out a specific program, but sought to determine if there was a pattern of objectionable programming that should be considered in relation to the renewal of Pacifica's licenses. The FCC determined that the programs, however provocative to some listeners, were not obscene and that to take action against them would create a situation where "only the wholly inoffensive, the bland, could gain access to the radio microphone or TV camera."[41]

Other FCC actions in subsequent years varied from a nominal fine of $100 against public radio station WUHY for an interview in which the Grateful

Dead's Jerry Garcia used a number of words that could be considered patently offensive, and $2,000 against WGLD in Oak Park, Illinois, for dialogue during one of the growing number of so-called topless radio shows. Topless radio became a staple in afternoon radio, in which disc jockeys-turned-talkers tried to lure greater audiences in the comparatively dead time prior to afternoon drive time by encouraging apparently bored and lonely women to call in with tales of their sex lives. During the 1970s, topless radio formats increased as the ratings for these afternoon shows continued to dominate their timeslots in many markets. Concomitantly, complaints from listeners also increased. In 1973 the FCC received 20,000 such letters, ten times the number in the previous year.[42]

The Commission, led by conservative chair Dean Burch, recently appointed by President Ronald Reagan, publicly attempted to get broadcasters and the public to gut the topless format by citing such material as the following from the errant WGLD program:

> **Female Listener:** I had a few hang-ups at first . . . but you know what we did . . . I have a craving for peanut butter . . . so I used to spread this on my husband's private parts, and after a while . . . I didn't need the peanut butter any more . . . we can try anything . . . any of these women that have called and they have hang-ups about this . . . they should try their favorite—you know—like . . .
>
> **Announcer:** Whipped cream, marshmallow . . .[43]

Determining that such programming does not fall into the excepted area of having artistic or literary merit, the FCC admonished broadcasters to avoid such material. Commissioner Nicholas Johnson consistently opposed the FCC's restrictions on what he felt were First Amendment rights and urged that if the speech violated any laws, the Justice Department should exercise jurisdiction. He said that the FCC was attempting to deal with indecent language as if it were obscene language. He stated: "The majority admits that indecent expression is something less than obscenity, yet the majority nevertheless asserts that it may outlaw indecent expression." He added that there was no clear definition of obscenity and that "if obscenity is so vaguely defined, then the indecency variant promulgated by the majority is a hopeless blur." He criticized the Commission for acting as a "Big Brother . . . allegedly capable of deciding what is and is not good for the American people to see and hear."[44] But his was a minority view.

Even then the Commission felt itself on shaky grounds, the definition of obscenity still vague enough to depend on the "I know it when I see it" interpretation. One of the coauthors of this book, with the FCC at that time, recalls how complaints would be examined first by appropriate staff members, with the initial determination and recommendation largely dependent on the personal evaluations—and attitudes—of those staff members. The FCC for some time had wanted better legal guidance and a clearer definition for its handling of obscenity and indecency complaints, and it had hoped for a definitive court test. Along with the fine against WGLD, the FCC stated, "we welcome and urge judicial consideration of our action."[45] But that was not to come for another few years and then would be hardly as satisfactory as the Commission wished.

Airing Grievances

The FCC had been applying whatever criteria the particular set of commissioners happened to agree on when determining whether to take action against a station for broadcasting indecent or obscene material. Needless to say, the judgments had varied with each new set of commissioners. From time to time stations had been fined, usually $200 per infraction. For years the FCC had hoped there might be an indecency/obscenity case that would reach the Supreme Court and produce a definition that could be a benchmark by which broadcasters could determine whether they might ultimately be fined by the FCC if they carried a given content. One of the authors of this book was with the FCC during that period, and frequently received inquiries from station managers and program directors describing the material they planned to air and asking whether they would be fined if they did so. The answer was standard: "As prohibited by the Communications Act, the Commission may not censor any programming; further, only you, as licensee, may have sole discretion as to what program material you will air. Therefore, we cannot tell you whether or not to air the material you describe or what the consequences, if any, might be, if you do. However, if we receive any complaints from listeners or viewers about specific content that you air and we investigate and find that it is indecent or obscene, then we may take action against your station." That, of course, left broadcasters out on a limb, and they, too, were eager for some closure on what constituted indecency and obscenity by FCC standards.

The process of getting an issue to the courts is simple. If the FCC imposes a negative judgment against a party, that party may sue the FCC in the federal district court. The losing side in any court decision may appeal to the next highest court—ultimately taking its case to the Supreme Court for the final decision. The FCC does not seek out obscenity cases. The Commission does not have sufficient budget to monitor the programming of all or, in reality, any stations in the country. Nor would it wish to. It depends on listener complaints, as noted above, to investigate any alleged wrongdoing. If a written complaint seems to have merit, the FCC will contact the station and attempt to determine the exact nature of the referenced material. If the evidence appears to indicate that the station did broadcast what in the opinion of the sitting FCC commissioners appears to constitute indecent or obscene materials, the FCC may then take action against the station. As in the old vaudeville skit "pay the $2 and go home," any station fined is likely to pay the fine rather than appeal. An appeal requires the services of a law firm and a likely minimum of tens of thousands of dollars in fees, considerably more than the average fine.

Congress also wanted a test case. During an oversight hearing by the Senate Communications Subcommittee in early 1973, the committee chair, Senator John Pastore, urged the FCC to find a test case. "Unless you put your foot down and have a test case, we'll never know [the extent of the FCC's authority to regulate indecency]."[46] FCC chair Dean Burch confirmed that the Commission had been looking for a test case for years and thought it had found it with the fine against WUHY for the Jerry Garcia interview. The FCC presented the following excerpts from the Garcia broadcast to show why it was displeased:

> Shit, man.
> I must answer the phone 900 fuckin' times a day, man.
> Right, and it sucks it right fuckin' out of ya', man.
> That kind of shit.
> It's fuckin' rotten, man.
> Political change is so fuckin' slow.[47]

The FCC acknowledged that some people might consider Garcia's presentation as part of a work of art. However, the FCC noted, "it is quite another thing to say that WUHY has the right to broadcast an interview in which Mr. Garcia begins many sentences with 'Shit, man' . . . an expression which conveys no thought, has no redeeming social value, and in the context of broadcasting, drastically curtails the usefulness of the medium for millions of people."[48]

However, there was no test case because the station paid the fine rather than take the case to the courts. In 1973, the same year of the WGLD topless radio fine, the FCC received the test case opportunity it was looking for.

NOTES

1. Robert L. Hilliard and Michael C. Keith, *The Broadcast Century and Beyond,* 3rd ed. (Boston: Focal Press, 2001), p. 81; Michael C. Keith, *Talking Radio: An Oral*

History of Radio in the Television Age (Armonk, N.Y.: M. E. Sharpe, 2000), p. 144; Robert J. Landry, *This Fascinating Radio Business* (New York: Bobb-Merrill, 1946), p. 91.

2. Donna Petrozzello, "Stern generates indecency fine . . . ," *Broadcasting and Cable*, October 21, 1996, p. 23.

3. Wayne Overbeck, *Major Principles of Media Law* (New York: Harcourt, 2002), p. 380.

4. *Miller v. California,* 413 U.S. 15 (1973).

5. Federal Communications Commission Fact Sheet, "FCC Takes Strong Stand on Enforcement of Prohibition Against Obscene and Indecent Broadcasts" (November 1987).

6. Overbeck, *Major Principles of Media Law,* p. 382.

7. Ibid.

8. Ibid.

9. Ibid.

10. Ibid.

11. Hilliard and Keith, *Broadcast Century and Beyond,* pp. 49–51.

12. 47 U.S. Code, par. 109.

13. 48 F. 2nd 128.

14. Ibid. Also see Milagros Rivera-Sanchez, "The Regulatory History of Broadcast Indecency (1907–1987)" (doctoral dissertation, University of Florida, 1993).

15. Rivera-Sanchez, "Regulatory History of Broadcast Indecency," pp. 54–55.

16. Congressional Record, January 14, 1938, p. 560.

17. "FCC on Mae West," *Time* magazine, January 24, 1938, pp. 51–52.

18. "Mae West's Name Banned," *New York Times,* December 25, 1937, p. 11.

19. "McNinch Warns Industry to Toe the Mark," *Broadcasting,* February 15, 1938, pp. 103–4.

20. "Citation for O'Neill Pulitzer Drama Sidetracked by FCC for Further Study," *Broadcasting,* October 15, 1938, p. 22.

21. Section 326, Communications Act of 1934.

22. 18 U.S. Code 1464.

23. Dwight L. Teeter and Bill Loving, *Law of Mass Communications: Freedom and Control of Print and Broadcast Media* (New York: Foundation Press, 2001), pp. 113–14.

24. 237 F. 2nd 796, 802, 2nd Cir. (1956).

25. *Roth v. United States,* 354 U.S. 476, 490, 77 Sup. Ct. 1304, 1312 (1957), as cited in Teeter and Loving, *Law of Mass Communications,* p. 115.

26. Ibid., pp. 115–16.

27. Overbeck, *Major Principles of Media Law,* p. 385.

28. Teeter and Loving, *Law of Mass Communications,* p. 117.

29. "KINM Cleared But Management Gets Sharp FCC Warning," *Broadcasting,* June 27, 1960, p. 72.

30. 383 U.S. 413.

31. 383 U.S. 463.

32. 390 U.S. 629.

33. FCC, 18 P&F Rad. Reg. 2nd, 865.
34. 413 U.S. 15.
35. Teeter and Loving, *Law of Mass Communications,* p. 125.
36. Ibid., p. 125–26.
37. Ibid., p. 126–27. *Miller v. California,* 413 U.S. 15, 23–24, 93 Sup. Ct. (1973).
38. Ibid., p. 127.
39. Ibid., p. 128.
40. Ibid., pp. 128–29. *Jenkins v. Georgia,* 418 U.S. 153, 160, 94 Sup. Ct. 2750, 2755 (1974).
41. T. Barton Carter, Marc A. Franklin and Jay B. Wright, *The First Amendment and the Fifth Estate: Regulation of Electronic Mass Media,* 5th ed. (New York: Foundation Press, 1999), pp. 223–24.
42. "Programming of Violent, Indecent, or Obscene Material," *Broadcast Management/Engineering (BM/E),* June 1975, pp. 22–24.
43. Ibid., pp. 224–25.
44. Jeremy H. Lipschultz, *Broadcast Indecency: F.C.C. Regulation and the First Amendment* (Washington, D.C.: Broadcasting and Cable, 1997), p. 39. See also Sonderling Broadcasting, 27 RR 2nd 285 (1973).
45. Lipschultz, *Broadcast Indecency,* p. 225.
46. "Pastore pushes FCC to move against 'indecent programs,'" *Broadcasting,* February 26, 1973, p. 50.
47. FCC, NAL against Eastern Educational Radio (WUHY-FM), 24 FCC 2nd 408 (1970).
48. Ibid.

CHAPTER 2

HOW MANY DIRTY WORDS?

In 1973 the FCC received a complaint from a man who was driving with his young son in New Jersey and heard a broadcast on a New York City noncommercial radio station, WBAI. WBAI was licensed to the Pacifica Foundation, an organization that operated several stations throughout the country and was known for its integrity—and bravery. For example, during the height of the cold war, most commercial stations carried programs about communism, but rarely, if ever, included a real, live communist in the discussion. Not so with Pacifica stations. The complainant alleged that at 2 p.m. one day his son inadvertently tuned into a WBAI broadcast on perceptions of language, and it included a monologue by comedian George Carlin, one he had used in nightclubs, entitled "Filthy Words." It is better known as the "Seven Dirty Words" case because in his routine Carlin describes the meanings and implications of seven words that he says cannot be uttered on the public airwaves: *shit, piss, fuck, cunt, tits, cocksucker* and *motherfucker*. The complaint was not on the man's behalf, but on behalf of his son, who he stated should not be subject to obscene material on the air during the times of day that young people are likely to be listening to or watching a broadcast station. A sample segment of the Carlin 12-minute monologue was aired by WBAI as an illustration during a program discussion of the public's general view of language:

> I was thinking one night about the words you couldn't say on the public airwaves, the ones you definitely couldn't ever. . . . and it came down to seven but the list is open to amendment and in fact has been changed by now. A lot of people pointed things to me, and I noticed some myself. The original seven words were shit, piss, fuck, cunt, cocksucker, motherfucker and tits. Those are the ones that will curve your spine, grow hair on your hands and maybe even

bring us, God help us, peace without honor—and a bourbon. And now the first thing that we noticed was that the word fuck was really repeated in there because the word motherfucker is a compound word and it's another form of the word fuck. Then you have the four-letter words from the old Anglo-Saxon fame. Uh, shit and fuck. The word shit is an interesting kind of word in that the middle class has never really accepted it and approved it. They use it like crazy but it's not really okay. It's still a rude, dirty old kind of gushy word. They don't like that but they say it, like, they say it, like, a lady now in a middle-class home, you'll hear most of the time she says it as an expletive, you know, it's out of her mouth before she knows. She says oh shit, oh shit, oh shit if she drops something. Oh, the shit hurt the broccoli. Shit. Thank you. Now the word shit is okay for the man. At work you can say it like crazy. Most figuratively. Get that shit out of here, will ya? I don't want to see that shit anymore. I can't cut that shit, buddy. I've had that shit up to here. I think you're full of shit myself. He don't know shit from Shinola. You know that? Always wondered how the Shinola people felt about that? Hi, I'm the new man from Shinola. Hi, how are ya? Nice to see ya. How are ya? Boy, I don't know whether to shit or wind my watch. Guess I'll shit on my watch. Oh, the shit is going to hit de fan. Built like a brick shit-house. Up, he's up shit creek. He's had it. He hit me. He hit me, I'm sorry. Hot shit, holy shit, tough shit, eat shit. Shit-eating grin. Uh, whoever thought of that was ill. He had a shit-eating grin. He had a what? Shit on a stick. Shit in a handbag. I always like that. He ain't worth shit in a handbag. Shitty. He acted real shitty. You know what I mean? I got the money back, but a really shitty attitude.[1]

The young son was 15 years old. The opinion of some that if he was not yet already familiar with the words in Carlin's routine, he must have spent his life locked in a closet, was not relevant. He was still considered a child and not an adult. The FCC found the Carlin routine to be patently offensive and indecent—although not obscene. The Commission decided that the material was inappropriate for the airwaves and placed a warning in WBAI's file. The FCC clarified its definition of indecency, while circumscribing its use in the broadcast media, as material that

> describes, in terms patently offensive as measured by contemporary community standards for the broadcast medium, sexual or excretory activities and organs, at times of the day where there is reasonable risk that children may be in the audience.[2]

On principle, WBAI and the Pacifica Foundation appealed, and the FCC's determination was reversed in the U.S. Court of Appeals. The 1977 U.S. Court of Appeals decision derided the FCC for violating section 326 of the Communication Act of 1934, which forbade censorship, and stated that the Commission was preventing "free and robust exchange of ideas on a wide range of issues and subjects by means of radio and television communications."[3] The court also found the FCC's action to be too vague and broad because the FCC did not clearly define what it meant by minors and it "sweepingly forbids any broadcast of the seven words irrespective of context however innocent or educational they may be. Clearly, every use of the seven words cannot be deemed offensive even as to minors."[4] The appeals court also stated that Carlin's words were not obscene, but merely crude statements and were not used to "titillate." It questioned the FCC's application of a so-called national standard.

> The Commission never solicited a jury verdict or expert testimony. Nor did it rely on polls or letters of complaint. The Commission simply recorded its conclusion that the words were indecent, thereby creating the suspicion that the national standard is in fact the composite of the individual Commissioners' standards or what they suppose are the national standards.[5]

The case reached the Supreme Court. Staff members at the FCC were delighted. Finally, they thought, there would be a definition of indecency for broadcasting; this was the first broadcasting case on the subject to reach the Supreme Court.

The Court issued a three-part decision in 1978. (See Appendix A at the end of this book.) First, it stated that the FCC did have authority to take action against a station for what it believed was indecent, but not obscene, speech. Second, it agreed with the FCC that this particular program segment was indecent, although not obscene, and should not have been broadcast during hours when children might be listening. And third—as broadcasters and regulators were waiting for a legal definition of indecency in broadcasting—the Supreme Court did not let the other shoe drop. It stated that all future cases on the subject would be considered on their individual merits. That meant, simply, that if any material other than the "Seven Dirty Words" routine was broadcast and the FCC took action against a station for such airing, the legitimacy of the FCC's action could be challenged and would have to be decided by the same procedure—an appeal reaching the federal courts and possibly the Supreme Court for a decision on the specific material of concern. In practical terms, the only material specifically designated as inappropriate for broadcasting during daytime hours is Carlin's "Filthy Words." Nevertheless, the Court decision established a principle regarding the broadcast of indecent material at times when children might be in the audience. Justice John Paul Stevens wrote the Court's opinion, which stated, in part:

> First, the broadcast media have established a uniquely pervasive presence in the lives of all Americans. Patently offensive, indecent material presented over

CHAPTER 2

the airwaves confronts the citizen, not only in public, but also in the privacy of the home, where the individual's right to be left alone plainly outweighs the First Amendment rights of an intruder. Because the broadcast audience is constantly tuning in and out, prior warnings cannot completely protect the listener or viewer from unexpected program content. To say that one may avoid further offense by turning off the radio when he hears indecent language is like saying that the remedy for an assault is to run away after the first blow. One may hang up on an indecent phone call, but that option does not give the caller a constitutional immunity or avoid a harm that has already taken place.

Second, broadcasting is uniquely accessible to children, even those too young to read. Although . . . [a] written message might have been incomprehensible to a first grader, Pacifica's broadcast could have enlarged a child's vocabulary in an instant. Other forms of offensive expression may be withheld from the young without restricting the expression at its source. Bookstores and motion picture theaters, for example, may be prohibited from making indecent material available to children. . . . The ease with which children may obtain access to broadcast material . . . amply justifies special treatment of indecent broadcasting.[6]

Justice William J. Brennan's dissent promulgated—but, as a minority view, did not establish—a different principle. Brennan wrote that

Whatever the minimal discomfort suffered by a listener who inadvertently tunes into a program he finds offensive during the brief interval before he can simply extend his arm and switch stations or flick the "off" button, is surely worth the candle to preserve the broadcaster's right to send, and the right of those interested to receive, a message entitled to full First Amendment protection.

I would place the responsibility and the right to weed worthless and offensive communications from the public airways where it belongs and where, until today, it resided: in a public free to choose those communications worthy of its attention from a marketplace unsullied by censor hand.

There lurks in today's decision a potential for reducing the adult population to hearing only what is fit for children.[7]

Brennan also suggested that the explanation of the seven words in the context of a serious study of language might be of value to some parents who want their children to understand the true meaning of such words rather than maintain for them a mysterious and potentially harmful taboo. He also chastised the majority opinion of the Court for its

depressing inability to appreciate that in our land of cultural pluralism, there are many who think, act, and talk differently from the Members of this Court, and who do not share their fragile sensibilities. It is only an acute ethnocentric myopia that enables the Court to approve the censorship of communications solely because of the words they contain.[8]

Although the Seven Dirty Words case is considered the seminal case in regard to broadcast indecency, between the initial complaint and the Supreme Court decision, another, frequently forgotten, FCC action set the tone for subsequent applications of the First Amendment to the electronic media. In a Notice of Apparent Liability to the University of Pennsylvania dated December 4, 1975,[9] the FCC found that the university's noncommercial radio station, WXPN-FM, had violated the standards the Commission had set forth "with respect to the broadcast of obscene or indecent matter." The Commission noted examples such as the following:

Male announcer: . . . on the air.
Female caller: Kiss my pussy, you dog you—
Male announcer: You're beautiful! You're a poet!
Female caller: Suck my pussy, you motherfu—
Male announcer: You're a poet! Don't hang up—keep going.
Female caller: Suck out my ass. Get a straw and strip it to the bone and suck out that motherfucker.

Another example cited by the FCC:
Male caller: We stopped into one of those porno stores on Market Street and we saw there the Greek Goddess—Not just two holes, but three—$29.95 rubber doll—
Male announcer: You mean in the mouth, in the butt and between the legs?
Male caller: That—as the man in the store described it—Not only has she got a mouth and a cunt, but she's got an asshole, too—(Laughter) . . .

And a further example:
Male announcer: Listen, you should call us more often and you should let your son listen to it, and you should teach your son that for him to beat-off at his age is good—for him to say fuck is good—for him to want to go to bed with you is healthy—for him to want to screw you, a la etcetera, is healthy—
Female caller: You know, he—he does want to go to bed with me.
Male announcer: Oh, you should give him all the physical attention you can give him now, so he won't be starved for it and go out raping later.

Female caller: Oh, he gets plenty of physical attention. I mean, he— he—

Male announcer: When was the last time you blew him?

The FCC fined the station the standard $2,000 and two weeks later issued an order for a hearing on whether the station's license should be revoked.[10] (Ultimately, it was not.) Interestingly, the FCC's decision was not based on traditional political philosophies. The two dissenting commissioners were Robert E. Lee, a strong conservative, and Benjamin Hooks, a strong liberal.

That the Seven Dirty Words decision did not solve the definition problem was evident a decade later in another situation involving, coincidentally, Pacifica. The same Pacifica radio station, WBAI in New York, planned to do a reading of James Joyce's *Ulysses* at 11 p.m. one night. Without telling the FCC the name of the novel, it asked whether it could present passages containing the words "kissing my bottom," "put it in me from behind," "lovely young cock," "stick his tongue seven miles up my hole" and "fucked yes and damned well fucked too." The FCC refused to advise WBAI whether or not it could present a reading with such language. WBAI presented it anyway, and the FCC took no action on the grounds that the questionable material was presented after midnight, within the bounds of the safe harbor for so-called adult, or indecent, programming.[11]

From the time of the Seven Dirty Words decision in 1978 to the present time—into the twenty-first century—the FCC and Congress have been running a marathon of deregulation in everything but their perceptions of indecency. Whether hypocrisy, political opportunism or more conservative national morality, or combinations of all have been the motivating factors is arguable. Deregulation began in earnest under a Democratic president, Jimmy Carter, in the late 1970s, implemented by his FCC chair, Charles Ferris. The social consciences that marked the 1960s and early 1970s began to disappear as the FCC actions appeared to more and more serve the private rather than the public interest. Public interest groups hoped for better times with Carter's appointment of Ferris in 1977; however, their hopes were dashed as Ferris moved even further away from public interest regulation to proindustry deregulation, reversing many of the proconsumer gains initiated when President John Kennedy appointed Newton Minow chair of the FCC in 1961, gains that continued in subsequent years as part of the Kennedy-Minow legacy.[12] Ferris, however, left another kind of bequest, described by *Broadcasting* magazine as a "laissez-faire legacy." The FCC, under his leadership, was described by Ralph Nader as one of the worst agencies in Washington.[13]

The "Right" Thing to Do

Deregulation galloped apace during the Ronald Reagan administrations, with a relaxation of the antimonopoly, multiple ownership rules, the discontinuance or vitiation of the program service requirements of broadcast stations, the relaxation of the number of commercial minutes permitted per hour, the elimination of requirements for the ascertainment of community needs by stations, the rescinding of program log requirements, the authorization of product identification and logos for public broadcasting underwriters, the abolition of the Fairness Doctrine and the replacement of stations' license renewal applications, which required a showing of having operated in the public interest, with a postcard-size form. Within a few years even cable television, which had been under the regulatory jurisdiction of the FCC, was virtually totally deregulated under the Cable Communications Policy Act of 1984, giving the cable industry free rein on fees and providing (or not) services to cable subscribers.

During the same period, beginning in 1976, sex became television's biggest rating booster. The *Charlie's Angels* series spawned a plethora of "jiggle" or "T and A" programs. Citizen and professional organizations, such as the National Parents-Teachers Association and the American Medical Association, expressed concern about too much sex in the media, and the National Association of Broadcasters was pressured into adding to its television code prohibitions concerning obscenity and profanity. However, the code was voluntary and had little effect on programming and was later abolished.[14]

For some the introduction of legislation and agency rules regarding indecent content was out of a sincere desire to protect children. For others that motive opened up an opportunity to concurrently bar material they didn't want adults exposed too, either. The various laws designed to protect children did both in some cases, resulting in ultimate findings of unconstitutionality. The Protection of Children Against Sexual Exploitation Act of 1977 was sufficiently narrowly defined to fall into the category of protection against obscene material. Child pornography, per se, is banned. But subsequent Acts, such as Title V of the Telecommunications Act of 1996, the Communications Decency Act (CDA); the Child Pornography Prevention Act of 1996 (hurriedly enacted when the CDA was declared unconstitutional); and the Child Online Protection Act of 1999 (COPA) were written so broadly they infringed on adults' rights to receive adult material and encountered First Amendment problems in the courts. It was in 1968 that the Supreme Court rendered a seminal decision regarding minors and obscene material. In *Ginsberg v. New York,* the Court ruled that a

Store owner's conviction under New York criminal obscenity statute that bars knowing sale to those under seventeen years of age of materials "harmful to minors" whether or not such materials would be obscene for adults is constitutionally valid, since state authority to control conduct of children exceeds its authority over adults, since New York's adjusted definition of obscenity for minors is based on such authority, and since the term "harmful to minors" gives an adequate notice of prohibited conduct and is therefore not impermissibly vague.[15]

A further case that established the principle of protection of children was *New York v. Ferber* in 1982, which affirmed a state's right to prosecute anyone who depicted children in sexual acts, without first having to prove that the materials are obscene. The Supreme Court made it clear that "the need to control child pornography was so compelling that the states were free to enact laws that might be unconstitutional under other circumstances."[16] As discussed in this chapter, the protection of children continues to be the key rationale in attempting to control "dirty discourse," including efforts involving the Internet. In its discussion of the CDA, for example, the Supreme Court observed that "pornography on the Internet is a flourishing business, with [in 1996] about 28,000 different Web sites generating almost $925 million in revenues per year."[17]

For more than a decade following the Seven Dirty Words case, the FCC appeared to be content with the status quo. It carried its concerns with indecent programming no further and rarely took action against stations for such programming. While the topless radio format per se abated somewhat, more formal programs emphasizing sex began to grow. "Shock jocks"—epitomized later by the Howard Stern and Don Imus genre—created more and more concern on the part of citizen organizations, ranging from children's advocates to right-wing fundamentalist religious groups. Pressures on Congress, relayed to the FCC, made the Commission take notice.

Capitalizing on their connections to the Reagan administration and to members of Congress such as Senator Jesse Helms, the religious right and other right-wing groups made special attempts in 1986 to pressure the FCC into interpreting the Seven Dirty Words case more broadly, rather than in the narrow limitations of the Supreme Court's decision. The National Federation for Decency (NFD), led by right-wing representative Donald Wildmon, and Morality in Media (MIM) picketed the FCC headquarters to call attention to their campaign. They also generated mass complaints from their followers. Even a conservative such as FCC chair Mark Fowler, who succeeded in dismantling almost all consumer protection and public interest regulations at the FCC, was targeted by Wildmon as not being assiduous enough in enforcing indecency provisions, and Wildmon was prepared to oppose

Fowler if the latter sought another term as FCC chair.[18] Typical of the organized right-wing pressure on the FCC, broadcasters and advertisers was the following flyer distributed to members of allied organizations by Wildmon.[19]

URGENT!!!
Your help is needed!

From: Donald Wildmon
Executive Director
National Federation for Decency
Tupelo, Mississippi 38803

The Federal Communications Commission has said it will prosecute stations which air obscene and/or indecent programming. We need your help in monitoring the Howard Stern Show which airs from 6:00 A.M. until 10:00 A.M. on radio station WYSP in Philadelphia.

Here is how you can help. Listen to the program. (If at all possible tape the program.) If you feel that any part of Mr. Stern's program is obscene or indecent, write James McKinney, Chief, Mass Media Bureau of the Federal Communications Commission and say so.

Be sure to give as many specific details as to why it was indecent—what was said, etc. Spell it out in detail. (That is the reason you need to tape the program.) Send along the tape to Mr. McKinney if possible.

In your letter to Mr. McKinney, be sure to mention the station on which the program was aired, the time of the program, and the date. Mail this information to: James McKinney, Chief, Mass Media Bureau, Federal Communications Commission, 1919 M Street, Washington, D.C. 20554.

PLEASE HELP WITH THIS PROJECT! THE FCC NEEDS LOTS OF ACCURATE, INFORMATIONAL LETTERS FROM LISTENERS IN AND AROUND PHILADELPHIA.

The religious right and other right-wing pressure groups did have an impact on the FCC. On November 24, 1987, in the definition/enforcement statement noted earlier, the FCC, "after a 12 year hiatus, has made it clear that it intends to take enforcement actions against broadcasters who air obscene or indecent programming in violation of the law." The publicly distributed statement (see Appendix B at the end of this book) reaffirmed three indecency rulings from the previous April against three broadcast stations.[20]

One of these stations, ironically (or, perhaps, not surprisingly), was a Pacifica station in Los Angeles. It aired the play *Jerker*, which features conversations that include sexual attitudes and visions of two homosexuals who are dying of AIDS. The Commission found the material patently indecent and possibly obscene.[21] Here are some excerpts from *Jerker,* as quoted by the FCC in coming to its decision.

> Yeah, it was loving even if you didn't know whose cock it was in the dark or whose asshole you were sucking.

> I'll give you the gentlest fuck west of the Mississippi.

> We cuddled and played around a bit before he started working on my ass. I remember he was kneeling between my legs and he worked my asshole with lube for the longest time—just getting it to relax so there was no tension, no fear.

> He lowered himself on top of me and slid his dick in all the way, but so gently, so smoothly, there wasn't even a bit of pain.

> His cock felt warm inside me—and full—so nice and full. So he began sliding his cock back and forth inside of my ass—but so gently, so gently.

> I don't think I've ever had such a gentle, sensitive fuck before or after. Well, he must have gone at it for twenty minutes at the very least—and then he whispered to me, "You're gonna feel me come inside of you." And I did, man, I could feel the cum pulse up his shaft inside of my ass. I could count the pulses and it felt warm and good.

The Commission asked the Department of Justice to look into the degree of obscenity for possible prosecution. The Justice Department took no action.

The second station was cited for airing a song, "Makin' Bacon," that the Commission considered to be offensive because of references to sexual organs and activities. The following lyrics were quoted by the FCC in its decision.[22]

> Makin' bacon, makin' bacon, makin' bacon, makin' bacon
> A ten-inch cropper with a varicose vein
> Makin' bacon is on my mind
> Come here baby, make it quick
> Kneel down there and suck on my dick
> Makin' bacon is on my mind
> Makin' bacon is on my mind
> Turn around baby, let me take you from behind
> Makin' bacon is on my mind
> With your blue, blue knickers, you look so neat
> Makin' bacon is on my mind
> Bend over baby, gonna give you my meat
> Makin' bacon is on my mind
> Get down baby on your hands and knees

Take my danish and give it a squeeze
Makin' bacon is on my mind
Makin' bacon is on my mind
Turn around baby. Let me take you from behind
Makin' bacon is on my mind
Hey, baby got something to chew
Deep throat, baby, it's good for you
Makin' bacon is on my mind

The FCC found that the song was patently offensive with "several clearly discernible references to sexual organs and activities."[23]

The third citation was against Infinity Broadcasting and its Howard Stern show,[24] which was to become a principal target of FCC indecency rules implementation. And to be used in this and future instances as a warning to other "shock jock" shows as well. The morning radio show was on the air from 6 a.m. to 10 a.m. Monday through Friday and, according to the FCC, had "specific references to masturbation, ejaculation, breast and penis size, sexual intercourse, oral-genital contact, sodomy, bestiality, menstruation, and testicles."[25] Six examples quoted by the FCC in its decision are

Stern: God, my testicles are like down on the floor. Boy, Susan, you could really have a party with these. I'm telling you honey.
Ray: Use them like Bocce balls.

★ ★ ★

Stern: Let me tell you something, honey. Those homos you are with are all limp.
Ray: Yeah. You've never even had a real man.

★ ★ ★

Susan: No. I was in a park in New Rochelle, N.Y.
Stern: In a park in New Rochelle? On your knees?
Susan: No, no.
Ray: And squeezing someone's testicles, probably.

★ ★ ★

Stern: (talking to a caller) I'd ask your penis size and stuff like that, but I really don't care.

★ ★ ★

Stern: (in a discussion about lesbians) I mean, to go around porking other girls with vibrating rubber products and they want the whole world to come to a standstill.

★ ★ ★

Stern: Have you ever had sex with an animal?
Caller: No.
Stern: Well, don't knock it. I was sodomized by Lambchop, you know the puppet Shari Lewis holds? Baaaah. That's where I was thinking that

Shari Lewis instead of like sodomizing all the people at the academy to get that shot on the Emmys she could've had Lambchop do it.

The findings in these three cases clearly broadened the interpretation of indecency developed in the Seven Dirty Words case—exactly what the religious right pressured the FCC to do. But the FCC was not unanimous. Commissioner Patricia Diaz Dennis noted that in Shakespeare's *Macbeth* and *Taming of the Shrew* there are scenes that "refer to excrement and to sex in fairly graphic terms," but she didn't think that the Commission would want to bar such plays from prime-time airing on television.[26]

Freedom Time

The FCC also established what it called a "safe harbor" for so-called adult programming, hours that the Commission presumed children would not be watching or listening—from midnight to 6 a.m. In other words, adult programming, or programming that might be considered by some to be indecent, could not be broadcast between the hours of 6 a.m. and midnight. At no time could so-called obscene programming be broadcast.[27] The safe harbor provision was argued in the courts, which upheld the FCC's safe harbor concept, but questioned the narrow six-hour window. At the same time, Congress, yielding to conservative pressure groups, directed the FCC to ban indecent programming entirely from the airwaves. Civil liberties and public interest groups convinced the courts to stay the congressional ban pending further FCC study. Nevertheless, in 1990 the FCC issued a 24-hour ban on indecent programming. Less than a year later the U.S. Court of Appeals found the total ban unacceptable and directed the FCC to

---

Ken Donaldson
KRTS, Houston, Texas

As a rock-ribbed libertarian type, I say no, the government has no business censoring broadcasters, unless the speech in question endangers the public (for example, airing a bogus bomb threat). In the United States, we should let the marketplace decide what speech is acceptable. If the public doesn't like what is being aired, it can "vote with its pocketbook," and simply not listen to a station or patronize its advertisers. In my opinion we have ceded far too many of our freedoms and abdicated far too much of our responsibility to the federal government.

---

reestablish a reasonable safe harbor. Not to be outdone, Congress then attached a midnight to 6 a.m. requirement to a 1992 bill funding public broadcasting. Back and forth the safe harbor times went among the FCC, the courts and Congress, and at one time the restriction was even completely eliminated. In the continuing safe harbor saga, the FCC established a midnight to 6 a.m. time, which was thrown out by the courts, and then an 8 p.m. to 6 a.m. period, which was also thrown out by the courts, then back to a midnight to 6 a.m. period. In 1993 the U.S. Court of Appeals reaffirmed the FCC's right to establish a safe harbor, but moved the time to 10 p.m. to 6 a.m. The safe harbor issue finally reached the Supreme Court. A variety of organizations, ranging from the American Civil Liberties Union to Action for Children's Television, argued that the best protection for children was the maintenance of the First Amendment's guarantees of freedom of speech and press. Peggy Charren, president of Action for Children's Television—the constituency that the safe harbor mandate purportedly was designed to protect—said, "The way the FCC has defined indecency could do in 'Bullwinkle.' It's amazing that just when we're instructing people throughout the world about the beauty of free speech, we're doing away with it in this country."[28]

The Supreme Court let stand two U.S. Court of Appeals decisions affirming the FCC's authority to establish safe harbor standards for the ostensible purpose of protecting children in the audience. The Commission then established a safe harbor of 10 p.m. to 6 a.m., which exists at this writing.[29] In 1996 the Supreme Court refused to hear a challenge to the 1992 amendment to the Public Telecommunications Act that established a restricted period.[30] The finalization—up to that time—of indecency restrictions appeared to fly in the face of precedent in some key cases. Although the appeal argued that "the 6 A.M. to midnight ban is unsupported by any evidence of harm to minors and is not narrowly tailored to serve the government's asserted interests," the U.S. Court of Appeals verdict upheld by the Supreme Court stated that "we find that the government has a compelling interest in protecting children under the age of 18 from exposure to indecent broadcasts."[31]

Attorney and cable producer Regina Ramsey noted that upholding such First Amendment restrictions occurred only if the restrictions "both further a substantial government interest and are narrowly tailored to achieve only that aim." She cited two cases, one in which the court stated that "mere speculation of harm does not constitute a compelling state interest" and another in which the Supreme Court noted that the First Amendment needs "breathing space to survive," implying that vague regulations are unacceptable. She further noted that in 1991 the FCC affirmed its dismissal of an indecency complaint against a newscast that broadcast phone conversations of alleged mobsters in which profanity was abundant.[32] Such analyses, however, did not deter Congress, a court or the FCC from its mission vis-à-vis perceived indecent content.

At first the FCC issued warnings to stations—as early as 1987 to two stations that carried the Howard Stern program and about which the FCC had received listeners' complaints. However, Stern's material got, if anything, even more coarse, and in 1992 the FCC fined Infinity Broadcasting Company, whose stations carried Stern's programs, the largest fine in history, $600,000. That didn't stop Stern or Infinity. Or the FCC. The total of fines reached $2 million. But Stern's ratings and Infinity's profits continued to grow, in large part because of the publicity generated by the FCC's actions. Some critics suggested that Infinity got more than $2 million worth of publicity out of it all.

A number of other stations, however, concerned that they too might be fined, pleaded with the FCC for a new, clarified statement on what constituted indecency. But, for some reason, the FCC did not issue such a clarification for another decade—until 2001—and in the interim continued to fine stations for infractions that sometimes were even accidental, absent a clear, binding definition of what was impermissible on the air.

Many groups and individuals tried to fathom the FCC's indecency concepts. One syndicated article described it as follows:

> How would you like to be told that if you said the wrong thing you would lose your livelihood, and then when you asked for some guidance as to what the "wrong thing" might be, they told you that they couldn't tell you in advance, but that they'd have to wait until you spoke, and if you said the wrong thing they'd tell you then. And take away your livelihood.[33]

Nevertheless, the FCC attempted to show that it meant business with its 1987 statement on indecency, and entertained and seriously examined the plethora of complaints that began to pile up. By 1989 it had a backlog of 95 complaints that could not be summarily or easily dismissed. Acting on its then safe harbor principle of 8 p.m. to 6 a.m., it cited eight stations for their daytime programming, and the other complaints were finally dismissed because the broadcasts took place during the safe harbor period. The offending material was not confined to any given geographical area. Two stations in Miami were fined $10,000 and $2,000 respectively for airing material deemed indecent on talk shows hosted by popular radio personality Neil Rogers. A station in Las Vegas was fined $2,000, one in Los Angeles $6,000, and others in New York, Cleveland, St. Louis, and Paris, Arkansas, were given warnings. What kind of content was found to be indecent? Substituting candy brand names for body parts. Pitching a beer for lesbians. Joke songs and fake commercials with offending material. The new crackdown was led by FCC chair Alfred Sikes, a staunch conservative newly appointed by President Ronald Reagan. Sikes defended the FCC's actions in a speech about indecency at a National Association of Broadcasters convention by saying, "Ask yourself whether Thomas Jefferson, or James Madison, or others, had such materials or circumstances in mind when the First Amendment was being crafted." On the other hand, the manager of one of the stations fined for the Neil Rogers show challenged the FCC's determination that the program violated contemporary community standards. The manager stated that the ratings showed Rogers to be the most popular AM talk-show host in South Florida.[34]

Television was not neglected. In 1988 the FCC decided that the film *Private Lessons,* which had been aired on a Kansas City TV station, was indecent because the "story line of the seduction of a 15-year-old boy by an older woman, together with the inclusion of explicit nudity, would have commanded the attention of children."[35] In 1990 the FCC spent a year investigating allegations of indecency against a highly praised series imported from the BBC, *The Singing Detective.* Communications attorney Robert Corn-Revere, who was with the FCC at the time, later stated that it was "the most egregious" example of FCC censorship following the Commission issuance of its 1987 indecency guidelines.[36] Corn-Revere wrote that

> To the extent the FCC seriously considered merit as an important factor in making indecency determinations, "The Singing Detective" did not present a close case . . . But the FCC did not consider the program as whole. Indeed, the Commission did not even know what the show was about. Its review was riveted on images of nudity and a short scene in which a child witnesses a non-graphic sexual encounter.[37]

To Each His Own

In the meantime Congress continued to seek restrictive legislation on what many of its members considered obscene speech—the perception of obscenity varying, of course, according to each legislator's background and beliefs. In 1988 Congress upset many civil liberty organizations and individuals dedicated to the First Amendment. A Senate bill entitled the Child Protection and Obscenity Enforcement Act of 1988 was pushed during the last weeks of the Reagan administration by a coalition that included right-wing extremists, purportedly to combat child pornography. While none of the major opposing organizations questioned the importance of fighting child pornography, they did question the overall impact on everyone's free speech. One such organization, Americans for Constitutional Freedom, stated:

> The right-wing extremists call it an "anti-obscenity" bill. But because the definition of obscenity is so vague and the bill's penalties are so extreme, it will have a chilling effect on the creative content of all forms of literature, art, movies, plays and music. It is also an invitation to "moral" vigilante groups to intimidate local video and bookstore owners.[38]

Public and governmental concern was exacerbated in 1992 with the debut of *NYPD Blue*, a program that included realistic language, sexual connectivity and partial nudity. The religious right attempted to organize a nationwide boycott of the program even before it went on the air. A number of ABC affiliates succumbed to the pressure and refused to carry the initial program and, in some cases, subsequent programs. But it received critical acclaim for its artistic and entertainment values and shot up in the ratings, including in some of the geographical areas that generated some of the strongest complaints about it.[39] Nevertheless, it prompted more demands for tougher regulation on sex in the media. In a way, it was a prime example, at the turn of the twenty-first century in the United States, of the Victorian hypocrisy that marked both pre- and post-Victorian England. Perhaps Noel Coward said it best when he commented on the success of, and protest against, the sexual content of his play *Private Lives*, which debuted in 1924. Critical reviews described the play as "tenuous . . . brittle . . . delightfully daring." Coward noted that the reviews plus the play's "irreverent allusions to copulation" caused "a gratifying number of respectable people to queue up at the box office."[40]

In 1995 a federal court of appeals affirmed both the FCC's definition of indecency, as promulgated in 1992, and the restriction of so-called adult—sometimes considered by some as indecent—programming to the 10 p.m. to 6 a.m. safe harbor. Communication law firms attempted to clarify the FCC's posture for their clients. One of the leading Washington, D.C., firms, Haley, Bader and Potts, issued a "Primer on Indecency" (see Appendix C at the end of this book), which stated that "the FCC's indecency standard is both vague and complex."[41]

Also in 1995 a peculiar series of events related to the Howard Stern program resulted in the FCC levying a series of heavy fines through Notices of Apparent Liability (NALs) against Stern's parent organization, Infinity Broadcasting, which subsequently paid the highest single amount of money to the government for having broadcast allegedly indecent programming, but not one cent in fines. When is a fine not a fine? A series of Stern's programs aired in 1994 were found by the FCC to contain language that describes sexual and excretory activities and organs in patently offensive terms at times when there was a "reasonable" risk that children may have been in the audience. Infinity challenged the fines and announced that it would sue the FCC—as legally provided for—in the federal district court. At the last minute Infinity offered to "donate" $1.7 million to the FCC in exchange for the Commission vacating all NALs. Infinity agreed to re-educate all of its on-air personalities about the FCC's indecency standards, but neither Infinity nor Stern were required to admit any wrongdoing regarding the programs that had been the subjects of the NALs. The largest single broadcasting fine in history turned out not to be a fine![42]

Federal concern with indecency in the mass media was not limited to broadcasting. The final years of the twentieth century and the beginning years of the twenty-first marked increased activity, even hyperactivity, on the part of Congress and the FCC regarding allegedly indecent discourse, in words and pictures, in all media. Because of the lengthy bureaucratic process required to finalize an action against a station (due process protects stations as well as individuals), many indecency and obscenity cases appear to be dormant for years, and the public doesn't find out about them until and if some dramatic action, such as the fines against Howard Stern, takes place. A formal complaint to the FCC about program content must be in the form of a written allegation accompanied by a detailed description of the content in question. Formal complaints are comparatively few, considering the need to provide the FCC with either a written transcript of the offending material or an audio- or videotape of the program. If the FCC finally does investigate a complaint and finds the broadcaster liable, it then issues a Notice of Apparent Liability, citing a fine or other action. Sometimes it takes months and even years after the infraction for the notice to be sent. After a 30-day period for a given broadcaster's formal response to the allegation and the action, the FCC goes ahead with the proposed action or modifies it. This may also take months and even years. If the broadcaster challenges the action in the courts by suing the FCC, it may take another few years for the case to be heard and/or resolved. So, even as this is being written, indecency cases from the twentieth century are still pending.

Acts of Decency

The FCC and Congress made certain there could be many indecency cases. The Telecommunications Act of 1996 included landmark legislation concerning indecency in the media, with the inclusion of the Internet as a forbidden sphere and strengthened regulations for cable. But even before that,

cable was the subject of federal action. In 1987, even as the FCC was man-
dating stronger controls over broadcast indecency, the Supreme Court
decided that state and local governments may not restrict local cable systems'
carriage of indecent programming, even nudity and sex acts (multiple ownership of cable systems—multiple-systems owner, or MSO—is permissible,
but cable distribution is local).[43] The case in point was a landmark decision.
A Utah law restricted sexually explicit programming on cable to the hours
between midnight and 7 a.m. The Utah Cable Television Programming
Decency Act permitted sanctions against anyone who "as a continuing course
of conduct . . . knowingly distributed indecent material within this state over
any cable television system or pay for viewing television programming." The
federal courts found that the law was too broad in its attempts to ban nonobscene material. Utah had used the Seven Dirty Words decision as its rationale for the law. It appeared that any additional attempts by any states to censor
nonobscene cable programming would be held unconstitutional.[44]

The Cable Television Consumer Protection and Competition Act of 1992
somewhat modified this restriction on censorship, giving cable operators
the option of banning or not banning "patently offensive material" on any
channels they leased for commercial purposes. The act also allowed cable
operators to censor sexually oriented programs on any of their access
channels—public, education and government. (See Appendix D at the end of
this book.) Within a month the FCC issued proposed rules to implement the
act. The intended regulations were "designed to restrict access by children to
indecent programming on leased access channels of cable systems" and to
"enable cable operators to prohibit use of channel capacity on the public,
educational, or governmental access channels ('PEG channels') for programming which contains obscene material, sexually explicit conduct, or
material soliciting or promoting unlawful conduct."[45] The cable operator
would no longer be immune from liability for access channel material
deemed obscene and would be authorized to enforce a written and published
policy of prohibiting programming that the cable operator reasonably
believes describes or depicts sexual or excretory activities or organs in a
"patently offensive manner as measured by contemporary community standards." The cable operator would also be expected to exclude from leased
access channels any programming it considers to be indecent. The proposed
rule would require the cable operator to put on a single channel all indecent
programming, to block that channel unless a subscriber specifically requested
its reception, and to inform cable subscribers if a given program is considered indecent according to FCC standards.[46] Several years later, however, in
1996, the courts overturned this provision of the 1992 Cable Act.[47]

It was in the 1996 Telecommunications Act, backed by both Republicans
and Democrats, that alleged indecency was sledge- hammered by Congress—

in broadcasting and cable and on the Internet. One provision required cable systems to either scramble any channels with sexually explicit adult programs or restrict them to a 10 p.m. to 6 a.m. safe harbor. In 2000 the Supreme Court found this provision unconstitutional, noting that a blocking device was available for parents who did not want their children to watch such programming. In the majority opinion, Justice Anthony Kennedy noted that "even where speech is indecent and enters the home, the objective of shielding children does not suffice to support a blanket ban if the protection can be accomplished by a less restrictive alternative." In sum, it was a violation of the First Amendment to deny nonobscene programming to adults when children could be protected by means other than blanket censorship.[48] The 1996 act also required the blocking of audio and video of sexually explicit channels, except to those homes that subscribe to them, with fines up to $100,000 for transmitting obscene material. Four years later, however, in suits brought by the Playboy and Spice cable channels, the Supreme Court found that the requirement blocking or scrambling channels with sexually oriented materials was unconstitutional. It said that "laws designed or intended to suppress or restrict the expression of specific speakers contradict basic First Amendment principles."[49]

Another key provision of the Telecommunications Act of 1996 established the V-chip and a rating system for broadcast channels. Responding to increasing complaints and personal perceptions about sex, violence and language available to children over television, Congress mandated that all but the smallest television sets manufactured after June 1999 be equipped with a V-chip that blocks any program rated by the distributing network or station as containing material unsuitable for children. To receive such programs for adult viewing, the adult in the household would be required to enter an accessibility code. The act also required the broadcasting industry to develop, within a year, a rating system that enabled one to judge whether any given program contained too much sex, profanity or violence for children. The industry at first dragged its heels on agreeing on a rating system; many industry leaders considered such a requirement an intrusion on their First Amendment rights. The FCC set a deadline: if the industry did not develop an acceptable rating system, then the FCC would develop one and impose it on the field. The industry hastened to come up with a system. Perhaps as a compromise possible in the shortest time with the least contention, it adapted the motion picture industry rating system. TVY signified suitability for very young children, TVY7 for children over seven years of age, TVG for children of all ages, TVPG for programs that might need parental judgment and guidance, TV14 for programs that might be considered unsuitable for children under 14, and TVMA for programs some might consider unsuitable for children under 17 years of age. Parents, professionals, consumer advocates and many members of Congress found these ratings too vague and devoid of indicating what the objectionable content might be. Within months—by mid-1997—the industry developed a letter rating system: S for sexual content, V for excessive violence, L for unsuitable language, D for suggestive dialogue and FV for fantasy violence. Except for NBC and a number of cable networks, the industry adopted the letter ratings and showed the appropriate letters in a corner of the screen at the start of a program.

First Amendment advocates were strongly concerned. *Broadcasting and Cable* magazine noted some of their concerns:

> The requirements infringe on broadcasters' First Amendment rights of free speech. It would be virtually impossible to rate and code every television program. Television programs that are labeled as violent or with adult themes would frighten away advertisers. Implementing the V-chip requirement would force networks to favor sitcoms against serious drama because the latter might well attract S and/or V labels.

Critic Brian Burke noted that "instead of empowering parents or strengthening their influence in America's cultural landscape, the V-chip challenges parental authority and places them in an untenable position, holding their own against the relentless wave of commercial exploitation from outside, while fighting an adversarial war to suppress their child's innate desire to experience the forbidden world . . . if you keep children from seeing obscene, indecent or violent behavior, what will happen to them when they turn 17 or 18 and have to go out into the real world? . . . the v-chip proposes to keep the children gagged and blindfolded on the banks until some arbitrary age and then casting the bodies into the rapids and expecting them to swim intelligently upstream."[50] Researcher and teacher Aaron Furgason concluded that "the V-chip should be found unconstitutional . . . it is supposed to make it easier for parents to monitor what their children are watching. . . . in reality just the opposite is happening . . . what the V-chip ultimately will do is to keep parents and children from communicating with one another on what is good and what is bad behavior."[51]

Another concern about the V-chip, even for its advocates, is that children and especially teenagers might find ways of bypassing the V-chip. In addition, there was justifiable concern by its advocates that relatively few homes were actually using the V-chip.[52] One study revealed that of the 40 percent of the homes that have the V-chip or another program-blocking device, only about half actually use it.[53]

A third key First Amendment issue in the Telecommunications Act of 1996 was Title V of the act, better known as the Communications Decency Act of 1996 (CDA). This act was aimed at "dirty" content on the Internet. It prohibited not only obscenity but also "indecent" and "patently offensive" material anywhere on the Internet where such material might be accessible to children. One of the provisions of the CDA forbade use of any telecommunications device to make, create, solicit or transmit

> any comment, request, suggestion, proposal, image or other communication which is obscene or indecent, knowing that the recipient of the communication is under 18 years of age, regardless of whether the maker of such communication placed the call or initiated the communication.[54]

And in another provision it prohibited use of

> any interactive computer service to display in a manner available to a person under 18 years of age, any comment, request, suggestion, proposal, image, or other communication that, in context, depicts or describes, in terms patently offensive as measured by contemporary community standards, sexual or excretory activities or organs, regardless of whether the user of such service placed the call or initiated the communication.[55]

Anyone transmitting such material—with "indecent" and "patently offensive" still catch-all words not specifically defined—would be subject to a fine of $25,000 and two years in jail. The religious right, strong backers of the bill, insisted that it would ban only hardcore and child pornography. In addition to an inherent disagreement about what constituted indecency or was patently offensive, the law provided no exception for material that might be considered of scientific, artistic, political, literary or social value. For example, if a woman logged on to the Internet to exchange information on breast cancer, she would appear to be breaking the law. Similarly, so would a man who logged on to exchange information about prostate cancer. Both would be transmitting material about sexual or excretory organs and functions. Much of Shakespeare, as well as other great works of art, drama and literature, would be banned.

The moment the bill was passed by Congress and signed into law by President Clinton, it was challenged in the courts by a large group of diverse organizations, ranging from Internet companies to publishers to the American Library Association to the American Civil Liberties Union. They made the point that the law was so broad that virtually anything related even vaguely to sexual or excretory organs or functions would fall under it.[56] It is significant that the CDA was pushed through Congress at the last minute as part of the 1996 Telecommunications Act with no hearings to provide alternate points of view or questions about its constitutionality. The act never went into effect because a federal court immediately stayed its implementation pending a hearing. Within months of its passage a federal appeals court issued an injunction against it, stating it violated both the First and Fifth Amendments to the Constitution. The court said the Internet deserved the "broadest possible" First Amendment protections and that it was the "most participatory marketplace of mass speech that this country—and indeed the world—has yet seen." The court noted that any regulation of the content of the Internet "could burn the global village to roast the pig."[57] It also said that the Internet merits "the broadest possible" First Amendment protections and that it was the "most participatory marketplace of mass speech that the country—and indeed the world—has yet seen."[58]

A year later the Supreme Court ruled that the CDA was, indeed, unconstitutional.[59] The conservative Supreme Court ruling reflected the true meaning of conservatism: to conserve the guarantees of freedom in the U.S. Constitution. It stated that the Internet, like newspapers and books, was entitled to the highest form of First Amendment protection. Justice John Paul Stevens stated that "The interest in encouraging freedom of expression in a democratic society outweighs any theoretical but unproven benefit of censorship." Several justices found the law unconstitutionally too broad and vague.[60] The key issue was indecency. The banning of obscenity in any and all media was not challenged. It should be noted that the Supreme Court did not hold the CDA unconstitutional in its entirety. It upheld provisions relating to obscenity, as, for example, in a 1999 decision where it ruled that obscene e-mails were prohibited but that indecent e-mails were not.[61] A few years after that the Supreme Court had to act again, this time on the matter of "virtual indecency" on the Internet.

Undeterred by the Supreme Court's ringing reaffirmation of the First Amendment in its CDA decision, including its assertion that "the interest in encouraging freedom of expression in a democratic society outweighs any theoretical but unproven benefit of censorship," Congress within months enacted the Child Pornography Prevention Act, which banned child pornography in any form on the Internet. Online distributors of any such material that could be interpreted as harmful to minors were subject to six months in jail and $50,000 in fines. Many of the members of the coalition that brought the suit against the CDA joined together to fight this new bill. In April 2002 the Supreme Court rendered a decision. It "struck down a federal law banning computer-generated images of minors engaging in sex."[62] The ruling does not change the ban on obscene material or the pornographic presentation of real children. It stated that computer-generated or manipulated photographic images not involving real children do not violate the Constitution and banning them "prohibits speech that records no crime" and that the cultural issue of teenagers having sex has been explored and celebrated in art, literature, documentaries and mainstream films.[63] The Supreme Court found that the language of the act was overly broad and punishes works that have redeeming social value, and the Court chastised Congress for making it a crime to express an idea.[64]

Even as the challenge to the Child Pornography Prevention Act of 1996 was going through the courts, Congress passed another law restricting material that might affect minors. Passed despite the finding by its own experts that it would likely be found unconstitutional, the Children's Internet Protection Act (CIPA), enacted in December 2000, required libraries to equip computers accessible to children—that is, computers available to the public in libraries—with software that blocks any material deemed to be pornographic. Libraries that fail to install appropriate blocking devices would lose federal grants that pay for their access to the Internet. The continuing problem is, of course, the interpretation of what is porn. For the third time organizations dedicated to free speech coalesced to seek an injunction to prevent the implementation of the law. Groups such as the American Civil Liberties Union and People for the American Way, library associations and Internet web site operators opposed the FCC and the Institute of Museum and Library Sciences. (See Appendix E at the end of this book.)

The case, *Multnomah County Library v. United States,* was heard in Philadelphia, and in May 2002 the CIPA was found to be unconstitutional. With much of the same reasoning it used when it found the 1996 Cyberspace Decency Act unconstitutional, the court stated that CIPA was "invalid under the First Amendment" because it blocked access to legitimate web sites, at the same time permitting access to some pornography sites. The justices determined "that it is currently impossible . . . to develop a filter that neither underblocks nor overblocks a substantial amount of speech."[65] The decision noted that there

> are more than 100,000 pornographic web sites that can be accessed for free and without providing any registration information, and tens of thousands of websites contain child pornography . . . the widespread dissemination of hardcore pornography [is] within the easy reach, not only of adults who have every right to access it (so long as it is not legally obscene or child pornography), but also of children and adolescents to whom it may be quite harmful.[66]

The court accepted the argument of the plaintiffs that the use of the filter would abrogate the First Amendment rights of adults by denying access that might provide legitimate health information, such as data on sexually transmitted diseases and breast cancer. American Library Association official Emily Sheketoff stated that "this technology is not protecting . . . children. The only way to protect children is to make sure they are educated, so they can have a safe, responsible experience."[67]

In April 2001 the FCC issued a Policy Statement entitled "Industry Guidance on the Commission's Case Law Interpreting 18 U.S.C. Par. 1464 and Enforcement Policies Regarding Broadcast Indecency."[68] (See Chapter 5 for a detailed description.) The policy relates only to indecent programming and not obscenity or profanity. This Policy Statement (at this writing) governs FCC actions on this subject. The Statement affirms that obscene speech cannot be broadcast at any time, but that indecent speech is protected by the First Amendment. It also notes that the government must identify a compelling interest for any regulation regarding indecency and further that interest with the least restrictive means. It adds that the courts have, within certain limitations, upheld the FCC's authority to regulate indecent speech. The Statement affirms the FCC's authority to take measures against indecent materials broadcast outside of the court-sanctioned safe harbor of 10 p.m. to 6 a.m. The FCC definitions are reclarified: "the material alleged to be indecent must fall within the subject matter scope of our indecency definition—that is, the material must describe or depict sexual or excretory organs or activities" and "the broadcast must be patently offensive as measured by contemporary community standards," with "the determination as to whether certain programming is patently offensive is not a local one and does not encompass any particular geographical area . . . [It is] that of an average broadcast viewer or listener and not the sensibilities of any individual complainant." The policy takes into account the full context of the material. For example, "explicit language in the context of a *bona fide* newscast might not be patently offensive, while sexual innuendo that is sufficiently clear to make the sexual meaning inescapable might be." The Policy Statement notes the principal factors that have proven most significant in past cases of indecency: "the *explicitness or graphic nature* of the description or depiction of sexual or excretory organs or activities; whether the material *dwells on or reports at length* descriptions of sexual or excretory organs or activities; *whether the material appears to pander or is used to titillate, or whether the material appears to have been presented for its shock value.*" It states that no single factor provides the basis for a given decision, but notes that "the more explicit or graphic the description or depiction, the greater the likelihood that the material will be considered patently offensive," and that "merely because the material consists of double entendre or innuendo . . . does not preclude an indecency finding if the sexual or excretory import is unmistakable."

The Policy Statement additionally includes information on enforcement, emphasizing the following points: (1) the FCC does not monitor broadcasts for indecent materials but bases its actions on complaints received from the public; (2) a complaint, to be considered, must have full information, such as the station's call letters, the date and time of the broadcast, and a tape or transcript of the offending material; (3) the broadcast must fall outside of the safe harbor hours and within the FCC's definition of indecency. If the above criteria are met, the FCC will evaluate the material for its patent offensiveness. If the material meets that test, then the FCC may issue a letter of inquiry (LOI) to the station in question, seeking further information, or may issue a Notice of Apparent Liability (NAL). Any fine may be appealed. If an appeal is lost and the licensee refuses to pay the fine, the FCC may refer the matter to the Department of Justice. Finally, in this Policy Statement, the FCC cites a number of examples of indecent broadcast material for which penalties were levied, which, coupled with the analysis of the Commission's approaches and procedures, "provides a framework by which broadcast licensees can assess the legality of airing potentially indecent material."[69]

Continuing arguments dominate this latest FCC pronouncement on indecency. Former FCC attorney Robert Corn-Revere, commenting on the Statement, wrote that "obscenity hinges on 'community standards'; indecency, on FCC's . . . in other words, the FCC's broadcast-indecency standard remains today just what it was before the Commission issued its guidance to the broadcast industry: clear as mud . . . provides little guidance for the future."[70]

Some complaints to the FCC are frivolous, reflecting the Victorian attitudes of the complainant or the organized pressure of a vested interest group seeking to impose its beliefs on the rest of America. For example, some years ago the FCC was deluged with thousands of postcards and letters containing similar language that protested a series of programs presented by a medical school in California over a public television station. The programs were designed to provide basic health information in lay language to the general public. The complaint campaign, made up of the members and supporters of a right-wing religious group, claimed outrage that on one of the programs a physician explained that masturbation was not harmful, contrary to what some fundamentalists would like us to believe. More recently, in 2002, "the FCC dismissed complaints that the ABC television network's broadcast of the Victoria's Secret fashion show, which featured scantily dressed models, violated the Commission's indecency rules."[71] The FCC received hundreds of protesting e-mails and about 20 formal complaints. In dismissing the allegations the FCC said the complainants had not proved that "the sexual aspects of the material" were, in context, so graphic or explicit as to be patently offensive.[72]

Rarely is the FCC unanimous in its judgment of what is indecent, or even in its issuance of policy statements on indecency. The First Amendment always looms large when any restriction is contemplated, albeit legal restrictions as authorized by case (court decisions), statute (enacted by Congress) or administrative (federal agency rules) law. Commissioner Susan Ness said that the broadcast indecency statute compels the FCC to reconcile two competing fundamental obligations: (1) to ensure that the airwaves are free of indecent programming material during prescribed hours when children are most likely to be in the audience; and (2) to respect the First Amendment rights of broadcasters regarding program content. . . . Even words that might be construed as indecent are subject to some constitutional protection against government regulation.[73]

Some FCC commissioners express impatience at what they consider foot dragging on the part of the Commission in enforcing existing standards regarding indecency. For example, Commissioner Gloria Tristani dissented from issuance of the 2001 Policy Statement and chastised the Commission for what she considered its failure to act on previous and pending indecency cases. She called the Policy Statement a diversion from the lack of enforcement. She stated that "it would better serve the public if the FCC got serious about enforcing the broadcast indecency standards."[74]

And in 2002 FCC Commissioner Michael Copps warned the broadcast industry that the government might have to step in if the industry didn't reduce what he considered a proliferation of raunch on the airwaves. He condemned what he called a wave of "patently offensive programming invading" America's homes. He criticized the FCC for its "dismal record of going after offenders." He stated that "the industry can fix the problem voluntarily. If it won't, the government may have to halt the race to the bottom."[75]

Urged on by Commissioner Copps, the FCC in 2002 took increasingly stronger stands on allegedly indecent programming. He urged stations to voluntarily tape programs and hold them for 60 days in case of indecency complaints. Although Canada and the United Kingdom have had a comparable requirement for years, it doesn't seem likely that required or voluntarily compliance with such a rule will make much headway in the United States.[76]

Subsequently, however, the FCC took the stance that a station would be considered guilty of an indecency violation alleged in a formal complaint unless it could prove its innocence. David Solomon, chief of the Commission's Enforcement Bureau, stated that "If a station can't refute information in the complaint, we'll assume the complainant got it right."[77] Some broadcasters felt that this was pressure to force stations to keep tapes, as Copps had proposed. This was part of a pattern of increased concern with and attention to indecency complaints on the part of the FCC. In all of 2001 there were about 280 formal complaints, and after investigation, the FCC found just seven worthy of a Notice of Apparent Liability. In early 2002 the FCC listed some 40 indecency complaints per month, but Commissioner Copps insisted that his office alone gets 30 complaints a day and that the Commission is, in fact, getting "hundreds or thousands" of such complaints.[78] In 2002 indecency fines included a $14,000 imposition on a Chicago station for "morning-show segments featuring a porn star describing a fetish sex act and another in which women described oral-sex techniques, accompanied by a soundtrack of women moaning."[79]

Just as strongly, however, many officials and critics have criticized the FCC for being too assiduous in its pursuit of indecent programming, alleging violations of basic First Amendment rights. One of the most vocal has been Nicholas Johnson, first as an FCC commissioner and more recently as writer, law professor and lecturer on the media.

In a 1994 case involving the Turner Broadcasting System (TBS), the Supreme Court stated, "a government body seeking to sustain a restriction on . . . speech must demonstrate that the harms it recites are real and that its restriction will in fact alleviate them to a material degree."[80]

Perhaps an editorial in the *Miami Herald* best summed it up. The editorial, in part, stated:

> The Federal Communications Commission isn't the first regulatory agency to test the limits of its authority. And the regulated—from Wall Street brokers to Main Street bankers—often test their regulators' limits, too . . .
>
> The FCC is different from other regulators in one crucial respect: It touches upon First Amendment rights whenever it delves into program content.
>
> Granted, only the absolutists among civil libertarians would argue for an "anything goes" standard in a medium that can intrude upon unwilling listeners. Even in that camp, there's little quarrel with the long-standing ban against outright obscenity.
>
> Yet when the issue becomes "indecency" rather than obscenity, a troubling degree of additional subjectivity creeps in. Lawmakers and the courts have had a tough enough time defining obscenity. Defining "indecency" is an even greater challenge because it dwells in a vast miasma somewhere between the obscene and the merely tasteless. . . .
>
> Defining indecency is only half the problem. The other is fashioning enforcement mechanisms so that the cure doesn't turn out to be worse than the disease. The courts—the institution responsible for striking a balance when rights are in conflict—must handle these cases with care. Free-speech rights are fragile, and, once shattered, not easily reconstructed.[81]

NOTES

1. *FCC v. Pacifica Foundation*, 438 U.S. 726, 98 Sup. Ct. 3026 (1978).
2. Dwight L. Teeter and Bill Loving, *Law of Mass Communications: Freedom and Control of Print and Broadcast Media* (New York: Foundation Press, 2001), p. 679; Pacifica Foundation, 56 FCC 2nd 94 (1975).

3. *Pacifica Foundation v. FCC*, 556 F. 2nd 9 (1977).
4. Ibid.
5. Ibid.
6. *FCC v Pacifica*, 438 U.S. 726, 98 Sup. Ct. 3026 (1978).
7. Ibid.
8. Ibid.
9. Federal Communication Reports, FCC 75-1333 (1975).
10. Federal Communication Reports, December 18, 1975, FCC 75-1405, docket no. 20677.
11. Marjorie Heins, *Not in Front of the Children: Indecency, Censorship, and the Innocence of Youth* (New York: Hill and Wang Publishing, 2001), pp. 115–16.
12. Robert L. Hilliard and Michael C. Keith, *The Broadcast Century and Beyond*, 3rd ed. (Boston: Focal Press, 2001), p. 217.
13. Ibid., p. 233.
14. Ibid., p. 218.
15. *Media Law Reporter*, vols. 1–15 (Washington, D.C.: Bureau of National Affairs), p. 632.
16. Wayne Overbeck, *Major Principles of Media Law* (New York: Harcourt, 2002), p. 357.
17. Peter Jacobson, "Legislative Update: The Child Online Protection Act," *Journal of Art and Entertainment Law*, spring, 1999.
18. Milagros Rivera-Sanchez, "The Regulatory History of Broadcast Indecency (1907–1987)" (doctoral dissertation, University of Florida, 1993), pp. 268–72.
19. Ibid., p. 272.
20. See Appendix A at the end of this book.
21. 2 FCC Record 2698, 62 RR 2nd 1191 (1987).
22. 2 FCC Record 2703, 62 RR 2nd 1199 (1987).
23. Ibid.
24. 2 FCC Record 2705, 62 RR 2nd 1202 (1987).
25. 2 FCC Record 2706, 62 RR 2nd 1202 (1987).
26. Heins, *Not in Front of the Children*, p. 113.
27. FCC Fact Sheet, "FCC Takes Strong Stand" (November 1987).
28. Robert Goldberg, "Smut Haters Level Sights at Broadcasters," *Wall Street Journal*, July 23, 1990.
29. Hilliard and Keith, *Broadcast Century and Beyond*, pp. 267–68, 278, 281, 292; Teeter and Loving, *Law of Mass Communications*, pp. 680–83.
30. Linda Greenhouse, "Curb on Smut Is Allowed," *New York Times*, January 9, 1996, p. A5.
31. "Court allows limits on indecent radio, TV shows," May 28, 1996, http://www.usatoday.com/news/court/nscot029.htm.
32. Regina Ramsey, "The FCC's Indecency Policy" (an academic paper, 1991).
33. Bill Cosford, "Trying to fathom FCC's indecency," *Boston Globe*, December 23, 1987, p. 42.
34. Juan Carlos Coto, "Fines for Indecency Rock Miami Radio," *Miami Herald*, October 27, 1989, p. 1A.

35. Heins, *Not in Front of the Children*, p. 119.
36. Ibid.
37. Ibid.
38. Public letter from Americans for Constitutional Freedom, August 26, 1988.
39. Ibid., p. 278.
40. Playbill for *Private Lives*, J. Howard Wood Theatre, Sanibel, Florida (March 2002).
41. "Primer on Indecency," issued by Haley, Bader and Potts, November 18, 1995.
42. FCC Docket MM-828 (1995).
43. Overbeck, *Major Principles of Media Law*, p. 474; *Wilkinson v. Jones*, affirmed in 480 U.S. 926 (1987).
44. Al Kamen, "High court bars Utah ban on 'indecent' cable shows," *Boston Globe*, March 24, 1987.
45. FCC Docket MM-92-258 (November 5, 1992).
46. Ibid.
47. Overbeck, *Major Principles of Media Law*, p. 475.
48. Ibid., pp. 475–76. *United States v. Playboy Entertainment Group*, 529 U.S. 803, 120 Sup. Ct. (2000).
49. Teeter and Loving, *Law of Mass Communications*, pp. 683–85; *United States v. Playboy Entertainment Group*.
50. Brian Burke, "The Significance of the V-Chip," http://www.cep.org.
51. Aaron Furgason, "Telecommunications Act of 1996" (Media Control and Regulation Class at Emerson College, 1997).
52. Ibid., pp. 458–60.
53. Teeter and Loving, *Law of Mass Communications*, p. 687, citing a study by the Annenberg Public Policy Center at the University of Pennsylvania.
54. Communications Decency Act, enacted by U.S. Congress February 1, 1996, text in its entirety on http://www.epic.org/cda/cda.html.
55. Ibid.
56. Ibid., pp. 400–402.
57. Information sheet issued by People for the American Way, "Federal Court Affirms First Amendment Protections on the Internet" (summer 1996).
58. Ibid.
59. *Reno v. ACLU*, 521 U.S. 844.
60. Overbeck, *Major Principles of Media Law*, p. 400.
61. *Apollo Media Corporation v. Reno*, 526 U.S. 1061.
62. Lyle Denniston, "Justices reject ban on 'virtual' child porn," *Boston Globe*, April 17, 2002, p. A1.
63. Ibid.
64. Ibid.
65. Robert O'Harrow Jr., "U.S. Court Overturns Internet Smut Law," *Boston Globe*, June 1, 2002, p. A1.
66. Ibid., A16.
67. Ibid.
68. FCC, file no. EB-00-IH-0089, March 14, 2001.

69. Ibid.
70. Robert Corn-Revere, "Eye of the beholder," *Broadcasting*, April 16, 2001 (web site).
71. "FCC says lingerie show broadcast is not illegal," *Boston Metro*, March 26, 2002, p. 3.
72. "A victory for scantily clad," *Broadcasting and Cable*, March 25, 2002, p. 6.
73. Federal Communications Commission Policy Statement on broadcast indecency, 1992.
74. Ibid.
75. David Hinckley, "Copps Swears Airwaves Will Be Policed," *New York Daily News*, February 7, 2002.
76. David Hinckley, "Radio Stations Wary of Taping All Shows," *New York Daily News*, January 21, 2002, p. 84.
77. Bill McConnell, "New rules for risqué business," *Broadcasting and Cable*, March 4, 2002, p. 5.
78. Ibid.
79. Ibid.
80. *Turner Broadcasting System, Inc. v. FCC*, 114 Sup. Ct. 2445, 2470 (1994).
81. "Indecency on the Air," editorial in the *Miami Herald*, November 1, 1989, p. 22A.

CHAPTER 3

CROCK JOCKS TO SHOCK JOCKS

The developers of really dirty discourse on radio were, in most part, disc jockeys who tried to enhance their record-playing roles with increasingly expanded commentary between records. The commentaries eventually morphed into more talk than music and after that into what we now call "talk radio." At first they titillated. Then, as the competition got tougher, they shocked. Harvard Professor Murray Levin stated that "when I studied talk radio there was no issue that aroused as much anger and emotion as homosexuality. The talk-show hosts, they knew this. They would talk more about it than the subject warranted. They'd get heated debates and would push people to further extremes. That boosted ratings."[1]

Some of them moved early into talk formats, which were manipulated to display what they thought they had and what they wanted their audience to believe they had—a special knowledge of politics and economics and social problems. Anyone with more than a passing knowledge of public affairs could well apply to them their own epithets and in most cases accurately say that they were simply a crock-full! Many of the jocks not only pontificated egotistically, but mean-spiritedly as well. They demeaned guests, callers, public figures and the general public. They deliberately attempted to shock. It is not surprising that some of them expanded or adapted their repertoires to the areas of sex and profanity and that dirty discourse became the format of choice. Sydney Head and Christopher Sterling observed that "shock radio deliberately aims at outraging conservative listeners by violating common taboos and desecrating sacred cows. Shock radio's contempt for adult authority and social tradition tends to attract listeners younger than the usual talk radio audience."[2]

Tom Leykis, the Los Angeles shock jock icon, said that the successful talk show has got to deal with personal relationships and not with ordinary, everyday, general topics. That approach, he believes, tends toward a voyeuristic prodding into the "sex lives" of the audience. "Whether the content is a male listener describing his sexual conquest of the night before, or a female relating her conflicted feelings about sharing the details of a sexual affair she had with one of her bridesmaids with her husband, such talk tends to repel older people while attracting those who thought they were 'music-only' listeners."[3]

Some of the early dirty discourse that roused listeners' passions and raised Congress's and the FCC's ire would be considered mild compared with later material. In the early 1970s period of so-called topless radio, in which women listeners were invited and sometimes goaded into discussing their sex lives on call-in talk shows, their intimate revelations resulted in official vilification, fines, threats and the quick disappearance of that format. When FM radio began to grow, its higher-quality sound and stereo signal taking AM's music programs, AM turned to talk as an alternative. More and more women tuned in the late morning and early afternoon talk shows. For broadcasters it was a way of attracting a younger female demographic, with more expendable funds than the older demographic that usually listened to what had been talk or discussion programs. At first the callers would phone the stations in the evening, and their talks with the host or hostess would be taped for playback the next day, edited by the station to conform with the format and content orientation of the given show. Understandably, even when the topic dealt with sex, the spontaneity often seemed forced or entirely missing. The answer was to do the phone-in interviews and discussions live. Such programs grew in popularity, and the format spread nationwide, with the former deejays who were most adept at getting callers to be explicit, outrageous and, most of all, shocking becoming stars not as music jocks, but as shock jocks. Although, as described in this chapter, FCC pressure resulted in the early demise of the format, it returned some years later in another form. Discussions of personal sex lives and predilections became a staple of both radio and TV. The only difference is that now a host had an M.D. or a Ph.D. after his or her name. A decade after topless radio ostensibly disappeared, Dr. Ruth Westheimer was heard on radio in New York conducting live candid intimate sessions with callers. And a decade after that Dr. Laura Schlessinger was doing somewhat the same thing in national syndication.[4]

Over the Topless

Topless radio is generally acknowledged to have begun with the program *Feminine Forum* on radio station KGBS, Los Angeles, in 1971, hosted by a personality named Bill Ballance. (More about Ballance and *Feminine Forum* later.)

However, sexual content on talk shows began much earlier; these shows and their stations became the targets of fines by the FCC for indecent programming. For example, in 1958 the FCC began a proceeding to revoke the license of a station in Denver because an announcer had talked about "flushing pajamas down the toilet" (accompanied by a flushing toilet sound effect), "inflating cheaters with helium" and "the guy who goosed the ghost and got a handful of sheet." The station apologized, fired the announcer and kept its license.[5]

In 1959 radio station KINM, Boulder, Colorado, broadcast the following after playing a record entitled *I Ain't Never:* "Gee, I ain't, either, sure would like to sometime." And after receiving a postcard from a listener noting that she took KINM radio with her everywhere: "I wonder where she puts KINM radio when she takes a bath—I may peek—watch yourself, Charlotte." That got the station a cease and desist order from the FCC.[6]

The next year radio station WDKD in South Carolina broadcast the following comments on the Charlie Walker show. Walker was certainly not a shock jock nor did his program resemble the later topless format. But he was very good at implying sex in his dialogues without actually mentioning sexual terms.

I seen something last night that I wanted. I wasn't too bashful to go get it, I was just too smart. She had her husband with her. My momma didn't raise no foolish young'uns.

★ ★ ★

Careful drivers can have accidents. Careful boyfriends can have accidents too.

★ ★ ★

I don't wanta save everything I get my hands on. I had my hands on something last night and I guarantee you boy I didn't want to save it. It's that you better believe.

★ ★ ★

This boy was lovin' this gal good and he says, "Darling, will you marry me?" And she says, "Well, I don't know. Tell me, do you want a home?" And he says, "Honey, I'm a regular homebody." And she says, "And what about children?" And he says, "Oh, honey, I just love children." And she says, "Well, in that case, I'll marry you if you like children. We'll be in business in about six months." They're gettin' a head start.

★ ★ ★

Betsy says it is that not only will she flirt with dynamite, but it is that if it's single, she'll propose to it. Betsy says it is that she don't mind marrying a stick of dynamite if he's got a long fuse.

★ ★ ★

You farmers better get off of it and get out there and get in at them tobacco fields. We don't want no other crop failures this year. It is that we don't want any farmers to have any crop failures. I know about eight farmers' daughters that I hope like the devil that have a crop failure. All I got to say is they better have one. If they don't have a crop failure, I'm gonna have a heart failure.[7]

That material proved to be a factor in WDKD later losing its license.

One of the early shock jocks who established the rude, crude persona for many others who were to follow was Joe Pyne. An original crock jock, Pyne held forth with far right-wing views on any and all subjects, violently and insultingly disagreeing with his guests and callers. The more shocking he was, the higher were his ratings. In the mid-1960s he had both a radio show in syndication to more than 250 stations and a television show syndicated by Metromedia. Although he didn't concentrate on sex, he didn't shy away from it, and many of his guests (like the purported bishop he goaded into admitting he had sexual affairs) confided their sexual secrets on his show. One of his shticks was to invite prostitutes on his show and berate them, all the while making sure there was enough graphic discussion of their professional expertise. He didn't shy away from profanity, either. His viciousness was his trademark. One of the coauthors of this book was a guest on the Joe Pyne show early in Pyne's career. It was in 1953, the day the Rosenbergs were executed for allegedly spying for the Soviet Union. When this coauthor walked into the Wilmington, Delaware, nightclub where the program originated, Pyne was crowing with great glee. "They burned those bastards tonight. I hope it was slow and painful. It's about time. We finally incinerated those commies." And on and on with much laughter.

A half-a-dozen years later the same coauthor was on the Joe Pyne show again. This time he and Pyne were in agreement. The topic was censorship of radio and television. Pyne, who died of cigarette smoking at an early age, left a legacy of nastiness as part of the talk radio act, most popularly epitomized today by Howard Stern.

Larry Solway was an early shock jock who wrote a book about his experiences, *The Day I Invented Sex*. He was working in Canada in the 1960s when he was prodded into being more controversial. Controversial became equated with sex. A look at some of the dialogue of his programs reveals that it is much milder than that heard on a Dr. Laura–type program, but at that time it was to many listeners quite scandalous.

Woman: I believe that "free sex" is all right if both parties are responsible. But you find a lot of people who just want sex. It becomes unfair to say you don't want to have sex—because then they don't want to know you. Sometimes that leaves me thinking there's something wrong with me.

Larry: These men who leave you thinking there's something wrong with you are really busy "promoting" you. Telling you that sex is free is one of the oldest con lines in the world. What you have to ask is: "All right, what am I going to get out of it? I know what you're going to get out of it. You're going to have an orgasm. Lucky you. But what about me?"

Woman: I know that. But when I was brought up I was told about sex the way Dr. Reuben tells it in the book. I was told that the thing-ma-billy went in the thing-ma-jig and that was it.

Larry: Do you feel more liberated but no more promiscuous as a result of reading the book?

Woman: I still can't get by my upbringing. That's why books like this are so very helpful. If there were more books brought out to tell you more about sex. I don't mean go and have sex on every occasion, but when you do come to the decision of having sex, you've got that extra bit of knowledge. You don't want to have sex and not know what it's all about, not to be able to fulfill your partner.

Larry: What frightens you about the act of intercourse?

Woman: I think the fear of pregnancy. I know girls can go on the pill.

Larry: Is that all that frightens you?[8]

One of the topics Solway frequently dealt with was masturbation.

Larry: Have you ever masturbated?

Woman: No.

Larry: Do you know what it is?

Woman: (Stumbling, almost inarticulate) I've had the urge, but I've never done it because I kind of felt it was something I shouldn't do.

Larry: (Reading from Reuben's book) "A woman who never reaches orgasm any other way can almost always achieve a climax with a vibrator . . . The reflex pathways that determine the sexual climax are reinforced over and over again until orgasm is no longer a sometime thing, but occurs regularly like clockwork . . . Once a woman is capable of reaching orgasms with regularity by this method she is ready for the next stage. What's that? Transferring the reflex mechanism to sexual intercourse. Masturbation re-establishes the association between pleasurable sensations and stimulation of the genitals. The obvious sequel is to extend that association by copulation itself."[9]

Needless to say, many if not most of the listeners were shocked. Yet today probably no one would even raise an eyebrow, taking the exchange at face value, a therapeutic discussion principally from a recognized medical work. There were other preshock jocks who set the groundwork for what would eventually be called dirty discourse, but as can be seen from Solway's work, it was quite far from anything indecent. It was in the early 1970s that the real shock jock format took its first steps.

To Shock in Earnest

The manager of radio station KGBS in Los Angeles, Ray Stanfield, programmer Rose Hutton, program director Ron Martin and on-air personality Bill Ballance are generally credited with having invented topless radio in 1971. One of the coauthors of this book recalls driving through Pennsylvania in the 1950s and hearing afternoon radio shows in which female callers recounted their personal and intimate sex problems and solutions. However, it wasn't until the 1970s that entire programs that encouraged graphic detail and profane language took hold on a regular basis. Also called "X-rated radio," the name of the format became controversial in itself. Some critics defined the format as purely dirty discourse, in which only women callers were allowed to talk on a given sexual subject. Their call-in comments were neither screened nor delayed. Defenders of the format said that the subject matter was not "sex talk" but discussions of male-female relationships. Ray Stanfield, an originator of the format, later stated that "we do not have a sex talk show on this station. We have a clever interviewer on the air, talking to callers about man-woman relationships. Sex is an occasional by-product. But when the subject turns sexual, it is never handled in bad taste."[10]

Stanfield stated that topless radio shows, within a year and a half originating on a daily basis on some 60 stations throughout the country, were stolen and bastardized from his station's Bill Ballance show.[11] Stanfield recalled that in attempting to revamp a format that was drawing too few listeners, he decided to orient talk radio to younger audiences. "What appeals most to young women? And the obvious answer, of course, was young men. We wanted to put on the air light, humorous conversations about the relationships between men and women."[12] At first a pretaped show with the title *Feminine Forum* took calls from female listeners; it was found to be dull. A former rock deejay, Bill Ballance, was asked to do a live midday version. It was an overnight success, and Storer Broadcasting, which owned KGBS, introduced the format at five of its other stations. Other stations followed. In California KNEW called its version *California Girls*, on Dallas's KLIP it was the *Dave Ambrose Show*, in Washington, D.C., the *Scott Burton Show*. Bill Ballance's show itself became one of the country's leading syndicated programs.[13] And, despite disclaimers, Ballance set the tone for the *Feminine Forum* clones. Examples of the topics discussed, a different one each day: "Who first turned you on?" "What place do you like to do it best?" "Was your virginity important to you?" Ballance often invited his female listeners to "stroke my stallion ganglia," and when one listener asked him to explain what he meant, he told her he could arrange a "private showing."[14]

The clones were pretty much alike, with the on-air personality providing the principal difference. One of the most successful was the *Dave Ambrose Show* in Dallas, with topics such as "Is your virginity important to you?" "How do you turn on your man?" "How would you confront the 'other woman'?" "Is sex really all that great?"[15] Following is an example of the call-in dialogue for the question "How do you turn on your man?"

Caller: The wine kiss-off.
Ambrose: The wine kiss-off? What's that?
Caller: I pour some wine on the right place and then I kiss it all off.[16]

The host of *California Girls*, Don Chamberlain, elicited tragic and comic comments both, all of them quite revealing. One caller, when asked who first turned her on, responded that it was her father when she was a child. Another caller said that 50 years earlier she and the people she worked with used to frantically have sex constantly behind the office switchboard like "sex maniacs."[17]

Of the stations that adopted and adapted the *Feminine Forum* format and approach, the one that was ultimately to reap the most notoriety was WGLD in Chicago. Using virtually the same title as Bill Ballance's show, WGLD put on a five-hour-per-day, five-day-per-week program entitled *Femme Forum*, hosted by Morgan Moore. There was nothing subtle about the content.

Moore: Okay, Jennifer, how do you keep your sex life alive?
Caller: Well actually, I think it's pretty important to keep yourself mentally stimulated . . . you think about how much fun you're going to be having . . . if that doesn't work there are different little things you can do.
Moore: Like?
Caller: Well, like oral sex when you're driving is a lot of fun—it takes the monotony out of things.
Moore: I can imagine.
Caller: The only thing is you have to watch out for truck drivers.
Moore: Okay, that sounds like good advice.
Caller: Try it sometime. You might like it.
Moore: Try it, you'll like it! What else, my dear?
Caller: Oh, well—that's about enough for now.[18]

On a program dealing with the question "How important is oral sex in your particular sex life?" the following exchange occurred:

Caller: . . . of course, I had a few hangups at first about—in regard to this, but you know what we did? I have a craving for peanut butter all that time, so I used to spread this on my husband's privates and after a while, I mean, I didn't even need the peanut butter anymore.
Moore: Peanut butter, huh?
Caller: Right. Oh, we can try anything, you know, any, any of these women that have called and they have, you know, hangups about this, I mean, they should try their favorite, you know, like, uh . . .
Moore: Whipped cream, marshmallow . . .
Caller: You know, I mean, it's a little messy, but outside of that, it's great.[19]

On that same program some callers spoke of their hang-ups concerning their partners' climaxing "when I go down on him," some stating that they never got over their aversions to "swallowing it." Another caller said that "initially what I was afraid of was the climaxing, the end of it. I thought I'd choke to death, you know . . . [but I] come to find out it not only can taste good, but it isn't all that much." And still another caller spoke of her husband's hang-up about oral sex: "He was afraid that I was going to bite it off."[20]

On another *Femme Forum* show masturbation was the topic. Some women callers explicitly described both the natural and artificial means they used to achieve a "climax." Some others insisted that masturbation improved their relationships with their spouses. And still others detailed how masturbation was the only way they could reach a "climax" or "sexual satisfaction."[21] One on-air exchange during that program included the following:

Caller: . . . your program does arouse me—so does your voice.
Moore: Take a cold shower, will you?
Caller: Oh, no—I took care of it already.
Moore: Oh, boy! Thank you.[22]

Burning Ears

While some listeners found topless radio funny and bizarre, others didn't. As topless radio proliferated, so did complaints from the public. Even the National Association of Broadcasters (NAB) began to worry. At that time the NAB had voluntary codes of conduct (long since abolished) for its member stations, and in March 1973 the radio code board, as a follow-up to its having urged its members several months earlier to "avoid sensationalism" in their topless radio shows, mandated the code authority to "increase its monitoring to cover sex-oriented talk programs and questionable lyrics to help determine the extent to which member stations are carrying such material and to help determine the status of such material under radio code standards."[23]

Defenders of the format claimed that it helped more people than it offended. Bill Ballance stated that he believed he helped people: "They are conversationally intimate with me because they can't communicate with their husbands. The show brings out a lot of marital discord that has been simmering below the surface."[24] George Duncan, then president of Metromedia's radio division, said that there "is no question that this country is in the process of changing its societal mores. Sex education in the school was a violently controversial topic only five years ago. But now sex taught as health education is entirely proper. Now we have people discussing sex on the radio, and it was to be expected. Radio is a reflective medium."[25] Dallas host Dave Ambrose said, "It's time radio kicked and screamed its way into the 20th century. Why can television, which is the same type of public media, talk about the same subjects at the same time of day—soap operas—and we can't? . . . Far from being irresponsible broadcasting, this kind of radio can be the most responsible type. We're into the serious aspects of daily living."[26] Ken Gaines of KNEW said, "A large portion of the world has opened up to these women for whom the world has never been a very open place."[27] One caller to *California Girls* stated that "at first I thought your show was just kind of kooky and left it at that. But you've been getting into areas lately that really concern us. I'm finding out a lot of things about myself I didn't know before."[28] The Peat, Marwick and Mitchell consulting firm conducted a study of callers to Bill Ballance's *Feminine Forum*, the mother of all topless radio, and found that they were "a representative cross-section of the southern California female population, with the distinction of being significantly above average in education, income, quality of residence and level of occupation. Their specific characteristics indicate a stable and mature group, with vested family interests, a fairly conservative outlook on marriage, as shown by lower divorce rates than the national average, and social habits denoting upper middle class. None of the callers considered her interview to be in poor taste, salacious or in any way offensive. Practically all said it had been fun."[29]

But for many people it was not at all fun. Congress was irate. Some of the public were irate. The FCC was irate. In March 1973 the FCC reported receiving some 2,000 letters complaining about objectionable programming.[30] Senate Subcommittee on Communications chair John Pastore wanted the FCC to revoke a license as a warning and a means of getting the topless format off of radio.[31]

House Subcommittee on Communications chair Torbert MacDonald told FCC chair Dean Burch at a congressional hearing that

> I hope you go after them [broadcasters with topless radio shows] because I told you privately and in public, before this, unless something is done, the Congress, whether it likes the role or not, will have to get into the role of becoming a censor, which the Congress has no business being. But somebody has to do something. . . . You have the quickest clout of anybody. Just tell them, if this continues, that you are going to see to it that it is stopped by lifting a number of licenses. If lifting one for a test case is not enough, why don't you lift 25 at a crack? They won't all settle and you will get a test case.[32]

A week later Burch addressed the annual convention of NAB and said, in part:

> What I am talking about is the prurient trash that is the stock-in-trade of the sex-oriented, radio talk show, complete with the suggestive, pear-shaped tones of the smut-hustling host. I am talking about three, four, five solid hours of titillating chit-chat—scheduled during daytime hours—on such elevating topics of urgent public concern as the number and frequency of orgasms (during a single sitting, so to speak) or the endless varieties of oral sex (including practical tips on learning to love it) or a baker's dozen of other turn-ons, turn-offs and turn-downs.[33]

Burch also warned broadcasters that "the boundaries of the First Amendment may next be tested in the context of the right to broadcast garbage—and don't kid yourselves—it will be tested" and that "if electric voyeurism is what the authors of the Constitution had in mind, I'll eat my copy."[34]

Obscenity is Indecency?

Burch's outrage was matched by that of many others—ordinary citizens, VIPs and most of the FCC commissioners. On the same day of Burch's speech, March 28, 1973, the FCC issued a Notice of Apparent Liability (NAL) against WGLD and *Femme Forum*. Although the allegation against WGLD was not indecency, which fell within the FCC's purview, but obscenity, which under criminal law was under the jurisdiction of the Justice Department, the FCC nevertheless decided this was going to be its test case.

The FCC inquiry would be closed to the public, with only one of the seven FCC commissioners, Nicholas Johnson, opposed to the action, which he called an inappropriate application of the FCC's regulatory responsibility. He called Burch's NAB speech "a despicable bit of government censorship and delivered in a masterfully professional style."[35] Protesting a closed-door meeting in which the commissioners heard a 25-minute excerpt of WGLD *Femme Forum* programs, Johnson declared that "it's not for us to proclaim that something can't be said over the air."[36]

The FCC fined the owner of WGLD, Sonderling Broadcasting, the maximum fine for the two programs it reviewed, a total of $2,000, and urged Sonderling to take the Commission to court as a test case so that a judicial determination could be made of both the FCC's authority and the challenged content. Sonderling, however, declined to do so.

The FCC stated that *Femme Forum* was an excellent example of broadcast obscenity:

> If discussions in this titillating and pandering fashion of coating the penis to facilitate oral sex, swallowing of semen at climax, overcoming fears of the penis being bitten off, etc., do not constitute broadcast obscenity within the meaning of 18 USC 1464, we do not perceive what does or could.[37]

The Commission further noted that

> We have no doubt the explicit material set out above is patently offensive to contemporary community standards for broadcast matter . . . We also believe that the dominant theme here is clearly an appeal to prurient interest . . . We do not believe that there is redeeming social value here. This is not a serious discussion of sexual matters, but rather titillating, pandering exploitation of sexual materials . . . It would make no sense to say that a broadcaster can escape the proscription against obscenity if he schedules a three, four, or five hour talk program, and simply intersperses the obscenity—so critical for the ratings—with other, non-obscene material.[38]

Commissioner Johnson dissented, characterizing the FCC as the Federal Censorship Commission for "penalizing a station because of the content" of its programs.[39] He stated,

> In the instant case, the majority focuses only on portions of the challenged program, makes absolutely no attempt to delineate the relevant "community" in question, and makes no effort whatsoever to determine the nature of the relevant community's standards.[40]

He claimed additionally that the courts, not the regulatory agencies, "are more competent to determine whether particular forms of expression fall within the unprotected category" and that any action regarding obscenity cases properly belonged with the Department of Justice.[41] He added,

FCC regulation of obscenity is dangerous not only because this agency is, as the instant case painfully reveals, incompetent to deal with the problem, but also because such regulation causes a "chilling effect" of enormous proportions on all forms of broadcast expression.[42]

Even before the actual fine on April 11, the March 28 NAL had a strong and immediate effect on the topless radio format and programs. Sonderling Broadcasting, when paying the fine, sent a letter to the FCC stating that

We have been made aware of the comments made by Senator Pastore, Congressmen Staggers and MacDonald and the Chairman's speech to the NAB convention on Wednesday, March 28 . . . we were apprised of the resolution passed by the NAB relating to sex-oriented programs . . . The very same day new rules were initiated and top management decreed that the "Femme Forum" talk program would be continued as part of the over-all programming of WGLD, but that, effective the same day, all sex-related subjects would be banned.[43]

This was a long nail in the coffin of topless radio. Three months later *Femme Forum* went off the air, and six months after that its importance to the station was magnified as the call letters of WGLD were changed and a new format was instituted for the entire station.[44] Even on the day the fine was levied on Sonderling Broadcasting, an FCC official suggested that although "we have no way of knowing . . . it appears nearly all of the topless shows have disappeared."[45] In May, a survey by NAB concluded that there was "little evidence of sex-oriented talk programming" on the air any longer and that what there was appeared to be cognizant of "audience sensibilities and good taste."[46] In a period spanning little more than 20 months, topless radio rose from nothing into its zenith and then surreptitiously crashed into ashes. It would rise again years later in the form of radio and TV hosts ostensibly providing psychological and physical health information, and as part of the routines of the shock jocks. In 1973, however, a headline in *Broadcasting* magazine summed up the FCC's actions for many people: "The net effect of Sonderling: FCC diminishes broadcast freedom yet another cubit."[47]

Raunchy Radio

A decade after topless radio was forced from the airwaves, a new phenomenon of dirty discourse resurrected sex radio's popularity. "Raunch radio," hosted by shock jocks, spread just like topless radio had before, despite—or perhaps, because of—a conservative era in America punctuated by the election of Ronald Reagan to the U.S. presidency. Listeners to shock jock shows

> ## Terry
> ## Lex and Terry Morning Radio Network
>
> This is probably a shock coming from me given the type of show I'm involved with, but yes I do think the government should have the right to prevent broadcasters from using language or material it considers offensive to the public. There should be some established guidelines. The real problem is that the "guidelines" aren't really defined. What one person finds offensive is another person's cup of tea. There isn't a firm outline in place, so the FCC can just pick and choose what it wants to condemn and fine. On the whole, I think it does a pretty good job given the mandate it is given. I believe in freedom of speech and will fight for it. I believe that the guidelines should allow for shows like ours that provide the type of adult entertainment that the listener wants. I feel there is a responsibility to stay away from anything that promotes hate of a person's race or sexual orientation. Broadcasters can do some serious damage if that is their intention. There's a fine line to walk and it can be a very ambiguous path.

"are barraged by sexually explicit references, cultural and ethnic attacks, off-color listener telephone calls, and sexually based interviews and antics."[48] Coauthor of this book Michael Keith scrutinized both raunch radio and shock jocks in a section of his book *Talking Radio*.[49] Keith noted that "today the reputed 'shock jocks of raunchy radio' have legions of loyal fans and high ratings in cities across the country and their attitude toward those who take umbrage at what they do over the air is perhaps best summed up by the self-proclaimed 'king of all media,' Howard Stern, in a conversation with a disgruntled caller: 'Hey, dial another fucking [sic] station . . . fool! Don't mess with my freedom of speech . . . Asshole [sic]'!" In a series of interviews Keith established a sense of both the content of and attitudes toward the format of shock jocks' shows. Walter Cronkite, news anchor, reporter and writer, described it this way: "They call it shock radio, but what they are basically about is hard-core pornography." Steve Allen, entertainer, author and composer felt the same way: "It's a grave error to assume that fundamentalist religious believers or political conservatives are the only critics of Stern and the thousand-and-one other examples of sleaze presently so dominant in our culture. I personally take liberal or progressive positions on a good many social issues, but I don't know of any conservative who is more revolted than I am by the present sleaze-flood." And about Howard Stern, Allen said, "I will oppose to the death what his incredible dependence on vulgarity of the grossest sort is doing to the American consciousness, of both children and adults. Unlike the social critic, Lenny Bruce . . . Stern has little to say about the conditions of life on our troubled planet." Writer and producer Sam Dann stated that "the climate exists for this kind of radio because moral, ethical, and even intellectual standards have all but disappeared." Conservative commentator Paul Harvey expressed his concern this way: "Our beautiful language has meant so much to us . . . For anybody to dirty it up, for anyone to drag his bedroom into the environment, I find inexcusable . . . such on air excess . . . is ultimately its own undoing."

And now for the other side of the story. Keith quoted producer and writer Dick Orkin: "I think Stern is unique because he knows he is pushing and testing the limits—a veritable Lenny Bruce of the blue ether. And, like Bruce, he is witty and clever and in some perverse way he reminds us of radio's strength as an up-close and intimate medium." Stan Freberg, entertainer, producer and writer, said that "I hate the whole shock-jock thing . . . But, despite all this, I think Stern is a very funny guy, who does make people listen to the medium. I'm a great fan of Don Imus, too." Peter Wolf, recording artist and programmer, was quoted as follows: "Shock jocks like Stern have their place on the dial, and they should be allowed to be there, I think . . . what is all the hubbub about anyway? Maybe the only downside is that there are just too many imitators on the air." Archivist and deejay Shel Swartz summed up the bottom line, quoting a radio performer friend whose program was loaded with sexual innuendo and profanities: "today you're either outrageous on the air or you're out of work." What, if anything, should be done about shock jocks? In *Talking Radio*, Keith included a comment from his coauthor of this book. It expresses a view they articulated in a number of books they have written, including one that reveals and analyzes what many consider a far dirtier discourse than any sexual repartee, the promulgation of hate and violence, as detailed in *Waves of Rancor: Tuning in the Radical Right*. That comment, from *Talking Radio*: "The airwaves should be available and accessible to everybody, regardless of point of view, as long as they are not used to inspire hatred or prejudice."

King of all Raunch

Let's look at Howard Stern and see what all the fuss is about. Stern is considered by many to be the king of the current crop of shock jocks. He has gotten more publicity than any of the others and more notoriety for his outrageous treatment of sex and language on his shows—indecency and profanity and, according to many critics, even the verboten obscenity. His radio shows go beyond sound and are frequently visual, in the studio and in the minds of his listeners. For example, "it is not unusual for Howard Stern and his on-air staff to cajole a female guest into disrobing as Stern details her anatomy for his listening audience."[50] He has been described as working without an obvious script, with his trademark long hair and sunglasses, and interspersing rambling commentary with sharply aimed insults. The *New York Times* noted that "Over the years, Mr. Stern has enthusiastically pushed the boundaries of permissible conduct on the air waves. His routines are spiced with talk about masturbation, the size of sexual organs, and an array of other sexual topics. Mr. Stern has also disparaged virtually every ethnic group in the country."[51]

The Howard Stern show earned for its owner, Infinity Broadcasting, the highest fines ever imposed by the FCC for indecency; it also earned the largest audiences for programs cited by the FCC as indecent. Of concern was not only the content, but the fact that his programs have been aired at times of day when children might be listening. These fines first reached a record $105,000, and when Stern continued to violate the FCC's indecency standards, they went up to $600,000, and by 1993 totaled over $1 million.[52] Numerous NALs, with forfeitures, were issued. Cited among the warnings issued to Infinity was Stern's use of the words *penis* and *vagina* over the air. How did Stern respond? Here is an example from one of his programs, a dialogue between Stern and his on-air partner, Robin Quivers:

> **Quivers:** You'd better be a good boy.
> **Stern:** No, I can't be good because it's the weekend.
> **Quivers:** You're going to lose all of us our jobs.
> **Stern:** You'd think I'd say "penis"?
> **Quivers:** Oh, no.
> **Stern:** I don't care what the FCC says. Where is the FCC?
> **Quivers:** Somebody stop him.
> **Stern:** Hey, FCC, "penis."
> **Quivers:** Put your hand over his mouth.
> **Stern:** I don't care, it's the weekend, baby.
> **Quivers:** It's a stampede in there, you can't say that. (Stampede sound effect.)
> **Stern:** Yeah, I don't care. I do draw the line at "vagina." Whoa, whoa, I can't believe I just said that word.
> **Quivers**: That's it, here they come.
> **Stern:** Oh, ooh, here comes the thought police. I don't believe it, baby. Oh, my goodness. Oh, look at those horses. They're going to trample over you, Robin.[53]

An example of an NAL sent by the FCC to Infinity Broadcasting was a May 1994 letter assessing a $200,000 fine for indecent material on two specific Howard Stern shows, one in December 1993 and the other in January 1994. (See Appendix F at the end of this book.) This was an unusually large fine for indecency violations, but the FCC's reasoning, as stated in the NAL, was because of "the apparent pattern of indecent broadcasting exhibited by Infinity over a substantial period since our initial indecency warning."[54] Many skeptics have said that Infinity deliberately persisted in such programming because the value of national publicity generated far exceeded the cost of the fines. Here are samples of the offending dialogue cited by the FCC in this particular NAL, with four stations noted as the subjects of the complaints.

Stern: We're allowed to masturbate. What is this? Suddenly I have to wither up and die, be Ward Cleaver.
Male Voice: Friday and Saturday night it makes you feel better.
Stern: Thank you.
Quivers: It's just . . .
Stern: How come we . . .
Quivers: Oh, you wouldn't do it if she knew?
Stern: No. It's embarrassing.
Male Voice: She would like me to, but I can't.
Stern: How do you, how do you . . . ?
Male Voice: I could never do it with a woman watching.
Stern: What happens? You go to bed at the same time or no?
Male Voice: Sometimes, sometimes not.
Stern: Sometimes you go to bed earlier cause we have to get up early.
Male Voice: Whatever.
Stern: So you go to bed and then you wake up.
Male Voice: Sometimes I can't get to sleep, you know?
Stern: Right, and you wake up in the middle of the night and your wife is laying there sleeping, you can tell when she's asleep.
Male Voice: And you say, well I won't wake her and I'll be very calm.
Quivers: Quiet.
Male Voice: And by the end, you're not.
Stern: And you do it right, and you do it right in the bed?
Male Voice: Sure.
Quivers: You don't even get up?
Male Voice: No. Where am I going to go?
Stern: Don't you . . . ?
Male Voice: Take a little precaution.
Stern: Right.
Male Voice: You know.
Quivers: What's the precaution?

Male Voice: A Dixie cup, all right? What do you mean?

Quivers: (laughs)

Stern: Takes a Dixie cup.

Male Voice: Some things you don't have to discuss.

Stern: He uses his sock. He has a sock.

Male Voice: Then I discard it. I don't put it in the wash.

Stern: Right, right, that's good, you bury it in the back yard with Jessica Hahn's lingerie.[55]

And the second offensive piece:

Male Voice: I came home after a band job late at night with this girl that I used to be with once in a while and she performed an act, you know, and I was drunk out of my mind, of course.

Quivers: Of course.

Stern: Of course.

Male Voice: The next day, as I recall, I kind of remember as it was happening that there was gagging going on, but this can happen . . .

Stern: Right.

Male Voice: . . . in such a thing and the next, you know what I'm saying? I mean . . .

Quivers: Oh, I know what you're saying, okay?

Stern: And she was gagging, right? Okay, yeah, she was gagging . . .

Male Voice: So she must have left that night.

Stern: And that's because you're such a monster.

Male Voice: Well, of course.

Stern: Yeah, right, I've seen you. Nobody's gagging on anything.

Male Voice: So obviously it could have been for some other reason.

Stern: Yeah.

Male Voice: Which we'll see it was.

Stern: You were all proud of yourself cause she was gagging.

Male Voice: Hey.

Stern: Right, you were like, oh.

Male Voice: Probably sobered me up.

Stern: Right.

Male Voice: So she left either that morning or the night before, whatever, but then I wanted to go to the bathroom.

Stern: Oh, oh.

Male Voice: And as I'm sitting there . . .

Stern: Little vomit.

Male Voice: I look down and in my lower area hair is like hunks.

Stern: Hunks? Aw, alright, alright, alright, I don't want to hear about this. Oh, my God. Oh, that's disgusting, Oh, you always have to outdo everyone, don't you?

Male Voice: There's Cheerios.

Quivers: Hey Gary, your girl just vomited on the bed.

Stern: So you look down and there was vomit all over you.

Male Voice: The big chunks.

Stern: Wow.

Quivers: Oh.

Male Voice: I mean, oh Jesus, it was like the most horrendous thing ever.[56]

Infinity appealed the fines as they were levied and brought court challenges on constitutional grounds.[57] More infractions occurred. Finally, the FCC threatened to revoke the licenses of Infinity's stations if the alleged indecencies continued, warning that "any future infractions would place Infinity's continuing fitness as a Commission licensee in question."[58] Unexpectedly, in 1995 Infinity offered to forego further litigation and settle the pending indecency fines levied from 1989 through 1994 for $1.7 million. Under the FCC-Infinity agreement, Infinity admitted no wrongdoing or liability for the still-outstanding fines. The president of Infinity, Mel Karmazin, stated that he believed that if litigation continued, the courts would ultimately find Stern's material protected by the First Amendment and not indecent, but he wanted to "conserve the time, expenses and human resources" of both Infinity and the FCC from further litigation. The FCC said, "that Infinity has conformed its conduct or at least changed its ways was an important fact in us agreeing that this settlement is in our interests."[59]

Was this the end of the indecency struggle between the FCC and Howard Stern? Not by a long shot. This settlement, the largest amount ever paid to the FCC for a violation, took care of a number of pending NALs—but there were still some outstanding against non-Infinity stations that carried Stern's program, and in subsequent years there would be more NALs issued. In 1997 CBS was the target, the Stern program originating at one of its stations. The NAL was accompanied by a number of examples of dialogue from Stern's shows, compiled by the FCC staff. Nothing in the content seemed to have changed. Was this material obscene? Was it indecent and offensive because it was aired during the forbidden 6 a.m. to 10 p.m. period? Did it meet the "patently offensive" as judged by "contemporary community standards" criteria? Or should it have been protected under any circumstance by the First Amendment?

Stern: . . . I'm ready for sex. Cause I purposely didn't play with myself on Friday.

Quivers: Really?

Stern: Or Saturday.

Quivers: You're storing up.

Stern: Yeah, even during the computer sex, as tempted as I was, I didn't, you know.

Quivers: Like a squirrel you're saving your nuts.

★ ★ ★

Stern: So I start dancing with her, right? And I'm rubbing, now don't forget, she doesn't have any panties on, I'm rubbing her legs while I'm dancing, and I'm squeezing her ass, and lifting the dress up a little bit, once in a while my arm slides into the wrong place, you know what I mean?

Quivers: Oh, dear.

Stern: You know what I mean? I'm manipulating her, spreading her cheeks, right? Come on, you know you like this, Robin.

Quivers: You are wacky.

Stern: Look at you.

Quivers: You're . . .

Stern: You're a little flush right now.

Quivers: Just go on with your story.

Stern: Want to take your shirt off? You like this, don't you? Come on, this is good, compliment me.

★ ★ ★

Stern: I know, so then I'm like, you know I'm rubbing her legs and she's getting into it and I'm like, you know, and I even like I was pulling down her top a little bit and kissing her and you know what I mean? And she was really turned on.

Quivers: Uh, huh.

Stern: Really turned on.

Quivers: How do you know?

Stern: Then I bent her over the bed, like I bent her, I just bent her over.

Quivers: Uh, huh.

Stern: Now she, she was totally open to me.

Male Voice: Totally vulnerable.

Stern: Totally vulnerable like you do it. Totally, like when the police get you up against the car?

Quivers: There you go.

Stern: Yeah, all bent over the car.

Quivers: You're mine.

Stern: And I start manipulating, doing everything I've learned over the years, which isn't much.

Quivers: All your expertise.

Stern: Right.

Quivers: At play.

Stern: All my expertise are in my hands. And she was writhing.

Quivers: Oh.

Stern: Oh, boy, had her going. Writhing with pleasure. But I was all sexed up from the computer.

Quivers: She doesn't know that, though.

Stern: Then she was losing her balance. It was so good.

Quivers: I thought she was bent over.

Stern: Yeah, but she was, I don't know, she was shaking.

Quivers: Got weak in the knees.

Stern: She got weak, she couldn't stand up. I was busy. I had two busy thumbs.

Quivers: Oh, dear.

Stern: Thumbs, look at my thumb, Robin.

Quivers: Please, I don't want to see it.

Stern: Come here.

Quivers: I don't want to watch.

Stern: Look at that, huh.

Quivers: I'm not looking at that.

Stern: Look how long it is, isn't that pretty?

Male Voice: Two of them.

Stern: There you go, two of them.

Quivers: Oh, shut up, you two.

Stern: Two of them, Atilla the Thumb.

Quivers: I don't know what he's talking about.

Stern: You know, you've been there.

Quivers: I've never been in thumb territory.

Stern: Well, let me tell you, she was, she hadn't been, either, after 20 years she hadn't been in thumb territory. Well, she was digging, let me tell you something, then I got her down on the bed and then with the vibrators, thumbs.

Quivers: Good lord, you needed vibrators then?

Stern: And, oh yeah, and you should, and the vibrator disappeared, if you know what I mean, and . . .

Male Voice: Question.

Stern: My tongue was used.

★ ★ ★

Stern: Pictures of Janah Jamerson, the porno star.

Quivers: Uh, huh.

Stern: And Jackie said to me, you think her dad, if you showed him five pictures of vaginas, could he pick out his daughter's vagina?

Quivers: Oh, dear.

Stern: So I asked him to hold on cause I want to see if he can do it.

Quivers: Oh, you're going to do it.

Stern: Yeah.

Quivers: You got other magazines?

Stern: Yeah. I got a picture of her vagina and a couple of other vaginas.

Male Voice: Alien vaginas.

Stern: Alien vaginas.

Quivers: Oh, he says he censors. He doesn't look at hers.

Stern: Yeah, but he knows her from when he used to change her diaper and stuff. Did it look that different?

Quivers: Yes, I would think so.

Stern: Why, they matured or something?

Male Voice: You could guess.

Stern: I wonder if he's ever gotten it on with a girl that his daughter has gotten it on with.

Quivers: Now there's a question cause I'm beginning to think that Janah was bringing those girls home for herself.

Stern: And then dad got.

Quivers: And dad got them.[60]

Sometimes it took years for the FCC to catch up with the complaints or find them valid. In 1998, for example, the FCC issued an NAL against the following 1993 Stern material:

Stern: The legs, rolling around on a Jaguar all sexed up. That Jaguar must have stunk for three days. I'm watching.

Quivers: I don't think she's a smelly person.

Stern: No, but you know girls have a special scent, that they leave, when they're all hot and they're not wearing panties and they're laying all over a car. Panty juice. I always look at my wife's panties. There's always something going on there, too.

Quivers: Oh.

Stern: She always.

Quivers: [Boy oh boy.]

Stern: What do you mean, boy oh boy?

Quivers: Panties.

Stern: These women have all kinds of stuff going on.

Quivers: Like yours are crystal clean.

Stern: I never like, there's always like junk going on in my wife's panties.

Quivers: Let me see yours right now.

Stern: Fine. What are you saying?

Quivers: I want to see yours right now.

Stern: I'll tell you, I don't have the stuff, you know, I have some leakage, I'll admit.

Quivers: (laughs)

Stern: I think she's leaking from everywhere.

Quivers: (laughs)

Stern: No, sometimes I look at my wife's underpants and I go, yeah, I really shouldn't look at her underpants because it's kind of a turn off. You know what I mean? There's lots going on.

Quivers: I don't know why you're doing that.

Stern: She always has pads and stuff. I don't know what's going on. It's always a two-sided surprise. You got, like stuff going on in your underpants, right?

Quivers: Everybody does.

Stern: Really? God, it's disgusting.[61]

Some critics feel that Stern's really indecent remarks go beyond the FCC's concept of sex and language. For example, after his principal talk-show rival, Don Imus, was hospitalized with a collapsed lung, Stern said on the air, "I hope he dies."[62] Even as this is written, in the early years of the twenty-first century, Stern continues to be a principal shock jock, his manner and material unabashed and the stations that carry his programs prime targets for FCC NALs and fines. Yet Stern himself has said that "I always resented the term 'shock jock' that the press came up with for me . . . because I never intentionally set out to shock anybody. What I intentionally set out to do was to talk as I talk off the air, to talk the way guys talk sitting around a bar."[63]

Clones and Echoes

Nevertheless, his style has been copied by many and developed simultaneously or even before him by some. Other jocks who have achieved similar notoriety, albeit in smaller or limited markets in most cases, are Steve Dahl, Gary Meier, Jonathon Brandmeier and Danny Bonaduce.[64]

Don Imus uses essentially the same style. But Imus is considered by many to have been the first authentic shock jock, the papa of shock jocks. Imus began in California in 1968 and after being fired a couple of times ended up with Infinity, ironically Howard Stern's company. Imus's signature comments are "Are you naked?" and "How's your Donkey Kong, baby?"[65] Calling himself the I-Man, Imus has had a long-running feud with Stern. He maintains that Stern imitated him, while Stern calls Imus one of his "many imitators." Imus claims to appeal to the intelligentsia and that Stern is a "garbage mouth."[66] During the 1980s and 1990s, while they went head to head, Stern's ratings far outdistanced Imus's, yet Imus remained Stern's foremost competitor for king of the shock jocks. Imus was promoted as the sophisticated alternative to Stern and in the late 1990s made an effective comeback. In fact, *Newsweek*, taking note of his apparently changed approach, has called him a "former shock jock."[67] His routines include commentary on political figures and discussions with journalist guests. His routines are not as raunchy as Stern's and emphasize more commonly discussed situations, such as Senator Ted Kennedy's alleged drinking problems and former President Clinton's alleged sexual promiscuity.[68]

America is full of local shock jocks, some of them with programs that are syndicated, none of them with the national reputation or appeal of Stern and Imus. But in their own markets some are as popular as Stern and the I-Man. One example is Erich "Mancow" Mueller, whose show originated in Chicago. (Mueller has been fined for on-air obscenity.) One description of his style: "His irreverent image of ethnic and cultural slurs, coupled with references to bodily functions, has led to a wide following in his markets. His broadcast sidekick, 'Turd,' provides on-the-street antics and interviews."[69]

Another example is Doug Tracht, broadcasting in the Washington, D.C., area as the Greaseman, a character Tracht developed who is ostensibly "a woodsman who blundered into the city, ate from dumpsters and found work spinning records on the radio while squatting on the toilet."[70] The Greaseman show has been described as "an adolescent dream-scape pocked with disease, dripping in bodily fluids, and cocked to explode with violence."[71] While the content and innuendo in his shows are somewhat similar to Stern's, Tracht eschews the kind of language Stern uses, finding euphemisms that don't shock the puritans as much or draw the ire of the FCC. For example, whereas Stern will say "breast" and "penis," Tracht will say "ta-tas" and "hydraulics."[72] In addition, he employs different routines, such as the character Fudgeman, who, with his assistant Throbin, saves the world from deviant behavior; the Bet the Bomb Bays quiz, in which listeners try to stump the Greaseman, "but if you don't, you best drop them pants"; the Rag Nad stories about the Greaseman's half–space alien love child; and an account of how Greaseman and his father picked up and enjoyed ugly women.[73]

While hundreds of shock jocks attempt to compete with Stern in local markets, the Greaseman had been one of the more successful—until 1999. Shock jocks' vocabularies, by and large, include not only sexual profanity, but frequently racist and ethnic epithets and slurs. In 1999 Tracht made a racist slur and was fired. After a year of abject apologies, he began trying to make a comeback. The nature of the shock jock business was expressed by Howard Stern when asked about Tracht's firing; he said that if Tracht had his [Stern's] ratings, Tracht might have gotten away with it![74]

Challengers to Stern have come and gone, but a couple of new jocks on the block, making their mark in the first few years of the new century, threatened to dethrone the king. The press has noted that they "may be the first real local threat to the longtime dominance of Howard Stern on the air."[75] In a matter of months becoming the highest-rated afternoon talk hosts in the New York area (Stern's morning program still garners the highest ratings of any talk show in the market), Opie (Gregg Hughes) and Anthony (Anthony Cumia) quickly developed a national reputation. In fact, Stern has complained that he isn't permitted to use language on his show that Opie and Anthony used with abandon. And the rivalry in the New York market built up (perhaps as a publicity gimmick?) to the point where one of Stern's ardent fans left a bomb threat on Opie's answering machine and was arrested for doing so. Opie and Anthony started their collaboration in Boston, were fired and moved to New York. They go beyond "sex, smells and excretion" into public visual stunts and other subject matter that has some critics saying that they've gone beyond Howard Stern in vulgarity. They attract a young male audience who enjoy "the kind of talk that was once limited to locker rooms and particularly nasty bars."[76] Anthony noted that "when you say we're so gross that you have to turn it [the radio] off, there are five or 10 people who just have to listen."[77]

Opie and Anthony's stunts include people eating live mice and stuffing women into 55-gallon drums, in addition to carrying sex and profanity to the edge.[78] They get women to disrobe in the studio (a Howard Stern staple, too), "do gay bashing, comedy bits about AIDS, have whipped cream bikini contests, and rate 'moms' they would like to have sex with."[79] Their signature stunt is called WOW, or "Whip 'Em out Wednesday," in which they encourage women listeners who are in cars to flash their breasts at other motorists.[80] They also sponsored a WOW contest that offered $1,000 to the first female who exposed her breasts on the *Today* show. And someone did. A woman standing in the crowd outside the NBC studio at Rockefeller Plaza "unbuttoned her shirt, yanked it open, and exposed her breasts to millions of viewers" as the camera panning the crowd reached her.[81] They're not the only shock jocks WOWing their listeners, however. Tom Leykis in Los Angeles asks his male listeners every Friday "to flash their headlights as a signal to female listeners in other cars to flash their breasts."[82]

All of this has made these shock jocks so successful that a 2001 syndication deal with, no surprise, Infinity, put Opie and Anthony in the vanguard of shock jocks with national exposure, ahead of leading competitors such as Erich Mueller, known as Mancow in Chicago, and Todd Clem, known as Bubba the Love Sponge in Tampa.[83] Opie and Anthony's style has been described as "frat house radio,"[84] and *Brill's Content* magazine put them on a continuum with a pantheon of the leading practitioners of rude and crude.[85] The program director of a Boston station that picked up their syndicated show reflected what appears to be the feeling about Opie and Anthony wherever their program is aired when he said, "people will be outraged, shocked, and amused."[86]

In the summer of 2002, people were more than outraged when Opie and Anthony pulled what was considered their most shocking on-air stunt. They arranged and broadcast a live account of a couple having sex in New York's St. Patrick's Cathedral. After three days of furious criticism from religious and lay groups and from government and broadcasting officials, they were fired by WNEW. Infinity Broadcasting, the station's owner, then canceled the national syndication of their show. It didn't take long for some wags to ask, if priests who had sex with altar boys in cathedrals were not fired, why were Opie and Anthony? Who did WNEW hire to replace them? Hardly a paragon of modest content: Los Angeles shock jock Tom Leykis.

In an interview, Opie put the criticism of the Opie and Anthony show in perspective. "Look at 'Hogan's Heroes,'" he said, "a sitcom about those wacky, lovable Nazis. And they say we're twisted."[87]

Professor, critic and writer of telecommunications Christopher Sterling commented to this book's authors on the long-range implications of the Opie and Anthony event:

Michael Harrison
Publisher, *Talkers Magazine*

I dislike the term "shock jock" but admit it has become the generic phrase to describe talk show hosts of the Howard Stern/Opie and Anthony ilk. There are really few talented—and thus successful—perveyors of the form. That's why Howard Stern is the *only* talker on *his* NYC station (as well as many of those that carry him in syndication) and that's why WNEW-FM will not be able to make it with this type of talk sans Opie and Anthony. Sadly, Opie and Anthony have given the colorful but sparse genre of bad taste a bad name. They might have ruined it for other talk artists of the shock jock school who aspire to follow in the great Howard Stern's large, muddy footsteps.

Such pushing of the "good-taste envelope" will unfortunately continue, given the radio business's desperate push for audience amidst more stations and some indications of declining listenership. Combined with a clear decline in demonstrated radio industry ethics, many stations will continue to dive for the bottom line in both taste and revenues. The FCC can or will do little about such cases. In the August 2002 WNEW-FM "Opie and Anthony" case, it may not even assess a fine, given that the program was quickly suspended and then cancelled, and station officials were suspended as well. The First Amendment (and Section 326 of the Communications Act of 1934) severely limit what the FCC can do about media content. More immediate, however, is the Commission's demonstrated unwillingness to even deal with "public interest" issues in potentially obscene content unless there is strong public or (even more influential) Congressional pressure to take some action. In a deregulatory age of not trusting government agencies, such pressure seems unlikely.

Wolves in She's Clothing

Although not as popular or as abundant as male shock jocks, there have been some female shock jocks. Female talk show hosts have been around a long time—about as long as radio. But their talk shows, up until the feminist movement of the 1970s, consisted mainly of stereotyped topics such as cooking and recipes, house cleaning, clothing and makeup, and care of children. The concentration was on homemaking. The pressures from feminists, individuals and organizations, and the pioneering efforts of women media personalities like Barbara Walters changed the topics and formats into coverage of legal issues, the environment, women's rights, local politics, the school system and other issues that helped open doors for women. There were some women disc jockeys, but not many. Although vastly outnumbered by their male counterparts, some competed effectively. As music got more raucous with the advent of rock and roll, so did the deejay commentaries, a freeing of language and ideas reflecting the freedom and beat of the new music. In their quest for the highest ratings in a given market, the male deejays tried to startle their audiences, then, going a step further, to electrify, sometimes by offending, sometimes with shocking material. They succeeded. However, the attitudes of society allowed listeners to accept from males what they would not accept from females, and the shock jock profession became virtually totally male. Women broadcast personalities sometimes used their sexual attraction through a sultry voice, a come-hither Mae West inflection. But rarely was heard a raunchy word.

In the 1960s a New York station, WNEW, experimented with a schedule of all-female disc jockeys and called it "Sexpot Radio." But it lasted only 18 months. Even so, what was called "chick talk" appealed to some stations, and a few hired and promoted women into key roles. Sally Jessy Raphael was one, offering advice on a variety of topics, sometimes covering material that would have been condemned by some if discussed as frankly on some of the male talk shows. As shock radio grew in the 1980s, a few women joined the movement. Considered by many the first so-called "shockette," Carolyn Fox, on a station (WHJY-FM) in Providence, Rhode Island, adapted her generally liberal views to sex and language even before Howard Stern became a national figure. In the early 1990s she was frequently referred to as the only female shock jock. She paved the way for a number of other women who entered the shock jock field.[88]

Darian O'Toole was considered in the late 1990s "one of a handful of outspoken and sexually candid women heard on modern adult and modern rock radio."[89] Her morning program was top rated in the San Francisco market. Sara Trexler in Austin, Texas, Caroline Corley in Denver and Kelly Walker in Detroit were other female shock jocks who were highly successful in the 1990s. Some of the female shock jocks first began on male shock jock programs, and some continue in that role. A prime example is Robin Quivers, who has worked with Howard Stern for many years.[90] Female jocks' program content is much the same as that of male shock jocks—locker room–type humor but from the female point of view.[91]

Sarah Clark, cohost of a highly rated morning show in San Francisco, said, "Let's face it. Sex is the bottom line—no pun intended . . . And you know that when you get any five women together, it gets just as nasty, maybe worse, than guys." She feels that "guys seem to love hearing a woman talk about sex. It's a fantasy."[92] Darian O'Toole said that "the conversations I have on the air are the same as the conversations I have with my friends. I can refer to my group of guys as my 'bevy of stud muffins.' A guy doing the same thing to women would be considered sexist." She feels that women jocks should be intelligent and articulate to get the respect of listeners, that she got away from the two traditional female stereotypes, the "whiskey-drinking chain-smoking biker babes . . . [and] the breathy phone-sex girls."[93] Jamie White, on a Denver station, stated that although men think that women are generally prudes, "when I go out with my girlfriends—surprise—we talk about sex." She thinks the image of a bunch of guys in a locker room as being most raunchy is exaggerated. "That's nothing compared to six women out having a few drinks. We give details that men don't. . . . If my friend Bob is suffering from a low sperm count or premature ejaculation, he's not going to call his friend Larry for advice. However, if I'm having a heavier-than-normal period or I want to recommend a new vibrator I just got, I'll call my friend Carla right away and talk about it on the air."[94]

But female shock jocks face problems and restrictions that males don't. The expectations of listeners are different. Kelly Walker, who was highly successful in Detroit, said that "It's a boys club. Guys can talk about T&A and lesbian stuff. If I did, I'd be considered a real asshole. I also don't think I can talk about how good I got it last night, because I'd be considered a whore." Sara Trexler noted that "I don't feel any sexism really in terms of what I can and can't do. But my gut says if a woman says something and a man says the same thing, people think that when the woman says it that it's dirtier." Several female shock jocks said that if they spend too much time on sex alone on one show or have too many programs in a row emphasizing sex that it seems to generate some unnecessary negative response. As did most female talent on shock talk programs, Jamie White found it "personally difficult for me to find my way. I feel that men in general are intimidated by strong women, and I find that when I talk like a real woman I upset more men than women. I used to shock my partners, who used to want me to shut up and do the news."[95]

Indecency on radio is frequently one of the key topics at meetings of women in broadcasting. Recently at such a meeting in San Francisco, a number of highly visible on-air women discussed the approaches women should and shouldn't take. Corey Foley stated that "You should be down to earth and real. But you don't have to be disgusting to be real. Sometimes the gross stuff people do is unnecessary. You can be entertaining without being gross." Kristi Thomas said, "You can be entertaining while being family friendly. You just have to work harder. You have to be prepared. You just don't walk in the studio and settle back into old traditions like talking about strippers for four hours." And Alicia Kaye stated that "if you're normal and you behave like the person who's listening to you, people will like you better. But if you act like you're too sexy and not for real, then people tune out."[96]

Cleaner Air?

Is the content of shock jock shows changing? As the old century was turning into the new, opinion was mixed. Some thought there was a trend toward less indecency. Doug Shane, a former morning deejay and program director, said, "I think it's gotten more sedate. . . . Even Howard Stern has become more mainstream. I think the jocks have gotten more mainstream because the [large media] companies have more invested, they don't want to risk fines." He added they don't want even one station to be investigated because that might make the entire multistation company a target.[97] On the other hand, Jim Villanucci, of the *Jim and Julie* radio show in Las Vegas, said that they have moved more into a "hot talk" format that's designed to appeal to a younger, 25–54, audience, to whom he can "talk on the radio like I would to my buddies in a bar."[98] And Ken Johnson, half of the *Johnson and Tofte* morning show, said that he's been able to get away with more on the air, that "we have more free reign than we used to. I don't know if there are seven dirty words you can't use or not. There could be five or 50, there are so many permutations."[99] His show, incidentally, drew an FCC fine against his station for references to anal sex and excretory bodily functions.

<h1 style="text-align:center">NOTES</h1>

1. Steve Emmons, "Just What Do Talk Shows Listen For?" *Los Angeles Times*, May 10, 1995, p. E-1.
2. Sydney Head and Christopher Sterling, *Broadcasting in America*, brief ed. (Boston: Houghton Mifflin, 1991), p. 270.
3. Susan Eastman and Douglas Ferguson, *Broadcast/Cable/Web Programming* (Belmont, Calif.: Wadsworth, 2001), p. 403.
4. Philip Auter, "Topless Radio," http://lists.fitzroydearborn.com/py/comment/get_comment/radio/topless.radio?sid=.
5. Marjorie Heins, *Not in Front of the Children: Indecency, Censorship, and the Innocence of Youth* (New York: Hill and Wang Publishing, 2001), p. 92.
6. John Carlin, "The FCC Versus 'Topless Radio'" (master's thesis, University of Florida, 1974).
7. Ibid.
8. Larry Solway, *The Day I Invented Sex* (Toronto: McClelland and Stewart, 1971), p. 29.
9. Ibid., p. 109.
10. "Touchiest topic on radio now: talk about sex," *Broadcasting*, March 19, 1973, p. 118.
11. Ibid.
12. Ibid.
13. Ibid., p. 119.
14. "Sex on the Dial," *Newsweek*, September 4, 1972, p. 90.
15. "Debate in Dallas: radio sex shows—smut or service?" *Broadcasting*, October 23, 1972, p. 35.
16. Ibid.
17. "Sex on the Dial."
18. Carlin, "FCC Versus 'Topless Radio.'"
19. Ibid.
20. Ibid.
21. Ibid.
22. Pamela Sybert, "Confessions and Concessions: The Short Exciting Life of Sex-Talk Radio, 1971–1973," paper presented to the Association for Educational Journalism and Mass Communication (AEJMC) convention, Atlanta, August 10–13, 1994.
23. "Code boards push button new projects," *Broadcasting*, April 2, 1973, p. 29.

24. "Sex on the Dial."
25. "Touchiest topic on radio now: talk about sex," *Broadcasting,* March 19, 1973, p. 119.
26. Ibid.
27. Ibid.
28. Ibid.
29. Ibid.
30. Sybert, "Confessions and Concessions."
31. *Broadcasting,* February 26, 1973, p. 50.
32. Subcommittee on Communications, Interstate and Foreign Commerce Committee, House of Representatives hearing, March 14, 1973.
33. Address by FCC chair Dean Burch to the annual convention of NAB, Washington, D.C., March 28, 1973.
34. Ibid.
35. Sybert, "Confessions and Concessions."
36. "F.C.C. Will Study Obscene Shows On Radio and TV," *New York Times,* March 28, 1973, p. 1.
37. FCC, NAL, FCC 73–401, April 11, 1973.
38. Ibid.
39. "Sonderling will pay forfeiture, avoid court test of FCC's anti-topless edict," *Broadcasting,* April 16, 1973, p. 8.
40. FCC, NAL.
41. "Sonderling will pay forfeiture."
42. Ibid.
43. Letter to Wallace Johnston, chief of the FCC's Broadcast Bureau, from Egmont Sonderling, president of Sonderling Broadcasting, April 11, 1973; also see Michael Sokolski, "WGLD: A Case Study of FCC Censorship" (master's thesis, Northern Illinois University, 1978).
44. Sokolski, "WGLD."
45. "Topless Radio Revisited," *Television Digest,* April 23, 1973, p. 42.
46. "Sex talk is muted on radio-code stations," *Broadcasting,* June 4, 1973, p. 55.
47. Len Zeidenberg, "Perspectives on the News," *Broadcasting,* April 23, 1973, p. 42
48. Charles Feldman, "Shock Jocks," http://lists.fitzroydearborn.com/py/comment/view_comment/radio/shock.jocks?sid=, consulted March 24, 2002.
49. Michael C. Keith, *Talking Radio: An Oral History of Radio in the Television Age* (Armonk, N.Y.: M. E. Sharpe, 2000), pp. 144–49.
50. Feldman, "Shock Jocks."
51. Hiley Ward, *Mainstreams of American Media History* (Boston: Allyn and Bacon, 1997), p. 382.
52. Robert L. Hilliard and Michael C. Keith, *The Broadcast Century and Beyond,* 3rd ed. (Boston: Focal Press, 2001), pp. 273, 277–78.
53. FCC, NAL [docket and date unavailable].
54. FCC, NAL, May 20, 1994, FCC 94–21.
55. Ibid.
56. Ibid.

57. Sydney Head, Christopher Sterling and Lemuel Schofield, *Broadcasting in America*, 7th ed. (Boston: Houghton Mifflin, 1994), pp. 373–74.

58. T. Barton Carter, Marc A. Franklin and Jay B. Wright, *The First Amendment and the Fifth Estate: Regulation of Electronic Mass Media*, 5th ed. (New York: Foundation Press, 1999), p. 273.

59. Sandra Sobieraj, "Howard Stern producer pays $1.7 million in FCC indecency case," *Detroit News*, September 2, 1995.

60. FCC, NAL, June 4, 1997, DA 97-1286, 1800C1-JEE.

61. FCC, NAL, June 4, 1998, 1800C1-CMW/JEE.

62. Hilliard and Keith, *Broadcast Century and Beyond*, p. 277.

63. Feldman, "Shock Jocks."

64. Ibid.

65. "Who is Don Imus," http://www.meretrix.com/stern/html, consulted May 12, 2002.

66. Michael McGovern, "Showing Claws—Imus, Stern on FCC Warning," *New York Daily News*, April 17, 1987, p. 4.

67. Feldman, "Shock Jocks."

68. Matthew Randazzo, "Imus vs. Stern," September 5, 2001, www.baptizingbyfire.com/aae/imusstern/imusstern.htm.

69. Feldman, "Shock Jocks."

70. Marc Fisher, "Greaseman Oozes Back Into Washington," *Washington Post*, May 15, 1997, p. B01.

71. Ibid.

72. Ibid.

73. "FAQ: The Greaseman," Institute of Information and Computing Sciences (ICS), June 28, 2001, http://www.csruu.nl/wais/html/na-dir/greaseman-faq.html.

74. Frank Ahrens, "The Silenced Greaseman," *Washington Post*, March 9, 2000, p. C01.

75. Peter Goodman, "On The Throne/Howard's Still King, But These Guys Are Selling By The Gross," *Newsday*, August 7, 2000, p. B03.

76. Ibid.

77. Ibid.

78. Ibid.

79. Anthony Violanti, "Rude, Crude, and Coming to WBUF-FM," *Buffalo News*, September 5, 2001, p. C6.

80. Paul Brownfield, "Can Opie, Anthony Find a Home in L.A.," *Los Angeles Times*, July 20, 2001, part 6, p. 26.

81. Tom Zucco, "Woman greets Today viewers with bare breasts," *St. Petersburg Times*, August 3, 2000, p. 2B.

82. Susan Tyler Eastman and Douglas Ferguson, *Broadcast/Cable/Web Programming* (Belmont, Calif.: Wadsworth, 2002), p. 403.

83. Clea Simon, "Media Talk: A New Breed of Trash Talkers on the Radio," *New York Times*, June 25, 2001, sec. C, p. 9.

84. Violanti, "Rude, Crude, and Coming to WBUF-FM."

85. Brownfield, "Can Opie, Anthony Find a Home."

86. Jim Sullivan, "Opie & Anthony add drive-time pop to WBCN," *Boston Globe*, date unknown.

87. Alex Beam, "Encounter: Opie and Anthony . . . ," *Boston Globe* (magazine), December 30, 2001, p. 8.

88. Donna Halper, *Invisible Stars* (Armonk, N.Y.: M. E. Sharpe, 2002) [some of the material in this paragraph is adapted from this book]; and from an essay by Phylis Johnson, "Female Radio Personalities and Disc Jockeys," http://lists. fitzroydearborn.com.py/comment/view_comment/radio/female/personali ties.djs?sid=PGPDvcAAAGMAAG4helE (site consulted March 18, 2002).

89. Kevin Carter and Marc Schiffman, "More Women Talk the Shock Talk: Different Limits Apply to Female Jocks," *Billboard*, January 17, 1998, pp. 71–72.

90. Halper, *Invisible Stars*.

91. Ibid.

92. Carter and Schiffman, "More Women Talk the Shock Talk."

93. Ibid.

94. Ibid.

95. Ibid.

96. Pamela Davis, "Women in radio speak up," *St. Petersburg Times*, April 20, 2001.

97. Ken White, "Has the shock gone out of radio?" *Las Vegas Review Journal*, March 31, 1998 (on-line).

98. Ibid.

99. Ibid.

CHAPTER 4

STRANGE MUSIC FILLS THE AIR . . .

Artists and most of the stations would say "people's music". "Strange and demented music" is what the FCC and many of the group owners would say.

Read the following concern, for example: "We have all been taught to believe that 'music soothes the savage breast,' but we have never stopped to consider that an entirely different type of music might invoke savage instincts. . . . America is facing a most serious situation regarding its popular music. Welfare workers tell us that never in the history of our land have there been such immoral conditions among our young people . . . the blame is laid on . . . music and its evil influence on the young people of to-day. . . . if this music is in any way responsible for the condition and the immoral acts . . . then it is high time that the question should be raised: 'Can music ever be an influence for evil?' "[1] Gangsta rap? Hip-hop? Alternative? No. This was written in 1921 about jazz. "Down with jazz" was as frequent a cry with the same kinds of groups then as "down with rap" is now.

A typical example of broadcast executives' attitudes toward music occurred in, perhaps appropriately, Boston, where blue-pencilers reigned longer than any place in the country. In 1931, on now-venerable station WBZ, then part of the Westinghouse system, a bandleader was cut off the air after he began singing a song entitled "Here Comes the Missus." The bandleader, Joe Rines, declared that nothing in the lyrics of the song could be construed as objectionable and that "anybody who can see a double meaning . . . must be looking especially for it."[2] The program director of the station, John L. Clark, had earlier stated the content credo for the station, one reflected at many stations:

The danger lurks like a slow, insidious poison in the lyrics of songs. Day by day, hour by hour, as drops of water wear away the hardest rocks, the words of cheap songs beat against the ears and the minds of impressionable listeners, attacking the moral strata, weakening and undermining the very foundations of morality. . . .

Fortunately, we have an alert Federal Radio Commission, the Clergy, and Public Opinion, as well as the columns—all too few—of fearless radio critics. The youth of today will be the men and women of tomorrow whom radio will influence to an amazing degree. We must see to it that the infamous dirt of cheap songs and gags does not besmirch the good name of broadcasting, that the air be kept pure and wholesome, and that parenthood be unafraid at any hour to turn on the switch or move the dial, for fear of "off-color" remarks or lyrics. Radio—the powerful, all-persuasive voice! Let's keep it clean![3]

But, as noted at the beginning of Chapter 1, times change, and what was considered indecent or profane then is not even given a second listen today.

Sour Notes

First Amendment freedoms, government censorship and self-censorship all are alive (though not necessarily healthy) in today's world of broadcasting.

More than the dirty discourse of topless radio and shock jocks, music has for a much longer time and in greater quantity been the subject of indecency complaints and formal and informal action. Over the years its aggravation of what, at a given time, may be considered contemporary community standards has continued unabated. Even some otherwise progressive defenders of civil liberties believe the lyrics of many songs have gone too far. For example, the late Steve Allen, in his book *Vulgarians at the Gate: Trash TV and Raunch Radio*, expressed great concern with music on the air, despite or perhaps because of his own reputation as the composer of hundreds of songs. He began a chapter entitled "Popular Music and Recordings" with a quote from gold-album rapper Mos Def: "In terms of what certain media outlets show you, it's very one-dimensional. It's not just hip-hop music—TV and movies in general are very narrow. Sex, violence, the underbelly, with junkies, prostitutes, alcoholics, gamblers. The new trend today is depravity."[4] Allen noted a Newsweek poll in which a substantial majority of respondents said that rap music has too much sex.[5] Allen cited as examples the lyrics of a number of songs, including the following by the Geto Boys:

> Her body's beautiful, so I'm thinking rape
> Shouldn't have had her curtains open so that's her fate
> Leavin' out her house, grabbed the bitch by her mouth
> Drug her back in, slammed her down on the couch
> Whipped out my knife, said "if you scream, I'm cuttin."

Opened her legs and commenced to fuckin;
She begged me not to kill her, I gave her a rose
Then slit her throat and watched her shake till her eyes closed
Had sex with her corpse before I left her . . .[6]

Allen noted the following from the song "Pop That Pussy" by 2 Live Crew:

Hot damn. Shit. Look at the ass on that bitch. Look at the titties . . . All you ladies are 'hos [whores] . . . I like big booty and big old titties. Bitch, you know you've been fucked by many. Come and be my private dancer. I've got some money if that's what gets you off, and if you can't fuck that day, baby, just lay back and open your mouth. 'Cause I have never met a girl that I loved in the whole wide world . . .[7]

And another by Tupac Shakur called "Tha Lunatic":

Oh, shit! Jumped on my man's dick. Heard he had a 12-inch, now the bitch is lovesick. Who's to blame? The guy or the groupie . . . now she wants to do me. Hoo-wee, this is the life—new bitch every night.[8]

One can understand Allen's concerns, especially when songs such as these are aired during hours when children may be listening and, as he said, the music is "infectious" and the rhythms would tend to draw audiences. An Internet deejay show playlist in the year 2000 further illustrates, through titles, the content of much current music. (See Appendix G at the end of this book.)

Yet times change, and songs considered just as obscene 70, 60, 50 and even 20 years ago would not be considered even indecent today. An early action by the FCC was against WJZ, an NBC radio station in New York that in 1935 broadcast, as part of a program sponsored by the government of Mexico, a song entitled "En Elogia de Silves" ("In Praise of Silves"). The FCC received a number of complaints and extreme pressure from some government officials. The Catholic magazine *America* called the presentation "a filthy piece of unabashed pornography." Congress was outraged and even translated and included some of the lyrics in the Congressional Record:

Greetings to Silves, friend
And ask her if she has
Memory of my love
In her sweet adobe.
Oh, how many nights I passed there
Beside a girl
Of well-shaped and graceful form,

Of firm and wide thighs!
Oh, how many women wounded
My soul there with loves!
Like sharp arrows were
Their sweet glances.
Oh, how many nights also
I passed by the side of the water
With the lovely singer
In the solitary meadow!
Then was she wont to sing to me
Between kisses
Some warlike song
To the sound of my guitar;
And my heart then
Shook with ardor
As in battle is heard
The shock of arms.
But my greatest delight
Was when she stood naked
Of her flowing garments
And, like a bending branch
Of a willow, uncovered to me
Her beauty, an unfolding rose
Which breaks its bud
And displays all its loveliness.[9]

Although the FCC did not find the song had the "tendency to deprave and corrupt the morals" and was therefore neither obscene nor indecent,[10] the incident prodded both the FCC and Congress to address seriously the matter of indecent, obscene or profane material on the airwaves.

A look at some of the censored materials through the years provides not only an overview of the FCC's changing perceptions and enforcement of the obscenity, indecency and profanity section of the Communications Act of 1934, but a view, as well, of the changing mores in American society.[11] A definitive view is found in Eric Nuzum's book, *Parental Advisory: Music Censorship in America*, in which detailed information on the items below may be found.

Words in the Music

In the 1950s Dean Martin's "Wham Bam, Thank You, Ma'am," Dottie O'Brien's "Four or Five Times," Rosemary Clooney's "Mambo Italiano" and Billie Holiday's singing of Cole Porter's "Love for Sale," among other records, were banned by stations and/or networks because they were deemed too suggestive or in poor taste. The Boston Catholic Youth Organization lobbied disc jockeys not to play what it considered obscene songs. And a number of radio stations ran announcements stating that they were not airing certain songs in the interest of community morals. That was also the decade when the *Ed Sullivan Show* restricted shots of Elvis Presley to only the waist up and Congress considered legislation requiring all songs to be screened by a committee before being broadcast. One station lost its license because it played songs that the FCC found too suggestive. In Memphis one channel was available for two stations, WREC and WMPS. In the comparative hearing to see which station would best serve the public interest, WMPS was determined to have aired six songs over a two-month period that were, according to the FCC, "certainly in less than good taste," with lyrics with a double meaning and vulgarity. The license went to WREC.[12]

In the 1960s the Rolling Stones' "I Can't Get No Satisfaction" was banned by many stations for being too suggestive, as was The Who's "Pictures of Lily" because the lyrics have references to masturbation, and Van Morrison's "Brown Eyed Girl" because of lyrics that mention premarital sex and teenage pregnancy. In order to appear on the Ed Sullivan Show, the Rolling Stones had to alter the lyrics of "Let's Spend the Night Together" to "let's spend some time together."

The 1970s saw not only a continued concern on the part of many of the stations and much of the public, but renewed FCC anxiety, especially in light of the Jerry Garcia and the Seven Dirty Words cases, as discussed in Chapters 1 and 2. President Richard Nixon and Vice President Spiro Agnew even got into the act, condemning the lyrics in rock music and prompting an increase in broadcasters' censorship. And an organization calling itself the Movement to Restore Democracy wanted all rock music banned in the United States because it believed such music was aiding the spread of socialism in the country. Record companies increased their altering of lyrics of some recorded songs, even without the consent of the writer or recording artist, if they felt the material might result in the recording being banned by radio stations. They leaned over backward to avoid even marginal lyrics. For example, Chrysalis Records arbitrarily and secretly changed Jethro Tull's "Locomotive Breath" because a lyric said "got him by the balls." Further examples include the banning by radio stations of Bob Dylan's "George Jackson" because the word *shit* was mentioned in the lyrics, the banning of John Denver's "Rocky Mountain High" under the presumption that the word *high* referred to the taking of drugs, the refusal of stations to play Loretta Lynn's "The Pill" because any reference to birth control was felt to be indecent, and the RKO stations' barring of Rod Stewart's "Tonight's the Night" until the lyrics "spread your wings and let me come inside" were eliminated.

Much of the official concern with music lyrics went beyond indecency or even obscenity. The concern was with political content, with many of the performers openly condemning Nixon's pursuit of the war in Vietnam and toleration of racism and sexism in the United States. By condemning these artists as purveyors of a drug culture and dirty discourse, and with the cooperation of broadcast executives, networks and stations, the White House and congressional pressure managed to get banned not only the kind of obscene lyrics referred to by Steve Allen at the beginning of this chapter, but dissident political content, as well. In early 1971, clearly influenced by Nixon's and Agnew's stands, the FCC issued a public notice warning stations that if they didn't check the content of the songs they played, it would raise "serious questions as to whether continued operation of the station is in the public interest."[13]

The Commission listed a number of songs it considered unacceptable. Though it later stated that the list was not an official attempt to ban any of the songs, broadcasters obeyed, some banning all music with references to sex or politics. Commissioner Nicholas Johnson dissented from the Public Notice, saying that the FCC was "harassing the youth culture" and acceding to the White House's "attempt to divert the American people's attention from the Vietnam war, hunger, poverty, racism, urban blight and other political problems."[14] The Yale Broadcasting Company took the FCC to court over the public notice edict, but the federal courts decided that the FCC had the authority to do what it did. Supreme Court Justice William O. Douglas dissented, stating that "the Government cannot, consistent with the First Amendment, require a broadcaster to censor its music any more than it can require a newspaper to censor the stories of its reporters."[15]

Aside from radio and TV stations censoring music they feared was too controversial, either in terms of sex and profanity or political content, the record companies were even more zealous in their attempts to change lyrics and avoid covers that they thought might discourage some stations from playing their albums or singles. MCA even sent stations a letter urging them not to play Al Hudson's "Let's Talk" because of what it considered sexually suggestive lyrics.

Music to Our Fears

The 1980s, reflecting the nation's regression under Ronald Reagan into the conservatism of an earlier age, saw more officials, organizations and citizen groups try to censor the content of radio and television stations, including music.[16] President Reagan suggested that "reactionary" and "obscene" rock music should not be protected by the First Amendment. Led by Tipper Gore and other prominent wives of key Washington politicians, an organization called Parents Music Resource Center (PMRC) was established and immediately began a campaign to hide, censor and ban music considered indecent or violent. PMRC had a strong influence on record companies and distributors and on broadcast stations. Surgeon General C. Everett Koop condemned of rock music as "saturated with what I think is going to make them have trouble having satisfying relationships with the opposite sex . . . when you're raised with rock music that uses both pornography and violence." A group called Women Against Pornography condemned "the sexist and violent content of rock videos." The president of the National Association of Broadcasters (NAB), Eddie Fritts, wrote to the major record companies urging them to include lyric sheets with all records sent to radio stations. Pat Roberston, during his presidential campaign, demanded regulation of the content rock music played on TV or radio. All over the country many local groups and individuals called for the removal of MTV from their cable systems. (In one city the City Council made MTV blockers available free to all citizens; a grand total of 40 people got them.) Ironically, MTV even censored itself. In one instance, it demanded that the Fuzztones change its use of the word *rubbers*, because it could be construed as a reference to condoms, before it would air the group's video. Stations censored such songs as George Michael's "I Want your Sex" and Olivia Newton John's "Physical."

Perhaps the most ludicrous example of the fear and paranoia occurred when Meyer Music Markets placed a warning sticker stating "explicit lyrics" on Frank Zappa's *Jazz from Hell Album* album—which was entirely instrumental.

The last decade-plus has seen an emphasis on censoring violence in music, although there is still concern with sex. The "explicit lyrics" warning sticker on albums has resulted in many chain and individual music sellers removing many artists from their shelves. These include large companies such as Wal-Mart, Disc Jockey, and Waxworks. Recording companies have attempted to avoid the warning label by more carefully screening the lyrics of the music that they distribute. Early in the 1990s, for example, MCA, Arista, Atlantic, Columbia, Elektra, EMI and RCA set up committees to check all upcoming releases for material that might be found objectionable.[17] Rap music was regarded as the principal culprit. A number of municipalities banned concerts that featured rap artists, and in some cases rap performers were even arrested in nightclubs where their material was deemed obscene. An example was the Birmingham, Alabama, County Commission, which passed a resolution to "eliminate violent, vulgar concerts" from the area's convention complex. Radio stations were pressured to stop playing rap. Even the Speaker of the House of Representatives, Newt Gingrich, exerted his influence in an interview in *Broadcasting and Cable* magazine by urging advertisers not to place ads on stations that played rap music. MTV was a special target. Several cable multiple-system owners (MSOs) dropped MTV from their listings and substituted less controversial music networks. Interestingly, the popularity of MTV among subscribers forced most of these systems to restore MTV not too long after they dropped it. MTV itself tried to soften its image by censoring material it thought might result in complaints. For example, in a heavily promoted "Madonnathon" day, MTV removed Madonna's video "Justify My Love" on the grounds that it included scenes of sadomasochism, homosexuality, cross-dressing and group sex.

The FCC, in its 1987 statement of its authority regarding, and definition of, indecency (see Chapter 2), included music as a target. It even fined a Chicago station for a listener's singing of a song entitled "Kiddie Porn" on a call-in show. And it took similar action against a Miami station for playing songs with the titles of "Candy Wrapper" (which used the brand names of candies as descriptions of sexual organs and functions), "Walk with an Erection" and "Penis Envy." The last was a feminist satire by the rock group Uncle Bonsai[18] and had lyrics like

> I'd take it to parties
> I'd stretch it and stroke it
> and shove it at smarties
> I'd take it to pet shows
> and teach it to stay
> I'd stuff it in turkeys
> on Thanksgiving Day[19]

The X in Lyrix

But perhaps the most significant occurrence in terms of music censorship was the arrest of the owner of a store in Florida (and in other states, as well) that sold 2 Live Crew's album *As Nasty as They Wanna Be*. In 1990 a U.S. district court in southern Florida ordered a ban on the distribution or sale of *As Nasty as They Wanna Be* because it found the music video obscene. A few days after the court decree, a music store owner sold a copy to an undercover police agent. And shortly after that the three members of 2 Live Crew were arrested for a concert performance (restricted to adults) on the grounds that they were disseminating obscene material. The storeowner was convicted. The 2 Live Crew members were not, their attorney having convinced the jury that rap music represented a serious African-American art form and that the language was not obscene in the context of black culture.[20] (All this occurred, perhaps not so coincidentally, at about the same time that the direc-

Michael Waite
WJBR-FM, Wilmington, Delaware

This truly is a matter for our courts or Congress to decide, since the question really does deal with a constitutional issue, the right of free speech. To have the U.S. government (in the guise of the FCC) be the barometer for what is or isn't fit for public consumption is in complete opposition to some of the basic principles our country was founded on. Standards in our country have changed, and I don't know if our federal bureaucracy is contemporary enough to reflect those changes. I'd much rather see us as an industry regulate ourselves, but unfortunately that's never going to happen, especially given the current climate in our business. I believe the bigger concern or question for broadcasters is this: Must we pander to the lowest common denominator in an attempt to get ratings? Just because a few years ago one broadcaster pushed the limits of what was "acceptable" we now have fifty copycats who keep attempting to push the envelope to get a little dirtier, a little sleazier, or to find a way to use more swear words in a four hour time slot than the next guy. What in the hell has happened to us? I swear I am not a prude, but these days I'm ashamed to be a part of our business. What happened to the principals that are supposed to be a part of our license agreements? Do we "serve the public good" by having women invited onto the airwaves to answer the sexual whims of a talk show host? Has anyone's life ever been changed for the better by watching a train wreck? My biggest fear is how far all this will go. What's acceptable today was not five years ago, so what will the next decade bring. God help us all!

tor of the Cincinnati Contemporary Arts Center was criminally prosecuted for holding a showing of Robert Mapplethorpe's photographs, which were judged by many to be obscene and/or pornographic and proved to be a factor in a new strict censorship policy for grants given by the National Endowment for the Arts. The swing to conservatism of the country as a whole was reflected in the restricted freedoms for the arts.) The music store owner appealed his conviction. In what became a key case regarding government censorship and its definition of obscenity, *Luke Records v. Navarro* reached a federal appellate court.[21] The original hearing before the local judge elicited testimony that the *As Nasty as They Wanna Be* video contained over "a dozen references urging violent sex, some 200 descriptions of women as either 'bitches' or 'hos' (whores), 115 explicit terms for male or female genitalia, 87 descriptions of oral sex, 4 extensive descriptions of group sex, all within a general theme glorifying the debasement and humiliation of women."[22] The appeals court decided that the local federal district judge who found the material obscene had not shown that he had the "artistic or literary background to find that the work lacked 'serious artistic, scientific, literary or political value.'"[23] The appeals court noted that the arresting sheriff who initiated the case also did not have the background to judge whether the album was obscene in the first place and that the district judge had based his determination of what were contemporary community standards on his own limited experience as a resident of south Florida. The album was found not to be legally obscene.[24]

Whether the case clarified or muddied the interpretation of contemporary community standards is arguable; it did, however, establish that those standards must go beyond a limited local view. The Cincinnati art gallery director also was found not guilty. However, a fallout of the case was a Supreme Court decision in 1998 on the new, restrictive rules of the National Endowment for the Arts (NEA); the decision stated that the NEA's requirement that all grantees sign anti-obscenity pledges was not unconstitutional and not a restriction of First Amendment free speech.[25]

All of this had a chilling effect on lyricists, performers, music publishers and recording companies, distributors and stations. Although the 2 Live Crew acquittal stopped the prosecution of other music sellers and concert organizers throughout the country who had fallen under similar 2 Live Crew nets, few wanted to risk arrest, prosecution and huge attorney fees to attain acquittal because another sheriff or judge felt it was a duty to halt what he or she might consider a violation of local obscenity standards.

None of this, however, stopped the FCC in its efforts to rid the airwaves of what it considered obscene music or, if aired other than in the presumably child-proof safe harbor of 10 p.m. to 6 a.m., indecent music. Buoyed by its April 2001 Policy Statement on indecency (see Chapter 2) and goaded by two of its five members to more strongly enforce indecency standards, the Commission became more assiduous in hunting down dirty discourse. Interestingly, a number of noncommercial college radio stations also have been on the receiving end of FCC sanctions. Even a few years before the 2001 crackdown, WSUC, the radio station of the University of the State of New York at Cortland, was fined $23,750 (later reduced to $4,200) for playing a song entitled "Yodeling in the Valley." The lyrics contain descriptions of sexual organs and of oral and anal sex.[26]

A Notice of Apparent Liability (NAL) and fine was issued against the FM station of the State University of New York for playing the rap song "I'm Not Your Puppet," which the Commission decided made explicit references to sexual intercourse "in patently offensive terms."[27]

Other stations that received NALs and fines in 2001 included WQAM in Miami for "Uterus Guy," judged to be lewd; KROQ-FM, Los Angeles, for "You Suck," described as graphic and explicit; KSJO-FM, San Jose, for inescapable sexual and excretory meaning in a song sung to the theme song of *The Beverly Hillbillies;* and KGB-FM, San Diego, for "Sit on My Face."

Alleged confusion by the FCC about the difference between indecency and political satire was the subject of the appeal by KBOO-FM, Portland, Oregon, against a fine for playing "Your Revolution," a rap song with lyrics by poet Sarah Jones. The song, which denounced sexual degradation of women, is considered a parody of rap that encourages casual and reckless sexual behavior and, in context, contains a number "of vulgar references . . . designed to pander and shock."[28] Her lyrics paraphrase lyrics from rap songs in order to show them up as misogynist and shallow.[29] KBOO stated that "Your Revolution" is a "feminist attack on male attempts to equate political 'revolution' with promiscuous sex" and, as such, has to be viewed in its contemporary cultural context. Some critics consider this particular song, in a program that discusses music and political speech, to be political speech.[30]

In 2002 Sarah Jones filed suit against the FCC on the grounds that it violated her First Amendment rights. It is extremely rare for an artist to get involved in such a case; usually the station itself assumes the entire burden. Jones stated that the association of her name with "sexual indecency is not something I can just let sit there, partly in light of the fact that other material is played ad infinitum on mainstream radio airways that's really problematical. I'm not one for censorship, but let's not use a double standard that victimizes certain voices." (See Appendix H at the end of this book for the complete NAL for playing "Your Revolution.")

Eminent Trouble

Possibly the most notorious NAL and fine thus far in this new century for allegedly indecent music was the $7,000 fine levied against KKMG-FM in Colorado Springs for playing the Eminem rap "The Real Slim Shady." Even though the song aired was an expurgated version with a number of expletives deleted, the FCC still found that it contained offensive sexual material. Here is an excerpt from what the Commission objected to:

Feminist women love Eminem
Slim Shady, I'm sick of him
Look at him, walking around grabbing his you know what, flippin' the you know who
"Yeah, but he's so cute, though"
Yeah, probably got a couple of screws up in my head loose

But the worse is what's going on in your parents' bedroom
Sometimes I want to get on TV and just let loose, but can't
But it's cool for Tom Green to hump a dead moose;
My bum is on you lips
My bum is on you lips
And if I'm lucky you might give it a little kiss
And that's the message we deliver to little kids
And expect them not to know what a woman's [BLEEP] is
Of course, they're gonna know what intercourse is
by the time they hit fourth grade
they got the Discovery Channel, don't they?
We ain't nothin' but mammals
Well, some of us cannibals
It's funny, cause at the rate I'm goin'
When I'm 30 I'll be the only person in the nursing home flirting
Pinching nurses asses when I'm [BLEEP] or jerkin'
Said I'm jerkin' but this whole bag of Viagra isn't workin'[31]

Citadel Broadcasting, the station's owner, insisted that the song, as played in its unexpurgated version, was not indecent, but a "caustic" comment on social justice and hypocrisy. The FCC insisted that even with the expletives removed, the song had unmistakable references to female sex organs and functions, masturbation and bestiality. Citadel said those depictions, if examined in the context of the entire piece, were not shocking.[32] The FCC, however, stated in its May 31, 2001, Order that airing of the song by Citadel had not been restricted to the safe harbor of 10 p.m. to 6 a.m. and that "the edited version of the song contains unmistakable offensive sexual references . . . intended to pander and shock . . . that the broadcast of the edited version of 'The Real Slim Shady' was willful and repeated . . . although Citadel contends that it attempted to render the song suitable for broadcast through editing, we believe that the licensee failed to purge a number of indecent references."[33] One of the problems resulting from this FCC action was expressed by Citadel attorney Kathleen Kirby: "The danger involved is that folks at the station level can't take comfort in the fact that something labeled 'radio edit version' is in compliance with the FCC's rules."[34] Accordingly, attorneys for some of the biggest station group owners in the country, including Clear Channel, Infinity and Citadel, advised their clients to remove from their playlists even the cleaned-up version of the "The Real Slim Shady."[35] Recording Industry of America director Hilary Rosen stated: "It would be a disgrace if the FCC were to impose a violation on a radio station because they didn't like the 'suggestive' nature of a song. That goes right to the heart of idea-based censorship."[36] As it turned out, in early 2002 the FCC reversed its decision to fine KKMG for its airing of "The Real Slim Shady."[37]

The FCC's threats generated something, in the eyes of some, at least as bad as government censorship: self-censorship. Some of the findings presented in research papers on radio and music censorship by students in a course taught by one of this book's authors are put forth in the following paragraphs.

About half of America's Top 40 stations refused to play "The Ballad of John and Yoko" in 1969 because they were concerned about blasphemy in the chorus, "Christ, you know it ain't easy."

As noted earlier in this chapter, Loretta Lynn's song "The Pill" was refused airplay by many stations—most ironically, predominantly by country music stations—that believed many listeners with conservative attitudes would be turned off by any reference to birth control, no less the obvious reference to sexual organs and functions. Some performers themselves compromised the integrity of music (and, perhaps, themselves) by changing lyrics to avoid offending anyone. One example was Pat Boone's avoidance of the sexual implications in Tutti Frutti's recording of "Boy, Don't You Know What She Do to Me." He changed Little Richard's lyrics "boy, you don't know what she doin' to me" to "pretty little Susie is the girl for me."

As radio made a local resurgence in the early 1960s, following its serious setback in the 1950s when television took its major network formats and stars, the Radio Trade Practices Committee urged that the NAB Radio Code Committee screen all popular songs for "raw sex and violence." Songs like the Drifters' "Honey Love" and the Midnighters' "Work with Me, Annie" were found offensive by some stations and removed from their lists. Even political and government leaders, as discussed in Chapter 2, got involved. For example, Governor Matthew Welsh of Indiana called the song "Louie, Louie" pornographic and asked stations in his state to ban it.

Reflecting the drug culture of the 1960s and early 1970s in the United States, a number of recording artists included references to drugs in their works, some obvious, some vaguely implied. Could one consider references to drugs indecent? Lists of drug-oriented songs were developed and sent to stations, with concomitant pressure not to play the offending tunes.

As noted earlier in this chapter, John Denver's "Rocky Mountain High" was one them. So was "Puff the Magic Dragon" and the Beatles' "Yellow Submarine." Taking heed of the FCC's warning not to play drug-oriented rock songs, stations banned any song that even appeared to have a drug message. One such song banned by some stations was Brewer and Shipley's "One Toke over the Line." With its references to marijuana, it became a Top 10 hit.

The Parents Music Resource Center had a strong impact for a while, particularly through its letters to citizens, music stores, recording companies and the press all over the country. It pressured for labeling of music and albums and for a lyric rating system similar to that for the movies. It pushed stations not to play the songs of its "filthy 15" list of artists, which included Madonna, Prince, Black Sabbath, Sheena Easton and AC/DC, among others, all highly popular.

To avoid being blacklisted, many artists modified their works to avoid overt indecency or profanity; however, that made little difference. Even the sanitized versions of songs were frequently boycotted. Some of the largest retailers of music recordings, such as HMV and Tower, refused to stock even the expurgated versions of songs, and many station managers fearfully followed suit. So frightened were some stations that they even banned instrumentals by suspect artists. The manager of New York radio station WBLS explained that "radio has a responsibility to the community at large and to the listeners. These are public airwaves . . . so if there is a greater concern growing out there regarding the content of music in general, we need to listen to that concern."[38]

The United States was not the only country to acquiesce to self-censorship. In fact, most countries, through their direct ownership and operation of broadcast stations or their strong governmental control over public or privately owned stations, keep a close eye on all content, especially political speech, but also any material that effective pressure groups, individual politicians or powerful families might consider indecent. For example, in a number of Muslim countries the very appearance of a female on television or radio is considered indecent. Even that old standby of on-air freedom, the British Broadcasting Company (BBC), succumbed. The BBC doesn't necessarily overtly ban a song; it simply quietly keeps it off its playlist.[39] The history of such soft-banning goes back decades. Perhaps the song "Je T'aime," banned in 1969, is the best-known example. With suggestive heavy breathing, the lyrics urged the listener to go "entre tes reins"—English translation, "between your kidneys." This was interpreted to promote anal sex.

In the early 1970s a song whose title and lyrics referred to prostitution, "Honky Tonk Angel," was kept off the air. A song entitled "Homosapien" was banned in the 1980s because of the lyric "homo superior in my interior." Another example of a song banned in Britain through self-censorship was "I Can't Control Myself." There was apparently more concern over the title and a "dirty" sound made by the artist than the reference to carrots shaped like penises. Even the Beatles' "I Am the Walrus" was banned because of the line "Boy, you been a naughty girl, you let your knickers down." In another famous case, in 1983 a well-known deejay played the song "Relax," apparently not having checked the lyrics, which include passages such as "relax, just do it, when you want to suck to it, relax, just do it, when you want to come." By the time the BBC caught on and banned it, it had climbed to number two on the charts, and the publicity over its banning moved it up to the number one song in the country.[40]

Profanity as well as perceived indecency kept records off the BBC airwaves. Some of the titles are "The Man Don't Give a Fuck," the Dead Kennedys' "Too Drunk to Fuck" and Fatboy Slim's "Fucking in Heaven." Other titles included "Fucking Up," "Fuckin' in the Bushes" and "Fucking Ada"—most of these by well-known and popular groups. A song by Prince, "Sexy Motherfucker," had its title changed to "Sexy MF," and the song "Don't Marry Her, Fuck Me" was changed to "Don't Marry Her, Have Me."[41] The "F word" apparently is the bête noir of broadcast music. One is tempted to think of Allen Sherman's book *Rape of the A.P.E.*, in which he devotes several pages to the repetition of one word, *fuck*. After one reads it repetitiously for minutes on end, the word becomes meaningless. Did Sherman have a point that has escaped most of the rest of the world?

Words in Time

Like the rest of the world, the BBC was sensitive, when pressured, to political speech in songs as well. Perhaps the most ironic incident was one that spanned 25 years and is making headlines even as this is being written. In 1977, at the silver jubilee of Queen Elizabeth II, the Sex Pistols' recording of "God Save the Queen" was banned from the air because of its allegedly "treasonous sentiments." Although the royal family objected to it, the public didn't, and it reached number two in the charts.[42] In 2002, at the Queen's golden jubilee, the Sex Pistols were asked to reprise "God Save the Queen," reportedly without objection from Buckingham Palace. Have times changed or have people changed?

Policing of lyrics is not easy, even if one wanted to do so. It requires someone to listen to all new songs before they are played. Personnel resources, especially at small stations, make this difficult, if not impossible. In some cases the deejay (particularly at noncommercial college stations), the screener, or the on-air person may not have the background or sophistication to understand the meaning of some of the lyrics. In some cases, especially with rap, the exact words can sometimes be blurred and incomprehensible to the person doing the screening. Even well-meaning self-censorship is still censorship and needs a defense. One large multiple-owner, responding to criticism for its list of banned songs, said it was merely a list put together to indicate where some of the sensitivities might be.[43]

Is censorship of music necessary? Advisable? Does such censorship work? One view: "Nearly all media select their content based on what they believe their audiences want. No matter how well intentioned, no government censor can expect to stop TV or radio stations from giving their audiences what they seek. In the end, censors will only offend more people than they help, and at too high a price."[44]

Expert on broadcast indecency Eric Nuzum said that "censors believe that an artist's right to self expression is superseded by a community's right to protect itself . . . Early on music censors were concerned that music condoned premarital sex, lewd dancing and wild behavior. Since then, popular music has expanded the variety of messages it expresses, and the censor's list of objectionable topics has expanded right along with it. Sex, religion, politics, drugs, race, and violence—all taboo in the censor's eyes."[45]

Perhaps the most telling argument regarding censorship, and possibly the best and last words for anyone contemplating censorship, is what happened in the late 1980s when the PMRC persuaded music companies to put warning labels on recordings. As one newspaper's headline blared: "Warning labels boost record sales."[46] For decades, movie producers, publishers and anyone else who wanted to distribute a work with questionable content looked with hope to the country's last official municipal censor in Boston. "Banned in Boston" meant a bonanza of sales throughout the country. Everyone, it seems, wanted the forbidden fruit. The head of the Music Plus chain, Mitch Perliss, remarked that putting warning stickers on albums helped sales of those albums because it "adds an element of danger," adds more excitement to the music.[47] Some mediocre and even very poor films, books and other works had huge sales and made small and large fortunes simply because they were banned in Boston. When 2 Live Crew's As Nasty as They Wanna Be was banned, a sanitized version was produced for airplay, As Clean as They Wanna Be. Nasty turned out to be the sixth best-selling album in the country; Clean, with its extensive airplay, was forty-fifth.[48]

Yet, as Eric Nuzum said, "censorship is a natural side effect of free speech. Therefore, as long as we maintain our right to free expression, we can always expect to see censors close behind. Watch your back."[49]

NOTES

1. Anne Shaw Faulkner, "Does Jazz Put the Sin in Syncopation," *Ladies' Home Journal*, August, 1921, pp. 16, 34.
2. *Boston American*, November 25, 1931.
3. "Keep Radio Clean," *Radiolog*, November 15, 1931, p. 6.
4. Steve Allen, *Vulgarians at the Gate: Trash TV and Raunch Radio* (Amherst, N.Y.: Prometheus Books, 2001), p. 243.
5. Ibid., p. 244.
6. Ibid., pp. 248–49.

7. Ibid., p. 251.

8. Ibid., p. 253.

9. "Independent Offices Appropriation Bill, 1937," Exhibit 3, *Congressional Record*, January 15, 1936, vol. 80, pt. 1, 419.

10. *Congressional Record*, Exhibit 9, July 31, 1935, vol. 79, pt. 11, 12203–4.

11. Most of the material noted is from Eric Nuzum, "A Brief History of Banned Music in the United States," www.ericnuzum.com/banned.html, consulted December 11, 2001. This material is ostensibly from Eric Nuzum's book *Parental Advisory: Music Censorship in America* (New York: HarperCollins, 2001).

12. FCC, 10 P&F Rad. Reg., 1351, 1358 (1955).

13. Marjorie Heins, *Not in Front of the Children: Indecency, Censorship, and the Innocence of Youth* (New York: Hill and Wang Publishing, 2001), p. 95.

14. Ibid., p. 96.

15. Ibid., p. 97.

16. See note 8.

17. Ibid.

18. Heins, *Not in Front of the Children*, p. 119.

19. Ibid.

20. Dwight L. Teeter and Bill Loving, *Law of Mass Communications: Freedom and Control of Print and Broadcast Media* (New York: Foundation Press, 2001), pp. 138–39; and "Rap Members Found Not Guilty in Obscenity Trial," *New York Times*, October 21, 1990, p. 1.

21. *Luke Records v. Navarro*, 960 F. 2nd 134, 11th Cir. (1992).

22. Teeter and Loving, *Law of Mass Communications*, p. 138.

23. Ibid.

24. Wayne Overbeck, *Major Principles of Media Law* (Fort Worth: Harcourt Brace, 1999), pp. 345, 357.

25. Ibid., p. 345. See also *National Endowment for the Arts v. Finley*, U.S. Lexis 4211, 1998.

26. "Explicit rap song finally leads to FCC fine," *Student Press Law Center Report*, Winter, 1998–99, p. 29.

27. Lawrence Etling, "Indecency In Music Broadcasting," *Feedback*, Winter, 2002, p. 55.

28. Bill McConnell, "FCC hip-hop deep in #@!*," *Broadcasting and Cable*, July 9, 2001, p. 28.

29. Neil Strauss, "Songwriter, Citing First Amendment, Sues F.C.C. Over Radio Sanctions," *New York Times*, January 30, 2002, p. B1.

30. K. Chapelle, www.plastic.com/music/o1/05/18/2025238.shtml, May 18, 2001.

31. FCC, NAL, EB-00-IH-0228, May 31, 2001, and cited in *Broadcasting and Cable*, June 11, 2001, p. 56.

32. McConnell, "FCC hip-hop deep in #@!*."

33. FCC, NAL, EB-00-IH-0228, May 31, 2001, and cited in *Broadcasting and Cable*, June 11, 2001, p. 56.

34. Pamela McClintock, "FCC fines radio station for Eminem song," Reuters.com, June 6, 2001.

35. McConnell, "FCC hip-hop deep in #@!*."
36. McClintock, "FCC fines radio station."
37. Strauss, "Songwriter," p. B8.
38. Boston College student research papers, citing Stephanie Lopez, "J-Lo, Eminem Create Some 'Real' thorny Issues for R&B Radio," *Airplay Monitors*, July 27, 2001.
39. "Village of the Banned: the Music Auntie Beeb Didn't Want You to Hear," http://www.bubblegum.com/features/banned.html, consulted June 16, 2001.
40. Ibid.
41. Ibid.
42. Ibid.
43. Jennifer Barrs, "List didn't Ban Songs, Clear Channel Says," *Tampa Tribune*, September 19, 2001, p. 12.
44. "FCC Censors Turn Up Volume, Drown Out Free Speech," *USA Today*, July 10, 2001, p. 11A.
45. Nuzum, "Brief History of Banned Music."
46. Ryan Murphy, "Warning labels boost record sales," *Boston Globe*, September 6, 1989, p. 75.
47. Ibid.
48. Ibid.
49. Nuzum, "Brief History of Banned Music."

CHAPTER 5

YOU HAVE TO PAY TO PLAY

If you're a broadcaster today and call the FCC and ask if you will be fined if you air a given piece of material between 6 a.m. and 10 p.m. that might be considered indecent, you won't get an answer. Not to your question, anyway. You will be told that the FCC does not censor and that all broadcast material must be determined by the licensee. The only exception is the Seven Dirty Words. This situation is, in fact, as frustrating for the FCC staff as it is for the station manager or program director who must make the decision on whether to air the material in question. In April 2001 in an effort to clarify the problem, the FCC issued a Policy Statement in which it tried to explain the legal basis for its indecency actions, analyzed some of the key factors in judging what is indecent, offered examples of material that has been found indecent and resulted in a warning or fine, and described the process it uses for enforcing its indecency standards.[1]

The Policy Statement provides the following statutory basis for FCC action: "It is a violation of federal law to broadcast obscene or indecent programming." Specifically, Title 18 of the U.S. Code, section 1464 (18 U.S.C. par. 1464) prohibits the utterance of "any obscene, indecent or profane language by means of radio communication. Congress has given the FCC the responsibility for administratively enforcing [this provision]. In doing so the Commission may revoke a station license, impose a monetary forfeiture, or issue a warning." The Statement cites *FCC v. Pacifica Foundation* (the Seven Dirty Words case) as one of the key judicial decisions that shaped its policy and approved its definition that has "remained substantially unchanged since: language or material that, in context, depicts or describes, in terms patently offensive as measured by contemporary community standards for the broadcast medium, sexual or excretory activities or organs." The Statement further notes that the courts instructed the FCC "to limit its ban on the broadcasting of indecent programs to the period 6:00 a.m. to 10:00 p.m. to insure the government's compelling interest in the welfare of children."

The Statement analyzes indecency determinations and notes that "the broadcast must be patently offensive" and that the determination "is not a local one and does not encompass any particular geographic area" [but] "is that of an average broadcast viewer or listener and not the sensibilities of any individual complainant." It further states that the full context in which the questionable material appears is critical (for example, explicit language in a bona fide newscast might not be patently offensive), but persistent sexual innuendo and meanings might be patently offensive.

The Offending Words

Under various headings, the Policy Statement provides examples. Under its first heading, "Explicitness/Graphic Description Versus Indirectness/ Implication," it states that "The more explicit or graphic the description or depiction, the greater the likelihood that the material will be considered patently offensive. Merely because the material consists of double entendre or innuendo, however, does not preclude an indecency finding if the sexual or excretory import is unmistakable." The following are examples of material that the FCC found indecent.

WYSP-FM, Philadelphia—*Howard Stern Show:*

God, my testicles are like down to the floor . . .
you could really have a party with these . . .
Use them like Bocci balls.

As part of a discussion of lesbians:

I mean to go around porking other girls with vibrating rubber products . . .
Have you had sex with an animal? Well, don't knock it. I was sodomized by Lambchop.

The FCC said that the program consisted of "vulgar and lewd references to the male genitals and to masturbation and sodomy broadcast in the context of . . . 'explicit references to masturbation, ejaculation, breast size, penis size, sexual intercourse, nudity, urination, oral-genital contact, erections, sodomy, bestiality, menstruation, and testicles.'"

WSUC-FM, Cortland, New York—*I'm Not Your Puppet* Rap Song:

The only thing that was on my mind, was just shoving my dick up this bitch's behind. I looked at the girl and said, babe, you ass ain't nothing but a base hit.

I'm going to have to get rid of your ass, yeah, 'cause you're on my dick, dick, ding-a-ling. Popped my dick in her mouth, and we rocked it back and forth. Now that she sucked my dick and Tony fuck you in the ass. I pulled out my dick, popped it in her mouth, and she sucked it.

The FCC concluded that the language used in the broadcast "describes sexual activities in patently offensive terms and is therefore indecent."

WQAM-AM, Miami—"Uterus Guy" Song:

I don't want to grow up, I'm a uterus guy. I want to spend a week or so right here between your thighs. Inhale your clam, with my head jammed by your quivering, crushing gams. No, I don't want to get up or get a towel to dry, cause I wouldn't be a uterus guy. I don't want to get up, I'm a uterus guy and I know where to lick and chew exactly where you like. You'll have more fun when I make you come, with my nose between your thighs.

The FCC held that the "song's sexual import is lewd, inescapable and understandable."

KROQ-FM, Los Angeles—"You Suck" Song:

I know you're really proud cause you think you're well hung but I think it's time you learn how to use your tongue. You say you want things to be even and you want things to be fair but you're afraid to get your teeth caught in my pubic hair. If you're lying there expecting me to suck your dick, you're going to have to give me more than just a token lick . . . Go down baby, you suck, lick it hard and move your tongue around. If you're worried about babies, you can lower your risk, by giving me that special cunnilingus kiss . . . you can jiggle your tongue on my clit. Don't worry about making me have an orgasm . . . You asshole, you shit. I know it's a real drag, to suck my cunt when I'm on the rag . . . You tell me it's gross to suck my yeast infection. How do you think I feel when I gas on your erection?

The FCC said that this material "graphically and explicitly describes sexual and excretory organs or activities."

WXTB-FM, Clearwater, Florida—*Bubba, the Love Sponge:*

Most women don't like swallowing, but I do. The trick is you need to swallow at the right time. Do it when you're deep throating . . . I like the pleasure giving, I like a pleasure giving woman who really, really likes to enjoy giving oral . . . She does more than just go up and down, she's creative by licking, nibbling and using overall different techniques . . . The sexy turn on for me is when I . . . expel into my partner's mouth . . .

I don't mind giving BJs . . . if a man doesn't get off, that means he wasn't quite excited by my techniques.

The FCC fined the station for that one.

The Commission has also fined stations where the material is less explicit or relies principally on innuendo if the sexual or excretory meaning is unmistakable and clear. Some examples:

KLOL-FM, Houston—*Stevens and Pruett Show:*

The doctor was talking about size. The man complained earlier that he was so large that it was ruining his marriages. Big is good if the guy knows how to use it. She is so big she could handle anything. Some of these guys, a very few of them, a handful are alike . . . two hands full. Twelve inches, about the size of a beer can in diameter. So, how could you handle something like that? It's actually ruined marriages. A big organ for a big cathedral. Somebody big is just going to have to find somebody that's big.

The FCC finding: "While the licensee may have substituted innuendo and double entendre for more directly explicit sexual references and descriptions in some instances, unmistakable sexual references remain that render the sexual meaning of the innuendo inescapable."

KGB-FM, San Diego—"Candy Wrapper" Song: .

I whipped out my Whopper and whispered, Hey, Sweetheart, how'd you like to Crunch on my Big Hunk for a Million Dollar Bar? Well, she immediately went down on my Tootsie Roll and you know, it was like pure Almond Joy. I couldn't help but grab her delicious Mounds . . . this little Twix had the Red Hots . . . as my Butterfinger went up her tight little Kit Kat, and she started to scream Oh, Henry, Oh, Henry. Soon she was fondling my Peter Paul, and Zagnuts and I knew it wouldn't be too long before I blew my Milk Duds clear to Mars and gave her a taste of the old Milky Way . . . I said, Look . . . why don't you just take my Whatchamacallit and slip it up your Bit-O-Honey. Oh, what a piece of Juicy Fruit she was, too. She screamed, Oh, Crackerjack. You're better than the Three Musketeers! As I rammed My Ding Dong up her Rocky Road and into her Peanut Butter Cup. Well, I was giving it to her Good 'n Plenty, and all of a sudden, my Starburst . . . she started to grow a bit Chunky and . . . Sure enough, nine months later, out popped a Baby Ruth.

The FCC said, "While the passages arguably consist of double entendre and indirect references, the language used in each passage was understandable and clearly capable of a specific sexual meaning and, because of the context, the sexual import was inescapable." One commissioner said, "notwithstanding the use of candy bar names to symbolize sexual activities, the titillating and pandering nature of the song makes my thought of a candy bar peripheral at best."

KSJO-FM, San Jose—Song to the Tune of the *Beverly Hillbillies* Theme Song:

Come and listen to a story about a man named Boas, a poor politician that barely kept his winky fed, then one day he's poking a chick and up from his pants came a bubbling crude Winky oil. Honey pot. Jail bait . . . so he loaded up his winky and he did it with Beverly Big Breasts. Only 15 years old.

The FCC determination: "Even in cases of double entendre not only was the language understandable and clearly capable of a specific sexual or excretory meaning, but because of the context, the sexual and excretory import was inescapable."

KMEL-FM, San Francisco—*Rick Chase Show*, "Blow Me" Song:
Blow me, you hardly even know me,
Just set yourself below me and blow me, tonight.
Hey, a handy would certainly be dandy,
but it's not enough to slow me,
hey, you gotta blow me all night.
Hey, when you pat your lips that way,
I want you night and day,
when you hold my balls so tight.
I want to blow my love, hey,
with all my might.

The FCC found that the lyrics were quite explicit and dwelled on a description of sexual organs and activities.

KGB-FM, San Diego—"Sit on My Face" Song:

Sit on my face and tell me that you love me.
I'll sit on your face and tell you that I love you, too.
I love to hear you moralize
when I'm between your thighs. You blow me away.
Sit on my face and let me embrace you.
I'll sit on your face and then I'll love you truly.
Life can be fine, if we both sixty-nine.
If we sit on faces, the ultimate place to play,
we'll be blown away.

Despite being sung with an English accent, the lyrics were found by the FCC to be indecent.

WWKX-FM, Woonsocket, Rhode Island—*Real Deal Mike Neil Show:*

Douche bag, hey, what's up fu(BLEEP)ck head? . . . You his fuck (BLEEP) ho or what? You his fuck (BLEEP) bitch man, where you suck his dick every night? . . . Suck some di(BLEEP)ck make some money for Howard and pay your pimp okay?

The FCC said that despite the seeming attempt at editing, the bleeps were ineffective, coming within or after a word, and the words were recognizable and indecent.

The FCC presented examples of indirect, as opposed to explicit, material that it did not consider indecent. Both items, the first entitled "Elvis" and the second "Power, Power, Power," were broadcast by WFBQ-FM/WNDE-AM in Indianapolis.

As you know, you gotta stop the King, but you can't kill him . . . So you talk to Dick Nixon, man you get him on the phone and Dick suggests maybe getting like a mega-Dick to help out, but you know, you remember the time the King ate mega-Dick under the table at a 095 picnic . . . you think about getting a mega-Hoagie, but that's no good because, you know, the King was a karate dude.

★ ★ ★

Power! Power! Power! Thrust! Thrust! Thrust! First it was Big Foot, the monster car crunching 4 × 4 pickup truck. Well, move over, Big Foot. Here comes the most massive power-packed monster ever! It's Big Peter! Big Peter with 40,000 Peterbilt horsepower under the hood. It's massive! Big Peter! Formerly the Big Dick's Dog Wiener Mobile. Big Peter features a 75-foot jacked up monster body. See Big Peter crush and enter a Volvo . . . strapped himself in the cockpit and put Big Peter through its paces. So look out Big Foot! Big Peter is coming! Oh, my God! It's coming! Big Peter!

The Commission, looking at both scripts as a whole, decided that the "surrounding contexts do not appear to provide a background against which a sexual import in inescapable."

Another type of material the Commission gave examples of dealt with dwelling and repetition as opposed to a fleeting reference. The Commission stated that "repetition of and persistent focus on sexual or excretory material [were] factors that exacerbate the potential offensiveness of the broadcasts. In contrast, where sexual or excretory references have been made once or have been passing or fleeting in nature, this characteristic has tended to weigh against a finding of indecency." Here are two examples where the material was repetitive or dwelt upon and was found to be indecent.

WXTB-FM, Clearwater, Florida—*Bubba, the Love Sponge:*

Could you take the phone and rub it on you. Chia Pet? Oh, let me make sure nobody is around. Okay, hang on a second. (Rubbing noise.) Okay, I did it. . . . Now, that really your little beaver? That was mine. Your what. That was my little beaver. Oh, I love when a girl says beaver. Will you say it again for me, honey, please? It was my little beaver . . . Will you say, Bubba come get my beaver? Bubba, would you come get my little beaver? . . . tell me that doesn't do something for you. That is pretty sexy . . . bring the beaver. It will be with me. We got beaver chow. I can't wait, will you say it for me one more time? Say what? My little beaver or Bubba come get my little beaver? Okay, Bubba come get my beaver. Will you say, Bubba come hit my beaver? Will you say it? Bubba, come hit my beaver. That is pretty sexy, absolutely. Oh, my God, beaver.

And from another *Bubba, the Love Sponge* program that drew a fine for dealing explicitly with excretory organs and activities in a way that was patently offensive:

Well, it was nice big fart. I'm feeling very gaseous at this point, but there so far has been no enema reaction, as far as . . . There's been no, there's been no expelling? No expelling. But I feel mucus rising. . . . Can't go like. (Grunting sound.) Pushing, all I keep doing is putting out little baby farts . . . on the toilet ready to go . . . Push it, strain it. It looks normal. Just average, average. Little rabbit one. Little rabbit pellets. I imagine maybe, we'll break loose. Push hard, Cowhead. I'm pushing, I got veins popping out of my forehead. Go ahead, those moles might pop right off. You can tell he's pushing. I'm out of breath. One more, last one. One big push.

For contrast the FCC Policy Statement offers the following examples of a fleeting reference that was not considered indecent. In the first example the FCC noted that the utterance was fleeting and isolated, and in the second the news announcer used only a single expletive.

WYBB-FM, Folly Beach, South Carolina—*The Morning Show:*

The hell I did, I drove mother-fucker. Oh, oh.

KPRL-AM/KDDB-FM, Paso Robles, California—News Announcer Comment:

Oops, fucked that one up.

On the other hand, the Commission made the point that sometimes a fleeting reference may be indecent, as with the following examples:

KUPD-FM, Tempe, Arizona—Announcer Joke:

What is the best part of screwing an eight-year-old?
Hearing the pelvis crack.

WEZB-FM, New Orleans—Announcer Joke:

What's the worst part of having sex with your brother?
. . . You got to fix the crib after it breaks and then you got to clean the blood off the diaper.

KLBJ-FM, Austin, Texas—Deejay Comments:

Suck my dick you fucking cunt.

A third FCC approach to judging indecency, as delineated in the Policy Statement, is whether or not the material is presented in a pandering or titillating manner or is used for shock value. For clarification, here is the statement quoted from the Supreme Court decision in the Seven Dirty Words case: "The language employed is, to most people, vulgar and offensive . . . a sort of verbal shock treatment." The manner of presentation of the material is also a factor in the FCC's judgment. Following are some of its examples.

KLOL-FM, Houston—*Stevens and Pruett Show:*

Sex survey lines are open. Today's question, it's a strange question and we hope we have a lot of strange answers. What makes your hiney parts tingle?

When my husband gets down there and goes (lips noise) . . . I love oral sex . . . Well, my boyfriend tried to put Hershey kisses inside of me and tried to lick it out and it took forever for him to do it.

The FCC fined the station for "explicit description in a program that focused on sexual activities in a lewd, vulgar, pandering and titillating manner."

WEBN-FM, Cincinnati—*Bubba, the Love Sponge:*

All I can say is, if you were listening to the program last night you heard Amy and Stacy . . . come in here, little lesbians that they are. Little University of Cincinnati ho's and basically that we come over and watch them. We got over to the house . . . They start making out a little bit. They go to bed. They get, they start, they're starting like a mutual 69 on the bed. Guido all of a sudden whips it out . . . Rather than take care of each other . . . Guido is like knee deep with the butch bitch and all of a sudden here is the fem bitch looking at me. Hot. I get crazy. I hook up a little bit. Then Guido says, hey, I done got mine, how about we switching? So I went into the private bedroom with the butch bitch and then got another one.

The FCC imposed a fine for the above material.

WXTB-FM, Clearwater, Florida—*Bubba, the Love Sponge:*

Take the phone and I want you to rub it on it hard. I want to hear the telephone, okay? Okay, honey. (Rubbing noises.) You hear that? A little bit longer,

> ## Scott Vanderpool
> ## KISW-FM, Seattle, Washington
>
> Personally, I am far less concerned about the rights of corporate FCC
> license holders to air "cuss" words which are uttered by potty mouthed,
> sex-chat talk shows and more concerned about the corporate takeover
> of the airwaves. From a legal standpoint, I suppose the "all laws nec-
> essary and proper" bit in the constitution does give Congress, and in
> turn the FCC, the right to ban words that a large segment of the pop-
> ulation finds offensive. I mean the Supreme Court has repeatedly said
> that even though millions of Americans smoke marijuana regularly
> (which causes far less societal damage than alcohol consumption) the
> moral values of those who want to continue the prohibition against
> marijuana outweigh those of whom want to smoke it. So why should
> it be any different for Americans who feel it is their god-given right to
> cuss on the radio? Then we have the issue concerning the control of
> the broadcastable band of the electromagnetic spectrum, which really
> should be considered a public resource. It's just "air," after all, and yet
> Congress divvied it up and sold it to the highest bidder, and it recently
> has removed most of the regulations that kept large corporate entities
> from gobbling up the whole thing. I am far more concerned with the
> fact that programming diversity is becoming nonexistent than I am
> about a stray "fuck" or "shit" in a song slipping out over the air. Monop-
> oly of the airwaves is a far greater subversion of the constitution than
> the so-called censorship of the broadcast bands by the government.

though, please. I'm on the edge right now. A little bit faster. (Rubbing noises.)
You get that? That's nice. Could you do it again and then scream my name
out, please? Like you're having an orgasm? Yeah. Go ahead. Okay. (Rubbing
noises.) Mm mm. That's it? It's got to be longer than that. Ginny, come on,
work with me. Be a naughty girl. Be a little shitty bitch that you are. One more
time. Okay. (Rubbing noises.)

This material, too, resulted in a fine.

The FCC noted that even where language might be explicit or graphic or
vulgarly repetitive, the context of the material may not make it indecent.
Such determinations usually occur in programs that are serious or artistic
and not deliberately "shock jock" in nature. On KING-TV, Seattle, the
program *Teen Sex: What about the Kids?* broadcast portions of a sex education
class at a local high school. It included demonstrations with very realistic sex
organ models, and it simulated various methods of birth control. There were

also frank discussions of sexual topics. The FCC ruled that although the program dealt explicitly with sexual issues and included highly graphic sex organ models, "the material presented was clinical or instructional in nature and not presented in a pandering, titillating or vulgar manner." Following are other examples that were investigated after complaints were filed.

WABC-TV, New York—*Oprah Winfrey Show*, "How to Make Romantic Relations with Your Mate Better":

Okay, for all you viewers out there with children watching, we're doing a show today on how to make romantic relations with your mate better. Otherwise known as s-e-x. . . . I'm very aware there are a number of children who are watching and so we're going to do our best to keep this show rated "G" but, just in case, you may want to send your kids to a different room. And we'll pause for a moment while you do that . . . According to experts and recent sex surveys the biggest complaints married women have about sex are . . . their lovemaking is boring . . . American wives all across the country have confessed to using erotic aids to spice up their sex life and . . . thousands of women say they fantasize while having sex with their husbands . . . And most women say they are faking it in the bedroom. [Quiz:] I like the way my partner looks in clothing . . . I like the way my partner looks naked . . . I like the way my partner's skin feels . . . I like the way my partner tastes . . . [Psychologist and panelists:] do you know that you can experience orgasm, have you experienced that by yourself? No, I have not . . . Okay, one of the things that, well, you all know what I'm talking about . . . You need at least to know how to make your body get satisfied by yourself. Because if you don't know how to do it, how is he going to figure it out? He doesn't have your body parts. He doesn't know.

While the content was similar to that of shock jocks who discuss masturbation, the FCC stated that subject matter alone does not constitute indecency. Whereas some people might find even a clinical discussion of the subject to be offensive, the material was not considered indecent in the context of this presentation.

KTVI-TV, St. Louis—*Geraldo Rivera Show*, "Unlocking the Great Mysteries of Sex"

We have seen such a slew of sex books . . . "Your G-spot," "How to Have Triple Orgasms." One of the biggest myths . . . either we go all the way or we do nothing . . . he just missed an opportunity to make love, not all the way . . . but to share a moment of passion and a moment of closeness . . . It's important that a man learn to use the penis the way an artist uses a paintbrush . . . and if a woman is also willing to learn how to move her vagina . . . With good control of PC muscles, a man can separate orgasm from ejaculation and have more than one orgasm . . . Really great sex is always based on feeling safe enough with your partner to open up. Passion is just the expression of a tremendous sense of connection you feel. If you think sex is pleasurable, try making love and having sex at the same time for turning pleasure into ecstasy.

As with the *Oprah* selection, the FCC conceded that although the above material might be offensive to some, in context it was not indecent. While the subject matter was not different from a shock jock discussion of the same subject, the manner of presentation was not pandering or titillating and did not include profanity.

A bona fide news story is exempt from the indecency criteria applied to other formats. The following is an example.

WSMC-FM, Collegedale, Tennessee—*All Things Considered:*

Mike Schuster has a report and a warning. The following story contains some very rough language. [The news story contained an excerpt from a wiretap of a telephone conversation during which organized crime figure John Gotti used the words *fuck* and *fucking* 10 times in seven sentences.]

The FCC stated that the language was an integral part of a bona fide new story and that it did "not find the use of such [coarse] words in a legitimate news report to have been gratuitous, pandering, titillating or otherwise 'patently offensive.' "

The FCC received complaints about frontal nudity when the movie *Schindler's List* was shown on television. In specific cases involving two television stations that aired the film, the FCC ruled that full frontal nudity is not indecent per se. It depends on the context of the presentation. "The subject matter of the film, the manner of its presentation, and the warnings that accompanied the broadcast" made the nudity in *Schindler's List* not indecent in terms of FCC standards.

A number of stations protested Notices of Apparent Liability (NALs) and fines on the grounds that the materials the FCC found objectionable were allegedly part of news broadcasts or items. The Policy Statement presents some examples where the FCC found that not to be so.

KSD-FM, St. Louis—*The Breakfast Club:*

I've got this Jessica Hahn interview here in Playboy. I just want to read one little segment . . . the good part. "[Jim Bakker] has managed to completely undress me and he's sitting on my chest. He's really pushing himself, I mean the guy was forcing himself. He put his penis in my mouth . . . I'm crying, tears are coming, and he is letting go. The guy came in my mouth. My neck hurts, my throat hurts, my head feels like it's going to explode, but he's frustrated and determined, determined enough that within minutes he's inside of me and he's on top and he's holding my arms. He's just into this, he's inside me now.

Saying, when you help the shepherd, you're helping the sheep." (Air personality making sheep sounds.) This was rape. Yeah, don't you ever come around here, Jim Bakker, or we're going to cut that thing off.

The FCC noted that the station claimed the broadcast was newsworthy "banter by two on-air personalities reflecting public concern, criticism, and curiosity about a public figure whose reputedly notorious behavior was a widespread media issue at the time." The FCC stated, however, that "although the program . . . arguably concerned an incident that was at the time 'in the news,' the particular material broadcast was not only exceptionally explicit and vulgar, it was . . . presented in a pandering manner. In short, the rendition of the details of the alleged rape was, in context, patently offensive."

A similar claim of exemption on the basis of "public affairs" programming was made in the following example.

> KNON (FM), Dallas—"I Want to Be a Homosexual" Song:
>
> *But if you really want to give me a blowjob*
> *I guess I'll let you*
> *as long as you respect me in the morning.*
> *Suck it, baby.*
> *Oh, yeah, suck it real good . . .*
> *Are you sure this is your first rim job? . . .*
> *Stick it up your punk rock ass.*
> *You rub your little thing,*
> *when you see phony dikes in Penthouse magazine.*
> *Call me a faggo,*
> *call me a butt-loving fudge-packing queer . . .*
> *You rub your puny thing*
> *when you see something pass you on the street.*

The licensee said that the "the words and song constitute political speech aired in good faith attempt to present meaningful public affairs programming . . . to challenge those who would use such language to stigmatize . . . members of the gay community." The FCC was concerned that the material was presented at a time when children might be in the audience, that the station had "considerable discretion as to the times of the day . . . when it may broadcast indecent material . . . Consequently, we find unavailing [licensee] Agape's argument that, in essence, its duty to air public affairs programming required a mid-afternoon presentation of lyrics containing repeated, explicit, and vulgar descriptions of sexual activities and organs."

Sometimes material that is not obviously pandering or titillating, and is even oriented principally to a political rather than a sexual statement, can be found indecent by the FCC. The following is an example.

WIOD-AM, Miami, Florida—"Penis Envy" Song:

If I had a penis . . .
I'd stretch it and stroke it
and shove it at smarties . . .
I'd stuff it in turkeys
on Thanksgiving day . . .
If I had a penis, I'd run to my mother
comb out the hair and compare it to brother.
I'd lance her, I'd knight her, my hands would indulge.
Pants would seem tighter
and buckle and bulge.
(Refrain)
A penis to plunder, a penis to push,
'cause one in the hand is worth one in the bush.
A penis to love me, a penis to share,
to pick up and play with when nobody's there . . .
If I had a penis . . . I'd force it on females,
I'd pee like a fountain.
If I had a penis, I'd still be a girl,
but I'd make much more money
and conquer the world.

The Commission stated "that it is not necessary to find that the material is pandering or titillating in order to find that its references to sexual activities and organs are patently offensive. Moreover, humor is not more an absolute defense to indecency . . . than is music or any other one component of communication."

The April 2001 Policy Statement also explains the FCC's enforcement process. It notes that "the Commission does not independently monitor broadcasts for indecent material. Its enforcement actions are based on documented complaints of indecent broadcasting received from the public." For a complaint to be considered, it must include (1) a full or partial tape or transcript or significant excerpts of the program, (2) the date and time of the broadcast, and (3) the call sign of the station involved. If the complaint does not include these items or if it appears that the program was aired during the safe harbor period or if the material appears not to fall within the scope of the Commission's indecency definition, it is usually dismissed. If the complaint is not dismissed, the material is analyzed by the FCC staff for "patent offensiveness." The disposition may be (1) denial of the complaint, (2) a letter of inquiry (LOI) to the licensee seeking further information, (3) issuance of an NAL with a monetary forfeiture, or (4) referral of the complaint to the full Commission (i.e., the five commissioners) for its action. The licensee may respond to both an LOI and an NAL with the reasons why it believes the material in question is not indecent. A licensee has the legal right to refuse to pay a fine and may sue the FCC in a U.S. district court. (See Appendices I and J at the end of this book for examples of complete NALs, one for a song and the other for a telephone call-in program.)

Divergent Views

While a majority of the Commission approved the Policy Statement, it was clear from some commissioners' statements that there was great diversity on the approach the FCC should take in dealing with alleged indecency on the airwaves. Commissioner Susan Ness stated that "Understandably, the public is outraged by the increasingly coarse content aired on radio and television, at all hours of the day, including times when children are likely to be listening or watching. . . . Despite an onslaught of on-air smut, the Commission necessarily walks a delicate line when addressing content issues, and must be careful not to tread on the First Amendment. . . . Release of this Policy Statement alone will not solve the festering problem of indecency on the airwaves. However, it is entirely within the power of broadcasters to address it—and to do so without government intrusion. . . . It is time for broadcasters to consider reinstating a voluntary code of conduct."

Commissioner Harold Furchtgott-Roth stated that "Commission action to enforce the indecency guidelines would set the stage for a new constitutional challenge regarding our authority to regulate content. . . . Today, the video marketplace is rife with an abundance of programming, distributed by several types of content providers. A competitive radio marketplace is evolving as well, with dynamic new outlets for speech on the horizon. Because of these market transformations, the ability of the broadcast industry to corral content and control information flow has greatly diminished. In my judgment, as alternative sources of programming and distribution increase, broadcast content restrictions must be eliminated."

The dissent of Commissioner Gloria Tristani stressed that "there is simply no proof that broadcast licensees are in need of this Policy Statement. No factual basis exists for concluding that confusion about the standards or overreaching enforcement by the FCC requires this Statement. . . . It would better serve the public if the FCC got serious about enforcing the broadcast indecency standards."

A *Broadcasting and Cable* report on the Policy Statement reflects the same kind of diversity, if not confusion. Reporting that the Statement was "intended to give clear-cut examples of acceptable and unacceptable broadcasts," it notes that "on-air depictions of morning show shock jocks or callers engaged in bestiality or oral sex were deemed illegal, while an 'Oprah' episode for hints for improving couples' sex lives was not." The report states that the specific examples given in the Statement were too clear-cut and that First Amendment lawyers felt they "provide no guidance for cases in which the lines between social commentary and irredeemable offensiveness are blurred."[2]

NOTES

1. FCC Policy Statement, "In the Matter of Industry Guidance on the Commission's Case Law Interpreting 18 U.S.C. Par. 1464 and Enforcement Policies Regarding Broadcast Indecency," EB-00-IH-0089, April 6, 2001 (adopted March 14, 2001).
2. Bill McConnell, "FCC hip-hop deep in #@!*," *Broadcasting and Cable*, July 9, 2001, p. 28.

CHAPTER 6

CRASS, BRASS AND ALAS

We live in what is generally regarded as a crass culture, so why should we expect that the media in that culture would be any less crass? Cynics among us would say that behind the broadcast industry's claim of First Amendment rights when confronted with what appears to be a dereliction of commitment to the public interest, convenience and necessity in some of its programming, is the industry's overriding concern for maximizing its bottom-line monetary profits. Others among us who are more inclined to be tolerant might say that some of the disturbing content displays an uninhibited brass, but in context does not violate a responsibility to the public interest. And some would say, alas, the cornerstones of democracy, the freedoms of speech and press, are being attacked and compromised by moralists who would impose their beliefs and judgments on the entire nation.

But that is what makes ballgames—and working democracies. The right to disagree and the right to make that disagreement heard. At the beginning of this twenty-first century, a sweeping wave of conservatism has compromised and in some cases even obliterated these rights. The September 11, 2001, terrorist attack on the United States made it possible for the federal government to label any political dissent as unpatriotic—or worse. Other government agencies are riding on the White House's coattails of attempting to convince—and, in fact, at least temporarily succeeding in convincing—the public that Big Brother in Washington, D.C., knows best. Taking advantage of the people's wartime-like reliance on the executive branch, even the FCC develops a symbiotic relationship with the public on issues of discourse on the media. The FCC feeds it the personal philosophy of the FCC commissioners and other government leaders, and receives echoes rather than a questioning of authority in return. It has always been thus. Even the presumably objective Supreme Court not only is subservient to politics (as in the 2000 presidential election), but reflects the country's attitude in its decisions. A study of Supreme Court decisions indicates that in times of a liberal attitude nationally a presumably conservative Court will reflect that liberality, and conversely, a presumably liberal Court will reflect the attitudes of a conservative time.

So we have censorship and we have self-censorship—although few would admit that either term properly describes its control of content. The urge and need to conform, to remain in the mainstream—and for the broadcast industry, not to antagonize a single potential customer of its advertisers' wares—is as much and perhaps more so the nature of media corporations as it is of individual citizens reluctant to make waves in their communities.

In 1935, before television and in the heyday of radio, Roger Baldwin, the director of the American Civil Liberties Union, declared that "there is radio censorship." He called for public opposition to violation of "civil rights of free speech over the air" and supported his view with a list of 100 cases of "private radio censorship."[1] While the concern was more with political speech than material that might be considered indecent, the latter was a component of the self-censorship imposed by the broadcasters. The director of programming for NBC at the time, John Royal, stated categorically that NBC does not censor. "We are careful whom we invite to broadcast," he said, "and once invited we would not expect to censor. We do not expect men and women in public life to say anything we would be ashamed of . . . We have no rule to see their manuscript in advance."[2]

CBS, on the other hand, stated that there are "no exceptions to the rule of submitting manuscripts in advance. If the speech is of a violent nature, leading executives and legal counsel decide whether it should be broadcast . . . Editorial responsibility is assumed by Columbia itself."[3] While the major concern here was controversial political comment (anything representing a liberal or left point of view was considered too controversial to air, such as a discussion of civil rights or southern lynchings or recognition of Russia), some new programs caused concern about indecency. Foremost was the "man in the street" interview format, becoming more and more popular at stations all over the country. NBC was worried that there was no way to control or prevent spontaneous profanity or obscenity by the public.[4] Another of NBC's taboos: "Obscene or off-color songs or jokes, oaths, sacrilegious expressions, and all other language of doubtful propriety must be eliminated."[5]

And the public got into it back then, just as self-appointed guardians of the public morals have been doing today. In 1934 the Catholic Church's Legion of Decency backed a number of women's groups in their attempt to "reform" the movies, and then helped organize some 25 women's organizations as the Women's National Radio Committee, with over 10 million members, for the purpose of reforming radio. In language eerily reflective of language today, the president of the group, J. Truman Ward, told the National Association of Broadcasters (NAB) convention in 1935 that stations should fire "breathless announcers," refuse to air commercials for products "which ladies and gentlemen of refinement would not freely discuss at the dinner table" and adopt CBS's plan for a citizens advisory board and guarantee that parents have access to "model programs" between the hours of 5 and 8 p.m. every day.[6] The Women's National Radio Committee made its point and its goal. Complaints by the committee to the FCC in 1935 resulted in New York radio station WMCA removing a "contraceptive jelly program" from the air. It pressured advertisers of laxative and feminine hygiene products not to advertise on radio, and CBS dropped commercials "involving unpleasant discussions of bodily functions."[7]

Not only discussions of sex, but the word *sex* itself was considered inappropriate for the airwaves. As an example, in 1930 the CBS network deleted the following sentence from one program that was part of a lecture series on philosophy: "Thomas Robert Malthus, arguing against his father, made some startling remarks about human nature and especially the strength of the sex impulse, which led people to marry as soon as they were able."[8] CBS's comment: "We are not permitted to mention sex over the radio."[9]

One can't help but wonder what these crusading critics and tiptoeing broadcasters would think if they could hear a Howard Stern show today.

A Guiding Hand

CBS developed a set of self-censorship guidelines in 1935 that was a forerunner in purpose, if not in content, of sensitivity protections of a half century later. The principal "don'ts" related to programs for children, including a ban on "off-color stories," "blasphemy" and "encouragement of parental or proper authority disrespect."[10] Within its statement concerning misrepresentation in advertising, CBS also banned "any product which describes graphically or repellently any internal bodily function, symptomatic results of internal disturbances, or matters which are generally unacceptable in social groups."[11] "Under the most controlled circumstances" only could syphilis be discussed or even mentioned, and mention of body odor, halitosis, and athlete's foot was completely barred. The network producers and editors were told that they must delete any material that might be considered unacceptable in "polite parlor conversation."[12]

A 1935 report on radio listed the following words as "too hot . . . you'll never hear them on the air: Belly, Diarrhea, Pimples, Infected areas, Expectant mothers, Pregnancy, Belching, Gagging, Gooey, Phlegm, Liverbile,

Blood, Pus, Cracked toes, Colon, Vomit, Scabies, Eruptions."[13] The "18 dirty words"? Self-censorship ran rampant, fleeing from every possible innuendo. For example, comedian Fred Allen had a routine about "The Full Moon Nudist Colony," Eddie Cantor frequently had nudist stories and Gracie Allen talked about "nudism helping a girl get a lot of things off her chest." Broadcast executives decreed that there shall be no more nudist jokes.[14] When asked about censorship, what did the executives at NBC and CBS say? "There is no censorship in broadcasting!"[15]

While the FCC, the networks and some church and civil organizations campaigned for censorship or self-censorship of radio, the public in general was against it. Following the Mae West incident, renewed efforts were made for careful control of radio content. The FCC thought it was "vulgar." A bill was being prepared in Congress that would more strictly monitor radio broadcasts. The chairman of the FCC, Frank R. McNinch, said that "of all means of entertainment . . . radio must have the highest standards" and that the broadcast of the Mae West episode would be a factor in the renewal of licenses for stations that carried the program.[16] But a Gallup poll found that 59 percent of the public was opposed to any government censorship of the medium and only 15 percent of those surveyed said they had been offended by radio programs they believed were "vulgar."[17]

Some union groups, such as the American Federation of Labor (AFL), went on record opposing government censorship, albeit for protection of political speech. The vice president of the AFL, Matthew Woll, stated that freedom to speak on the airwaves with no restriction, unlike in any other country in the world, "is something worth any struggle to protect and maintain . . . once the camel's head is in the tent it might not be long until the body follows."[18] And even some church groups, generally considered conservative on most issues, rallied for the protection of First Amendment rights. But, again, the orientation was toward political speech. The Federal Council of Churches of Christ in America, for example, issued a study, "Broadcasting and the Public," in which it decried any form of censorship and advocated a strict adherence to democratic control of the media in which licenses should remain with those broadcasters who serve the public "interest, convenience and necessity in the fullest measure." The report cautioned that "in a democracy freedom of speech is a priceless possession. No administrative government agency is wise enough to be entrusted with power to determine what people shall hear. Freedom of radio is almost if not quite as important as freedom of the press. If either is curtailed, our political and religious liberties are imperiled. For this reason we believe any attempt to regulate utterances over the radio by an administrative government agency, except within the canons of decency, propriety and public safety clearly defined by statute, is dangerous and contrary to public policy."[19]

At the same time, however, the FCC's gratuitous censuring of stations that broadcast material with sexual overtones or innuendo brought strong objections from the press and the public. A case in point was the broadcast of Eugene O'Neill's Pulitzer Prize–winning play *Beyond the Horizon* by the NBC Blue network. One of the stations that carried it was cited by the FCC for a hearing on its license. Public objection and condemnation by the press prompted the FCC to reverse itself the following week.[20] The hit-and-miss nature of judging indecency and the tug-of-war over censorship, self-censorship and no censorship seem to continue in much the same manner today. Is our society more crass today?

Multimedia Dirty Discourse

Controversy over content may be found today in every media distribution system. While commercial radio and, to a lesser extent, commercial television get the bulk of listener and viewer complaints and the attention of the FCC, cable, satellite, the Internet and—for some reason considered inappropriate—noncommercial or public radio are also targets of concern.

The seminal cases of findings of indecency were, in fact, about programs on noncommercial radio stations: WUHY and its Jerry Garcia interview and WBAI and the landmark Seven Dirty Words case. Perhaps because 80 percent of the noncommercial radio stations are licensed to colleges and universities, these licensees have taken special pains to try to prevent the broadcast of obscene material or the airing of indecent material outside of the safe harbor. Many of these stations are run, with the exception of a faculty adviser, by students of the college or university. As an example, one institution, Hiram College, developed a list of "inappropriate topics" for its campus radio station. All personnel are told that the following topics may not be discussed on air under any circumstance: "rape; sexual deviance; masturbation; prostitution or stripping; acts or graphic violence; offensive terms referring to sexual activity; insensitive references to suicide; promotion of drug use; promotion or irresponsible use of alcohol; insulting or degrading references to any on-campus groups; insulting or degrading references to any religious, ethnic or social group; hate speech of any kind." In addition, certain language is barred: "any slang term referring to genitalia or excretory organs; any slang term referring to sexual activity; any slang term referring to excrement; any racial, religious, sexist or heterosexist slurs; any form of hate speech."[21] At another college a campus "radio obscenity policy" stresses the need to confine all indecent material to the safe harbor time and that "all recorded music must be previewed and screened for lyric content prior to broadcast."[22] No more dirty discourse on college campuses?

The Internet has become the medium of choice for dirty discourse. As noted in Chapter 2, Congress has given rapt attention to the distribution of indecent and obscene materials in cyberspace and continues to seek legislation banning or controlling such materials that will pass constitutional muster. In a review of Frederick S. Lane III's book, *Obscene Profits: The Entrepreneurs of Pornography in the Cyber Age*, Bruce Headlam wrote: "From search results clogged with sex sites to e-mail boxes that fill up with 'XXX' subject lines to innocent-looking links that lead to red-light sites, pornography seems inescapable online."[23] Headlam noted that the book states that "A new wave of entrepreneurs . . . is threatening the hegemony of old-style men's publications like *Playboy* and *Penthouse* with not only the sheer amount of online images but also their explicitness" and that publishers like Larry Flynt are concerned about the inroads into their businesses.[24] In his book, Lane estimated that there are some 30,000 to 60,000 web sites oriented to sex, plus a host of phone-sex lines, chat rooms and video mail-order services. Headlam stated that sex sites on the Internet "not only look dirty, they feel dirty."[25]

The Internet spans a range of streaming programs that may be considered by some more or less indecent without necessarily being pornographic. One such enterprise is called "ToplessRadio.com." Building on the success of a site called "Naked News," ToplessRadio combines "beautiful women and great rock 'n roll." Its CEO and founder, Rich Schmidt, said, "You'll have beautiful, topless women, playing hit records interspersed with lifestyle pieces. There will be topless sports, topless Rock reports, and on."[26] Given the sexual content on the Internet, this appears to be one of the more innocuous programs. Some critics, however, think the most outrageous, indecent, obscene, profane web site is one operated by a government agency: the FCC. The FCC web site contains complete reports of the indecency cases it handles, including examples of the materials it considers indecent. Not entirely tongue-in-cheek, but certainly with satirical irony, one writer, J. D. Tuccille, stated that "In order to protect the minds of Americans from language that will, one supposes, cause their brains to melt out their ears, the FCC offers up vivid examples of the language, listed item after item completely out of context. That the language is presented in a medium other than those where it's forbidden doesn't change anything; it still enters people's brains to wreak whatever damage the FCC thinks it wreaks. . . . The oddity of banning supposedly 'bad' language from one medium while it's protected in another without apparent ill effect is increasingly emphasized by evolving information technology. Some language may be unpleasant, but it doesn't do any harm, and censorship makes less and less sense in a changing world."[27]

Perhaps as ironic but infinitely more amusing are the cyberspace adventures of the web sites of the Gardner and Dunstable police departments in

Massachusetts. People logging on to these sites find not police and safety information but pornography. It seems that both police departments forgot to renew their domain names and by the time they discovered their oversight the names had been sold to pornographic purveyors on other continents.[28]

Satellite distributors are not immune from prosecution for alleged indecent or obscene programs. Moreover, they can be charged in areas where they do not originate programming but where it can be received. This was established in 1990 when GTE Spacenet and U.S. Satellite Corporation were criminally indicted in Alabama for feeding X-rated films to cable pay-per-view systems. Specifically, the Exxstasy and Tuxxedo cable channels showed the films *Santa Comes Twice* and *Young Girls Do*, which were videotaped by some youngsters, shared with their schoolmates, and discovered by angry parents. Home Dish Satellite Network (HDSN) was forced to go out of business. The message to local law enforcement authorities and to satellite distributors was that "local obscenity standards can be enforced against offenders based outside their areas."[29] Finding movies, from any source, indecent or obscene had been established earlier by FCC actions. A key case occurred in 1988 when the FCC cited a television station for airing an unedited version of the film *Private Lessons* in prime time. The Commission found that "explicit nudity and scenes depicting sexual matters were dealt with in a pandering and titillating manner, which were neither isolated or fleeting." Although nudity per se was not necessarily indecent, the FCC said that nudity in concert with the explicit presentation of the seduction of a teenage boy by an older woman was indecent because it "would have commanded the attention of children."[30] In this particular case the FCC action became moot when a federal court negated the FCC's 24-hour ban on indecency and ordered the Commission to look into a reasonable safe harbor period.

Foreign-language broadcasts have also been targets of government and citizen concern. With the strong growth of Spanish-language radio, some hosts have tended to take advantage of the shock jock phenomenon to draw large audiences, while others lean over backwards to protect the Hispanic or Latino image. For example, in 2002 the National Hispanic Media Coalition in New York was preparing a complaint against a program entitled *El Vacilón de la Mañana* on a local radio station. A bleep button doesn't keep off the air the sexually explicit comments of callers. Even the program's host has warned callers to be circumspect about disturbing content, saying, "People are having breakfast."[31] In one instance "a caller identified as a four year old boy is egged on to use profanity by both his mother, who can be heard in the background, and one of the hosts, who tells him, 'say one of those little words of yours.' The boy complies with a string of expletives, to raucous laughter in the studio."[32] As one of the city's top radio shows, *El Vacilon* is expected by some to maintain especially high standards. As journalist Mireya

Navarro stated, "Spanish-language radio has a heightened obligation in New York to maintain high standards, both because there are relatively few stations, and because Spanish speakers tend to rely on radio for information and entertainment more than other groups."[33]

If there is a wish and a way to distribute indecent, obscene or pornographic material, someone will find them. Even station call letters are screened by the FCC before they are approved—call letters such as WSEX, KOCK, KUNT and any others one's imagination can conjure. Whether the response to such material should be censorship is another matter. The National Association of Broadcasters affirms and reaffirms its stand on violence, drugs and sex on the airwaves. In regard to sex, the NAB advocates the following principles:

> In evaluating programming dealing with human sexuality, broadcasters should consider the composition and expectations of the audience likely to be viewing or listening to their stations and/or to a particular program, the context in which sensitive material is presented and its scheduling. Creativity and diversity in programming that deals with human sexuality should be encouraged. Programming that purely panders to prurient or morbid interests should be avoided. Where a significant child audience can be expected, particular care should be exercised when addressing sexual themes. Obscenity is not constitutionally-protected speech and is at all times unacceptable for broadcast. All programming decisions should take into account current federal requirements limiting the broadcast of indecent matter.[34]

Stop the Stresses

Whether due to exploitation of media being exploited by the media, or due to an actual increase in dirty discourse, or due to greater sensitivity and direct personal observation or hearing by the public, or due to better organization and stronger lobbying by groups opposed to what they consider indecent material, the public weal appears to be continually rising in regard to media content.

Journalist Tom Maurstad, in 2002, syndicated his concern that "the marketing of outrage is television's latest trend."[35] He cited as one example the film *A Season on the Brink*, with "frequent and unbleeped use of" the word *fuck* and other obscenities. He quoted Matthew Felling of the Center for Media and Public Affairs in Washington, D.C.: "Shock used to be used to sell products; now shock is the product being sold. . . . The climb to the top of the ratings is turning into a race to the bottom of the barrel."[36] Maurstad stated that "it's become common practice for network dramas to open with cautions of 'strong language' and 'brief nudity.'" He noted the following comment from former NBC executive Andrew Bergstein: "In today's media marketplace, in which consumers choose from an expanding array of options—network, basic cable, premium cable, satellite TV, the Internet—the need to stand out drives programming decisions. In a variation on the entertainment industry motto, 'There's no such thing as bad publicity,' the backlash has become the payoff."[37] Maurstad asked where we are headed. "Is full frontal nudity an inevitability in the near future?" He quoted Felling's answer: "I don't think there's any question that it's coming. In lots of ways, we're already there."[38]

Religious groups in particular have built an increasing concern on such perceived content trends in the media. The Catholic Exchange, an Internet site, exhorts its constituents to take heed. "Even a staff writer for the normally left-leaning *Washington Post* appeared shocked to discover that the Federal Communications Commission intends on doing practically nothing to discourage vulgar language on the air."[39] (The inexplicable equating of "left-leaning" with vulgar language perhaps is more revealing of the radical right attitudes of the source than of the legitimacy of its attitudes toward language.) It alleges that the FCC has said that it will allow "even the F-word" on the air in certain circumstances.[40] One columnist, John Fay, complained about the proliferation of offensive material in sports programs. He cited as an example what happened to a woman who called in to a program, trying to win tickets to an Allman Brothers concert. The host "told the woman she had to do an impersonation of Meg Ryan's famous scene from 'When Harry Met Sally' to win. Well, first he asked for her measurements. The woman didn't want to do the Meg scene because her 2-year-old child was in the room. But [the host] wasn't giving up the tickets unless the woman gave in and did the dirty deed. She gave in. She got the tickets. And she was happy to win."[41] Fay concluded that "there's enough violence and drugs in sports that talkers are forced to discuss. Leave the sex out."[42]

Even students, presumably a bit more open-minded than the general public—assuming higher education opens one's mind—are concerned. Writing in *Capitalism Magazine*, Nicholas Hamisevicz said that "somewhere, Lenny Bruce is laughing" because the inconsistency of the FCC has allowed all kinds of vulgarity and obscenity on the air. He cited individual incidents of speech such as "sweet merciful crap" on *The Simpsons* and "shit happens" on *Chicago Hope*. He noted that radio station KKMG got fined for playing a "cleaned up" version of "The Real Slim Shady," that a play, *On Golden Pond*, was not fined for using one of George Carlin's Seven Dirty Words, but when David Letterman tried to comment on the word used in *On Golden Pond*, the word got bleeped. "No wonder Lenny Bruce is laughing," Hamisevicz said, "he knows that, as citizens in a free society, the joke's on us."[43] As an intern in the right-wing Heritage Foundation when he wrote the above, Hamisevicz represents the thinking of many right-wing students.

As a justification for their demands, a number of groups opposed to what they consider indecency and obscenity running rampant in the media point to former FCC commissioner Gloria Tristani's statement on the subject as she was leaving the FCC. Tristani, consistently taking the FCC to task for what she believed was lax enforcement of the indecency rules, said:

> In fierce competition for ratings, broadcasters are increasingly resorting to violent and sexually-oriented programming. The Commission needs to get serious about enforcing the law enacted by Congress to limit indecent material on the airwaves that reaches our children. The courts have repeatedly held that the Commission's indecency enforcement activities do not violate broadcasters' First Amendment rights because our rules are designed to protect children. Indecency enforcement can require the agency to make difficult judgment calls regarding language and context, but that is no reason for the Commission to shrink from enforcing the law.[44]

Some of the would-be censors justify their stands by stating that some commonly held beliefs about First Amendment protections are incorrect. Morality in Media, for example, offered the following "clarifications":[45]

1.   "If you don't want to be exposed to indecent programs on radio or TV, turn the dial."
Clarification: "The Supreme Court has rejected the 'turn the dial' argument."

2.   "If I can listen to a comedian's 'dirty words' in a nightclub act, why can't I have the same access to entertainment on my radio and TV?"
Clarification: "Indecent programming is prohibited by federal law, as is obscenity."

3.   "Who knows what the vague term 'indecency' means?"
Clarification: "Every broadcaster should know . . . The Federal Communications Commission has defined indecency quite clearly."

4.   "If the FCC is keeping indecency off the airwaves merely to protect children, won't adults be reduced to hearing and viewing only what is fit for children?"
Clarification: "The U.S. Supreme Court ruled in the 1978 FCC v. Pacifica . . . 'seven dirty words' . . . not just protecting children from such material, but also protecting adults from such assaults. . . . the Court went on to say that indecent speech offends 'for the same reason obscenity offends.'"

5.   "'Adult' (meaning indecent or obscene) programming should be permitted during late evening hours when children are sleeping."

Clarification: "There are substantial numbers of children in the listening audience at all hours of the night."

6. "It is up to parents to supervise their children and protect them from exposure to indecent broadcasting."

Clarification: "There is no feasible way for parents to protect their children from exposure to indecent programming, short of confining a child or teenager 24 hours a day in a sound-proofed isolation unit without radio or TV."

7. "Only those who pay for cableporn get it. If you don't want it, you don't have to order it."

Clarification: "That's not true. . . . The basic package in some areas automatically includes hardcore pornographic programming on public access channels."

8. "If you don't want to see cableporn, or if you don't want children to see such programming, get a lockout box or a TV with a V-chip."

Clarification: "I have no obligation to get a lockout box, a V-chip, or any other technological fix, to prevent being assaulted by obscene programming. The obligation is on the cable programmer not to transmit illegal pornography."

9. "The video industry says it rents and sells hundreds of millions of 'adult' video tapes each year. Doesn't this demonstrate community standards?"

Clarification: "The courts have found that, with regard to community standards, tolerance is not acceptance."

10. "Isn't the Internet a completely different medium from radio, TV, and newspapers? How could the same obscenity and indecency standards apply?"

Clarification: "William Bennett Turner [professor at the law school of the University of California at Berkeley] wrote recently, 'Material that is so gross as to fall within the Supreme Court's strict definition of obscenity [the *Miller* standard] is unprotected by the First Amendment regardless of the medium in which it appears.'"

Morality in Media also insists that "enforcement of the obscenity laws is not censorship." It stated that "the word 'censorship' means prior restraint of First Amendment rights by government. Enforcement of the Federal or State obscenity laws is NOT censorship because, first of all, the government is exercising no prior restraint on the pornographers. The porn purveyors are free to publish whatever they want, but if what they distribute or exhibit is obscene, they are, after the fact, subject to prosecution under the obscenity laws."[46]

Mike Gallagher
Salem Radio Network

There's not much that surprises me anymore. However, listening to "shock jocks" instruct women to put their cell phones down the front of their pants as I'm driving home from work in the New York City area is a sorry reminder of how low some radio stations will sink in order to achieve ratings and revenue. Even more shocking is the failure of the FCC to do anything about it. As a mainstream conservative, I'm not fond of more government intrusion in our lives. However, the radio airwaves do belong to the people, and most people don't expect their government to protect the airing of obscene and filthy language. Free speech advocates argue that if I don't like hearing the garbage that occasionally passes for entertainment on the radio, I can turn the dial. That argument ignores the very premise of the way radio stations are licensed in America. Radio stations are given a license by the federal government to air content on a particular frequency. To suggest that content can be obscene or pornographic is contrary to what is expected by the American people. Not only do I believe the government has the right to prevent profane material and language from being aired, I believe it has the obligation to do so.

Organizations such as Morality in Media have not only encouraged their constituents to file formal complaints with the FCC, but also provided instructions on how to do so. Some do this very effectively. Others sometimes write to the FCC and to newspapers and radio and television stations in such anger that their points are lost in the rancor. Here are some examples of both approaches.

To the FCC:[47]

May 24, 2000

Ms. Linda Blair
Federal Communications Commission
Radio Complaints
Mass Media Bureau
445 12th Street, SW
Room 2-A320
Washington, DC 20554

Dear Ms. Blair:

I am writing to officially file a complaint with the Federal Communications Commission (FCC) regarding the content of WKQX's "Mancow's Morning Madhouse" show, heard on Q101 FM, from 6 am until 10:30 pm, Monday through Friday here in Chicago.

The host, shock jock Eric "Mancow" Mueller, continues to cross all lines of decency, and blatantly ignored obscenity laws. Wednesday, May 24th, between 8:05 and 8:09 in the morning, Mancow aired a pre-record segment in which Heather, a Mancow personality, interviewed citizens on the streets of Chicago. In this segment Heather unabashedly asked a number of women "how do you feel about your vagina?" This interview was followed by a song in which the phrase "dripping wet" was continually repeated. This material is extremely indecent and inappropriate for broadcast on the public's airwaves.

The FCC is governed by Title 47, of which section 73.399 states: (a) No licensee of a radio or television broadcast station shall broadcast any material which is obscene. (b) No licensee of a radio or television broadcast station shall broadcast on any day between 6 a.m. and 10 p.m. any material which is indecent.

Furthermore, the FCC has defined broadcast indecency as language or material that, in context, depicts or describes, in terms patently offensive as measured by contemporary community standards for the broadcast medium, *sexual* or *excretory organs* or activities. The foregoing broadcasts mentioned here meet and/or exceed the definitions of indecent, and are within the prohibited time frame of 6:00 a.m. and 10:00 p.m. and are therefore subject to indecency enforcement action.

I urge the FCC to act on this documented case! Please enforce these rules and regulations for the citizens who own the airwaves that are being misused. Proactive measures must be taken against these types of abuses! Please act on my behalf!

Sincerely,

David Smith

3400 West 11th Street
Chicago, Illinois 60655

To the president:[48]

March 7, 2001

President George W. Bush
The White House
1600 Pennsylvania Avenue
Washington, DC 20500
Tel: 202-456-1414
Fax: 202-456-2461

Dear President Bush:

On behalf of more than six million American-Muslims we are writing to you to say we recognize that one of your most important responsibilities as President is to appoint, with the advice and consent of the Senate, Commissioners to sit on the Federal Communications Commission (FCC).

One of the FCC's important responsibilities is to enforce the Broadcast Indecency Law (18 U.S.C 1464) against TV and radio stations. The FCC's definition of broadcast indecency reads: "language or material that in context depicts or describes in terms patently offensive, as measured by contemporary community standards for the broadcast medium, sexual or excretory organs or activities."

We, therefore, are writing to urge you to appoint/reappoint only those Commissioners (including the FCC Chairman) who are committed to enforcing the Indecency Law effectively against both TV and radio stations. We believe that it is imperative for representatives of the American-Muslin community to be appointed as FCC Commissioners. While not every vulgarity or mention of sex on TV violates the Indecency Law, surely much of the barrage of cheap sex talk and action and vulgarity do so—particularly when large numbers of children are in the viewing audience. This type of education of our future generation through television is no doubt to have very harmful, if not dangerous, consequences for our nation.

Nevertheless, while the FCC has on occasion enforced the Indecency Law against radio stations, not one TV station has been fined for violating the Indecency Law in over 20 years!

The FCC may not be the only answer to the glut of morally offensive TV programming. As the Supreme Court has said, "There is a right of the nation to maintain a decent society"; and it is the FCC's job to curb indecency on broadcast TV.

In response to the question, "Do you think the TV industry rating system is an effective alternative to enforcing indecency laws or do you think the FCC needs to work harder to enforce existing indecency laws?," 59% of adult Americans said, "FCC WORK HARDER." (1998 Worldwide Wirthlin poll conducted for Morality in Media.)

Our nation's youth are the most vulnerable to the glut of exploitive sex and vulgarity on TV, but to a significant extent, the decline of TV standards has adversely affected all Americans. When appointing the Commissioners for FCC, you must keep in mind the historical fact that moral decline on a national level has caused the downfall of many civilizations. Anxiously awaiting your response.

Sincerely,

Ghazi Y. Khankan
Executive Director
Council on American-Islamic Relations

To members of Congress, in the form of an open letter from Morality in Media:[49]

May 1, 2001

Dear Member:

If ever there was a time for Congress to review the statutory role and effectiveness of the Federal Communications Commission in upholding standards of decency in broadcasting, it is now.

Radio stations that provide national and local platforms for grossly vulgar "shock jocks" have little to fear from the FCC; and no broadcast TV station has paid an indecency fine in over 20 years. By the end of this year, only Chairman Michael Powell may remain from the present Commission. Enforcement of the broadcast indecency law does not appear to be one of Mr. Powell's priorities.

On April 6, the FCC released a POLICY STATEMENT to provide guidance regarding "our case law interpreting 18 USC 1464 and our enforcement policies with respect to broadcast indecency." In 1994, the FCC agreed in federal court to publish such guidance but did not do so. Unable to bring indecency enforcement actions in court because of this failure, the FCC allowed the statute of limitations to run in three cases, even though it issued Notices of Apparent Liability. In addition to clarifying the indecency standards, the STATEMENT reiterates the FCC "enforcement policies," including the following:

> "The Commission does not independently monitor broadcasts for indecent material . . . [C]omplaints must generally include: (1) a full or partial tape or transcript of significant excerpts of the program . . . if a complaint does not contain the supporting material . . . it is usually dismissed."[MIM ed. Note: "must generally" and "usually" are best understood to mean must and always.]

Morality in Media does not expect the FCC to monitor all broadcasting for possible violations of the indecency law. But if the FCC can monitor TV programs to ensure compliance with ad limits during children's programming (see Public Notice, released 29 May 98), it can monitor to ensure compliance with the indecency law. We would add that on April 24, the Federal Trade Commission issued a follow-up report on the marketing of violent entertainment to children. In the FTC Release describing the report, we find the following: "This review, unlike the original study, relied on advertising monitoring rather than internal documents."

There is also no justification (statutory or constitutional) for requiring complainants to provide tapes or transcripts. Commissioner Gloria Tristani criticized this self-imposed barrier to effective enforcement in a May 18, 2000 Press Statement:

The Commission appears so averse to indecency cases, and has erected so many barriers to complaints from members of the public, that indecency enforcement has become almost non-existent. For instance, if a member of the public wants to file an indecency complaint, the Commission generally requires them to submit tapes, transcripts or significant excerpts of the offending material. This is surely an unreasonable burden to impose on the public. It means that the public cannot be protected from indecency on the public airwaves unless they have the foresight to have a tape recorder running when the offending language is broadcast. . . .

We assume there will be instances when the FCC must rely on complainants to provide a tape or transcript. But most TV programs are taped by licensees or program providers. Why then does the FCC routinely dismiss complaints about indecency because they do not include tapes or transcripts—when the FCC can obtain them from the licensee or provider?

There is no justification for the FCC's failure in appropriate cases to revoke or deny renewal of a license. Even the programming of radio "shock jocks" has not moved the FCC to revoke or refuse to renew a license. But as the Supreme Court pointed out in FCC v. Pacifica (1978):

"The prohibition against censorship unequivocally denies the Commission any power to edit proposed broadcasts in advance . . . The prohibition, however, has never been construed to deny the Commission the power to review the content of completed broadcasts in the performance of its regulatory duty . . . Judge Wright forcefully pointed out that the Commission is not prevented from canceling the license of a broadcaster who persists in a course of improper programming. He explained:

"This would not be prohibited 'censorship,' . . . any more than would be the Commission's considering on a license renewal application whether a broadcaster allowed 'coarse, vulgar, suggestive, double-meaning' programming; programs with such material are grounds for denial of a license renewal."

Nor is there justification for the FCC's failure to levy fines in sufficient numbers or amounts to deter violations. It would appear that the FCC issues just enough Notices of Apparent Liability relating to indecent radio broadcasts to deflect most criticism, but never enough in numbers and amounts to deter indecent programming.

And TV licensees might as well have diplomatic immunity as far as broadcast indecency is concerned. When it comes to ever increasing amounts (and explicitness) of TV sex and vulgarity, the FCC's inexplicable policy is: "See no evil, hear no evil."

It is time for Congress to exercise oversight of the FCC before the transformation of broadcasting is complete—from a medium that should be serving the public interest, into one that is polluting the public airwaves and endangering the welfare of children.

The Senate should question President Bush's Commission nominees about their views on TV sex, vulgarity and violence and on enforcement of the broadcast indecency law. Senate and House Committees must also conduct hearings to get answers to these questions:

Why did it take the FCC so long to issue "industry guidance" on broadcast indecency?

Why does the FCC issue so few Notices of Apparent Liability for indecency violations?

Why are indecency fines set too low to deter future violations?

Why doesn't the FCC revoke or refuse to renew a license in circumstances where violations are flagrant or persistent?

Why must complainants provide tapes or transcripts—even when licensees or TV programmers have tapes of programs?

Why does the FCC refuse to monitor programs to ensure compliance with the law?

Why are TV stations 'exempt' from the indecency law?

Undoubtedly, the primary concern about indecent broadcasting is its impact on the millions of children who spend hours each day listening to radios and watching TV. But broadcast indecency is also a quality of life issue that affects all citizens.

We are confident that the American people will fully support your diligent efforts to curb patently offensive, indecent programming on broadcast radio and television.

Robert Peters
President

Peter Knickerbocker
Vice President

Paul J. McGeady
General Counsel

A letter from a concerned citizen to a radio network:[50]

Brenda Donnellan
••
February 25, 1999

Frank Hoffman, General Manager
West Virginia Public Radio
600 Capitol Street East
Charleston, WV 25301

Dear Mr. Hoffman:

I find a large part of the programming on West Virginia Public Radio to be of extremely leftist persuasion—no surprise since it is a joint effort of government, corporations and tax-free foundations—and I resent my tax money (both federal and state) being used to support it. To add insult to injury (literally!) the programming is becoming more and more vulgar (as in "locker room" language and crude expressions). Examples:

Several times last week I heard promo excerpts from a weekend program of a man telling somebody, "You can sing the d__n phone book if you want to!" It would be bad enough to broadcast it once on Saturday morning, but playing it over and over all week was very offensive.

The often raunchy Prairie Home Companion reached a new low a few weeks ago when Keillor cut loose with several vulgar phrases, e.g., "go p__s up a rope."

Please don't tell me to just turn my radio off. I don't like it. Decent people have been turning off their radios and TVs for several years now, ignoring the smut being broadcast. This has allowed trashy "entertainment" to proliferate and become mainstream and "acceptable" so that today's children think the stuff is normal.

While I'm wound up, please allow me to mention another item that irked me. Commenting on the incident of the official using the word "niggardly" (for which faux pas he was unreasonably and excessively punished), a young lady accused him of being guilty of "puttin' on airs" because he used an uncommon word. In other words, to speak like an educated person will only cause a man to be ridiculed. Our society has been turned upside-down. Quality has lost its meaning. Everything good and admirable and honored is despised, while everything vile, obscene and depraved is esteemed. The media (intentionally or not) have helped change our attitudes and our talk. I beg you to stop what you have been doing and instead promote wholesome and decent programs.

Yours truly,
c.c.
National Public Radio
Senator Robert C. Byrd, West Virginia
Senator John D. Rockefeller, IV, West Virginia
Congressman Allan Mollohan, West Virginia
West Virginia Senator Donna Boley
West Virginia Senator Frank Deem
West Virginia Delegate Larry Border
Governor Jesse Ventura, Minnesota

And newspapers are not exempt from ireful complaints:[51]

Subject: re: Wash. Post article

Dear Mr. Geiger:

I read your article "Fed up with all the TV trash?" in the *Washington Post* . . . at a time when I am so outraged, I could just scream. TV is not alone in this disgraceful exhibition of sex and violence.

I can't believe the gutter talk on radio (i.e., Victoria Jones, Imus and shock jock Howard Stern). I "station surf" to find something decent to listen to as I work through my mornings. Is the use of the word penis, over and over again and its description, peeing and with whom and all the other disgusting dialogue really necessary? It seems that each station tries to outdo the other in gutter talk . . . all for the sake of the "ratings share" which means, of course, money in their pockets.

What has happened to the English language? We have SO distorted the first amendment of free speech, I think our forefathers are probably turning over in their graves.

All the garbage that is being heard by our impressionable young people is giving them license to converse with the same expletives that they hear on the radio and TV and accept as normal.

We monitor and restrict TV in our house, but our daily lives and our main society are so polluted with obsenities [*sic*].

Everywhere one turns, one is confronted with sex, violence, explicit pictures in newspapers, magazines and yes, even childrens [*sic*] books.

There is no way a child or children can be monitored 24 hours a day. Even schools are no longer havens of decency.

When are we going to get some educational programs for our children to view???

I am, a concerned parent,

Hope Bazaco

Sound Solutions

Although the degrees of concern vary and concepts of what constitutes indecency differ, complainants look for solutions. Most proposed solutions seek a "big brother" approach in which the government takes direct action—coincidentally an approach most of its advocates would abhor in any situation other than the control of speech. Some propose self-censorship. Others seek technological solutions. And still others would have listeners and viewers "just say no."

In one instance the Donnelly Corporation of Grand Rapids, Michigan, banned workers on its assembly lines from listening to a radio talk program, *Love Phones*, with "Dr. Judy," on the grounds that the show deals with sex, love and relationships, including extramarital sex and sexual dysfunctions. A company official stated that the show was banned because its contents contradict many of the company's values, "The fact is that sexually explicit radio talk shows have no place in a work setting like the one at Donnelly. The programs are deeply offensive and embarrassing to many employees. They disrupt the ability of our work teams to function together smoothly and cooperatively." When workers tried to tune in to the program, they were told to turn it off.[52]

Technological solutions include hardware like the Eventide Model BD500 Obscenity Delay. Promotional material describes it as follows:

> Eventide's patented automatic catch-up feature, first introduced on our now classic BD955, solves the problem of getting back into delay after a segment is "DUMPED." The DUMP button is pushed to prevent an obscenity or other undesirable utterance from reaching the air. The obscenity is deleted and delay goes to zero. Then, without further operator intervention, the unit starts imperceptibly adding delay back into the program audio, with no program interruption. Thus, the delay "safety margin" is automatically rebuilt.[53]

Internet sites have more recently created the most concern, with Congress continually seeking legislation that would suppress what it considers inappropriate material in cyberspace. One solution would be the imposition of fees high enough to keep potential offenders off the net. Such a proposal has been considered by the U.S. copyright office, albeit for the protection of intellectual property rather than for censorship purposes. One cyberspace radio station expressed its opposition this way: "A proposed ruling by the U.S. Copyright office could impose webcast fees so high that they would force XXX Radio Network & many other Internet radio stations—including many community and non-profit stations—to cease online operations."[54] XXX Radio, one of many similar operations on the Internet, is unabashed about its content and promotes itself as "a streaming broadcast of songs about life, sex, death, sex, food, sex and deviant sex. It's not a place for listeners with delicate ears."[55]

Another approach to protecting children from what is considered indecent material on the Internet is to build web sites only for children, "a children's zone populated only by Web sites deemed safe."[56] Sites that are deemed suitable for children under 13 would get special "kids.us." Internet addresses. Software would enable parents to restrict children to those sites. Some critics think such sites would get "zero traffic." Others say that this could block out content not especially oriented to children, but critical to their development, such as encyclopedias and other reference materials.[57]

Some concerned citizens are saying just tune out the bad stuff. One commentary quotes Professor Dennis Baron, "In the last 40 years that I've been observing the use of profane speech, I've seen a growing tolerance for its use in public context—such as on television and on radio and in music and in films and theater."[58] How to solve the "proliferation of public profanity"? On the web site of Probe Ministries, its president said, "I recommend that you listen to Christian Radio."[59]

Nimby

The United States does not stand alone in its concern with indecency in the media. In varying degrees, every country in the world with media systems has expressed similar misgivings and sought solutions. Here are a few examples. In 1973, in an effort to provide access to the media for groups that felt they had been denied the opportunity to air their views, the British Broadcasting Company set aside 40 minutes of late night airtime for this purpose. One of its restrictions, however, was a ban on the presentation of obscene or indecent material.[60] Prior to the authorization of private stations in the United Kingdom, a concern was that the increase of stations would result in an increase of audience-seeking programs similar to the topless radio and shock jock formats in the United States, which, in turn, would lead to looser morals and behavior. But private stations were authorized, and a report in the late 1990s found that "despite speculation, there is little evidence that an increase in the number of stations available for listeners to choose from has led to increased promiscuity."[61]

One of Europe's most popular TV formats, although considered indecent by many, made its way from Italy into the schedules of a number of other countries. It was a quiz show in which the contestants had to remove an article of clothing every time they gave an incorrect answer. The winner was the person who was the last one not to be absolutely nude.

Finland, however, trumped this strip video TV program. A threesome (two men and a woman or two women and a man) making love is one of the most titillating sexual fantasies for many people. Relatively few people actually experience it except in their imaginations. In Finland, however, radio listeners could hear it live. A radio station put blankets and pillows on the floor of its studio, placed microphones in strategic places, and broadcast the ménage à trois, as it occurred, on a morning program. Audiences across the country could not only hear the bodily movements, the sighs, the breathing and the groans of the three participants, named Haidi, Miia, and Kaide, but also expletives and cries like, "Oh, God, Kaide, give it to me!" Apparently, there was not as much concern with the content of the program as with the fact that when people heard it they would stop what they were doing in order to listen, causing a disruption in traffic and normal services. The legal implications related to the protection of children from pornographic material—and any child with a radio on could hear it all. And to another Finnish law, which bans any sexual activity that causes a public nuisance![62]

Even in the Holy Land anger erupted at what is perceived as indecency on the media. What kind of indecency? The Hadassah Medical Center offered sexual advice to callers, in a program similar to that of Dr. Ruth Westheimer in the United States. It featured a noted Israeli sexologist, Dr. Yaakov Meir-Weil. The program was taken off the air after pressure and alleged threats from the "haredim," representing strong religious objections. Most listeners were disappointed. The director of a hospital sex therapy clinic, Dr. Uri Wernik, put it in perspective. "The idea of sexuality is supposed to have a certain degree of modesty attached to it, but proper discussions of it should not bother people, even in religious circles." And a regular listener said that "it was nice to know that if you had a question, you had someone to turn to where you didn't have to feel embarrassed. After all, everyone has questions, and it's not the kind of thing you talk about at the Shabbat dinner table. It was nice to have a forum for such things. The haredim obviously are busy having sex, judging by the number of children they have, and it would seem to me they could benefit from such a program, since they're much less likely to talk among themselves about such things."[63]

Sex shows are reaching places remote from their U.S. shock jock origins. Even in Vietnam. A program called *Window on Love*, a radio call-in show dealing with sex, was going strong at the turn of the new century on the national Radio Voice of Vietnam.

Canada has followed the U.S. approach to regulating indecency, obscenity and profanity, but with tighter restrictions. The Canadian Broadcast Standards Council (CBSC) and the Canadian Radio-Television and Telecommunications Commission (CRTC) develop and implement rules regarding program content. As might be expected, in recent years one of their major concerns has been the *Howard Stern Show*, syndicated to stations in Canada since 1997. Complaints about the Stern show have related not only to the presumed indecent content but to his alleged denigration on occasion of Canada and Canadians. In dealing with complaints about Stern, the CBSC issued an analysis of its laws and their application to the case. It cited the responses to complainants of stations carrying Stern. One such response stated that "while the overall objective of the Howard Stern show is to amuse and entertain through comedy, this is sometimes done through comments which some may find shocking or outrageous. Such comments are, of course, intended to be humorous, and are in no way intended to be serious commentary on social or political issues."[64]

The CBSC clarified the differences between U.S. and Canadian approaches to media speech.

> The CBSC considers it appropriate to draw certain distinctions between Canadian and American approaches to the free speech issue which might result in the non-acceptability of a broadcast in one country and the acceptability of the same program in the other. In broadcast terms, the texts of the First Amendment in the American Bill of Rights and the first and second sections of the Canadian Charter of Rights and Freedoms are materially different. The American approach is far more sweeping. It provides that

>> Congress shall make no law respecting an establishment of religion, or prohibiting the free exercise thereof; or abridging the freedom of speech, or of the press; or the right of the people peaceably to assemble, and to petition the Government for a redress of grievances.

> In Canada freedom of expression is nowhere declared to be absolute. In the Canadian Charter of Rights and Freedoms, Section 2(b), which declares the existence of the fundamental freedoms "of thought, belief, opinion and expression, including freedom of the press and other media of communication," these freedoms are subject to the limitation imposed in Section 1, which declares:

>> The Canadian Charter of Rights and Freedoms guarantees the rights and freedoms set out in it subject only to such reasonable limits prescribed by law as can be demonstrably justified in a free and democratic society.

The Canadian Broadcasting Act differs from the U.S. Communications Act of 1934 and the Telecommunications Act of 1996 in that, according to the CBSC, the latter have no provisions that purport to restrict free speech, while the Canadian Broadcasting Act "clearly restricts untrammelled freedom of expression" as follows:

> A licensee shall not broadcast
> (a) anything in contravention of the law;
> (b) any abusive comment that, when taken in context, tends or is likely to expose an individual or group or class of individuals to hatred or contempt on the basis of race, national or ethnic origin, colour, sex, sexual orientation, age or mental or physical disability;
> (c) any obscene or profane language;
> (d) any false or misleading news.

The CBSC went on to say that "free speech without responsibility is not liberty." It further noted that "the Canadian approach to broadcast speech is far more cautious [than the American approach] and reflective of the need to respect other Canadian values." On this basis, it quoted pertinent selections from Stern's programs.

Howard Stern: It's a big day! I'm in Montreal and in Toronto! Turn it on baby! Got a little penis, baby? Yeah, baby, conquering Canada! Yeah, and Robin, too! Yeah, baby! There's a lot of angry people but we're on in Canada! Hey, I'm singing, Frig the French! Screw the French! You're going to have to listen to Americans now! Screw your culture and we're invading your ass. For as long as it lasts! Sorry!

The CBSC also cited sexist comments, such as:

Howard Stern: Hey, I got to take a break. Spice girls are here.
Robin Quivers: Oh, they are?
Howard Stern: Yeah, they're little knockouts. Little pieces of ass. I wonder what they're doing here. I don't know their music but I don't care. I want to get in their pants.

And another:

Howard Stern: You cow!
Caller Patricia: Well, you're a son of a bitch, asshole. Why don't you stick your head where the sun don't shine?
Howard Stern: Maybe I will. Why don't you come down here? All you want to do is bend over a chair and get a good high, hard one anyway, you horny cow. That's your problem. No penis. Hey, you left, huh? Coward! Hum . . .

And a further example:

Howard Stern: Yeah, Spike Lee. But now she wants to shut up. Oh, I just wanna take that piece of ass body, put tape over her mouth, and do things to her. [Playing sound effects of a woman in a sexual encounter throughout the following passage.] And have her lay by my pool in a bikini and have her come out and service me. And I'm laying by my pool, in comes that nude with just a pair of heels. And then like, I reach in, I yank out her vocal chords and then she just orally satisfied me by the pool. Oh, she's a totally mute Kim. And she's totally nude.

The CBSC then cited several sections from the Canadian Association of Broadcasters Code of Ethics, including the following:

Recognizing that stereotyping images can and do cause negative influences, it shall be the responsibility of broadcasters to exhibit, to the best of their ability, a conscious sensitivity to the problems related to sex-role stereotyping, by refraining from exploitation and by the reflection of the intellectual and emotional equality of both sexes in programming.

And:

Television and radio programming shall refrain from the exploitation of women, men and children. Negative or degrading comments on the role and nature of women and children in society shall be avoided.

Last Laugh

On the grounds of "abusive or discriminatory comments directed at French-Canadians and other identifiable groups . . . sexist remarks or observations . . . unsuitable language or descriptions of sexual activity during a broadcast period when children could be expected to be listening to radio," both stations carrying the *Howard Stern Show* were found guilty.[65]

NOTES

1. "Censors: ACLU Declares Radio Gags Speakers With Red Tape," *News-Week*, September 14, 1935, p. 25.
2. Ibid.
3. Ibid.
4. "Interviews: Unexpurgated Comment of Man in the Street," *News-Week*, July 13, 1945, p. 29.
5. H. B. Summers, *Radio Censorship* (New York: H. W. Wilson, 1939), p. 116.
6. "Women: Hand That Rocks the Cradle Shakes Warning Finger at Radio," *News-Week*, July 13, 1935, p. 29.
7. Ibid.
8. Summers, *Radio Censorship*, p. 166.
9. Ibid.
10. "Radio: Good Taste: Blue Pencils of Censors Are Always Genteel," *News-Week*, April 3, 1937, p. 30.
11. Ibid.
12. Ibid.
13. Robert Eichberg, "Too Hot To Broadcast," *Radio Stars*, January, 1935, p. 23.
14. Ibid., p. 77.
15. Ibid., p. 22.
16. George Gallup, "Radio Public Seen Against A Censor," *New York Times*, February 11, 1938, sec. 4, p. 4.
17. Ibid.

18. "Freedom of Radio Vital, Says Woll," *Broadcasting*, October 15, 1938, p. 22.

19. "Churches Hold No Public Body Is Qualified to Censor Radio," *Broadcasting*, October 15, 1938, p. 22.

20. "Citation for O'Neill Pulitzer Drama Sidetracked by FCC for Further Study," *Broadcasting*, October 15, 1938, p. 22.

21. WHRM, Hiram College Radio Station, http://143.206.107.71/www/whrm/operapptwo.asp. Site consulted June 14, 2001.

22. "Campus Radio Obscenity Policy for All Programs," http://www.db.erau.edu/campus/student/weru/training/coc/obscenity.html. Site consulted December 11, 2001.

23. Bruce Headlam, "How the Web Changed the Smut Business." Publisher and date not available.

24. Ibid.

25. Ibid.

26. "Uncovering Topless Radio's Nude TV," *Streaming Magazine*, July 2001, p. 40.

27. "Short Take: Naughty words and the FCC," April 17, 2001, http://civilliberty.about.com/news/issues/civilliberty/library/briefs/bl041701.htm.

28. "Porn firm takes over police tip site," *Boston Globe*, April 11, 2002.

29. Marvin R. Bensman, *Broadcast/Cable Regulation* (Washington, D.C.: University Press of America, 1990). Bensman cites *Variety*, November 5, 1990, p. 41.

30. Ibid.

31. Mireya Navarro, "Latino Radio Gaining Popularity and Scrutiny," *New York Times*, August 13, 2001, p. A1.

32. Ibid., p. A17.

33. Ibid.

34. Advisory Committee on Public Interest Obligations of Digital Television Broadcasters, "Appendix C: Statement of Principles of Radio and Television Broadcasting," issued by the Board of Directors of the National Association of Broadcasters, http://www.benton.org/PIAC/appc.html, posted January 22, 1999.

35. Tom Maurstad, "TV on brink of putting payoff before principles," *News-Press* (Florida), March 12, 2002.

36. Ibid.

37. Ibid.

38. Ibid.

39. Ed Vitagliano, "FCC Hard-of-Hearing to Indecency Complaints," May 25, 2001, www.e3mil.com/vm/index.asp?_id=43&art_id=7326.

40. Ibid.

41. John Fay, "Vulgar talk radio absolutely $#@!&," *Cincinnati Inquirer*, July 4, 1999, http://enquirer.com/editions/1999/o7/04/spt_vulgar_talk_radio.html.

42. Ibid.

43. Nicholas Hamisevicz, "Clearing the Airwaves," *Capitalism Magazine*, October 13, 2001, www.capitalismmagazine.com/2001/october/her_airwaves.htm.

44. "Gloria Tristani Officially Steps down from the FCC. On Her Way Out the Door, Tristani Comments on Indecency and LPFM," *Radio Ink*, September 10, 2001, www.radioink.com/Headlineentry.asp?hid=58961&pt=ink+Headlines.

45. "Clichés about Pornography in the Electronic Media: Radio, Television, Cable, Video, Cyberspace," http://moralityinmedia.org/cliches.htm. Site consulted July 16, 2001.

46. "Enforcement of the Obscenity Laws is Not Censorship," http://moralityinmedia.org/censorsh.htm. Site consulted June 12, 2001.

47. http://www.safeplace.net/ccv/docs/fcccomplaint2.htm.

48. CAIR-NY, http://www.cair.ny.com/NEWSREL/20010307-broadcast.html.

49. "An Open Letter to the Members of Congress re: FCC Failure to Enforce the Broadcast Indecency Law," News Release from Morality in Media, May 1, 2001.

50. Brenda Donnellan, "My Letter to West Virginia Public Radio," February 25, 1999, www.eurekanet.com/~brendonnell/pubrad.html.

51. Letter dated October 27, 1995, http://ftp.fcc.gov/Bureaus/Mass_Media/Filings/Kids_TV_93-48/93480336.txt.

52. "Workers told to tune out radio sex show," Associated Press, June 6, 1996, http://detnews.com/menu/stories/51346.htm.

53. "Eventide Model BD980 Obscenity Delay," www.eventide.com/broadcast.bd980bro.htm. Site consulted July 16, 2001.

54. XXX Radio Network, www.firtyboogie.com/main.php3. Site consulted May 12, 2002.

55. Ibid.

56. "If they build domain, will kids come?" CNN.com/Sci-Tech, May 12, 2002.

57. Ibid.

58. Kerby Anderson, "Proliferating Profanity," June 20, 2000, www.probe.org/docs/c-profanity.html.

59. Ibid.

60. "BBC reserves time for late-night access," *Broadcasting*, February 26, 1973, p. 50.

61. www.rab.co.uk.

62. Jack Boulware, "Three-way radio," Salon.com, June 16, 2000, www.salon.com/sex/world/2000/06/16/finland/.

63. Aryeh Dean Cohen, "Israeli call-in sex radio program nixed; threats are suspected," *Jerusalem Post Service*, December 5, 1997, in *Jewish Bulletin of Northern California*, www.jewishsf.com/bk971205/isex.htm.

64. CBSC, decisions of October 17, 1997, (station CHOM-FM) and October 18, 1997 (station CILQ-FM). www.cbsc.ca/english/decision/971017.htm.

65. Ibid.

CHAPTER 7

TIT FOR TAT

So easily manipulated is the American public by the media that one event, in 2004, comparatively innocuous compared to most media fare watched daily by children and adults alike—material you have already encountered in this book and material not "blue" enough to mention here, ranging from afternoon soap operas to evening sitcoms and dramas—became a *cause célèbre* that galvanized politicians, religious organizations, pressure groups, and the public in general into an all-out assault on media content that even remotely might be considered indecent. So all-encompassing was this assault that many television stations cancelled showings of highly praised films such as Steven Spielberg's *Saving Private Ryan* for fear that some of its content might be considered indecent and subject a given station to FCC sanctions.

What was this cataclysmic event that aroused almost universal cries of horror and vigilante accusations that the media were corrupting America's family values and leading its youth into paths of degradation? During the half-time entertainment at the 2004 Super Bowl football game, seen not only in the United States, but also by an estimated 100 million viewers throughout the world, singer Janet Jackson's black leather costume top was ripped off by her co-performer Justin Timberlake, exposing a portion of her right breast. The explanation that it was a "wardrobe malfunction" was generally dismissed. A firestorm followed, far greater than any reaction to many other TV programs that have featured, during prime time, partial frontal nudity, total rear nudity and simulated nude sex, including exposures of more than one breast.

Why the sudden onrush of indignation? One explanation stems from the tenor of the times. Under the presidency of George W. Bush and the control of Congress by the Republican party, America had turned far to the right, with political radicals and religious fundamentalists for the first time in many years given places of power and influence in the governance of the country.

The media, albeit always conservative, was now even more right wing, and fed the appetites of the extremists. It was an optimum moment for them. In 2003 almost all complaints of indecent material on radio and television— 99.8%—came from one source, the Parents Television Council, led by arch-conservative Brent Bozell. Aside from the complaints about the Janet Jackson caper, about the same percentage of all complaints in 2004 also came from the Parents Television Council.[1]

The increase of indecency complaints was consistent with the increase of right-wing power in the United States. In 2000 the FCC received only 111 such complaints. In 2002 it had jumped dramatically to 14,000. In 2003 it increased exponentially to 240,000. The Janet Jackson "wardrobe malfunc-tion" was a principal factor in the 2004 total of 1.07 million indecency complaints. In 2005 the FCC announced that it was overhauling its complaint-processing system in order to deal with the continuing deluge.[2]

The reaction to the Super Bowl event was immediate. The FCC chair immediately phoned the president of Viacom—owner of CBS, which aired the presentation, which was produced by MTV—expressing his outrage. The National Football League president said new League policies would preclude similar half-time happenings in the future. CBS and MTV both made public apologies.[3] Nevertheless, the FCC, under continued government and public pressure, ultimately fined CBS $550,000 for the incident—the largest fine of a TV broadcaster up to then. Viacom protested the fine as "illogical" and, with CBS, said that it had apologized and that it did not believe that the inci-dent violated FCC indecency rules.[4]

The Janet Jackson uproar put the FCC on a path of righteous indignation at virtually every radio and TV utterance or showing that might be consid-ered indecent. Radio jocks were especially susceptible to the FCC's wrath and stations immediately leaned over backwards to avoid even the appearance of indecency on the air. Many instituted "zero-tolerance" policies supplemented by delay mechanisms that would permit the bleeping out of any suspect material. *Talkers* magazine publisher called it an "alarming, serious issue" that has resulted in a "radical repression, a loss of nuance all across the dial."[5]

Nevertheless, the fining marathon was on. Fines as an effective lever to prevent indecency on the air prompted Congress to act, with the Senate rapidly passing legislation raising the indecency fine to $275,000 per incident (up from $27,500 for stations and $11,000 for performers) to a maximum of $3 million per day. The House version designated $500,000 per incident. In the fall of 2004, the Senate and House failed to reach a compromise, with the legislation therefore failing passage. However, members of both bodies averred that they would revive the bills, which they did in early 2005. Similar bills were introduced in the House and Senate. The House passed the Broad-cast Decency Enforcement Act of 2005, the subtitle of which read "To increase the penalties for violations by television and radio broadcasters of the prohibitions against transmission of obscene, indecent, and profane material, and for other purposes." The House bill passed by an overwhelming margin and included not only the $500,000 per incident maximum fine, but also made individuals, such as performers, personally liable, and authorized the revocation of a station's license for three violations. The Senate bill, which differed from the House's mainly in the maximum amount of fine per incident, $275,000, had not yet been passed by the Senate at this writing.[6]

The American Federation of Television and Radio Artists (AFTRA) warned that the legislation would have "an immediate and significant chilling effect on artistic freedom."[7] An indication of what was to come in the Jackson aftermath is a comparison of indecency fines levied by the FCC on radio and television programs in recent years: 2000—$48,000; 2001—$91,000; 2002—$99,400; 2003—$440,000; 2004—$7.9 million.[8]

But even before Congress could enact a law raising the fines, station owners cracked down. Some examples: Clear Channel, owner of more than 1200 radio stations, removed the Howard Stern show from six of its stations after the FCC proposed a $495,000 fine against Stern. A day later Clear Channel fired a radio team for a sexually explicit routine satirizing the FCC's attitude toward indecency. Clear Channel had already agreed to pay a $755,000 fine for indecent programming by the *Bubba, the Love Sponge* show and fired its host, Todd Clem.[9] Clear Channel later settled a number of fines for a total of $1.75 million—the largest settlement collected by the FCC for indecency violations up to that time.[10] CBS cancelled the 2004 "Victoria's Secret" annual fashion show for fear of FCC allegations of indecency.[11] The FCC fined Emmis Communications $42,000 for indecent programming on its Chicago stations.[12] Emmis later settled a number of FCC indecency fines for $300,000.[13] The FCC proposed fines totaling $1.5 million against Infinity Broadcasting for its Howard Stern programs.[14] Another FCC proposed fine was $220,000 against two Kansas radio stations for a program with local strippers and interviews with porn stars.[15] A reporter on the CBS television station in New York was fired for using the "f" word, after he thought he was off the air, to two men who were harassing him during his live, outside report.[16] Perhaps one of the most significant FCC actions representing the pressures of the Janet Jackson aftermath was its reversal of a previous decision not to fine the music personality Bono for using the "f" word on an awards telecast. The word was used just once and apparently inadvertently, considered not indecent under the FCC's "fleeting and isolated" policy (see Chapter 5). Post-Jackson, the policy was reconsidered and new judgments were applied retroactively.

On the other hand, the FCC did not act blindfolded with knee-jerk decisions. Nor did it act with a partisan political agenda. For example, Democrat

Commissioner Copps supported a crackdown on indecent material at least as strongly as did Republican chair Michael Powell and his Republican successor, Kevin Martin.

Not all complaints were automatically found valid. For example, a number of complaints by the Parents Television Council that the use of the nickname for Richard as an insult was indecent were dismissed. The FCC stated that although some material may appear to be tasteless to many, it is not necessarily "patently offensive."[17] The FCC also dismissed a complaint that women kissing and faking sexual intercourse on the sitcom *Will and Grace* was indecent, inasmuch as both women were clothed and the sequence did not attempt to "pander, titillate or shock the audience." It also denied a Parents Television Council complaint that a scene in *Buffy the Vampire Slayer* was indecent because it simulated two of the characters having intercourse. The FCC decided that the depiction was not "sufficiently graphic or explicit to be deemed indecent."[18] As was feared by many stations, many complaints to the FCC alleged that showings of *Saving Private Ryan* were indecent because they contained profane language. The FCC decided that the offensive language was not indecent in the context of the film in which it was presented.[19] One football-related incident was on the verge of becoming another Janet Jackson furor when it was defused by the FCC. An advertisement on ABC's *Monday Night Football* program depicted *Desperate Housewives* star Nicollette Sheriden, clad only in a towel, seeking out Philadelphia Eagles star Terrell Owens in the team's locker room, ostensibly to seduce him. In the sequence, her back to the camera, she flings open the towel. The audience does not see her presumably nude body. The FCC decided that the material was not sufficiently explicit or graphic to be considered indecent.[20]

While broadcasters scurried to shore up their content against allegations of indecency, many attacked the FCC's actions. Viacom president and chief operating officer Mel Karmazin said that "just because you don't like the words 'anal sex' doesn't make it indecent . . . if it doesn't appeal to you, shut the radio off."[21] Todd Clem, who performed as "Bubba the Love Sponge," stated that "it saddens me the knee-jerk reaction to a wardrobe malfunction our government is putting radio through . . . the government is on a right-wing religious witch-hunt. I may have been the first fired, but there will be more—and the only people who are suffering are the consumers."[22] Emmis Radio's president, Rick Cummings, stated that the FCC had been highly inconsistent in its judgment of what programming should or should not be fined for indecency. He noted that the current furor was part of the continuing issue of "indecency vs. free speech and the first amendment," and referred to a statement by FCC chair Powell, prior to Powell's reaction to the Super Bowl incident, that if parents believe their children shouldn't be listening to something on the air, they should turn it off.[23] Citadel Broadcasting's chief operating officer, Judy Ellis, stated that "government that decides what we can hear and see is a very frightening thing. Questioning where the government is going on the indecency issue isn't a pro-indecency position; it's about honoring free speech and the first amendment."[24] The founder and chief executive officer of the Oxygen cable network told a cable convention that "I don't think we should use the word indecency; we should call it what it is: censorship."[25] Stephen King, in a radio interview, summed up the objections of many in the various media industries to the FCC's crusade:

> I think it's nonsense . . . What I think about it is a word that I don't want to use on the radio or I'll get you guys in trouble . . . It makes me angry and it's silly and what happened to Howard Stern is silly . . . I don't listen to him—I think he's silly—but at the same time I think he ought to have a right to be silly on the radio . . . this is America. It's a free country and we're supposed to have the right of free speech . . . the way that it works in America or the way it's supposed to work in America—if he's [Stern] saying stuff that you don't like, if it offends you, you got a hand, you reach out, take hold of the knob, turn it off. He's gone—goodbye . . . You don't need a politician in your living room to say you got to put a Band-Aid over that guy's mouth.[26]

Some of the shoring up took the form of mechanical and electronic devices. One such device, the "Guardian," eliminated profanity and other spoken material through an automated logging system. President Eugene Novacek of the ENCO Systems' "Guardian" described its speech recognition software as follows:

> There's one list for words to eliminate and [another] for words to log. Guardian constantly monitors the broadcast air feed using variable length delay settings. When a word or phrase from either list is detected, Guradian can bleep/mute and/or log the event. The date/time logging is enhanced by storing a small piece of the actual audio for future reference.[27]

The government efforts to more closely restrict broadcast content met with resistance from civil liberties groups, citizen organizations, and broadcasting associations, the latter not usually in league with the former two. For example, in May, 2004, a nonprofit, nonpartisan website, SaveRadioNow.org, was formed for four distinct purposes: (i) "to inform Americans about the actions of Congress and the FCC, and their impact upon free speech rights"; (ii) "to enable Americans to share ideas and opinions on this topic via chats, blogs, and meet-ups"; (iii) "to provide Americans with easy access to their elected Representatives and the FCC Commissioners so they can express their opinions"; (iv) to sign a petition that will be sent to the FCC as well as to all members of the Senate and House committees in charge of writing rules and enforcing policy."[28] Fred Jacobs, president of Jacobs Media, which funded the site, explained that "There is a large gap between the opinions about indecency that are being expressed by the FCC and Congress and what we're hearing from radio listeners in America . . . It is also noteworthy that these listeners (as determined by a poll) are suspicious of the politics behind this current environment aimed at ending 'indecency' on the radio."[29]

At about the same time, a petition was filed at the FCC from a conglomerate of groups such as the American Civil Liberties Union, Citadel Broadcasting, American Federation of Television and Radio Artists, National Federation of Community Broadcasters, Viacom, Fox Entertainment Group, Screen Actors Guild, and People for the American Way (see note 30 for complete list). The petition asked the FCC to reverse its decision to exercise greater control over and deal more harshly with broadcast material it considers offensive. The petition expressed particular concern with the FCC's addition of "profanity" and "blasphemous" speech to its indecency concerns. Ralph Ness, president of the People for the American Way Foundation, one of the petitioners, stated that "FCC does not stand for Federal Commission of Censorship. The agency's recent power grab is intended to intimidate, and it is already squelching free speech. The petition is a key step in challenging the FCC's decision to unilaterally rewrite the First Amendment." Ness added, "It is astonishing that a federal agency would take unto itself the authority to punish speech it considers blasphemous. What does the First Amendment mean if federal bureaucrats can decide which public discussions are too irreverent? Which religious authorities will the FCC consult in deciding how big the fines should be for comments that offend someone's religious sensibilities? This is America, and we do not want to go down this road."[30]

How did the listening and viewing audience react to the FCC's crackdown? In the case of Howard Stern, his ratings in the largest markets had significant increases. However, Stern and Clem and other shock jocks and non-shock jocks saw the writing on the wall, handwriting that additionally revealed the gradual demise of terrestrial radio because of its abandonment of local service through massive consolidation[31] and opted to move to satellite radio. FCC indecency rules are not applied to cable and satellite distribution services. In late 2004 Stern signed a $500 million, five-year contract with Sirius satellite radio, beginning in 2006. Shock jocks Opie and Anthony, anathema to some broadcasters after their St. Patrick's Cathedral stunt, were among those who found new homes on satellite radio.

While some broadcasters fought the FCC's new repression and the anticipated congressional law, others saw them as a *fait accompli*. All, however, expressed concern over what they considered an unequal playing field. The FCC indecency rules applied only to regulated broadcast stations; they did not apply to cable or to satellite radio. Terrestrial radio, in particular, was at a disadvantage in programming content to certain demographic groups. It was (and continued to be) a double-edged sword: to ask Congress and the FCC to impose similar restrictions on cable and satellite, thus evening out the competition, but by doing so solidifying FCC and congressional control over content. Philip Lombardo, chair of the NAB Board, decried the different requirements for regulated and unregulated media. "Broadcasters today are living in a state of tremendous uncertainty," he said. "The FCC's inconsistent application of indecency rules—coupled with concern over a small number of what some would call 'tasteless' programs—has prompted unprecedented anxiety at every level of our business. . . . The breadth of this disparate treatment creates a confusion among both broadcasters and consumers. . . . when nearly 85% of households receive local television signals from cable or satellite, is it appropriate for only one medium—broadcasting—to face large fines and threats of license revocation? Does the average cable and satellite customer even differentiate between an over-the-air channel and a cable or satellite channel?"[32]

A Los Angeles radio company, Mt. Wilson FM Broadcasters, petitioned the FCC to apply an indecency provision similar to that for terrestrial radio to satellite digital radio. In denying the petition, the FCC stated that "the Commission does not impose regulations regarding indecency on services lacking the indiscriminate access to children that characterizes broadcasting."[33]

That did not stop Congress, however, and in mid-2005 some senators were considering introducing a bill that would include cable and satellite channels under FCC authority. The new chair of the FCC, Kevin Martin, agreed to the broadening of the Commission's indecency regulations. Representative Bernie Sanders, a consistent defender of First Amendment rights, introduced a bill that would prevent the FCC from thus extending its authority.[34]

In late 2005, however, the FCC was ready to release more stringent approaches related to indecency. Instead of notices to stations of apparent liability for airing indecent material (or denials of complaints regarding alleged indecent programming) handled by FCC staff offices, the FCC Commissioners were expected to deal with indecency actions directly. Because there is no statutory definition of indecency and determinations are made on the basis of past FCC rulings and, to a limited extent, past court decisions, it appeared that all cases should be heard at the highest FCC level.[35]

Whether the FCC's crackdown was working, whether broadcasters were massively self-censoring any materials that might even remotely be considered indecent, whether the listening and viewing public had grown tired of the hoopla and complaint fad exacerbated by the Janet Jackson caper, or whether American audiences had suddenly grown more sophisticated or more dedicated to First Amendment speech freedoms, the fact is that in mid-2005 the number of indecency complaints to the FCC dramatically

CHAPTER 7

decreased. In the second quarter of the year (April–June) the Commission received 6161 complaints compared to 157,016 complaints in the first quarter (January–March) of 2005.[36] But if, in fact, there were such changes, they appeared to be short-lived. In the third quarter of 2005 the FCC received 26,185 complaints, and an increase of 44,109 in the fourth quarter.[37]

In March, 2006, the FCC further demonstrated its hard-line approach to indecency with decisions based on 300,000 complaints concerning some 50 television programs from early 2002 into early 2005. Included was an affirmation of its earlier fine of CBS for the Janet Jackson incident, citations to such programs as *Without a Trace* and *The Surreal Life*, and the finding of profane language as indecent in a number of TV shows.[38] FCC Chair Martin stated that the FCC's actions "demonstrate the Commission's continued commitment to enforcing the law prohibiting the airing of obscene, indecent and profane material.[39]

As we write the end of this chapter, the indecency saga continues, with legislation still pending even as regulation tightens, with no immediate end in sight.

The fallout didn't disappear. Buoyed by the unrelenting media sensationalizing of the Janet Jackson incident even years after it occurred, politicians were virtually guaranteed press coverage of anything they did or said concerning indecency. While, as noted earlier, congressional attempts to censor the Internet were, with few exceptions, consistently found to be unconstitutional, senators and representatives didn't stop trying.[40]

At the FCC, Commissioners representing both political parties called for more direct involvement in decisions relating to indecency complaints, in most cases handled directly and solely by the Commission staff.[41] At the end of 2005, testifying before the Senate Committee on Commerce, Science and Transportation, which has oversight of the FCC, FCC Chair Kevin J. Martin stressed the need for government oversight over what children watched and heard on radio and television and called for legislation to curb what he considered indecent programming distributed via cable and satellite.[42]

After the 2004 Super Bowl incident, great pains were taken to see that a comparable incident didn't happen again, and The Rolling Stones' half-time presentation at the 2006 Super Bowl was carefully screened. Some called it censorship.

NOTES

1. "Most FCC Complaints Come From Single Group," *Radio Ink*, December 8, 2004, www.radioink.com/headlineentry.asp.
2. Ibid. and "FCC Looks to Speed Evaluation of Indecency Complaints," *Radio Ink*, February 14, 2005, www.radioink.com/headlineentry.asp.

3. Frank Ahrens and Lisa de Moraes, "FCC is Investigating Super Bowl Show," *The Washington Post*, February 3, 2004, p. A01. www.washingtonpost.com.

4. "FCC Set to Fine CBS for Janet Jackson Mishap," September 13, 2004; "FCC Fines CBS $550,000 for Super Bowl 'Wardrobe Malfunction'," September 29, 2004; "Viacom Disputes FCC Indecency Fine for Super Bowl Slip," November 15, 2004. *Radio Ink*, www.radioink.com/headlineentry.asp.

5. Mark Jurkowitz, "FCC Turns up Pressure and the Radio Industry Responds," *The Boston Globe*, April 17, 2004, pp. C1, 5.

6. See Broadcast Decency Enforcement Act of 2005, H.R. 310, 109th Congress.

7. "AFTRA: Fines Indecent," *Above and Below*, May 2004, pp. 1, 2.

8. Paul Davidson, "Indecent or Not? TV, Radio Walk Fuzzy Line," *USA TODAY*, June 3, 2005, p. 1B.

9. "Clear Channel Cans 'The Regular Guys' for Explicit Conversation," *Radio Ink*, April 12, 2004. www.radioink.com/headlineentry.asp.

10. "Clear Channel to Settle with FCC," *The News-Press*, June 10, 2004, p. D1.

11. "Latest 'Indecency' Casualty: Victoria's Secret Fashion Show," *Radio Ink*, April 13, 2004. www.radioink.com/headlineentry.asp.

12. "FCC Fines Emmis $42,000 for 6 Chicago Broadcasts," *Radio Ink*, April 23, 2004. www.radioink.com/headlineentry.asp.

13. "Emmis Settles FCC Indecency Issue for $300,000," *Radio Ink*, August 30, 2004. www.radioink.com/headlineentry.asp.

14. "RFCC may Fine Infinity $1.5 Million for Howard Stern Comments," *Radio Ink*, July 6, 2004. www.radioink.com/headlineentry/asp.

15. "FCC Proposed Fine for 'Twister' Broadcast," *Boston Globe*, December 23, 2004, p. A2.

16. *Radio Ink*, May 21, 2005. www.radioink.com/headlineentry.asp.

17. "FCC Dismisses 36 Indecency Complaints as not 'Patently Offensive'," *Radio Ink*, January 27, 2005. www.radioink.com/headlineentry.asp.

18. "FCC Says *Buffy*, *Will and Grace* Episodes 'Not Indecent'," *Radio Ink*, August 11, 2004. www.radioink.com/headlineentry.asp.

19. "FCC Denies Indecency Complaints Against Three TV Broadcasts," *Radio Ink*, March 1, 2005. www.radioink.com/headlineentry.asp.

20. "FCC Denies Indecency Complaint Against MNF Segment," *Radio Ink*, March 16, 2005. www.radioink.com/headlineentry.asp.

21. "Karmazin Defends Howard Stern's Broadcasts," *Radio Ink*, April 29, 2004. www.radioink.com/headlineentry.asp.

22. "'Bubba, the Love Sponge' Sees Indecency as 2004's Political, Religious 'Hot Button'," *Radio Ink*, April 12, 2004. www.radioink.com/headlineentry.asp.

23. "Emmis' Rick Cummings Says FCC has been 'Inconsistent on Indecency'," *Radio Ink*, April 12, 2004. www.radioink.com/headlineentry.asp.

24. "Citadel's Judy Ellis: Honor Free Speech and First Amendment," *Radio Ink*, April 14, 2004. www.radioink.com/headlineentry.asp.

25. *Radio Ink*, May 15, 2004. www.radioink.com/headlineentry.asp.

26. *Radio Ink*, June 9, 2004. www.radioink.com/headlineentry.asp.

27. "Profanity Elimination and Word Logging Device to be Unveiled," *Radio Ink*, April 7, 2004. www.radioink.com/headlineentry.asp.

28. "SaveRadioNow.org will Address Free Speech Issues," *Radio Ink*, May 4, 2004. www.radioink.com/headlineentry.asp.
29. Ibid.
30. "Free Speech Advocates Challenge FCC Rules," *Radio Ink*, April 20, 2004. www.radioink.com/headlineentry.asp. Petition signatories: American Civil Liberties Union, American Federation of Television and Radio Artists, Beasley Broadcasting Group, Citadel Broadcasting Corporation, The Creative Coalition, Directors Guild of America, Entercom Communications Corporation, The First Amendment Project, Fox Entertainment Group, Freedom to Read Foundation, Margaret Cho, Media Access Project, Minnesota Public Radio, The National Coalition Against Censorship, National Federation of Community Broadcasters, Penn & Teller, People for the American Way Foundation, Radio One Inc., The Recording Artists Coalition, Recording Industry Association of America, Screen Actors Guild, Viacom Inc., When in Doubt Productions, Writers Guild of America West.
31. See Robert L. Hilliard and Michael C. Keith, *The Quieted Voice: The Rise and Demise of Local Radio*. Carbondale, IL: Southern Illinois University Press, 2005.
32. "NAB Board Chairman Lombardo Rails Against 'Indecency Disconnect'," *Radio Ink*, February 7, 2005. www.radioink/headlineentry.asp.
33. "FCC Declines Indecency Rules for Satellite Radio," *Radio Ink*, December 17, 2004. www.radioink.com/headlineentry.asp.
34. Adam Thierer, "New World to Conquer," *Washington Post*, June 7, 2005. www.washingtonpost.com/ac2/wp-dyn=emailarticle; and Frank Ahrens, "Anti-Indecency Forces Opposed," *Washington Post*, March 26, 2005, p. D12.
35. John Eggerton, "FCC Seeks Indecency Clarity," *Broadcasting and Cable*, October 3, 2005. www.broadcastingcable.com/article/CA62.
36. "FCC Reports Indecency Complaints Down 96 Percent," *Radio Ink*, September 30, 2005. www.radioink.com/headlineentry.asp.
37. "Indecency Calls Rise in Q4, 05," *Radio Ink*, February 27, 2006. www.radioink.com/headlineentry.
38. http://fcc.gov/edocs, March 15, 2006.
39. Ibid.
40. In 2005 Republican Senator John McCain and Republican Representatives Michael Oxley and James Greenwood filed briefs with the Third Circuit Court of Appeals, supporting the Child Online Protection Act (COPA), which, on appeal, had been sent back to the Federal Appeals Court by the Supreme Court for reconsideration. The Third Circuit Court had found COPA to be an untenable violation of America's First Amendment rights to freedom of speech.
41. John Eggerton, *Broadcasting and Cable*, October 3, 2005. www.broadcastingcable.com/article/CA62.
42. "FCC's Martin Speaks at Senate Committee," *Radio Ink*, November 30, 2005. www.radioink.com/headlineentry.

CHAPTER 8

SPEAK THE SPEECH

To censor or not to censor? That is the question. Whether 'tis nobler to suffer sometimes outrageous speech in order to maintain the freedom thereof, or take arms against a sea of indecent matter and, by opposing, end it. A matter that neither Hamlet nor Bertold Brecht's Azdak in *The Caucasian Circle of Chalk* might easily solve. Passionate principles emanate from all sides of the controversy. Aside from the legal principles and the concerns that have generated the controversy, which have already been examined in this book, what are some of the philosophical or moral considerations?

In the 1939 book *Radio Censorship*, the matter is put into the open with three key questions: (1) "Should there be any attempt made, whatsoever, to censor programs—to eliminate the elements deemed contrary to the public interest?" (2) "If programs are to be censored, who should be the censor?" and (3) "Does program censorship exist, today?"[1] More than 60 years later, in this new book, we are asking the same questions, seeking still to find answers.

In the book *Commentaries on Obscenity* (written before even the rise of topless radio), a number of viewpoints are explored. One suggests that the restricting of sex materials from the public by the state has no clear justification. "The underlying assumption is that to [be exposed to] obscene material incites [one] to lustful thoughts [and that] lustful thoughts can result in anti-social behavior . . . [If a person is thus incited] to think about sex in any way except the conventional [the material] is obscene." It is suggested that the trend toward censorship of such material is an outgrowth of the continuation of Puritanism in both the United States and the United Kingdom.[2]

An additional viewpoint suggests that the principal basis for obscenity laws needs to be examined, that "one cannot assume, without consideration, that the Constitution forbids society to hold the view societies have held and continue to hold—that obscenity is immoral, that it corrupts morals and character of the persons exposed and the moral tone of a community, and should be suppressed to prevent such corruption."[3] This viewpoint goes on to suggest that obscenity laws should be considered, as well, in "relation to the freedom of the individual to obtain and indulge—at least privately—even in what others may consider obscene." The question is then asked whether "the morality that is the concern of obscenity laws . . . is still the law's business . . . whether the perpetuation by government of a morality religious in origin and having no present social purpose is a form of the establishment of religion . . . that perhaps the Constitution denies to government and to majorities the domain of the nonrational, leaving private morality to Church, to Home, and Conscience." The suggestion is made that "legislatures might be required to re-examine old laws based on moral and religious views of an earlier day, to identify motives and purposes for regulation presently acceptable, and to determine anew whether and which regulation is now called for."[4]

Another viewpoint cites adultery, fornication, sodomy, incest, prostitution, bigamy, abortion, open lewdness and obscenity as commonly perceived "offenses against morals." The argument is made that if these are differentiated from offenses against the "person" or against "property" or against "public administration," then sexual offenses do not truly violate moral principles. This viewpoint goes on to say that "the ordinary justification for secular penal controls is the preservation of public order" and that "what truly distinguishes the offenses commonly thought of as 'against morals' is not their relation to morality but the absence of ordinary justification for punishment by a non-theocratic state."[5]

Some critics see politics and political philosophies as the bases for government attempting to be a national nanny for media content. One critic referred to the Morality in Media call for "an indecency litmus test for the new FCC nominees" and for an investigation of what it considers the FCC's lax attitude toward indecency as a way to blame the media for many of society's ills and as a chill political wind blowing through Washington, D.C., in 2001. "The conservative Republican agenda beginning to take shape under George Jr. bears close watching. The last time the FCC cracked down on broadcast indecency, George Sr. was in the White House."[6]

Perceived Interests

The question of community standards and the public interest continue to be key issues in determining whether or not to censor. A critic notes that soap operas allegedly desensitize us to "sexual promiscuity, adultery, teenage pregnancies, murder and a host of other social sins," but the genre thrives, creating "human interaction and emotion to connect with its viewers."[7] Are these sins incompatible with contemporary community standards? Are they violations of society's moral beliefs and, therefore, patently offensive? A soap opera has never been cited for indecency. Concomitantly, what is expected to generate public concern sometimes doesn't, suggesting that many people's perceptions of contemporary community standards are no more than perceptions. A case in point: In a 2002 episode of the drama series *Once and Again*, two teenage girls kiss, a clear implication of a budding lesbian relationship. A station in conservative southern Florida, with many fundamental religionists, stated that it received not a single complaint. Some interviewees said that they've now seen gay relationships so many times in the media that they don't think of them as out of the ordinary and certainly not indecent. A minister said, "It's affirming for me to see that what's really happening in some teens' lives is being portrayed."[8]

T. Franklin Harris Jr., in an article in the *Freeman* entitled "Obscenity: The Case for a Free Market in Free Speech,"[9] examined the concept of a national contemporary community standard for obscenity. He cited the *Roth* and *Miller* cases as examples where the Supreme Court did not issue an objective national standard for obscenity, but by default left standards up to individual local communities. He asked, therefore, "If the Supreme Court should not force its artistic standards upon a diverse citizenry, why should mayors and city councilmen—or perhaps special censorship boards—have the ability to do so? . . . The community standard rule enshrines in law a purely arbitrary majoritarianism." Harris believes that two principles of justice are thereby violated, the rule of law and equality before the law. He stated that the definition of what is considered obscene is therefore an arbitrary one and that, concomitantly, so is the definition of what presumably comprises the community that makes up the standard for judging obscenity. Censorship, therefore, he concluded, clearly violates the principles of equality before the law.

Harris dealt with the concept of obscenity in a similar manner. He noted, as others have done, that sex in artistic works is censored on the grounds that its effect on the population can cause harm to the society. Yet, he noted, political speech is presumably not censored, and it can cause and has caused infinitely more harm to society. He also noted that to come to some determination as to what is obscene, we have to have some comparison; that is, to study what has been considered obscene previously. Even the most ardent antipornography advocates study the subject to be able to come to some conclusions as to what is obscene. "If human beings are to be fully realized moral agents, they must be free to make moral decisions on the basis of all available evidence. To deprive adults of the ability to make their own judgments is to turn the government into a nanny state and reduce adults to the moral equivalent of children." He believes that if obscenity is indeed evil, as some claim, it can be stamped as evil without it being banned as illegal because if it is made illegal, "law-abiding citizens will be unable to make their own judgments. Instead they will be like the parishioners of medieval churches: illiterate, without their own copy of text to interpret and discuss with others—and forced to rely upon blind faith in authority."

One Person's Poison is Another's . . .

Do programs acknowledged as indecent nevertheless serve a useful public interest purpose? When the Yale University radio station's *Rumpus Radio* was taken off the air for sexual references and profanity, a cohost of the program, Josh Kaplowitz, said, "visually impaired people can't enjoy the pleasures of pornographic magazines the way the rest of us can. We were providing a public service by tastefully describing several of the pictures in one particular magazine. We thought [the station] would be more responsive to that sort of social consciousness."[10]

Sometimes a clever play on words conveys the same meaning without the perceived obscenity or profanity. Woody Allen was quoted as saying, "Some guy hit my fender the other day, and I said unto him, 'Be fruitful, and multiply.' But not in those words." And Dorothy Parker once said, "Ducking for apples—change one letter and it's the story of my life." Lenny Bruce said, "I was arrested for using a ten-letter word that began with 'c,' and I would marry no woman who was not one." And on the *Tonight Show* Jack Paar asked Oscar Levant, "What do you think about pornography?" Levant's answer: "It helps."[11]

The issue of censorship has prompted not only arguments and debates, but serious academic exploration. The University of California radio network raised several questions: "Community voices on both sides [of the censorship issue] grew stronger. Were the issues blown out of proportion? Hyped up by the media? Or was this the start of a greater awareness? The flip side to censorship is education." The network held a forum, entitled "Day of Decency," for a discussion of the political, cultural, and social aspects of censorship, including censorship in the arts and music, self-censorship in the media, book burning and similar topics.[12] Not a bad approach for communities where censorship of the media is a key public issue.

Even in the conservative atmosphere of the first years of the twenty-first century, the conservative chair of the FCC, Michael Powell, in response to a question in 2002 about whether the Commission has gotten more lax about alleged indecent material on radio and television, answered: "I am always nervous [when dealing with indecency cases] . . . Indecency questions are the

Corey Deitz
Corey and Jay Show, Little Rock, Arkansas

The federal government acts on behalf of the people who own the airwaves by assigning licenses and renewing them. While a regulatory agency, the FCC also acts in a fiduciary capacity on behalf of citizens. The Commission should be responsive TO the people and not reactionary to their own opinions or those of special interest groups who might pressure it to act in a certain way. In the same way pornography is usually based on community standards so should the language used on local radio be judged. Listening to the radio is always a conscious choice. Offensive programming can be avoided or turned off. Listeners who choose to tune to a radio program that uses coarse language, sexual references, and even obscenities know exactly what they are getting and by tuning in create a community standard among themselves. Over the past 25 years what can be said on the radio without fear of regulatory reprisal or even community outrage has changed dramatically. It continues to morph. A quarter century ago you couldn't say "ass" without controversy. Today, you can say "asshole," "dick," "prick," "goddamn," "bastard," "son of a bitch," and more. In the not too distant future, I have no doubt that "shit" and "bullshit" will become acceptable. Edgy radio personalities reflect how their listeners act, react, and feel. They continually push these boundaries. Oddly enough, other words which were once quite common (not necessarily in a positive way) have become non-utterable. "Nigger" has become the "N" word and everyone is afraid to use it, even in a reasonable and intelligent context during a discussion. The word has all but vanished from speech as if it were written out of history. The government should defer to the community of listeners of a particular radio station when it comes to what it wishes to hear or not hear.

most subjective and most dangerous decisions the Commission is forced to make . . . unfettered speech about unpopular things is what America is all about."[13]

Another FCC commissioner, Rachelle Chong, spoke in a similar vein in a speech to the National Association of Broadcasters 1997 Radio Convention. She said:

As I complete my watch at the FCC, I would like to emphasize that our First Amendment tradition mandates that broadcasters must be free to present whatever programming they believe will best suit the needs of their local audiences. Except when there is a compelling government interest and it has chosen the most narrowly tailored way, government is forbidden from censoring your content or otherwise dictating categories of programming you must or must not show.

Having said that, I recognize that there are some limits on broadcast content that are part of the Communications Act, and have been upheld by the courts. These limits include obscenity, indecency, kids' educational programs, and some political broadcasting rules. Although the FCC must enforce such laws, it ought not expand the law to suit the whim of individual regulators. Our freedom as a nation is too important for that. And so, I . . . urge each of you speak out. Oppose government intrusion into your programming decisions. Don't sit quietly in your frog pot . . . Leap out of the pot, and voice your opposition to content regulation.[14]

Erik Barnouw, in his book *Mass Communication,* indicated the ineffectiveness of censorship:

Banning evil examples . . . does not ban it from life.
It may not strengthen our power to cope with it. It may have the opposite effect.

Code rules multiply, but they do not produce morality. They do not stop vulgarity. Trying to banish forbidden impulses, censors may only change the disguises in which they appear. They ban passionate love-making, and excessive violence takes its place.[15]

In a 1997 briefing paper, the American Civil Liberties Union analyzed freedom of expression in the arts and entertainment.[16] It offered the following definition of censorship:

Censorship, the suppression of word, images, or ideas that are "offensive," happens whenever some people succeed in imposing their personal political or moral values on others. Censorship can be carried out by the government as well as private pressure groups. Censorship by government is unconstitutional. In contrast, when private individuals or groups organize boycotts against stores that sell magazines of which they disapprove, their actions are protected by the First Amendment, although they can become dangerous in the extreme. Private pressure groups, not the government, promulgated and enforced the infamous Hollywood blacklists during the McCarthy period. But these private censorship campaigns are best countered by groups and individuals speaking out in defense of the threatened expression.

The ACLU briefing paper summarizes the history of censorship in the United States, noting the ambivalence of American society on the subject. It cites government attempts at censorship from the Comstock Law in 1873 to the Communications Decency Act in 1996 and, conversely, Supreme Court decisions that upheld our First Amendment rights to freely express what is in our imagination. Such decisions have been relatively broad, protecting artistic expression in books, theatrical works, paintings, posters, comic books and, by and large, television, radio, and music videos. The briefing paper notes that freedom of expression is governed by two principles.

> The first is "content neutrality"—the government cannot limit expression just because any listener, or even the majority of a community, is offended by its content. In the context of art and entertainment, this means tolerating some works that we might find offensive, insulting, outrageous—or just plain bad.

> The second principle is that expression may be restricted only if it will cause direct and imminent harm to an important societal interest. . . . Even then, the speech may be silenced or punished only if there is no other way to avert the harm.

The ACLU asked why censorship should be opposed, considering the content of some works of art—from violence and murder on television, to sexually explicit material on radio that degrades women, to graphic arts that insult religious and ethnic groups. It asked: "Why not let the majority's morality and taste dictate what others can look at or listen to?"

> The answer is simple and timeless: a free society is based on the principle that each and every individual has the right to decide what art or entertainment he or she wants—or does not want—to receive or create. Once you allow government to censor someone else, you cede to it the power to censor you, or something you like. Censorship is like poison gas: a powerful weapon that can harm you when the wind shifts.

Words of Tolerance

The authors of this book, when writing *Waves of Rancor: Tuning in the Radical Right,* encountered hate speech that literally turned our stomachs. Much of the hate speech went beyond cruel viciousness; it fomented violence that could maim and even kill designated groups and individuals. Yet, no matter how abhorrent we found it, we found even more abhorrent any censorship—which, given the political winds of a given time, could be used not only to stifle the extremists' speech but anyone's, including one's own speech. Even now, or especially now, in 2002 as this is written, the principles of free speech, press and assembly that mark our democratic country as different from most other countries in the world are under siege as a counterpoint to the threat of terrorism. We find it ironic that compromising our First Amendment rights, no matter what the circumstances, is exactly what our enemies would do and would want us to do.

We may abhor the flagrant obscenity, indecency and profanity we see and hear on television and radio, in films and books, and on cable and the Internet. But tolerance is the price we must pay for freedom. It is not too large a price.

NOTES

1. H. B. Summers, *Radio Censorship* (New York: H. W. Wilson, 1939).
2. Donald B. Sharp, ed. *Commentaries on Obscenity* (Metuchen, N.J.: Scarecrow Press, 1970), p. 11.
3. Ibid., p. 195.
4. Ibid., p. 209.
5. Ibid., p. 215.
6. "Keep Out," *Broadcasting and Cable*, May 14, 2001, www.findarticles.com/cf_O/moBCA/21_131/74823540/print.jhtml.7. Harold Bant, "Soap Operas: A Staple of Popular Culture," Ferris State University. www.ferris.edu/htmls/alumni/c&g/Apr96/soaps.htm. Site consulted June 16, 2001.
8. Joan D. LaGuardia, "Girls' kiss on ABC elicits little criticism," *News-Press* (Florida), March 14, 2002, p. E1.
9. T. Franklin Harris Jr., "Obscenity: The Case for a Free Market in Free Speech," *Freeman* 46, no. 9 (September 1996).
10. Perry Bacon, "Radio Comedy Hour Gets the Last Laugh," *Yale Daily News*, November 4, 1999, www.studentadvantage.lycos.com/lycos/archive/0.4681.cl-176.00.html.
11. "Pornography, Obscenity, Etc.," www.mcwilliams.com/books/aint/307.htm.
12. "R.O.C. on the Air! California Student Radio Blasts FCC, Censorship!" www.theroc.org/roo-mag/textarch/roc-o5/roc05-03.htm.
13. Holland Cooke, "What the Digital Revolution Means to Talk Radio," *Talkers Magazine*, May 2002, p. 8.
14. Rachelle Chong, "Content Regulation Heats Up: A Word to the Wise," remarks to the National Association of Broadcasters 1997 Radio Convention, September 19, 1997, New Orleans.
15. Erik Barnouw, *Mass Communication*, as quoted in Robert L. Hilliard, *Writing for Television, Radio, and New Media* (Belmont, Calif.: Wadsworth, 2000), p. 11.
16. "Freedom of Expression in the Arts and Entertainment," excerpts from ACLU Briefing Paper, no. 14 (1997).

APPENDICES

APPENDIX A

THE UNITED STATES SUPREME COURT

No. 77-528

FEDERAL COMMUNICATIONS COMMISSION

v.

PACIFICA FOUNDATION

Argued April 18, 19, 1978—Decided July 3, 1978

CERTIORARI TO THE UNITED STATES COURT OF APPEALS
FOR THE DISTRICT OF COLUMBIA CIRCUIT

[438 U.S. 726]

Syllabus

A radio station of respondent Pacifica Foundation (hereinafter respondent) made an afternoon broadcast of a satiric monologue, entitled "Filthy Words," which listed and repeated a variety of colloquial uses of "words you couldn't say on the public airwaves." A father who heard the broadcast while driving with his young son complained to the Federal Communications Commission (FCC), which, after forwarding the complaint for comment to and receiving a response from respondent, issued a declaratory order granting the complaint. While not imposing formal sanctions, the FCC stated that the order would be "associated with the station's license file, and, in the event subsequent complaints are received, the Commission will then decide whether it should utilize any of the available sanctions it has been granted by Congress."

In its memorandum opinion, the FCC stated that it intended to "clarify the standards which will be utilized in considering" the growing number of complaints about indecent radio broadcasts, and it advanced several reasons for treating that type of speech differently from other forms of expression. The FCC found a power to regulate indecent broadcasting, inter alia, in 18 U.S.C. §1464 (1976 ed.), which forbids the use of "any obscene, indecent, or profane language by means of radio communications." The FCC characterized the language of the monologue as "patently offensive," though not necessarily obscene, and expressed the opinion that it should be regulated by principles analogous to the law of nuisance, where the "law generally speaks to channeling behavior, rather than actually prohibiting it." The FCC found that certain words in the monologue depicted sexual and excretory activities in a particularly offensive manner, noted that they were broadcast in the early afternoon, "when children are undoubtedly in the audience," and concluded that the language, as broadcast, was indecent and prohibited by § 1464. A three-judge panel of the Court of Appeals reversed, one judge concluding that the FCC's action was invalid either on the ground that the order constituted censorship, which was expressly forbidden by § 326 of the Communications Act of 1934, or on the ground that the FCC's opinion was the functional equivalent of a rule, and, as such, was "overbroad." Another judge, who felt that § 326's censorship provision did not apply to broadcasts forbidden by § 1464, concluded that § 1464, construed narrowly as it has to be, covers only language that is obscene or otherwise unprotected by the First Amendment. The third judge, dissenting, concluded that the FCC had correctly condemned the daytime broadcast as indecent. Respondent contends that the broadcast was not indecent within the meaning of the statute because of the absence of prurient appeal.

Held: The judgment is reversed.

181 U.S.App.D.C. 132, 556 F.2d 9, reversed.

MR. JUSTICE STEVENS delivered the opinion of the Court with respect to Parts I-III and IV-C, finding:

1. The FCC's order was an adjudication under 5 U.S.C. § 554(e) (1976 ed.), the character of which was not changed by the general statements in the memorandum opinion; nor did the FCC's action constitute rulemaking or the promulgation of regulations. Hence, the Court's review must focus on the FCC's determination that the monologue was indecent as broadcast.
2. Section 326 does not limit the FCC's authority to sanction licensees who engage in obscene, indecent, or profane broadcasting. Though the censorship ban precludes editing proposed broadcasts in advance, the ban does not deny the FCC the power to review the content of completed broadcasts.
3. The FCC was warranted in concluding that indecent language within the meaning of § 1464 was used in the challenged broadcast. The words "obscene, indecent, or profane" are in the disjunctive, implying that each has a separate meaning. Though prurient appeal is an element of "obscene," it is not an element of "indecent," which merely refers to conconformance with accepted standards of morality. Contrary to respondent's argument, this Court, in Hamling v. United States, 418 U.S. 87, has not foreclosed a reading of § 1464 that authorizes a proscription of "indecent"

language that is not obscene, for the statute involved in that case, unlike § 1464, focused upon the prurient, and dealt primarily with printed matter in sealed envelopes mailed from one individual to another, whereas § 1464 deals with the content of public broadcasts.

4. Of all forms of communication, broadcasting has the most limited First Amendment protection. Among the reasons for specially treating indecent broadcasting is the uniquely pervasive presence that medium of expression occupies in the lives of our people. Broadcasts extend into the privacy of the home, and it is impossible completely to avoid those that are patently offensive. Broadcasting, moreover, is uniquely accessible to children.

MR. JUSTICE STEVENS, joined by THE CHIEF JUSTICE and MR. JUSTICE REHNQUIST, concluded in Part IV-A and IV-B:

1. The FCC's authority to proscribe this particular broadcast is not invalidated by the possibility that its construction of the statute may deter certain hypothetically protected broadcasts containing patently offensive references to sexual and excretory activities. Cf. Red Lion Broadcasting Co. v. FCC, 395 U.S. 367.

2. The First Amendment does not prohibit all governmental regulation that depends on the content of speech. Schenck v. United States, 249 U.S. 47, 52. The content of respondent's broadcast, which was "vulgar," "offensive," and "shocking," is not entitled to absolute constitutional protection in all contexts; it is therefore necessary to evaluate the FCC's action in light of the content of that broadcast.

MR. JUSTICE POWELL, joined by MR. JUSTICE BLACKMUN, concluded that the FCC's holding does not violate the First Amendment, though, being of the view that Members of this Court are not free generally to decide on the basis of its content which speech protected by the First Amendment is most valuable and therefore deserving of First Amendment protection, and which is less "valuable" and hence less deserving of protection, he is unable to join Part IV-B (or IV-A) of the opinion. STEVENS, J., announced the Court's judgment and delivered an opinion of the Court with respect to Parts I-III and IV-C, in which BURGER, C.J., and REHNQUIST, J., joined, and in all but Parts IV-A and IV-B of which BLACKMUN and POWELL, JJ., joined, and an opinion as to Parts IV-A and IV-B, in which BURGER, C.J., and REHNQUIST, J., joined. POWELL, J., filed an opinion concurring in part and concurring in the judgment, in which BLACKMUN, J., joined, post, p. 755. BRENNAN, J., filed a dissenting opinion, in which MARSHALL, J., joined, post, p. 762. STEWART, J., filed a dissenting opinion, in which BRENNAN, WHITE, and MARSHALL, JJ., joined, post, p. 777. [438 U.S. 729]

MR. JUSTICE STEVENS delivered the opinion of the Court (Parts I, II, III, and IV-C) and an opinion in which THE CHIEF JUSTICE and MR. JUSTICE REHNQUIST joined (Parts IV-A and IV-B).

This case requires that we decide whether the Federal Communications Commission has any power to regulate a radio broadcast that is indecent but not obscene.

A satiric humorist named George Carlin recorded a 12-minute monologue entitled "Filthy Words" before a live audience in a California theater. He began by referring to his thoughts about "the words you couldn't say on the public, ah, airwaves, um, the ones you definitely wouldn't say, ever." He proceeded to list those words and repeat them over and over again in a variety of colloquialisms. The transcript of the recording, which is appended to this opinion, indicates frequent laughter from the audience.

At about 2 o'clock in the afternoon on Tuesday, October 30, 1973, a New York radio station, owned by respondent Pacifica Foundation, broadcast the "Filthy Words" monologue. A few weeks later a man, who stated that he had heard the broadcast while driving with his young son, wrote a letter complaining to the Commission. He stated that, although he could perhaps understand the "record's being sold for private use, I certainly cannot understand the broadcast of same over the air that, supposedly, you control."

The complaint was forwarded to the station for comment. In its response, Pacifica explained that the monologue had been played during a program about contemporary society's attitude toward language, and that, immediately before its broadcast, listeners had been advised that it included "sensitive language which might be regarded as offensive to some." Pacifica characterized George Carlin as "a significant social satirist" who, "like Twain and Sahl before him, examines the language of ordinary people. . . . Carlin is not mouthing obscenities, he is merely using words to satirize as harmless and essentially silly our attitudes towards those words."

Pacifica stated that it was not aware of any other complaints about the broadcast.

On February 21, 1975, the Commission issued a declaratory order granting the complaint and holding that Pacifica "could have been the subject of administrative sanctions." 56 F.C.C.2d 94, 99. The Commission did not impose formal sanctions, but it did state that the order would be

"associated with the station's license file, and, in the event that subsequent complaints are received, the Commission will then decide whether it should utilize any of the available sanctions it has been granted by Congress."FN1 [438 U.S. 731]

In its memorandum opinion, the Commission stated that it intended to "clarify the standards which will be utilized in considering" the growing number of complaints about indecent speech on the airwaves. Id. at 94. Advancing several reasons for treating broadcast speech differently from other forms of expression,FN2 the Commission found a power to regulate indecent broadcasting in two statutes: 18 U.S.C. § 1464 (1976 ed.), which forbids the use of "any obscene, indecent, or profane language by means of radio communications,"FN3 and 47 U.S.C. § 303(g), which requires the Commission to "encourage the larger and more effective use of radio in the public interest."FN4

The Commission characterized the language used in the Carlin monologue as "patently offensive," though not necessarily obscene, and expressed the opinion that it should be regulated by principles analogous to those found in the law of nuisance, where the

"law generally speaks to channeling behavior more than actually prohibiting it. . . . [T]he concept of "indecent" is intimately connected with the exposure of children to language that describes, in terms patently offensive as measured by contemporary community standards for the broadcast medium, sexual or excretory activities and organs, at times of the day when there is a reasonable risk that children may be in the audience." 56 F.C.C.2d at 98.FN5

Applying these considerations to the language used in the monologue as broadcast by respondent, the Commission concluded that certain words depicted sexual and excretory activities in a patently offensive manner, noted that they "were broadcast at a time when children were undoubtedly in the audience (i.e., in the early afternoon)," and that the prerecorded language, with these offensive words "repeated over and over," was "deliberately broadcast." Id. at 99. In summary, the Commission stated: "We therefore hold that the language as broadcast was indecent and prohibited by 18 U.S.C. [§] 1464.FN6" Ibid.

After the order issued, the Commission was asked to clarify its opinion by ruling that the broadcast of indecent words as part of a live newscast would not be prohibited. The Commission issued another opinion in which it pointed out that it

"never intended to place an absolute prohibition on the broadcast of this type of language, but rather sought to channel it to times of day when children most likely would not be exposed to it." 59 F.C.C.2d 892 (1976). The Commission noted that its "declaratory order was issued in a specific factual context," and declined to comment on various hypothetical situations presented by the petition.FN7 Id. at 893. It relied on its "long-standing policy of refusing to issue interpretive rulings or advisory opinions when the critical facts are not explicitly stated or there is a possibility that subsequent events will alter them." Ibid.

The United States Court of Appeals for the District of Columbia Circuit reversed, with each of the three judges on the panel writing separately. 181 U.S.App.D.C. 132, 556 F.2d 9. Judge Tamm concluded that the order represented censorship and was expressly prohibited by § 326 of the Communications Act.FN8 Alternatively, Judge Tamm read the Commission opinion as the functional equivalent of a rule, and concluded that it was "overbroad." 181 U.S.App.D.C. at 141, 556 F.2d at 18. Chief Judge Bazelon's concurrence rested on the Constitution. He was persuaded that § 326's prohibition against censorship is inapplicable to broadcasts forbidden by § 1464. However, he concluded that § 1464 must be narrowly construed to cover only language that is obscene or otherwise unprotected by the First Amendment. 181 U.S.App.D.C. at 140–153, 556 F.2d at 24–30. Judge Leventhal, in dissent, stated that the only issue was whether the Commission could regulate the language "as broadcast." Id. at 154, 556 F.2d at 31. Emphasizing the interest in protecting children not only from exposure to indecent language, but also from exposure to the idea that such language has official approval, id. at 160, and n. 18, 556 F.2d at 37, and n. 18, he concluded that the Commission had correctly condemned the daytime broadcast as indecent.

Having granted the Commission's petition for certiorari, 434 U.S. 1008, we must decide: (1) whether the scope of judicial review encompasses more than the Commission's determination that the monologue was indecent "as broadcast"; (2) whether the Commission's order was a form of censorship forbidden by § 326; (3) whether the broadcast was indecent within the meaning of § 1464; and (4) whether the order violates the First Amendment of the United States Constitution.

I

The general statements in the Commission's memorandum opinion do not change the character of its order. Its action was an adjudication under 5 U.S.C. § 554(e) (1976 ed.); it did not purport to engage in formal rulemaking or in the promulgation of any regulations. The order "was issued in a specific factual context"; questions concerning possible action in other contexts were expressly reserved for the future. The specific holding was carefully confined to the monologue "as broadcast."

"This Court . . . reviews judgments, not statements in opinions." Black v. Cutter Laboratories, 351 U.S. 292, 297. That admonition has special force when the statements raise constitutional questions, for it is our settled practice to avoid the unnecessary decision of such issues. Rescue Army v. Municipal Court, 331 U.S. 549, 568 569. However appropriate [438 U.S. 735] it may be for an administrative agency to write broadly in an adjudicatory proceeding, federal courts have never been empowered to issue advisory opinions. See Herb v. Pitcairn, 324 U.S. 117, 126. Accordingly, the focus of our review must be on the Commission's determination that the Carlin monologue was indecent as broadcast.

II

The relevant statutory questions are whether the Commission's action is forbidden "censorship" within the meaning of 47 U.S.C. § 326 and whether speech that concededly is not obscene may be restricted as "indecent" under the authority of 18 U.S.C. § 1464 (1976 ed.). The questions are not unrelated, for the two statutory provisions have a common origin. Nevertheless, we analyze them separately.

Section 29 of the Radio Act of 1927 provided:

"Nothing in this Act shall be understood or construed to give the licensing authority the power of censorship over the radio communications or signals transmitted by any radio station, and no regulation or condition shall be promulgated or fixed by the licensing authority which shall interfere with the right of free speech by means of radio communications. No person within the jurisdiction of the United States shall utter any obscene, indecent, or profane language by means of radio communication." 44 Stat. 1172.

The prohibition against censorship unequivocally denies the Commission any power to edit proposed broadcasts in advance and to excise material considered inappropriate for the airwaves. The prohibition, however, has never been construed to deny the Commission the power to review the content of completed broadcasts in the performance of its regulatory duties.FN9 [438 U.S. 736]

During the period between the original enactment of the provision in 1927 and its reenactment in the Communications Act of 1934, the courts and the Federal Radio Commission held that the section deprived the Commission of the power to subject "broadcasting matter to scrutiny prior to its release," but they concluded that the Commission's "undoubted right" to take note of past program content when considering a licensee's renewal application "is not censorship."FN10 [438 U.S. 737]

Not only did the Federal Radio Commission so construe the statute prior to 1934; its successor, the Federal Communications Commission, has consistently interpreted the provision in the same way ever since. See Note, Regulation of Program Content by the FCC, 77 Harv.L.Rev. 701 (1964). And, until this case, the Court of Appeals for the District of Columbia Circuit has consistently agreed with this construction.FN11 Thus, for example, in his opinion in Anti-Defamation League of B'nai B'rith v. FCC, 131 U.S.App.D.C. 146, 403 F.2d 169 (1968), cert. denied, 394 U.S. 930, Judge Wright forcefully pointed out that the Commission is not prevented from canceling the license of a broadcaster who persists in a course of improper programming. He explained:

"This would not be prohibited "censorship" . . . any more than would the Commission's considering on a license renewal application whether a broadcaster allowed "coarse, vulgar, suggestive, double-meaning" programming; programs containing such material are grounds for denial of a license renewal."

131 U.S.App.D.C. at 150–151, n. 3, 403 F.2d at 173–174, n. 3. See also Office of Communication of United Church of Christ v. FCC, 123 U.S.App.D.C. 328, 359 F.2d 994 (1966).

Entirely apart from the fact that the subsequent review of program content is not the sort of censorship at which the statute was directed, its history makes it perfectly clear that it was not intended to limit the Commission's power to regulate the broadcast of obscene, indecent, or profane language. A single section of the 1927 Act is the source of both the anti-censorship provision and the Commission's authority to impose sanctions for the broadcast of indecent or obscene language. Quite plainly, Congress intended to give meaning to both provisions. Respect for that intent requires that the censorship language be read as inapplicable to the prohibition on broadcasting obscene, indecent, or profane language.

There is nothing in the legislative history to contradict this conclusion. The provision was discussed only in generalities when it was first enacted.FN12 In 1934, the anti-censorship provision and the prohibition against indecent broadcasts were reenacted in the same section, just as in the 1927 Act. In 1948, when the Criminal Code was revised to include provisions that had previously been located in other Titles of the United States Code, the prohibition against obscene, indecent, and profane broadcasts was removed from the Communications Act and reenacted as § 1464 of

Title 18. 62 Stat. 769 and 866. That rearrangement of the Code cannot reasonably be interpreted as having been intended to change the meaning of the anti-censorship provision. H.R.Rep. No. 304, 80th Cong., 1st Sess., A106 (1947). Cf. Tidewater Oil Co. v. United States, 409 U.S. 151, 162.

We conclude, therefore, that § 326 does not limit the Commission's authority to impose sanctions on licensees who engage in obscene, indecent, or profane broadcasting.

III

The only other statutory question presented by this case is whether the afternoon broadcast of the "Filthy Words" monologue was indecent within the meaning of § 1464.FN13 Even that question is narrowly confined by the arguments of the parties.

The Commission identified several words that referred to excretory or sexual activities or organs, stated that the repetitive, deliberate use of those words in an afternoon broadcast when children are in the audience was patently offensive, and held that the broadcast was indecent. Pacifica takes issue with the Commission's definition of indecency, but does not dispute the Commission's preliminary determination that each of the components of its definition was present. Specifically, Pacifica does not quarrel with the conclusion that this afternoon broadcast was patently offensive. Pacifica's claim that the broadcast was not indecent within the meaning of the statute rests entirely on the absence of prurient appeal.

The plain language of the statute does not support Pacifica's argument. The words "obscene, indecent, or profane" are written in the disjunctive, implying that each has a separate meaning. Prurient appeal is an element of the obscene, but the normal definition of "indecent" merely refers to nonconformance with accepted standards of morality.FN14

Pacifica argues, however, that this Court has construed the term "indecent" in related statutes to mean "obscene," as that term was defined in Miller v. California, 413 U.S. 15. Pacifica relies most heavily on the construction this Court gave to 18 U.S.C. § 1461 in Hamling v. United States, 418 U.S. 87. See also United States v. 12 200-ft. Reels of Film, 413 U.S. 123, 130 n. 7 (18 U.S.C. § 1462) (dicta). Hamling rejected a vagueness attack on § 1461, which forbids the mailing of "obscene, lewd, lascivious, indecent, filthy or vile" material. In holding that the statute's coverage is limited to obscenity, the Court followed the lead of Mr. Justice Harlan in Manual Enterprises, Inc. v. Day, 370 U.S. 478. In that case, Mr. Justice Harlan recognized that § 1461 contained a variety of words with many shades of meaning.FN15 Nonetheless, he thought that the phrase "obscene, lewd, lascivious, indecent, filthy or vile," taken as a whole, was clearly limited to the obscene, a reading well grounded in prior judicial constructions: "[T]he statute, since its inception, has always been taken as aimed at obnoxiously debasing portrayals of sex." 370 U.S. at 483. In Hamling, the Court agreed with Mr. Justice Harlan that § 1461 was meant only to regulate obscenity in the mails; by reading into it the limits set by Miller v. California, supra, the Court adopted a construction which assured the statute's constitutionality. [438 U.S. 741]

The reasons supporting Hamling's construction of § 1461 do not apply to § 1464. Although the history of the former revealed primary concern with the prurient, the Commission has long interpreted § 1464 as encompassing more than the obscene.FN16 The former statute deals primarily with printed matter enclosed in sealed envelopes mailed from one individual to another; the latter deals with the content of public broadcasts. It is unrealistic to assume that Congress intended to impose precisely the same limitations on the dissemination of patently offensive matter by such different means.FN17

Because neither our prior decisions nor the language or history of § 1464 supports the conclusion that prurient appeal is an essential component of indecent language, we reject Pacifica's construction of the statute. When that construction is put to one side, there is no basis for disagreeing with the Commission's conclusion that indecent language was used in this broadcast. [438 U.S. 742]

IV

Pacifica makes two constitutional attacks on the Commission's order. First, it argues that the Commission's construction of the statutory language broadly encompasses so much constitutionally protected speech that reversal is required even if Pacifica's broadcast of the "Filthy Words" monologue is not itself protected by the First Amendment. Second, Pacifica argues that, inasmuch as the recording is not obscene, the Constitution forbids any abridgment of the right to broadcast it on the radio.

A

The first argument fails because our review is limited to the question whether the Commission has the authority to proscribe this particular broadcast. As the Commission itself emphasized, its order was "issued in a specific factual context." 59 F.C.C.2d at 893. That approach is appropriate for courts as well as the Commission when regulation of indecency is at stake, for indecency is largely a function of context—it cannot be adequately judged in the abstract.

The approach is also consistent with Red Lion Broadcasting Co. v. FCC, 395 U.S. 367. In that case, the Court rejected an argument that the Commission's regulations defining the fairness doctrine were so vague that they would inevitably abridge the broadcasters' freedom of speech. The Court of Appeals had invalidated the regulations because their vagueness might lead to self-censorship of controversial program [438 U.S. 743] content. Radio Television News Directors Assn. v. United States, 400 F.2d 1002, 1016 (CA7 1968). This Court reversed. After noting that the Commission had indicated, as it has in this case, that it would not impose sanctions without warning in cases in which the applicability of the law was unclear, the Court stated:

"We need not approve every aspect of the fairness doctrine to decide these cases, and we will not now pass upon the constitutionality of these regulations by envisioning the most extreme applications conceivable, United States v. Sullivan, 332 U.S. 689, 694 (1948), but will deal with those problems if and when they arise.
395 U.S. at 396.

It is true that the Commission's order may lead some broadcasters to censor themselves. At most, however, the Commission's definition of indecency will deter only the broadcasting of patently offensive references to excretory and sexual organs and activities.FN18 While some of these references may be protected, they surely lie at the periphery of First Amendment concern. Cf. Bates v. State Bar of Arizona, 433 U.S. 350, 380–381. Young v. American Mini Theatres, Inc., 427 U.S. 50, 61. The danger dismissed so summarily in Red Lion, in contrast, was that broadcasters would respond to the vagueness of the regulations by refusing to present programs dealing with important social and political controversies. Invalidating any rule on the basis of its hypothetical application to situations not before the Court is "strong medicine," to be applied "sparingly and only as a last resort." Broadrick v. Oklahoma, 413 U.S. 601, 613. We decline to administer that medicine to preserve the vigor of patently offensive sexual and excretory speech. [438 U.S. 744]

B

When the issue is narrowed to the facts of this case, the question is whether the First Amendment denies government any power to restrict the public broadcast of indecent language in any circumstances.FN19 For if the government has any such power, this was an appropriate occasion for its exercise.

The words of the Carlin monologue are unquestionably "speech" within the meaning of the First Amendment. It is equally clear that the Commission's objections to the broadcast were based in part on its content. The order must therefore fall if, as Pacifica argues, the First Amendment prohibits all governmental regulation that depends on the content of speech. Our past cases demonstrate, however, that no such absolute rule is mandated by the Constitution.

The classic exposition of the proposition that both the content and the context of speech are critical elements of First Amendment analysis is Mr. Justice Holmes' statement for the Court in Schenck v. United States, 249 U.S. 47, 52:

"We admit that, in many places and in ordinary times, the defendants, in saying all that was said in the circular, would have been within their constitutional rights. But the character of every act depends upon the circumstances in which it is done. . . . The most stringent protection of free speech would not protect a man in falsely shouting fire in a theatre and causing a panic. It does not even protect a man from an injunction against uttering words that may have all the effect of force. . . . The question in every case is whether the words used are used in such circumstances and are of such a nature as to create a clear and present danger that they will bring about the substantive evils that Congress has a right to prevent.

Other distinctions based on content have been approved in the years since Schenck. The government may forbid speech calculated to provoke a fight. See Chaplinsky v. New Hampshire, 315 U.S. 568. It may pay heed to the "'common sense differences' between commercial speech and other varieties." Bates v. State Bar of Arizona, supra at 381. It may treat libels against private citizens more severely than libels against public officials. See Gertz v. Robert Welch, Inc., 418 U.S. 323. Obscenity may be wholly prohibited. Miller v. California, 413 U.S. 15. And, only two Terms ago, we refused to hold that a "statutory classification is unconstitutional because it is based on the content of communication protected by the First Amendment." Young v. American Mini Theatres, Inc., supra, at 52.

The question in this case is whether a broadcast of patently offensive words dealing with sex and excretion may be regulated because of its content.FN20 Obscene materials have been denied the protection of the First Amendment because their content is so offensive to contemporary moral standards. Roth v. United States, 354 U.S. 476. But the fact that society may find speech offensive is not a sufficient reason for suppressing it. Indeed, if it is the speaker's opinion that gives offense, that consequence is a reason for according it constitutional protection. For it is a central tenet of the First Amendment that the government must remain neutral in the marketplace of ideas.FN21 If there were any reason to believe that the Commission's characterization of the Carlin monologue as offensive could be traced to its political content— or even to the fact that it satirized contemporary attitudes about four-letter wordsFN22—First Amendment protection might be required. But that is simply not this case. These words offend for the same reasons that obscenity offends.FN23 Their place in the hierarchy of First Amendment values was aptly sketched by Mr. Justice Murphy when he said:

"[S]uch utterances are no essential part of any exposition of ideas, and are of such slight social value as a step to truth that any benefit that may be derived from them is clearly outweighed by the social interest in order and morality." Chaplinski v. New Hampshire, 315 U.S. at 572.

Although these words ordinarily lack literary, political, or scientific value, they are not entirely outside the protection of the First Amendment. Some uses of even the most offensive words are unquestionably protected. See, e.g., Hess v. Indiana, 414 U.S. 105. Indeed, we may assume, arguendo, that this monologue would be protected in other contexts. Nonetheless, the constitutional protection accorded to a communication containing such patently offensive sexual and excretory language need not be the same in every context.FN24 It is a characteristic of speech such as this that both its capacity to offend and its "social value," to use Mr. Justice Murphy's term, vary with the circumstances. Words that are commonplace in one setting are shocking in another. To paraphrase Mr. Justice Harlan, one occasion's lyric is another's vulgarity. Cf. Cohen v. California, 403 U.S. 15, 25.FN25

In this case, it is undisputed that the content of Pacifica's broadcast was "vulgar," "offensive," and "shocking." Because content of that character is not entitled to absolute constitutional protection under all circumstances, we must consider its context in order to determine whether the Commission's action was constitutionally permissible.

C

We have long recognized that each medium of expression presents special First Amendment problems. Joseph Burstyn, Inc. v. Wilson, 343 U.S. 495, 502–503. And of all forms of communication, it is broadcasting that has received the most limited First

Amendment protection. Thus, although other speakers cannot be licensed except under laws that carefully define and narrow official discretion, a broadcaster may be deprived of his license and his forum if the Commission decides that such an action would serve "the public interest, convenience, and necessity."FN26 Similarly, although the First Amendment protects newspaper publishers from being required to print the replies of those whom they criticize, Miami Herald Publishing Co. v. Tornillo, 418 U.S. 241, it affords no such protection to broadcasters; on the contrary, they must give free time to the victims of their criticism. Red Lion Broadcasting Co. v. FCC, 395 U.S. 367.

The reasons for these distinctions are complex, but two have relevance to the present case. First, the broadcast media have established a uniquely pervasive presence in the lives of all Americans. Patently offensive, indecent material presented over the airwaves confronts the citizen not only in public, but also in the privacy of the home, where the individual's right to be left alone plainly outweighs the First Amendment rights of an intruder. Rowan v. Post Office Dept., 397 U.S. 72. Because the broadcast audience is constantly tuning in and out, prior warnings cannot completely protect the listener or viewer from unexpected program content. To say that one may avoid further offense by turning off the radio when he hears indecent language is like saying that the remedy for an assault is to run away after the first blow. One may hang up on an indecent phone call, but that option does not give the caller a constitutional immunity or avoid a harm that has already taken place.FN27

Second, broadcasting is uniquely accessible to children, even those too young to read. Although Cohen's written message might have been incomprehensible to a first grader, Pacifica's broadcast could have enlarged a child's vocabulary in an instant. Other forms of offensive expression may be withheld from the young without restricting the expression at its source. Bookstores and motion picture theaters, for example, may be prohibited from making indecent material available to children. We held in Ginsberg v. New York, 390 U.S. 629, that the government's interest in the "wellbeing of its youth" and in supporting "parents' claim to authority in their own household" justified the regulation of otherwise protected expression. Id. at 640 and 639.FN28 The ease with which children may obtain access to broadcast material, coupled with the concerns recognized in Ginsberg, amply justify special treatment of indecent broadcasting.

It is appropriate, in conclusion, to emphasize the narrowness of our holding. This case does not involve a two-way radio conversation between a cab driver and a dispatcher, or a telecast of an Elizabethan comedy. We have not decided that an occasional expletive in either setting would justify any sanction or, indeed, that this broadcast would justify a criminal prosecution. The Commission's decision rested entirely on a nuisance rationale under which context is all-important. The concept requires consideration of a host of variables. The time of day was emphasized by the Commission. The content of the program in which the language is used will also affect the composition of the audience,FN29 and differences between radio, television, and perhaps closed-circuit transmissions, may also be relevant. As Mr. Justice Sutherland wrote, a "nuisance may be merely a right thing in the wrong place,—like a pig in the parlor instead of the barnyard." Euclid v. Ambler Realty Co., 272 U.S. 365, 383. We simply hold that, when the Commission finds that a pig has entered the parlor, the exercise of its regulatory power does not depend on proof that the pig is obscene.

The judgment of the Court of Appeals is reversed.

It is so ordered.

APPENDIX TO OPINION OF THE COURT

The following is a verbatim transcript of "Filthy Words" prepared by the Federal Communications Commission.

Aruba-du, ruba-tu, ruba-tu. I was thinking about the curse words and the swear words, the cuss words and the words that you can't say, that you're not supposed to say all the time, [']cause words or people into words want to hear your words. Some guys like to record your words and sell them back to you if they can, (laughter) listen in on the telephone, write down what words you say. A guy who used to be in Washington knew that his phone was tapped, used to answer, Fuck Hoover, yes, go ahead. (laughter) Okay, I was thinking one night about the words you couldn't say on the public, ah, airwaves, um, the ones you definitely wouldn't say, ever, [']cause I heard a lady say bitch one night on television, and it was cool like she was talking about, you know, ah, well, the bitch is the first one to notice that in the litter Johnie right. (murmur) Right. And, uh, bastard you can say, and hell and damn, so I have to figure out which ones you couldn't and ever and it came down to seven but the list is open to amendment, and in fact, has been changed, uh, by now, ha, a lot of people pointed things out to me, and I noticed some myself. The original seven words were shit, piss, fuck, cunt, cocksucker, motherfucker, and tits. Those are the ones that will curve your spine, grow hair on your hands and (laughter) maybe, even bring us, God help us, peace without honor (laughter) um, and a bourbon. (laughter) And now the first thing that we noticed was that word fuck was really repeated in there because the word motherfucker is a compound word and it's another form of the word fuck. (laughter) You want to be a purist it doesn't really, it can't be on the list of basic words. Also, cocksucker is a compound word and neither half of that is really dirty. The word—the half sucker that's merely suggestive (laughter) and the word cock is a halfway dirty word, 50% dirty—dirty half the time, depending on what you mean by it. (laughter) Uh, remember when you first heard it, like in 6th grade, you used to giggle. And the cock crowed three times, heh (laughter) the cock—three times. It's in the Bible, cock in the Bible. (laughter) And the first time you heard about a cock-fight, remember—What? Huh? naw. It ain't that, are you stupid? man. (laughter, clapping) It's chickens, you know, (laughter) Then you have the four letter words from the old Anglo-Saxon fame. Uh, shit and fuck. The word shit, uh, is an interesting kind of word in that the middle class has never really accepted it and approved it. They use it like, crazy but it's not really okay. It's still a rude, dirty, old kind of gushy word. (laughter) They don't like that, but they say it, like, they say it like, a lady now in a middle-class home, you'll hear most of the time she says it as an expletive, you know, it's out of her mouth before she knows. She says, Oh shit oh shit, (laughter) oh shit.

If she drops something, Oh, the shit hurt the broccoli. Shit. Thank you. (footsteps fading away) (papers ruffling)

Read it! (from audience)

Shit! (laughter) I won the Grammy, man, for the comedy album. Isn't that groovy? (clapping, whistling) (murmur) That's true. Thank you. Thank you man. Yeah. (murmur) (continuous clapping) Thank you man. Thank you. Thank you very much, man. Thank, no, (end of continuous clapping) for that and for the Grammy, man, [']cause (laughter) that's based on people liking it man, yeh, that's ah, that's okay man. (laughter) Let's let that go, man. I got my Grammy. I can let my hair hang down now, shit. (laughter) Ha! So! Now the word shit is okay for the man. At work you can say it like crazy. Mostly figuratively, Get that shit out of here, will ya? I don't want to see that shit anymore. I can't colt that shit, buddy. I've had that shit up to here. I think you're full of shit myself (laughter) He don't know shit from Shinola. (laughter) you know that? (laughter) Always wondered how the Shinola people felt about that (laughter) Hi, I'm the new man from Shinola. (laughter) Hi, how are ya? Nice to see ya. (laughter) How are ya? (laughter) Boy, I don't know whether to shit or wind my watch. (laughter) Guess, I'll shit on my watch. (laughter) Oh, the shit is going to hit de fan. (laughter) Built like a brick shit-house. (laughter) Up, he's up shit's creek. (laughter) He's had it. (laughter) He hit me, I'm sorry. (laughter) Hot shit, holy shit, tough shit, eat shit, (laughter) shit-eating grin. Uh, whoever thought of that was ill. (murmur laughter) He had a shit-eating grin! He had a what? (laughter) Shit on a stick. (laughter) Shit in a handbag. I always like that. He ain't worth shit in a handbag. (laughter) Shitty. He acted real shitty. (laughter) You know what I mean? (laughter) I got the money back, but a real shitty attitude. Heh, he had a shit-fit. (laughter) Wow! Shit-fit. Whew! Glad I wasn't there. (murmur, laughter) All the animals—Bull shit, horse shit, cow shit, rat shit, bat shit. (laughter) First time I heard bat shit, I really came apart. A guy in Oklahoma, Boggs, said it, man. Aw! Bat shit. (laughter) Vera reminded me of that last night, ah (murmur). Snake shit, slicker than owl shit. (laughter) Get your shit together. Shit or get off the pot. (laughter) I got a shit-load full of them. (laughter) I got a shit-pot full, all right. Shit-head, shit-heel, shit in your heart, shit for brains, (laughter) shit-face, heh (laughter) I always try to think how that could have originated; the first guy that said that. Somebody got drunk and fell in some shit, you know. (laughter) Hey, I'm shit-face. (laughter) Shitface, today. (laughter) Anyway, enough of that shit. (laughter) The big one, the word fuck that's the one that hangs them up the most. [']Cause in a lot of cases that's the very act that hangs them up the most. So, it's natural that the word would, uh, have the same effect. It's a great word, fuck, nice word, easy word, cute word, kind of. Easy word to say. One syllable, short u. (laughter) Fuck. (Murmur) You know, it's easy. Starts with a nice soft sound—fuh—ends with a kh. Right? (laughter) A little something for everyone. Fuck (laughter) Good word. Kind of a proud word, too. Who are you? I am FUCK. (laughter) FUCK OF THE MOUNTAIN. (laughter) Tune in again next week to FUCK OF THE MOUNTAIN. (laughter) It's an interesting word too, [']cause it's got a double kind of a life—personality—dual, you know, whatever the right phrase is. It leads a double life, the word fuck. First of all, it means, sometimes, most of the time, fuck. What does it mean? It means to make love. Right? We're going to make love, yeh, we're going to fuck, yeh, we're going to fuck, yeh, we're going to make love. (laughter) we're really going to fuck, yeh, we're going to make love. Right? And it also means the beginning of life, it's the act that begins life, so there's the word hanging around with words like love, and life, and yet, on the other hand, it's also a word that we really use to hurt each other with, man. It's a heavy. It's one that you have toward the end of the argument. (laughter) Right? (laughter) You finally can't make out. Oh, fuck you man. I said, fuck you. (laughter, murmur) Stupid fuck. (laughter) Fuck you and everybody that looks like you, (laughter) man. It would be nice to change the movies that we already have and substitute the word fuck for the word kill, wherever we could, and some of those movie cliches would change a little bit. Madfuckers still on the loose. Stop me before I fuck again. Fuck the ump, fuck the ump, fuck the ump, fuck the ump, fuck the ump. Easy on the clutch Bill, you'll fuck that engine again. (laughter) The other shit one was, I don't give a shit. Like it's worth something, you know? (laughter) I don't give a shit. Hey, well, I don't take no shit, (laughter) you know what I mean? You know why I don't take no shit? (laughter) Cause I don't give a shit. (Laughter)

If I give a shit, I would have to pack shit. (laughter) But I don't pack no shit cause I don't give a shit. (laughter) You wouldn't shit me, would you? (laughter) That's a joke when you're a kid with a worm looking out the bird's ass. You wouldn't shit me, would you? (laughter) It's an eight-year-old joke but a good one. (laughter) The additions to the list. I found three more words that had to be put on the list of words you could never say on television, and they were fart, turd and twat, those three. (laughter) Fart, we talked about, it's harmless. It's like tits, it's a cutie word, no problem. Turd, you can't say, but who wants to, you know? (laughter) The subject never comes up on the panel, so I'm not worried about that one. Now the word twat is an interesting word. Twat! Yeh, right in the twat. (Laughter)

Twat is an interesting word because it's the only one I know of, the only slang word applying to the, a part of the sexual anatomy that doesn't have another meaning to it. Like, ah, snatch, box and pussy all have other meanings, man. Even in a Walt Disney movie, you can say, We're going to snatch that pussy and put him in a box and bring him on the airplane. (murmur, laughter) Everybody loves it. The twat stands alone, man, as it should. And two-way words. Ah, ass is okay providing you're riding into town on a religious feast day. (laughter) You can't say, up your ass. (laughter) You can say, stuff it! (murmur) There are certain things you can say—its weird, but you can just come so close. Before I cut, I, uh, want to, ah, thank you for listening to my words, man, fellow, uh space travelers. Thank you man for tonight and thank you also. (clapping whistling)

POWELL, J., concurring

MR. JUSTICE POWELL, with whom MR. JUSTICE BLACKMUN joins, concurring in part and concurring in the judgment.

I join Parts I, II, III, and IV-C of MR. JUSTICE STEVENS' opinion. The Court today reviews only the Commission's holding that Carlin's monologue was indecent "as broadcast" at two o'clock in the afternoon, and not the broad sweep of the Commission's opinion. Ante at 734–735. In addition to being consistent with our settled practice of not deciding constitutional issues unnecessarily, see ante at 734; Ashwander v. TVA, 297 U.S. 288, 345–348 (1936) (Brandeis, J., concurring), this narrow focus also is conducive to the orderly development of this relatively new and difficult area of law, in the first instance by the Commission, and then by the reviewing courts. See 181 U.S.App.D.C. 132, 158–160, 556 F.2d 9, 35–37 (1977) (Leventhal, J., dissenting).

I also agree with much that is said in Part IV of MR. JUSTICE STEVENS' opinion, and with its conclusion that the Commission's holding in this case does not violate the First Amendment. Because I do not subscribe to all that is said in Part IV, however, I state my views separately.

I

It is conceded that the monologue at issue here is not obscene in the constitutional sense. See 56 F.C.C.2d 94, 98 (1975); Brief for Petitioner 18. Nor, in this context, does its language constitute "fighting words" within the meaning of Chaplinsky v. New Hampshire, 315 U.S. 568 (1942). Some of the words used have been held protected by the First Amendment in other cases and contexts. E.g., Lewis v. New Orleans, 415 U.S. 130 (1974); Hess v. Indiana, 414 U.S. 105 (1973); Papish v. University of Missouri Curators, 410 U.S. 667 (1973); Cohen v. California, 403 U.S. 15 (1971); see also Eaton v. Tulsa, 415 U.S. 697 (1974). I do not think Carlin, consistently with the First Amendment, could be punished for delivering the same monologue to a live audience composed of adults who, knowing what to expect, chose to attend his performance. See Brown v. Oklahoma, 408 U.S. 914 (1972) (POWELL, J., concurring in result). And I would assume that an adult could not constitutionally be prohibited from purchasing a recording or transcript of the monologue and playing or reading it in the privacy of his own home. Cf. Stanley v. Georgia, 394 U.S. 557 (1969).

But it also is true that the language employed is, to most people, vulgar and offensive. It was chosen specifically for this quality, and it was repeated over and over as a sort of verbal shock treatment. The Commission did not err in characterizing the narrow category of language used here as "patently offensive" to most people regardless of age.

The issue, however, is whether the Commission may impose civil sanctions on a licensee radio station for broadcasting the monologue at two o'clock in the afternoon. The Commission's primary concern was to prevent the broadcast from reaching the ears of unsupervised children who were likely to be in the audience at that hour. In essence, the Commission sought to "channel" the monologue to hours when the fewest unsupervised children would be exposed to it. See 56 F.C.C.2d at 98. In my view, this consideration provides strong support for the Commission's holding.FN1

The Court has recognized society's right to "adopt more stringent controls on communicative materials available to youths than on those available to adults." Erznoznik

v. Jacksonville, 422 U.S. 205, 212 (1975); see also, e.g., Miller v. California, 413 U.S. 15, 36 n. 17 (1973); Ginsberg v. New York, 390 U.S. 629, 636–641 (1968); Jacobellis v. Ohio, 378 U.S. 184, 195 (1964) (opinion of BRENNAN, J.). This recognition stems in large part from the fact that "a child . . . is not possessed of that full capacity for individual choice which is the presupposition of First Amendment guarantees." Ginsberg v. New York, supra at 649–650 (STEWART, J., concurring in result). Thus, children may not be able to protect themselves from speech which, although shocking to most adults, generally may be avoided by the unwilling through the exercise of choice. At the same time, such speech may have a deeper and more lasting negative effect on a child than on an adult. For these reasons, society may prevent the general dissemination of such speech to children, leaving to parents the decision as to what speech of this kind their children shall hear and repeat:

"[C]onstitutional interpretation has consistently recognized that the parents' claim to authority in their own household to direct the rearing of their children is basic in the structure of our society."

"It is cardinal with us that the custody, care and nurture of the child reside first in the parents, whose primary function and freedom include preparation for obligations the state can neither supply nor hinder." Prince v. Massachusetts, [321 U.S. 158, 166 (1944)]. The legislature could properly conclude that parents and others, teachers for example, who have this primary responsibility for children's wellbeing are entitled to the support of laws designed to aid discharge of that responsibility." Id. at 639. The Commission properly held that the speech from which society may attempt to shield its children is not limited to that which appeals to the youthful prurient interest. The language involved in this case is as potentially degrading and harmful to children as representations of many erotic acts.

In most instances, the dissemination of this kind of speech to children may be limited without also limiting willing adults' access to it. Sellers of printed and recorded matter and exhibitors of motion pictures and live performances may be required to shut their doors to children, but such a requirement has no effect on adults' access. See id. at 634–635. The difficulty is that such a physical separation of the audience cannot be accomplished in the broadcast media. During most of the broadcast hours, both adults and unsupervised children are likely to be in the broadcast audience, and the broadcaster cannot reach willing adults without also reaching children. This, as the Court emphasizes, is one of the distinctions between the broadcast and other media to which we often have adverted as justifying a different treatment of the broadcast media for First Amendment purposes. See Bates v. State Bar of Arizona, 433 U.S. 350, 384 (1977); Columbia Broadcasting System, Inc. v. Democratic National Committee, 412 U.S. 94, 101 (1973); Red Lion Broadcasting Co. v. FCC, 395 U.S. 367, 386–387 (1969); Capital Broadcasting Co. v. Mitchell, 333 F. Supp. 582 (DC 1971), aff'd sub nom. Capital Broadcasting Co. v. Acting Attorney General, 405 U.S. 1000 (1972); see generally Joseph Burstyn, Inc. v. Wilson, 343 U.S. 495, 502–503 (1952). In my view, the Commission was entitled to give substantial weight to this difference in reaching its decision in this case.

A second difference, not without relevance, is that broadcasting—unlike most other forms of communication—comes directly into the home, the one place where people ordinarily have the right not to be assaulted by uninvited and offensive sights and sounds. Erznoznik v. Jacksonville, supra at 209; Cohen v. California, 403 U.S. at 21; Rowan v. Post Office Dept., 397 U.S. 728 (1970). Although the First Amendment may require unwilling adults to absorb the first blow of offensive but protected speech when they are in public before they turn away, see, e.g., Erznoznik, supra at 210–211, but cf. Rosenfeld v. New Jersey, 408 U.S. 901, 903–909 (1972) (POWELL, J., dissenting), a different order of values obtains in the home.

"That we are often "captives" outside the sanctuary of the home and subject to objectionable speech and other sound does not mean we must be captives everywhere." Rowan v. Post Office Dept., supra at 738. The Commission also was entitled to give this factor appropriate weight in the circumstances of the instant case. This is not to say, however, that the Commission has an unrestricted license to decide what speech, protected in other media, may be banned from the airwaves in order to protect unwilling adults from momentary exposure to it in their homes.FN2 Making the sensitive judgments required in these cases is not easy. But this responsibility has been reposed initially in the Commission, and its judgment is entitled to respect.

It is argued that, despite society's right to protect its children from this kind of speech, and despite everyone's interest in not being assaulted by offensive speech in the home, the Commission's holding in this case is impermissible because it prevents willing adults from listening to Carlin's monologue over the radio in the early afternoon hours. It is said that this ruling will have the effect of "reduc[ing] the adult population . . . to [hearing] only what is fit for children." Butler v. Michigan, 352 U.S. 380, 383 (1957). This argument is not without force. The Commission certainly should consider it as it develops standards in this area. But it is not sufficiently strong to leave the Commission powerless to act in circumstances such as those in this case.

The Commission's holding does not prevent willing adults from purchasing Carlin's record, from attending his performances, or, indeed, from reading the transcript reprinted as an appendix to the Court's opinion. On its face, it does not prevent respondent Pacifica Foundation from broadcasting the monologue during late evening hours, when fewer children are likely to be in the audience, nor from broadcasting discussions of the contemporary use of language at any time during the day. The Commission's holding, and certainly the Court's holding today, does not speak to cases involving the isolated use of a potentially offensive word in the course of a radio broadcast, as distinguished from the verbal shock treatment administered by respondent here. In short, I agree that, on the facts of this case, the Commission's order did not violate respondent's First Amendment rights.

II

As the foregoing demonstrates, my views are generally in accord with what is said in Part IV-C of MR. JUSTICE STEVENS' opinion. See ante at 748–750. I therefore join that portion of his opinion. I do not join Part IV-B, however, because I do not subscribe to the theory that the Justices of this Court are free generally to decide on the basis of its content which speech protected by the First Amendment is most "valuable," and hence deserving of the most protection, and which is less "valuable" and hence deserving of less protection. Compare ante at 744–748; Young v. American Mini Theatres, Inc., 427 U.S. 50, 63–73 (1976) (opinion of STEVENS, J.), with id. at 73 n. 1 (POWELL, J., concurring).FN3 In my view, the result in this case does not turn on whether Carlin's monologue, viewed as a whole, or the words that constitute it, have more or less "value" than a candidate's campaign speech. This is a judgment for each person to make, not one for the judges to impose upon him.FN4 [438 U.S. 762]

The result turns instead on the unique characteristics of the broadcast media, combined with society's right to protect its children from speech generally agreed to be inappropriate for their years, and with the interest of unwilling adults in not being assaulted by such offensive speech in their homes. Moreover, I doubt whether today's decision will prevent any adult who wishes to receive Carlin's message in Carlin's own words from doing so, and from making for himself a value judgment as to the merit of the message and words. Cf. id. at 77–79 (POWELL, J., concurring). These are the grounds upon which I join the judgment of the Court as to Part IV.

ME. JUSTICE BRENNAN, with whom MR. JUSTICE MARSHALL joins, dissenting.

I agree with MR. JUSTICE STEWART that, under Hamling v. United States, 418 U.S. 87 (1974), and United States v. 12 200-ft. Reels of Film, 413 U.S. 123 (1973), the word "indecent" in 18 U.S.C. § 1464 (1976 ed.) must be construed to prohibit only obscene speech. I would, therefore, normally refrain from expressing my views on any constitutional issues implicated in this case. However, I find the Court's misapplication of fundamental First Amendment principles so patent, and its attempt to impose its notions of propriety on the whole of the American people so misguided, that I am unable to remain silent.

I

For the second time in two years, see Young v. American Mini Theatres, Inc., 427 U.S. 50 (1976), the Court refuses to embrace the notion, completely antithetical to basic First Amendment values, that the degree of protection the First Amendment affords protected speech varies with the social value ascribed to that speech by five Members of this Court. See opinion of MR. JUSTICE POWELL, ante at 761–762.

Moreover as do all parties, all Members of the Court agree that the Carlin monologue aired by Station WBAI does not fall within one of the categories of speech, such as "fighting words," Chaplinsky v. New Hampshire, 315 U.S. 568 (1942), or obscenity, Roth v. United States, 354 U.S. 476 (1957), that is totally without First Amendment protection. This conclusion, of course, is compelled by our cases expressly holding that communications containing some of the words found condemnable here are fully protected by the First Amendment in other contexts. See Eaton v. Tulsa, 415 U.S. 697 (1974); Papish v. University of Missouri Curators, 410 U.S. 667 (1973); Brown v. Oklahoma, 408 U.S. 914 (1972); Lewis v. New Orleans, 408

U.S. 913 (1972); Rosenfeld v. New Jersey, 408 U.S. 901 (1972); Cohen v. California, 403 U.S. 15 (1971). Yet despite the Court's refusal to create a sliding scale of First Amendment protection calibrated to this Court's perception of the worth of a communication's content, and despite our unanimous agreement that the Carlin monologue is protected speech, a majority of the Court FN1 nevertheless finds that, on the facts of this case, the FCC is not constitutionally barred from imposing sanctions on Pacifica for its airing of the Carlin monologue. This majority apparently believes that the FCC's disapproval of Pacifica's afternoon broadcast of Carlin's "Dirty Words" recording is a permissible time, place, and manner regulation. Kovacs v. Cooper, 336 U.S. 77 (1949).

Both the opinion of my Brother STEVENS and the opinion of my Brother POWELL rely principally on two factors in reaching this conclusion: (1) the capacity of a radio broadcast to intrude into the unwilling listener's home, and (2) the presence of children in the listening audience. Dispassionate analysis, removed from individual notions as to what is proper and what is not, starkly reveals that these justifications, whether individually or together, simply do not support even the professedly moderate degree of governmental homogenization of radio communications—if, indeed, such homogenization can ever be moderate given the preeminent status of the right of free speech in our constitutional scheme that the Court today permits.

A

Without question, the privacy interests of an individual in his home are substantial, and deserving of significant protection. In finding these interests sufficient to justify the content regulation of protected speech, however, the Court commits two errors. First, it misconceives the nature of the privacy interests involved where an individual voluntarily chooses to admit radio communications into his home. Second, it ignores the constitutionally protected interests of both those who wish to transmit and those who desire to receive broadcasts that many—including the FCC and this Court—might find offensive.

"The ability of government, consonant with the Constitution, to shut off discourse solely to protect others from hearing it is . . . dependent upon a showing that substantial privacy interests are being invaded in an essentially intolerable manner. Any broader view of this authority would effectively empower a majority to silence dissidents simply as a matter of personal predilections." Cohen v. California, supra, at 21.

I am in wholehearted agreement with my Brethren that an individual's right "to be let alone" when engaged in private activity within the confines of his own home is encompassed within the "substantial privacy interests" to which Mr. Justice Harlan referred in Cohen, and is entitled to the greatest solicitude. Stanley v. Georgia, 394 U.S. 557 (1969). However, I believe that an individual's actions in switching on and listening to communications transmitted over the public airways and directed to the public at large do not implicate fundamental privacy interests, even when engaged in within the home. Instead, because the radio is undeniably a public medium, these actions are more properly viewed as a decision to take part, if only as a listener, in an ongoing public discourse. See Note, Filthy Words, the FCC, and the First Amendment: Regulating Broadcast Obscenity, 61 Va.L.Rev. 579, 618 (1975). Although an individual's decision to allow public radio communications into his home undoubtedly does not abrogate all of his privacy interests, the residual privacy interests he retains vis-a-vis the communication he voluntarily admits into his home are surely no greater than those of the people present in the corridor of the Los Angeles courthouse in Cohen who bore witness to the words "Fuck the Draft" emblazoned across Cohen's jacket. Their privacy interests were held insufficient to justify punishing Cohen for his offensive communication.

Even if an individual who voluntarily opens his home to radio communications retains privacy interests of sufficient moment to justify a ban on protected speech if those interests are "invaded in an essentially intolerable manner," Cohen v. California, supra at 21, the very fact that those interests are threatened only by a radio broadcast precludes any intolerable invasion of privacy; for unlike other intrusive modes of communication, such as sound trucks, "[t]he radio can be turned off," Lehman v. Shaker Heights, 418 U.S. 298, 302 (1974)—and with a minimum of effort. As Chief Judge Bazelon aptly observed below,

"having elected to receive public air waves, the scanner who stumbles onto an offensive program is in the same position as the unsuspecting passers-by in Cohen and Erznoznik [v. Jacksonville, 422 U.S. 205 (1975)]; he can avert his attention by changing channels or turning off the set." 181 U.S.App.D.C. 132, 149, 556 F.2d 9, 26 (1977).

Whatever the minimal discomfort suffered by a listener who inadvertently tunes into a program he finds offensive during the brief interval before he can simply extend his arm and switch stations or flick the "off" button, it is surely worth the candle to preserve the broadcaster's right to send, and the right of those interested to receive, a message entitled to full First Amendment protection. To reach a contrary balance, as does the Court, is clearly to follow MR. JUSTICE STEVENS' reliance on animal metaphors, ante at 750–751, "to burn the house to roast the pig." Butler v. Michigan, 352 U.S. 380, 383 (1957).

The Court's balance, of necessity, fails to accord proper weight to the interests of listeners who wish to hear broadcasts the FCC deems offensive. It permits majoritarian tastes completely to preclude a protected message from entering the homes of a receptive, unoffended minority. No decision of this Court supports such a result. Where the individuals constituting the offended majority may freely choose to reject the material being offered, we have never found their privacy interests of such moment to warrant the suppression of speech on privacy grounds. Cf. Lehman v. Shaker Heights, supra. Rowan v. Post Office Dept., 397 U.S. 728 (1970), relied on by the FCC and by the opinions of my Brothers POWELL and STEVENS, confirms, rather than belies, this conclusion. In Rowan, the Court upheld a statute, 39 U.S.C. § 4009 (1964 ed., Supp. IV), permitting householders to require that mail advertisers stop sending them lewd or offensive materials and remove their names from mailing lists. Unlike the situation here, householders who wished to receive the sender's communications were not prevented from doing so. Equally important, the determination of offensiveness vel non under the statute involved in Rowan was completely within the hands of the individual householder; no governmental evaluation of the worth of the mail's content stood between the mailer and the householder. In contrast, the visage of the censor is all too discernible here. [438 U.S. 767]

B

Most parents will undoubtedly find understandable, as well as commendable, the Court's sympathy with the FCC's desire to prevent offensive broadcasts from reaching the ears of unsupervised children. Unfortunately, the facial appeal of this justification for radio censorship masks its constitutional insufficiency. Although the government unquestionably has a special interest in the wellbeing of children, and consequently "can adopt more stringent controls on communicative materials available to youths than on those available to adults," Erznoznik v. Jacksonville, 422 U.S. 205, 212 (1975); see Paris Adult Theatre I v. Slaton, 413 U.S. 49, 106–107 (1973) (BRENNAN, J., dissenting), the Court has accounted for this societal interest by adopting a "variable obscenity" standard that permits the prurient appeal of material available to children to be assessed in terms of the sexual interests of minors. Ginsberg v. New York, 390 U.S. 629 (1968). It is true that the obscenity standard the Ginsberg Court adopted for such materials was based on the then-applicable obscenity standard of Roth v. United States, 354 U.S. 476 (1957), and Memoirs v. Massachusetts, 383 U.S. 413 (1966), and that "[w]e have not had occasion to decide what effect Miller [v. California, 413 U.S. 15 (1973)] will have on the Ginsberg formulation." Erznoznik v. Jacksonville, supra at 213 n. 10. Nevertheless, we have made it abundantly clear that, "under any test of obscenity as to minors . . . , to be obscene, 'such expression must be, in some significant way, erotic.'" 422 U.S. at 213 n. 10, quoting Cohen v. California, 403 U.S. at 20.

Because the Carlin monologue is obviously not an erotic appeal to the prurient interests of children, the Court, for the first time, allows the government to prevent minors from gaining access to materials that are not obscene, and are therefore protected, as to them.FN2 It thus ignores our recent admonition that

"[s]peech that is neither obscene as to youths nor subject to some other legitimate proscription cannot be suppressed solely to protect the young from ideas or images that a legislative body thinks unsuitable for them." 422 U.S. at 213–214.FN3

The Court's refusal to follow its own pronouncements is especially lamentable, since it has the anomalous subsidiary effect, at least in the radio context at issue here, of making completely unavailable to adults material which may not constitutionally be kept even from children. This result violates in spades the principle of Butler v. Michigan, supra. Butler involved a challenge to a Michigan statute that forbade the publication, sale, or distribution of printed material "tending to incite minors to violent or depraved or immoral acts, manifestly tending to the corruption of the morals of youth." 352 U.S. at 381. Although Roth v. United States, supra, had not yet been decided, it is at least arguable that the material the statute in Butler was designed to suppress could have been constitutionally denied to children. Nevertheless, this Court found the statute unconstitutional. Speaking for the Court, Mr. Justice Frankfurter reasoned:

"The incidence of this enactment is to reduce the adult population of Michigan to reading only what is fit for children. It thereby arbitrarily curtails one of those liberties of the individual, now enshrined in the Due Process Clause of the Fourteenth Amendment, that history has attested as the indispensable conditions for the maintenance and progress of a free society." 352 U.S. at 383–384.

Where, as here, the government may not prevent the exposure of minors to the suppressed material, the principle of Butler applies a fortiori. The opinion of my Brother POWELL acknowledges that there lurks in today's decision a potential for "reduc[ing] the adult population . . . to [hearing] only what is fit for children," ante at 760, but expresses faith that the FCC will vigilantly prevent this potential from ever becoming a reality. I am far less certain than my Brother POWELL that such faith in the Commission is warranted, see Illinois Citizens Committee for Broadcasting v. FCC, 169 U.S.App.D.C. 166, 187–190, 515 F.2d 397, 418–421 (1975) (statement of Bazelon, C.J., as to why he voted to grant rehearing en banc); and even if I shared it, I could not so easily shirk the responsibility assumed by each Member of this Court jealously to guard against encroachments on First Amendment freedoms.

In concluding that the presence of children in the listening audience provides an adequate basis for the FCC to impose sanctions for Pacifica's broadcast of the Carlin monologue, the opinions of my Brother POWELL, ante at 757–758, and my Brother STEVENS, ante at 749–750, both stress the time-honored right of a parent to raise his child as he sees fit—a right this Court has consistently been vigilant to protect. See Wisconsin v. Yoder, 406 U.S. 205 (1972); Pierce v. Society of Sisters, 268 U.S. 510 (1925). Yet this principle supports a result directly contrary to that reached by the Court. Yoder and Pierce hold that parents, not the government, have the right to make certain decisions regarding the upbringing of their children. As surprising as it may be to individual Members of this Court, some parents may actually find Mr. Carlin's unabashed attitude towards the seven "dirty words" healthy, and deem it desirable to expose their children to the manner in which Mr. Carlin defuses the taboo surrounding the words. Such parents may constitute a minority of the American public, but the absence of great numbers willing to exercise the right to raise their children in this fashion does not alter the right's nature or its existence. Only the Court's regrettable decision does that.FN4

C

As demonstrated above, neither of the factors relied on by both the opinion of my Brother POWELL and the opinion of my Brother STEVENS—the intrusive nature of radio and the presence of children in the listening audience—can, when taken on its own terms, support the FCC's disapproval of the Carlin monologue. These two asserted justifications are further plagued by a common failing: the lack of principled limits on their use as a basis for FCC censorship. No such limits come readily to mind, and neither of the opinions constituting the Court serves to clarify the extent to which the FCC may assert the privacy and "children in the audience" rationales as justification for expunging from the airways protected communications the Commission finds offensive. Taken to their logical extreme, these rationales would support the cleansing of public radio of any "four-letter words" whatsoever, regardless of their context. The rationales could justify the banning from radio of a myriad of literary works, novels, poems, and plays by the likes of Shakespeare, Joyce, Hemingway, Ben Jonson, Henry Fielding, Robert Burns, and Chaucer; they could support the suppression of a good deal of political speech, such as the Nixon tapes; and they could even provide the basis for imposing sanctions for the broadcast of certain portions of the Bible.FN5

In order to dispel the specter of the possibility of so unpalatable a degree of censorship, and to defuse Pacifica's overbreadth challenge, the FCC insists that it desires only the authority to reprimand a broadcaster on facts analogous to those present in this case, which it describes as involving

"broadcasting for nearly twelve minutes a record which repeated over and over words which depict sexual or excretory activities and organs in a manner patently offensive by its community's contemporary standards in the early afternoon when children were in the audience." Brief for Petitioner 45.

The opinions of both my Brother POWELL and my Brother STEVENS take the FCC at its word, and consequently do no more than permit the Commission to censor the afternoon broadcast of the "sort of verbal shock treatment," opinion of MR. JUSTICE POWELL, ante at 757, involved here. To insure that the FCC's regulation of protected speech does not exceed these bounds, my Brother POWELL is content to rely upon the judgment of the Commission while my Brother STEVENS deems it prudent to rely on this Court's ability accurately to assess the worth of various kinds of speech.FN6 For my own part, even accepting that this case is limited to its facts,FN7 I would place the responsibility and the right to weed worthless and offensive communications from the public airways where it belongs and where, until today, it resided: in a public free to choose those communications worthy of its attention from a marketplace unsullied by the censor's hand.

II

The absence of any hesitancy in the opinions of my Brothers POWELL and STEVENS to approve the FCC's censorship of the Carlin monologue on the basis of two demonstrably inadequate grounds is a function of their perception that the decision will result in little, if any, curtailment of communicative exchanges protected by the First Amendment. Although the extent to which the Court stands ready to countenance FCC censorship of protected speech is unclear from today's decision, I find the reasoning by which my Brethren conclude that the FCC censorship they approve will not significantly infringe on First Amendment values both disingenuous as to reality and wrong as a matter of law.

My Brother STEVENS, in reaching a result apologetically described as narrow, ante at 750, takes comfort in his observation that "[a] requirement that indecent language be avoided will have its primary effect on the form, rather than the content, of serious communication," ante at 743 n. 18, and finds solace in his conviction that "[t]here are few, if any, thoughts that cannot be expressed by the use of less offensive language." Ibid. The idea that the content of a message and its potential impact on any who might receive it can be divorced from the words that are the vehicle for its expression is transparently fallacious. A given word may have a unique capacity to capsule an idea, evoke an emotion, or conjure up an image. Indeed, for those of us who place an appropriately high value on our cherished First Amendment rights, the word "censor" is such a word. Mr. Justice Harlan, speaking for the Court, recognized the truism that a speaker's choice of words cannot surgically be separated from the ideas he desires to express when he warned that

"we cannot indulge the facile assumption that one can forbid particular words without also running a substantial risk of suppressing ideas in the process." Cohen v. California, 403 U.S. at 26.

Moreover, even if an alternative phrasing may communicate a speaker's abstract ideas as effectively as those words he is forbidden to use, it is doubtful that the sterilized message will convey the emotion that is an essential part of so many communications. This, too, was apparent to Mr. Justice Harlan and the Court in Cohen.

"[W]e cannot overlook the fact, because it is well illustrated by the episode involved here, that much linguistic expression serves a dual communicative function: it conveys not only ideas capable of relatively precise, detached explication, but otherwise inexpressible emotions as well. In fact, words are often chosen as much for their emotive as their cognitive force. We cannot sanction the view that the Constitution, while solicitous of the cognitive content of individual speech, has little or no regard for that emotive function which, practically speaking, may often be the more important element of the overall message sought to be communicated." Id. at 25–26.

My Brother STEVENS also finds relevant to his First Amendment analysis the fact that "[a]dults who feel the need may purchase tapes and records or go to theaters and nightclubs to hear [the tabooed] words." Ante at 750 n. 28. My Brother POWELL agrees:

"The Commission's holding does not prevent willing adults from purchasing Carlin's record, from attending his performances, or, indeed, from reading the transcript reprinted as an appendix to the Court's opinion." Ante at 760.

The opinions of my Brethren display both a sad insensitivity to the fact that these alternatives involve the expenditure of money, time, and effort that many of those wishing to hear Mr. Carlin's message may not be able to afford, and a naive innocence of the reality that, in many cases, the medium may well be the message.

The Court apparently believes that the FCC's actions here can be analogized to the zoning ordinances upheld in Young v. American Mini Theatres, Inc., 427 U.S. 50 (1976). For two reasons, it is wrong. First, the zoning ordinances found to pass constitutional muster in Young had valid goals other than the channeling of protected speech. Id. at 71 n. 34 (opinion of STEVENS, J.); id. at 80 (POWELL, J., concurring).

No such goals are present here. Second, and crucial to the opinions of my Brothers POWELL and STEVENS in Young—opinions, which, as they do in this case, supply the bare five-person majority of the Court—the ordinances did not restrict the access of distributors or exhibitors to the market or impair [438 U.S. 775] the viewing public's access to the regulated material. Id. at 62, 71 n. 35 (opinion of STEVENS, J.); id. at 77 (POWELL, J., concurring). Again, this is not the situation here. Both those desiring to receive Carlin's message over the radio and those wishing to send it to them are prevented from doing so by the Commission's actions. Although, as my Brethren point out, Carlin's message may be disseminated or received by other means, this is of little consolation to those broadcasters and listeners who, for a host of reasons, not least among them financial, do not have access to, or cannot take advantage of, these other means.

Moreover, it is doubtful that even those frustrated listeners in a position to follow my Brother POWELL's gratuitous advice and attend one of Carlin's performances or purchase one of his records would receive precisely the same message Pacifica's radio station sent its audience. The airways are capable not only of carrying a message, but also of transforming it. A satirist's monologue may be most potent when delivered to a live audience; yet the choice whether this will in fact be the manner in which the message is delivered and received is one the First Amendment prohibits the government from making.

III

It is quite evident that I find the Court's attempt to unstitch the warp and woof of First Amendment law in an effort to reshape its fabric to cover the patently wrong result the Court reaches in this case dangerous, as well as lamentable. Yet there runs throughout the opinions of my Brothers POWELL and STEVENS another vein I find equally disturbing: a depressing inability to appreciate that, in our land of cultural pluralism, there are many who think, act, and talk differently from the Members of this Court, and who do not share their fragile sensibilities. It is only an acute ethnocentric myopia that enables the Court to approve the censorship of communications solely because of the words they contain. [438 U.S. 776]

"A word is not a crystal, transparent and unchanged, it is the skin of a living thought, and may vary greatly in color and content according to the circumstances and the time in which it is used." Towne v. Eisner, 245 U.S. 418, 425 (1918) (Holmes, J.).

The words that the Court and the Commission find so unpalatable may be the stuff of everyday conversations in some, if not many, of the innumerable subcultures that compose this Nation. Academic research indicates that this is indeed the case. See B. Jackson, "Get Your Ass in the Water and Swim Like Me" (1974); J. Dillard, Black English (1972); W. Labov, Language in the Inner City: Studies in the Black English Vernacular (1972). As one researcher concluded,

"[w]ords generally considered obscene, like "bullshit" and "fuck" are considered neither obscene nor derogatory in the [black] vernacular except in particular contextual situations and when used with certain intonations." C. Bins, "Toward an

Ethnography of Contemporary African American Oral Poetry," Language and Linguistics Working Papers No. 5, p. 82 (Georgetown Univ. Press 1972). Cf. Keefe v. Geanakos, 418 F.2d 359, 361 (CA1 1969) (finding the use of the word "motherfucker" commonplace among young radicals and protesters).

Today's decision will thus have its greatest impact on broadcasters desiring to reach, and listening audiences composed of, persons who do not share the Court's view as to which words or expressions are acceptable and who, for a variety of reasons, including a conscious desire to flout majoritarian conventions, express themselves using words that may be regarded as offensive by those from different socio-economic backgrounds.FN8 In this context, the Court's decision may be seen for what, in the broader perspective, it really is: another of the dominant culture's inevitable efforts to force those groups who do not share its mores to conform to its way of thinking, acting, and speaking. See Moore v. East Cleveland, 431 U.S. 494, 506–511 (1977) (BRENNAN, J., concurring).

Pacifica, in response to an FCC inquiry about its broadcast of Carlin's satire on "the words you couldn't say on the public . . . airways," explained that "Carlin is not mouthing obscenities, he is merely using words to satirize as harmless and essentially silly our attitudes towards those words." 56 F.C.C.2d at 95, 96. In confirming Carlin's prescience as a social commentator by the result it reaches today, the Court evinces an attitude toward the "seven dirty words" that many others besides Mr. Carlin and Pacifica might describe as "silly." Whether today's decision will similarly prove "harmless" remains to be seen. One can only hope that it will.

MR. JUSTICE STEWART, with whom MR. JUSTICE BRENNAN, MR. JUSTICE WHITE, and MR. JUSTICE MARSHALL join, dissenting.

The Court today recognizes the wise admonition that we should "avoid the unnecessary decision of [constitutional] issues." Ante at 734. But it disregards one important application of this salutary principle—the need to construe an Act of Congress so as to avoid, if possible, passing upon its constitutionality.FN1 It is apparent that the constitutional questions raised by the order of the Commission in this case are substantial.FN2 Before deciding them, we should be certain that it is necessary to do so. [438 U.S. 778]

The statute pursuant to which the Commission acted, 18 U.S.C. § 1464 (1976 ed.),FN3 makes it a federal offense to utter "any obscene, indecent, or profane language by means of radio communication." The Commission held, and the Court today agrees, that "indecent" is a broader concept than "obscene" as the latter term was defined in Miller v. California, 413 U.S. 15, because language can be "indecent" although it has social, political, or artistic value and lacks prurient appeal. 56 F.C.C.2d 94, 97–98.FN4 But this construction of § 1464, while perhaps plausible, is by no means compelled. To the contrary, I think that "indecent" should properly be read as meaning no more than "obscene." Since the Carlin monologue concededly was not "obscene," I believe that the Commission lacked statutory authority to ban it. Under this construction of the statute, it is unnecessary to address the difficult and important issue of the Commission's constitutional power to prohibit speech that would be constitutionally protected outside the context of electronic broadcasting.

This Court has recently decided the meaning of the term "indecent" in a closely related statutory context. In Hamling v. United States, 418 U.S. 87, the petitioner was convicted of violating 18 U.S.C. § 1461, which prohibits the mailing of "[e]very obscene, lewd, lascivious, indecent, filthy or vile article." The Court "construe[d] the generic terms in [§ 1461] to be limited to the sort of "patently offensive representations or descriptions of that specific 'hard core' sexual conduct given as examples in Miller v. California." 418 U.S. at 114, quoting United States v. 12 200-ft. Reels of Film, 413 U.S. 123, 130 n. 7. Thus, the clear holding of Hamling is that "indecent," as used in § 1461, has the same meaning as "obscene" as that term was defined in the Miller case. See also Marks v. United States, 430 U.S. 188, 190 (18 U.S.C. § 1465).

Nothing requires the conclusion that the word "indecent" has any meaning in § 1464 other than that ascribed to the same word in § 1461.FN5 Indeed, although the legislative history is largely silent,FN6 such indications as there are support the view that § 1461 and 1464 should be construed similarly. The view that "indecent" means no more than "obscene" in § 1461 and similar statutes long antedated Hamling. See United States v. Bennett, 24 F.Cas. 1093 (No. 14,571) (CC SDNY 1879); Dunlop v. United States, 165 U.S. 486, 500–501; Manual Enterprises v. Day, 370 U.S. 478, 482–484, 487 (opinion of Harlan, J.).FN7 And although §§ 1461 and 1464 were originally enacted separately, they were codified together in the Criminal Code of 1848 as part of a chapter entitled "Obscenity." There is nothing in the legislative history to suggest that Congress intended that the same word in two closely related sections should have different meanings. See H.R.Rep. No. 304, 80th Cong., 1st Sess., A104–A106 (1947).

I would hold, therefore, that Congress intended, by using the word "indecent" in § 1464, to prohibit nothing more than obscene speech.FN8 Under that reading of the statute, the Commission's order in this case was not authorized, and on that basis, I would affirm the judgment of the Court of Appeals.

FOOTNOTES

STEVENS, J., LEAD OPINION (FOOTNOTES)

1. 56 F.C.C.2d at 99. The Commission noted:
   "Congress has specifically empowered the FCC to (1) revoke a station's license (2) issue a cease and desist order, or (3) impose a monetary forfeiture for a violation of Section 1464, 47 U.S.C. [§§] 312(a), 312(b), 503(b)(1) (E). The FCC can also (4) deny license renewal or (5) grant a short term renewal, 47 U.S.C. [§§] 307, 308." Id. at 96 n. 3.
2. "Broadcasting requires special treatment because of four important considerations: (1) children have access to radios and in many cases are unsupervised by

parents; (2) radio receivers are in the home, a place where people's privacy interest is entitled to extra deference, see Rowan v. Post Office Dept., 397 U.S. 728 (1970); (3) unconsenting adults may tune in a station without any warning that offensive language is being or will be broadcast; and (4) there is a scarcity of spectrum space, the use of which the government must therefore license in the public interest. Of special concern to the Commission, as well as parents, is the first point regarding the use of radio by children." Id. at 97.

3. Title 18 U.S.C. § 1464 (1976 ed.) provides:

"Whoever utters any obscene, indecent, or profane language by means of radio communication shall be fined not more than $10,000 or imprisoned not more than two years, or both."

4. Section 303(g) of the Communications Act of 1934, 48 Stat. 1082, as amended, as set forth in 47 U.S.C. § 303(g), in relevant part, provides:

"Except as otherwise provided in this chapter, the Commission from time to time, as public convenience, interest, or necessity requires, shall—

★ ★ ★ ★

"(g) . . . generally encourage the larger and more effective use of radio in the public interest."

5. Thus, the Commission suggested, if an offensive broadcast had literary, artistic, political, or scientific value, and were preceded by warnings, it might not be indecent in the late evening, but would be so during the day, when children are in the audience. 56 F.C.C.2d at 98.

6. Chairman Wiley concurred in the result without joining the opinion. Commissioners Reid and Quello filed separate statements expressing the opinion that the language was inappropriate for broadcast at any time. Id. at 102–103. Commissioner Robinson, joined by Commissioner Hooks, filed a concurring statement expressing the opinion:

"[W]e can regulate offensive speech to the extent it constitutes a public nuisance. . . . The governing idea is that "indecency" is not an inherent attribute of words themselves; it is, rather, a matter of context and conduct. . . . If I were called on to do so, I would find that Carlin's monologue, if it were broadcast at an appropriate hour and accompanied by suitable warning, was distinguished by sufficient literary value to avoid being "indecent" within the meaning of the statute." Id. at 107–108, and n. 9.

7. The Commission did, however, comment:

" '[I]n some cases, public events likely to produce offensive speech are covered live, and there is no opportunity for journalistic editing.' Under these circumstances, we believe that it would be inequitable for us to hold a licensee responsible for indecent language. . . . We trust that, under such circumstances, a licensee will exercise judgment, responsibility, and sensitivity to the community's needs, interests and tastes." 59 F.C.C.2d at 893 n. 1.

8. "Nothing in this Act shall be understood or construed to give the Commission the power of censorship over the radio communications or signals transmitted by any radio station, and no regulation or condition shall be promulgated or fixed by the Commission which shall interfere with the right of free speech by means of radio communication." 48 Stat. 1091, 47 U.S.C. § 326.

9. Zechariah Chafee, defending the Commission's authority to take into account program service in granting licenses, interpreted the restriction on "censorship" narrowly:

"This means, I feel sure, the sort of censorship which went on in the seventeenth century in England—the deletion of specific items and dictation as to what should go into particular programs." 2 Z. Chafee, Government and Mass Communications 641 (1947).

10. In KFKB Broadcasting Assn. v. Federal Radio Comm'n, 60 App.D.C. 79, 47 F.2d 670 (1931), a doctor who controlled a radio station as well as a pharmaceutical association made frequent broadcasts in which he answered the medical questions of listeners. He often prescribed mixtures prepared by his pharmaceutical association. The Commission determined that renewal of the station's license would not be in the public interest, convenience, or necessity because many of the broadcasts served the doctor's private interests. In response to the claim that this was censorship in violation of § 29 of the 1927 Act, the Court held:

"This contention is without merit. There has been no attempt on the part of the commission to subject any part of appellant's broadcasting matter to scrutiny prior to its release. In considering the question whether the public interest, convenience, or necessity will be served by a renewal of appellant's license, the commission has merely exercised its undoubted right to take note of appellant's past conduct, which is not censorship." 60 App.D.C. at 81, 47 F.2d at 672. In Trinity Methodist Church, South v. Federal Radio Comm'n, 61 App.D.C. 311, 62 F.2d 850 (1932), cert. denied, 288 U.S. 599, the station was controlled by a minister whose broadcasts contained frequent references to "pimps" and "prostitutes" as well as bitter attacks on the Roman Catholic Church. The Commission refused to renew the license, citing the nature of the broadcasts. The Court of Appeals affirmed, concluding that First Amendment concerns did not prevent the Commission from regulating broadcasts that

"offend the religious susceptibilities of thousands . . . or offend youth and innocence by the free use of words suggestive of sexual immorality." 61 App.D.C. at 314, 62 F.2d at 853. The court recognized that the licensee had a right to broadcast this material free of prior restraint, but "this does not mean that the government, through agencies established by Congress, may not refuse a renewal of license to one who has abused it." Id. at 312, 62 F.2d at 851.

11. See, e.g., Bay State Beacon, Inc. v. FCC, 84 U.S.App.D.C. 216, 171 F.2d 826 (1948); Idaho Microwave, Inc. v. FCC, 122 U.S.App.D.C. 253, 352 F.2d 729 (1965); National Assn. of Theatre Owners v. FCC, 136 U.S.App.D.C. 352, 420 F.2d 194 (1969), cert. denied, 397 U.S. 922.

12. See, e.g., 67 Cong.Rec. 12615 (1926) (remarks of Sen. Dill); id. at 5480 (remarks of Rep. White); 68 Cong.Rec. 2567 (1927) (remarks of Rep. Scott); Hearings on S. 1 and S. 1754 before the Senate Committee on Interstate Commerce, 69th Cong., 1st Sess., 121 (1926); Hearings on H.R. 5589 before the House Committee on the Merchant Marine and Fisheries, 69th Cong., 1st Sess., 26 and 40 (1926). See also Hearings on H.R. 8825 before the House Committee on the Merchant Marine and Fisheries, 70th Cong., 1st Sess., passim (1928).

13. In addition to § 1464, the Commission also relied on its power to regulate in the public interest under 47 U.S.C. § 303(g). We do not need to consider whether § 303 may have independent significance in a case such as this. The statutes authorizing civil penalties incorporate § 1464, a criminal statute. See 47 U.S.C. §§ 312(a)(6), 312(b)(2), and 503(b)(1)(E) (1970 ed. and Supp. V). But the validity of the civil sanctions is not linked to the validity of the criminal penalty. The legislative history of the provisions establishes their independence. As enacted in 1927 and 1934, the prohibition on indecent speech was separate from the provisions imposing civil and criminal penalties for violating the prohibition. Radio Act of 1927, §§ 14, 29, and 33, 44 Stat. 1168 and 1173; Communications Act of 1934, §§ 312, 326, and 501, 48 Stat. 1086, 1091, and 1100, 47 U.S.C. §§ 312, 326, and 501 (1970 ed. and Supp. V). The 1927 and 1934 Acts indicated in the strongest possible language that any invalid provision was separable from the rest of the Act. Radio Act of 1927, § 38, 44 Stat. 1174; Communications Act of 1934, § 608, 48 Stat. 1105, 47 U.S.C. § 608. Although the 1948 codification of the criminal laws and the addition of new civil penalties changes the statutory structure, no substantive change was apparently intended. Cf. Tidewater Oil Co. v. United States, 409 U.S. 151, 162. Accordingly, we need not consider any question relating to the possible application of § 1464 as a criminal statute.

14. Webster defines the term as
"a: altogether unbecoming: contrary to what the nature of things or what circumstances would dictate as right or expected or appropriate: hardly suitable: UNSEEMLY . . . b: not conforming to generally accepted standards of morality: . . . ." Webster's Third New International Dictionary (1966).

15. Indeed, at one point, he used "indecency" as a shorthand term for "patent offensiveness," 370 U.S. at 482, a usage strikingly similar to the Commission's definition in this case. 56 F.C.C.2d at 98.

16. "[W]hile a nudist magazine may be within the protection of the First Amendment . . . , the televising of nudes might well raise a serious question of programming contrary to 18 U.S.C. § 1464. . . . Similarly, regardless of whether the "4-letter words" and sexual description, set forth in "Lady Chatterly's Lover," (when considered in the context of the whole book) make the book obscene for mailability purposes, the utterance of such words or the depiction of such sexual activity on radio or TV would raise similar public interest and section 1464 questions." Enbanc Programming Inquiry, 44 F.C.C. 2303, 2307 (1960). See also In re WUHY-FM, 24 F.C.C.2d 408, 412 (1970); In re Sonderlin Broadcasting Corp., 27 R.R.2d 285, on reconsideration, 41 F.C.C.2d 777 (1973), aff'd on other grounds sub nom. Illinois Citizens Committee for Broadcasting v. FCC, 169 U.S.App.D.C. 166, 515 F.2d 397 (1974); In re Mile High Stations, Inc., 28 F.C.C. 795 (1960); In re Palmetto Broadcasting Co., 33 F.C.C. 250 (1962), reconsideration denied, 34 F.C.C. 101 (1963), aff'd on other grounds sub nom. Robinson v. FCC, 118 U.S.App.D.C. 144, 334 F.2d 534 (1964), cert. denied, 379 U.S. 843.

17. This conclusion is reinforced by noting the different constitutional limits on Congress' power to regulate the two different subjects. Use of the postal power to regulate material that is not fraudulent or obscene raises "grave constitu-

tional questions." Hannegan v. Esquire, Inc., 327 U.S. 146, 156. But it is well settled that the First Amendment has a special meaning in the broadcasting context. See, e.g., FCC v. National Citizens Committee for Broadcasting, 436 U.S. 775; Red Lion Broadcasting Co. v. FCC, 395 U.S. 367; Columbia Broadcasting System, Inc. v. Democratic National Committee, 412 U.S. 94. For this reason, the presumption that Congress never intends to exceed constitutional limits, which supported Hamling's narrow reading of § 1461, does not support a comparable reading of § 1464.

18. A requirement that indecent language be avoided will have its primary effect on the form, rather than the content, of serious communication. There are few, if any, thoughts that cannot be expressed by the use of less offensive language.

19. Pacifica's position would, of course, deprive the Commission of any power to regulate erotic telecasts unless they were obscene under Miller v. California, 413 U.S. 15. Anything that could be sold at a newsstand for private examination could be publicly displayed on television.

   We are assured by Pacifica that the free play of market forces will discourage indecent programming. "Smut may," as Judge Leventhal put it, "drive itself from the market and confound Gresham," 181 U.S.App.D.C. at 158, 556 F.2d at 35; the prosperity of those who traffic in pornographic literature and films would appear to justify skepticism.

20. Although neither MR. JUSTICE POWELL nor MR. JUSTICE BRENNAN directly confronts this question, both have answered it affirmatively, the latter explicitly, post at 768 n. 3, and the former implicitly by concurring in a judgment that could not otherwise stand.

21. See, e.g., Madison School District v. Wisconsin Employment Relations Comm'n, 429 U.S. 167, 175–176; First National Bank of Boston v. Bellotti, 435 U.S. 765.

22. The monologue does present a point of view; it attempts to show that the words it uses are "harmless," and that our attitudes toward them are "essentially silly." See supra at 730. The Commission objects not to this point of view, but to the way in which it is expressed. The belief that these words are harmless does not necessarily confer a First Amendment privilege to use them while proselytizing, just as the conviction that obscenity is harmless does not license one to communicate that conviction by the indiscriminate distribution of an obscene leaflet.

23. The Commission stated:

   "Obnoxious, gutter language describing these matters has the effect of debasing and brutalizing human beings by reducing them to their mere bodily functions. . . . " 56 F.C.C.2d at 98. Our society has a tradition of performing certain bodily functions in private, and of severely limiting the public exposure or discussion of such matters. Verbal or physical acts exposing those intimacies are offensive irrespective of any message that may accompany the exposure.

24. With respect to other types of speech, the Court has tailored its protection to both the abuses and the uses to which it might be put. See, e.g., New York Times Co. v. Sullivan, 376 U.S. 254 (special scienter rules in libel suits brought by public

officials); Bates v. State Bar of Arizona, 433 U.S. 350 (government may strictly regulate truthfulness in commercial speech). See also Young v. American Mini Theatres, Inc., 427 U.S. 50, 82 n. 6 (POWELL, J., concurring).

25. The importance of context is illustrated by the Cohen case. That case arose when Paul Cohen entered a Los Angeles courthouse wearing a jacket emblazoned with the words "Fuck the Draft." After entering the courtroom, he took the jacket off and folded it. 403 U.S. at 19 n. 3. So far as the evidence showed, no one in the courthouse was offended by his jacket. Nonetheless, when he left the courtroom, Cohen was arrested, convicted of disturbing the peace, and sentenced to 30 days in prison.

In holding that criminal sanctions could not be imposed on Cohen for his political statement in a public place, the Court rejected the argument that his speech would offend unwilling viewers; it noted that "there was no evidence that persons powerless to avoid [his] conduct did in fact object to it." Id. at 22. In contrast, in this case, the Commission was responding to a listener's strenuous complaint, and Pacifica does not question its determination that this afternoon broadcast was likely to offend listeners. It should be noted that the Commission imposed a far more moderate penalty on Pacifica than the state court imposed on Cohen. Even the strongest civil penalty at the Commission's command does not include criminal prosecution. See n. 1, supra.

26. 47 U.S.C. §§ 309(a), 312(a)(2); FCC v. WOKO, Inc., 329 U.S. 223, 229. Cf. Shuttlesworth v. Birmingham, 394 U.S. 147; Staub v. Baxley, 355 U.S. 313.

27. Outside the home, the balance between the offensive speaker and the unwilling audience may sometimes tip in favor of the speaker, requiring the offended listener to turn away. See Erznoznik v. Jacksonville, 422 U.S. 205. As we noted in Cohen v. California:

"While this Court has recognized that government may properly act in many situations to prohibit intrusion into the privacy of the home of unwelcome views and ideas which cannot be totally banned from the public dialogue . . . , we have at the same time consistently stressed that "we are often 'captives' outside the sanctuary of the home, and subject to objectionable speech." 403 U.S. at 21.

The problem of harassing phone calls is hardly hypothetical. Congress has recently found it necessary to prohibit debt collectors from "plac[ing] telephone calls without meaningful disclosure of the caller's identity"; from "engaging any person in telephone conversation repeatedly or continuously with intent to annoy, abuse, or harass any person at the called number"; and from "us[ing] obscene or profane language or language the natural consequence of which is to abuse the hearer or reader." Consumer Credit Protection Act Amendments, 91 Stat. 877, 15 U.S.C. § 1692d (1976 ed., Supp. II).

28. The Commission's action does not by any means reduce adults to hearing only what is fit for children. Cf. Butler v. Michigan, 352 U.S. 380, 383. Adults who feel the need may purchase tapes and records or go to theaters and nightclubs to hear these words. In fact, the Commission has not unequivocally closed even broadcasting to speech of this sort; whether broadcast audiences in the late

evening contain so few children that playing this monologue would be permissible is an issue neither the Commission nor this Court has decided.

29. Even a prime time recitation of Geoffrey Chaucer's Miller's Tale would not be likely to command the attention of many children who are both old enough to understand and young enough to be adversely affected by passages such as: "And prively he caughte hire by the queynte." The Canterbury Tales, Chaucer's Complete Works (Cambridge ed.1933), p. 58, l. 3276.

POWELL, J., CONCURRING (FOOTNOTES)

1. See generally Judge Leventhal's thoughtful opinion in the Court of Appeals. 181 U.S.App.D.C. 132, 155–158, 556 F.2d 9, 32–35 (1977) (dissenting opinion).

2. It is true that the radio listener quickly may tune out speech that is offensive to him. In addition, broadcasters may preface potentially offensive programs with warnings. But such warnings do not help the unsuspecting listener who tunes in at the middle of a program. In this respect, too, broadcasting appears to differ from books and records, which may carry warnings on their face, and from motion pictures and live performances, which may carry warnings on their marquees.

3. The Court has, however, created a limited exception to this rule in order to bring commercial speech within the protection of the First Amendment. See Ohralik v. Ohio State Bar Assn., 436 U.S. 447, 455–456 (1978).

4. For much the same reason, I also do not join Part IV-A. I had not thought that the application vel non of overbreadth analysis should depend on the Court's judgment as to the value of the protected speech that might be deterred. Cf. ante at 743. Except in the context of commercial speech, see Bates v. State Bar of Arizona, 433 U.S. 350, 380–381 (1977), it has not in the past. See, e.g., Lewis v. New Orleans, 415 U.S. 130 (1974); Gooding v. Wilson, 405 U.S. 518 (1972).

   As MR. JUSTICE STEVENS points out, however, ante at 734, the Commission's order was limited to the facts of this case; "it did not purport to engage in formal rulemaking or in the promulgation of any regulations." In addition, since the Commission may be expected to proceed cautiously, as it has in the past, cf. Brief for Petitioner 42–43, and n. 31, I do not foresee an undue "chilling" effect on broadcasters' exercise of their rights. I agree, therefore, that respondent's overbreadth challenge is meritless.

BRENNAN, J., DISSENTING (FOOTNOTES)

1. Where I refer without differentiation to the actions of "the Court," my reference is to this majority, which consists of my Brothers POWELL and STEVENS and those Members of the Court joining their separate opinions.

2. Even if the monologue appealed to the prurient interest of minors, it would not be obscene as to them unless, as to them, "the work, taken as a whole, lacks

serious literary, artistic, political, or scientific value." Miller v. California, 413 U.S. 15, 24 (1973).

3. It may be that a narrowly drawn regulation prohibiting the use of offensive language on broadcasts directed specifically at younger children constitutes one of the "other legitimate proscription[s]" alluded to in Erznoznik. This is so both because of the difficulties inherent in adapting the Miller formulation to communications received by young children, and because such children are "not possessed of that full capacity for individual choice which is the presupposition of the First Amendment guarantees." Ginsberg v. New York, 390 U.S. 629, 649–650 (1968) (STEWART, J., concurring). I doubt, as my Brother STEVENS suggests, ante at 745 n. 20, that such a limited regulation amounts to a regulation of speech based on its content, since, by hypothesis, the only persons at whom the regulated communication is directed are incapable of evaluating its content. To the extent that such a regulation is viewed as a regulation based on content, it marks the outermost limits to which content regulation is permissible.

4. The opinions of my Brothers POWELL and STEVENS rightly refrain from relying on the notion of "spectrum scarcity" to support their result. As Chief Judge Bazelon noted below, "although scarcity has justified increasing the diversity of speakers and speech, it has never been held to justify censorship." 181 U.S.App.D.C. at 152, 556 F.2d at 29 (emphasis in original). See Red Lion Broadcasting Co. v. FCC, 395 U.S. 367, 396 (1969).

5. See, e.g., I Samuel 25:22: "So and more also do God unto the enemies of David, if I leave of all that pertain to him by the morning light any that pisseth against the wall"; II Kings 18:27 and Isaiah 36:12: "[H]ath he not sent me to the men which sit on the wall, that they may eat their own dung, and drink their own piss with you?"; Ezekiel 23:3: "And they committed whoredoms in Egypt; they committed whoredoms in their youth; there were virginity."; Ezekiel 23:21: "Thus thou calledst to remembrance the lewdness of thy youth, in bruising thy teats by the Egyptians for the paps of thy youth." The Holy Bible (King James Version) (Oxford 1897).

6. Although ultimately dependent upon the outcome of review in this Court, the approach taken by my Brother STEVENS would not appear to tolerate the FCC's suppression of any speech, such as political speech, falling within the core area of First Amendment concern. The same, however, cannot be said of the approach taken by my Brother POWELL, which, on its face, permits the Commission to censor even political speech if it is sufficiently offensive to community standards. A result more contrary to rudimentary First Amendment principles is difficult to imagine.

7. Having insisted that it seeks to impose sanctions on radio communications only in the limited circumstances present here, I believe that the FCC is estopped from using either this decision or its own orders in this case, 56 F.C.C.2d 94 (1975) and 59 F.C.C.2d 892 (1976), as a basis for imposing sanctions on any public radio broadcast other than one aired during the daytime or early evening and containing the relentless repetition, for longer than a brief interval, of "language that describes, in term patently offensive as measured by contemporary com-

munity standards for the broadcast medium, sexual or excretory activities and organs." 56 F.C.C.2d at 98. For surely broadcasters are not now on notice that the Commission desires to regulate any offensive broadcast other than the type of "verbal shock treatment" condemned here, or even this "shock treatment" type of offensive broadcast during the late evening.

8. Under the approach taken by my Brother POWELL, the availability of broadcasts about groups whose members constitute such audiences might also be affected. Both news broadcasts about activities involving these groups and public affairs broadcasts about their concerns are apt to contain interviews, statements, or remarks by group leaders and members which may contain offensive language to an extent my Brother POWELL finds unacceptable.

STEWART, J., DISSENTING (FOOTNOTES)

1. See, e.g., Johnson v. Robison, 415 U.S. 361, 366–367; United States v. Thirty-seven Photographs, 402 U.S. 363, 369; Rescue Army v. Municipal Court, 331 U.S. 549, 569; Ashwander v. TVA, 297 U.S. 288, 348 (Brandeis, J., concurring); Crowell v. Benson, 285 U.S. 22, 62.

2. The practice of construing a statute to avoid a constitutional confrontation is followed whenever there is "a serious doubt" as to the statute's constitutionality. E.g., United States v. Rumely, 345 U.S. 41, 45; Blodgett v. Holden, 275 U.S. 142, 148 (opinion of Holmes, J.). Thus, the Court has construed a statute to avoid raising a doubt as to its constitutionality even though the Court later in effect held that the statute, otherwise construed, would have been constitutionally valid. Compare General Motors Corp. v. District of Columbia, 380 U.S. 553, with Moorman Mfg. Co. v. Bair, 437 U.S. 267.

3. The Court properly gives no weight to the Commission's passing reference in its order to 47 U.S.C. § 303(g). Ante at 739 n. 13. For one thing, the order clearly rests only upon the Commission's interpretation of the term "indecent" in § 1464; the attempt by the Commission in this Court to assert that § 303(g) was an independent basis for its action must fail. Cf. SEC v. Chenery Corp., 318 U.S. 80, 94–95; SEC v. Sloan, 436 U.S. 103, 117–118. Moreover, the general language of § 303(g) cannot be used to circumvent the terms of a specific statutory mandate such as that of § 1464.

"[T]he Commission's power in this respect is limited by the scope of the statute. Unless the [language] involved here [is] illegal under § [1464], the Commission cannot employ the statute to make [it] so by agency action." FCC v. American Broadcasting Co., 347 U.S. 284, 290.

4. The Commission did not rely on § 1464's prohibition of "profane" language, and it is thus unnecessary to consider the scope of that term.

5. The only Federal Court of Appeals (apart from this case) to consider the question has held that "obscene" and "indecent" in § 1464 are to be read as parts of a single proscription, applicable only if the challenged language appeals to the prurient interest. United States v. Simpson, 561 F.2d 53, 60 (CA7).

APPENDIX A

6. Section 1464 originated as part of § 29 of the Radio Act of 1927, 44 Stat. 1172, which was reenacted as § 326 of the Communications Act of 1934, 48 Stat. 1091. Neither the committee reports nor the floor debates contain any discussion of the meaning of "obscene, indecent or profane language."

7. When the Federal Communications Act was amended in 1968 to prohibit "obscene, lewd, lascivious, filthy, or indecent" telephone calls, 82 Stat. 112, 47 U.S.C. § 223, the FCC itself indicated that it thought this language covered only "obscene" telephone calls. See H.R.Rep. No. 1109, 90th Cong., 2d Sess., 7–8 (1968).

8. This construction is further supported by the general rule of lenity in construing criminal statutes. See Adamo Wrecking Co. v. United States, 434 U.S. 275, 285. The Court's statement that it need not consider the meaning § 1464 would have in a criminal prosecution, ante at 739 n. 13, is contrary to settled precedent: "It is true . . . that these are not criminal cases, but it is a criminal statute that we must interpret. There cannot be one construction for the Federal Communications Commission and another for the Department of Justice. If we should give § [1464] the broad construction urged by the Commission, the same construction would likewise apply in criminal cases." FCC v. American Broadcasting Co., supra at 296.

APPENDIX B

FCC TAKES STRONG STANCE ON
ENFORCEMENT OF PROHIBITION AGAINST
OBSCENE AND INDECENT BROADCASTS

The Federal Communications Commission, after a 12 year hiatus, has made clear that it intends to take enforcement actions against broadcasters who air obscene or indecent programming in violation of the law. The Commission, on November 24, 1987, reaffirmed three April rulings that enforced a stringent application of the Criminal Code's prohibition of obscene broadcasts and its limitation on indecent broadcasts against three radio stations.

Obscene Broadcasts Prohibited at all Times
The FCC, in the April and November rulings, made clear that the broadcast of obscene programming is a criminal offense and that such broadcasts are banned from the airwaves at all times of the day. The Commission noted that obscene material is defined by the Supreme Court as follows:

(1) an average person, applying contemporary community standards, must find that the material, as a whole, appeals to the prurient interest;
(2) the material must depict or describe, in a patently offensive way as measured by contemporary community standards, sexual or excretory conduct; and
(3) the material, taken as a whole, must lack serious literary, artistic, political, or scientific value. *Miller v. California*, 413 U.S. l5 (1973).

Obscene speech is not protected by the First Amendment and cannot be broadcast at any time.
    In *its* April rulings, the Commission referred a broadcast by a Los Angeles radio station to the U.S. Justice Department for a possible obscenity prosecution. In July, however, the Justice Department declined to prosecute the station for obscenity

because the earlier confusion in the law would make it difficult to establish the criminal intent necessary to prevail in court.

Tougher Enforcement Regarding Indecent Broadcasts

By its April actions, which the Commission has reaffirmed, the Commission demonstrated that it intended to enforce the limitation against indecent broadcasts. Although under current law the Commission may not prohibit indecent programming altogether, the Commission prohibits broadcasters from airing indecent material at a time of day when there is a reasonable risk that children may be in the audience. The Supreme Court, in 1978, upheld this provision of the law. *FCC v. Pacifica Foundation*, 438 U.S. 726 (1978).

Prior to the April decisions, enforcement of the limitation against indecent broadcasts had been limited to those broadcasts that repeatedly used the "seven dirty words" made famous by a George Carlin comedy monologue. As a result of these policies, after 1975, no broadcaster was found in violation of the indecency limitation, until the current Commission acted in April 1987.

In April, the Commission announced that it would strengthen the enforcement of the limitation on indecent broadcasts by interpreting the law in a more sensible manner. It therefore announced that it would return to the actual definition of the term "indecency" affirmed by the Supreme Court in 1978. That term defines "indecency" as:

> language or material that depicts or describes, in terms patently offensive as measured by contemporary community standards for the broadcast medium, sexual or excretory activities or organs.

As a result, broadcasts that fit within this definition, not just these using the "seven dirty words," are subject to the indecency enforcement standards.

As noted above, however, under existing Supreme Court precedent, non-obscene broadcasts, even though sexually explicit, may not be banned altogether, but are subject to reasonable channeling requirements in order to restrict children's ability to hear or see them. Before the April decisions, precedent had indicated that the broadcast of this type of programming would be permissible after 10:00 p.m. In its April decisions, however, the Commission announced that there was still a reasonable risk of children in the audience even at 10:00 p.m. in the markets before it.

November Decisions Reaffirm Indecency Rulings

After the release of the April decisions, a group of broadcasters asked the Commission to reconsider those rulings, claiming that the Commission had misconstrued the law and that the rulings were unconstitutional. The group made numerous requests to the Commission, including asking the Commission to adopt a policy under which a broadcaster's decision to air a program would be considered reasonable and therefore not sanctionable unless the Commission had previously found that program indecent, and to return to the old precedent that non-obscene broadcasts could be made after 10:00 p.m.

On November 24, 1987, the Commission denied the broadcasters' requests, concluding that its April rulings had been correct. It specifically denied their requests to adopt a prospective only policy and to permit the broadcast of certain adult-oriented programming after 10:00, reaffirming its conclusion that there was still a reasonable risk of children in the audience at that time. It noted that adult-oriented programming that was not obscene could not be broadcast until after midnight.

The Commission concluded that current Supreme Court precedent precluded it from banning non-obscene programming from the airwaves altogether. Therefore, in light of the broadcasters' statements that without a specific hour the practical effect of the Commission's rulings was to ban non-obscene programming altogether, the Commission determined establishing a time after which certain adult, non-obscene programming could be broadcast was necessary to ensure that its enforcement actions would be upheld in court. (Two of its April rulings are already the subject of court appeals). The Commission noted that a fixed time of day would also allow parents to know when their supervision of children's viewing and listening habits would have to be increased.

The Commission emphasized, however, that obscene programming could never be legally broadcast and that indecent programming could not be legally broadcast before midnight when there was a reasonable risk that children may be in the audience. The bulk of complaints received by the Commission regarding indecent broadcasts involve programming aired prior to midnight, and the Commission will be focusing its ongoing enforcement efforts on these broadcasts, where the risk of children's exposure to indecent programming is the greatest.

-FCC-

APPENDIX C

HALEY, BADER & POTTS

Primer on Indecency

On June 30, 1995, a federal court of appeals upheld the FCC's definition of indecency and a federal statute winch prohibits the broadcast of indecent material between the hours of 6:00 a.m. and 10:00 p.m. Various groups, including the NACB, have asked the Supreme Court to review this decision. Unless the Supreme Court reverses the lower court decision, all indecent material must be broadcast during the "safe harbor" period, 10:00 p.m.–6:00 a.m.

In 1987, the FCC replaced its "seven dirty words" indecency standard with a broad "generic" definition of indecency. Since then, the Commission has levied indecency fines amounting to millions of dollars. Fines range from $2,000 to hundreds of thousands of dollars depending upon the nature of the violation. A college station which aired a single indecent rap song was fined $23,750.

The FCC's indecency standard is both vague and complex. The following memo gives some guidance as to its meaning by analyzing the definition and summarizing FCC rulings.

What does the FCC consider to be "indecent"?

The FCC considers a broadcast to be indecent if it contains: "language or material that, in context, depicts or describes, in terms patently offensive as measured by contemporary community standards for the broadcast medium, sexual or excretory activities or organs."

Gee, thanks. What does that mean?

Material is indecent if it offends the "average" broadcast viewer or listener. Examples of the Commission's finding include: popular songs which contain repeated references to sex or sexual organs (*e.g.*, "Penis Envy," "Walk with an Erection," "Erotic City," "Jet Boy, Jet Girl," "Makin' Bacon"); DJ banter concerning tabloid sex scandals (*e.g.*, Vanessa Williams' photographs in *Penthouse* and a honeymooner whose testicle was caught in a hot tub drain); discussions between DJs and callers concerning intimate sexual questions (*e.g.*, "What makes your hiney parts tingle?"; "What's the grossest thing you ever put in your mouth?"); dirty jokes or puns ("Liberace was great on the piano but sucked on the organ"); non-clinical references to gay or lesbian sex, masturbation, penis or breast size, sodomy, erections, orgasms, etc.; and the seven dirty words (shit, fuck, piss, cunt, cocksucker, motherfucker, tits). It appears that the Commission will consider almost any reference to oral or non-heterosexual sex to be indecent.

My station is in Los Angeles. Community standards are different than in Bell Buckle, Tennessee. Does that protect me?

No. The standard applied is a *national* standard based upon what the Commission believes to be indecent.

My station is completely oriented to a college audience. If we get a complaint, can't we simply show that children don't listen to our station?

No. The FCC has taken the position that all broadcast stations must comply with its indecency policy, no matter what their target audience. The only defense that the FCC will consider is a study which shows that there are no children listening to *any* station in the market at the time the indecent material aired.

The on-air staff at my station really toe the line. We make sure that none of the patter goes too far. Some of the songs that we air are a bit on the racy side, however. The Commission doesn't fine stations for airing nationally—distributed recordings by well-known artists, does it?

It sure does. It fined a station $25,000 for airing the now-infamous song, "Candy Wrapper" (a song in which various candy bar names symbolize sexual activities) and the Monty Python song "Sit on my Face", which contains the lyrics "Sit on my face and tell me that you love me. I'll sit on your face and tell you I love you too . . . life can be fine, if we both sixty-nine." The Commission fined a Las Vegas station $2,000 for airing a Prince song that repeatedly used the word "fuck."

My station had no intention of airing anything indecent. Somehow, a conversation between my DJ and a caller got a little bit bawdy. The Commission wouldn't fine me for that, would it?

Yes, it would. The Commission has repeatedly rejected arguments that the indecency policy interferes with the spontaneity of talk or call-in shows.

The statement made by the DJ was a one-time thing. He said an offensive word once, realized what he had done and moved on to a totally different topic. Doesn't the Commission recognize that people are human and might slip up now and then?

Sometimes. The Commission has dismissed complaints which merely cite the use of isolated words or phrases in a broadcast, and has stated that it would "not necessarily" take action against "the isolated use of unplanned expletives during live coverage of news or public affairs programs." As pointed out above, however, the Commission did fine a Las Vegas FM station $2,000 for a single broadcast of a Prince song which contained one indecent word.

A DJ at my station never actually used any "dirty" words, but he did an hilarious skit based on innuendo. The Commission can't get us for that, can it?

It sure can. Material may be indecent even if it does not contain graphic descriptions of sexual activity. An indirect allusion may be deemed offensive "if it is understandable and clearly capable of a specific sexual or excretory meaning which, in context, is inescapable." WIOD(AM), Miami was fined $10,000 for airing material such as "Candy Wrapper" and "Butch Beer" (a satiric commercial which, in the Commission's view, contained an "unambiguous . . . lesbian theme.") A station's humorous or ironic intent is not considered as a defense.

We were covering a discussion on the etiquette of condom use. Some of the language is pretty graphic. Doesn't the Commission recognize that a station should air programming that in other contexts could be considered indecent?

The Commission's definition of indecent programming explicitly recognizes that context *is* important. Material contained in political advertisements, news and public affairs programs has been found not to be offensive because of "context." The Commission denied a complaint against a political ad in which a mayoral candidate opposed the incumbent's proposal to buy a clock for the City Hall building with the rallying cry, "clocksuckers." It denied a complaint against a segment of "All Things Considered" featuring a wiretapped conversation with reputed gangster John Gotti, in which he repeatedly used variations of the word "fuck." It also denied a complaint against the telecast of a high school sex education class. But context is not an easily defined concept, nor a sure-fire defense. The Commission fined a station $4,000 for a program in which two DJs read from and commented on a *Playboy* interview with Jessica Hahn. In that ruling, it rejected arguments that the DJ's remarks were essentially news commentary and warned that "while the newsworthy nature of broadcast material and its presentation in a serious, newsworthy manner would be relevant contextual considerations in an indecency determination, they are not, in themselves, dispositive factors."

I doubt that anybody tuned in to the discussion of condom use just to get their kicks. I mean, the discussion was embarrassing rather than titillating. I thought that the Commission was only interested in the pandering skits that some of the drive-time DJs engage in?

Not true. Material may be indecent even if it is not pandering or titillating in nature. Songs such as "Penis Envy" and "Makin' Bacon" were held to be indecent because they contained lewd references to genital organs, even though those references may not have been titillating. In what may be the low point of the Commission's anti-indecency drive, it found that a licensee had aired indecent programming when it broadcast excerpts from a critically acclaimed play about a person dying of AIDS.

Doesn't the merit of a program count for something?

Although the Commission has said that the merit of a program is a factor to be assessed in determining whether a program is indecent, it has stressed the fact that merit is "simply one of many variables, and it would give this particular variable undue importance if we were to single it out for greater weight or attention than we give other variables." The Commission refused to issue a declaratory ruling that James Joyce's *Ulysses* was not indecent, and denied a complaint against a reading from *Ulysses* primarily on grounds that the reading occurred after midnight. More recently, it has equivocated on the question of whether political ads containing graphic depictions of abortions are indecent. No indecency complaint has yet been denied solely on the grounds that the material was meritorious.

November 18, 1995

This memorandum has been prepared for discussion at the NABC Conference and is intended for information purposes only. It does not constitute legal advice. If you have any questions concerning this memorandum, please contact John Crigler at Haley Bader & Potts at 703/841-0606

APPENDIX D

Before the
FEDERAL COMMUNICATIONS COMMISSION   FCC 92–498
Washington, D.C. 20554

In the Matter of
Implementation of Section 10 of the
Cable Consumer Protection and
Competition Act of 1992   MM Docket Ho. 92–258

Indecent Programming and Other Types
of Materials on Cable Access Channels

NOTICE OF PROPOSED ROLE MAKING

Adopted: November 5, 1992,   **Released:** November 10, 1992

Comment Date: December 7, 1992

Reply Comment Date: December 21, 1992

By the Commission:

Introduction

1.   On October 5,1992, Congress enacted a comprehensive cable television bill, the Cable Television Consumer Protection and Competition Act of 1992 ("Cable Act of 1992"), Pub. L. 102–385, which substantially alters existing provisions of the Communications Act that govern cable television. Generally, the Communications Act prohibits cable operators from exercising editorial control over the access channels on their systems.FN1 Section 10 of the new Act, however, permits cable operators voluntarily to prohibit indecent programming on the leased access channels on their system. Section 10 also requires, *inter alia*, the Commission to adopt regulations that (1) are designed to restrict access by children to indecent programming on leased

access channels of cable systems and (2) enable cable operators to prohibit use of channel capacity on the public, educational, or governmental access channels ("PEG channels") for programming which contains obscene material, sexually explicit conduct, or material soliciting or promoting unlawful conduct.

2.   Section 10 of the new Act also amends section 638 of the Communications Act (47 U.S.C. §558), which immunizes cable operators from liability for programming on access channels, by adding at the end of it "unless the program involves obscene material." Thus, if a program is obscene, a cable operator is no longer statutorily immune from liability for programs carried on the PEG or leased access channels of its system.FN2 This particular amendment becomes effective without further action by the Commission on December 4, 1992, i.e., 60 days after the new Act's enactment.FN3

3.   The purpose of this proceeding is to seek comment on the provisions discussed above that require implementing regulations. In the paragraphs below, we discuss in detail the statutory provisions and our proposals for implementation.

Leased Access Channels—Voluntary Prohibitions by Cable Operators

4.   Section 10 amends section 612(h) of the Communications Act, 47 U.S.C. §532(h), relating to cable leased access, to permit a cable operator to enforce a "written and published policy of prohibiting programming that the cable operator reasonably believes describes or depicts sexual or excretory activities or organs in a patently offensive manner as measured by contemporary community standards." This provision allows a cable operator, if it chooses, to exclude from leased access channels any programming that the operator "reasonably believes" is indecent.FN4 This statutory description of indecency in this section is analogous to the Commission's definition of indecency that have been applied in both the broadcast and common carrier telephone context and that have been upheld by the courts. See *Dial Information Services v.Thornburgh* 938 F.2d 1535 (2d Cir. 1991), *cert. denied*, 112 S. Ct. 966 (1992) and *Action for Children's Television v. FCC*, 852 F.2d 1332 (D.C. Cir. 1988). This statutory authority is self-executing and, therefore, a cable operator's authority to prohibit on leased access channels programming it reasonably believes to be indecent becomes effective on December 4, 1992.

Leased Access Channel—Indecent Matter Required To Be Blocked

5.   Section 10 of the new Act also amends section 612 of the Communications Act of 1934 (47 U.S.C. §532) by adding a new subsection (j) Subsection (j)(1) requires the Commission to promulgate regulations within 120 days of the date of enactment of that subsection designed to:

> limit the access of children to indecent programming, as defined by Commission regulations, and which cable operators have not voluntarily prohibited under subsection (h) by—
>
> (A) requiring cable operators to place on a single channel all indecent programs, as identified by program providers, intended for carriage on channels designated for commercial use under this section;
>
> (B) requiring cable operators to block such single channel unless the subscriber requests access to such channel in writing; and

(C) requiring programmers to inform cable operators if the program would be indecent as defined by Commission regulations.

Subsection (j)(2) provides that cable operators are required to "comply with the regulations promulgated pursuant to paragraph (1)."

6. We seek comment on the best way to effectuate these provisions. At the outset, we address the definitional issue posed by the new law. Under section 10, cable operators are required to block indecent programming "as defined by Commission regulations." Thus, Congress has left to the Commission the task of defining "indecent programming" for the purpose of implementing the above provision. Congress, however, has provided guidance to us by including a description of indecent programming in that part of Section 10 that permits cable operators, if they so choose, to exclude this type of programming on cable leased access on their systems. As noted earlier, this language is strikingly similar to the Commission's definitions of indecency that have been applied to broadcasting and the telephone medium.FN5 We propose, therefore, to track the definitional language used by Congress in the first part of section 10 which refers to programming "that describes or depicts sexual or excretory activities or organs in a patently offensive manner as measured by contemporary community standards."

7. In proposing a definition of indecent programming, we note that the Supreme Court in *FCC v. Pacifica Foundation*, 438 U.S. 726, 748 (1978), has stated that "each medium of expression presents special First Amendment problems." In light of this statement, we invite comment on whether we should state in this definition that the "community standards" test to be used is one which applies to the cable medium. We note that, in analogous areas, we have tailored our indecency definitions for broadcast programming and telephone communications to the standards applicable to those particular media. It is our intention to faithfully execute the provisions of the statute and, in this regard, we seek comment on how we may do so and also ensure that the statute is implemented in the most constitutionally permissible manner.

8. As set out above, section 10 specifically requires cable operators to place all indecent programming on a single leased access channel and to block access to that channel unless the subscriber requests access in writing. Thus, unlike recently enacted legislation aimed at regulation of indecent programming on broadcast stations,FN6 this legislation does not compel cable operators to prohibit indecent leased access programming during a specified period of the day. Instead of this type of "safe harbor" approach, it mandates a "blocking" approach similar in some respects to that contained in section 223 of the Act applicable to providers of indecent communications over common carrier telephone facilities. The explicit references in the legislative history to the "blocking" approach under section 223 reinforces that this type of regulation was deliberately chosen over the "safe harbor" approach that applies on the broadcast side.FN7

9. In essence, under section 10, children's exposure to indecent programs is effectively eliminated unless access to that leased access channel service is specifically requested in writing by the cable subscribing household. Our proposed regulations would codify these statutory requirements by requiring that cable operators place all

programming identified as indecent on a single leased access channel, employ appropriate blocking mechanisms, and permit access only if the subscriber so requests in writing. Commenters should provide any relevant suggestions or comments concerning appropriate blocking mechanisms and procedures relating to subscriber access. We also seek comment on our interpretation that, under section 624(d)(2)(A) of the Communications Act, cable operators would still be required to provide a "lock box," upon request, to a subscriber who has specifically requested access to this channel.FN8 It is our tentative view that Congress did not mean to preclude a person's right under that section to obtain a lockbox to control access to other cable services on the system or to limit access to this channel to others in the household.

10.   Under section 10 it is the program provider, not the cable operator, who must determine if a program is indecent and, hence, must be provided on the blocked channel. Because the cable operator is prohibited under section 612(c)(2) of the Communications Act from exercising editorial control over the leased access channels (unless under the new Act it enforces a written and published policy that prohibits indecent programming),FN9 it would appear that the cable operator has no power to require that indecent programming be carried on the blocked channel if the program provider does not identify the program as indecent and so inform the cable operator.FN10 We seek comment upon whether the above construction of the statute is correct and, if not, the reasons therefor.

11.   We also seek comment on whether the cable operator, consistent with section 612(c)(2)'s no censorship provision and with the new amendments under section 10, can require program providers to certify that their programming is not obscene or indecent (as defined by Commission regulations). We assume that cable operators who have a written and published policy of prohibiting indecent material may require such certifications. In view of cable operators' potential liability for carriage of obscene materials, we also assume that all cable operators can require program providers to certify that their programs do not contain obscene materials.

12.   Finally, as the statute expressly provides, programmers must inform cable operators if the material sought to be presented on a leased access channel of the system would be indecent as defined by Commission regulation. In order to comply with the single channel requirement, it is evident that cable operators must receive adequate advance notice in order to have sufficient time to channel such programming on their systems. We seek comment on what would be a reasonable time frame for the required notification by a program provider to the cable operator and on whether such notification should be made in writing. We also ask commenters to address whether a cable operator should be held harmless from liability under our proposed rules if it does not receive any, or timely, notification from a programmer. We also seek comment on any other requirements that should be adopted in order to effectuate the new law's provisions. For example, commenters should address whether a cable operator should be required to retain notifications for a prescribed period of time. We also invite commenters to bring to our attention any other matters not discussed in this notice that they believe have an important bearing on the Commission's proposed implementation of the statute.

Public, Educational, and Governmental Access Channels – Cable Operator-Imposed Prohibitions on Certain Types of Proramming

13.   Section 10 requires the Commission to promulgate within 180 days of the enactment of the Act regulations that enable a cable operator to prohibit the use of any public, educational, or governmental access facility "for any programming which contains obscene material, sexually explicit conduct, or material soliciting or promoting unlawful conduct."FN11 This section does not require the cable operator to refuse carriage of such programming on these channels but merely allows the cable operator the option of prohibiting such programming.FN12 As pointed out earlier, however, the newly-amended section 638 of the Act expressly provides that cable operators are no longer statutorily immune from liability for carriage of obscene materials on these channels.FN13

14.   We propose to codify in our rules the authority afforded to cable operators under this new statutory provision. One mechanism that a cable operator might use to enforce a policy of prohibiting this programming would be to require certifications by users or operators that no materials fitting into any of these statutory categories will be presented on these channels. We request comment on this approach. Commenters should also address whether our regulations should provide for any additional matters not expressly addressed in the statute. For example, commenters may wish to address whether specific procedures should be developed to govern disputes between the cable operator and programmer of these access channels. Because these channels are mandated and their conditions of use are defined at the local level, we propose that any such disputes should be handled at the local level. We invite interested persons to comment on these and any other aspects that they believe would be germane to proper implementation of this provision.

15.   This is a non-restricted notice and comment rulemaking proceeding. *Ex parte* presentations are permitted, except during the Sunshine Agenda period, provided they are disclosed pursuant to the Commission's rules. *See* 47 C.F.R. §§1.1202, 1.1203 and 1.1206(a). Pursuant to applicable procedures set forth in sections 1.415 and 1.419 of the Commission's Rules, interested parties may file comment on or before December 7, 1992, and reply comments on or before December 21, 1992. All relevant and timely comments will be considered by the Commission before final action is taken in this proceeding. To file formally in this proceeding, participants must file an original and four copies of all comments, reply comments, and supporting material. If participants want each Commissioner to receive a personal copy of their comments, an original plus nine copies must be filed. Comments and reply comments should be sent to the Office of the Secretary, Federal Communications Commission, 1919 M Street, N.W., Washington, D.C. 20554.

16.   As required by section 603 of the Regulatory Flexibility Act (Pub. L. No. 96–353, 94 Stat. 1164, 5 U.S.C. §601 *et seq.* (1981), the Commission has prepared an Initial Regulatory Flexibility Analysis (IRFA) of the expected impact on small entities of the proposals suggested in this document. The IRFA is set forth in Appendix B. Written public comments are requested on the IRFA. The comments must be filed in accordance with the same filing deadlines as comments on the rest of this *Notice of Proposed Rule Making*, but they must have a separate and distinct heading, designating

them as responses to the Initial Regulatory Flexibility Analysis. The Secretary shall send a copy of this *Notice of Proposed Rule Making*, including the IRFA, to the Chief Counsel for Advocacy of the Small Business Administration in accordance with section 603(a) of the Regulatory Flexibility Act.

17. Authority for this proceeding is contained in sections 4(i), 4(j), and 303(r) of the Communications Act of 1934, as amended, 47 U.S.C. §§154(i), 154(j), and 303(r) and section 10 of the Cable Television Consumer Protection and Competition Act of 1992, Pub. L. 102–385 (1992).

18. Further information on this proceeding may be obtained by contacting Stephen A. Bailey, Office of General Counsel, at (202) 254–6530.

FEDERAL COMMUNICATIONS COMMISSION
Donna R. Searcy
Secretary

NOTES

1. *See* section 611(e), of the Communications Act applicable to the public, educational, and governmental access channels and section 612(c) (2) of the Act applicable to commercial leased access channels.

2. Section 639 of the Communications Act, 47 U.S.C. §559, and 18 U.S.C. §1468 prohibit obscene matter on cable systems.

3. Section 15 of the new Act, which relates to the provision of unsolicited sexually explicit programs on "premium channels" that are offered as part of a cable subscriber promotional effort, also becomes effective 60 days after enactment. *See* FCC Public Notice "Self-Effectuating Provisions of the Cable Television Consumer Protection and Competition Act of 1992" (released November 5, 1992). That section amends section 624 (e) of the Communications Act by requiring that cable operators provide 30 days advance notice to subscribers regarding channels that offer X, NC-17, or R rated movies and to block these channels upon subscriber request.

4. *See* 138 CONG. REC. S646 (daily ed. January 30, 1992)

5. See Infinity Broadcasting Corp., 3 FCC Rcd 930, 936 n.6 (1987), remanded on other grounds sub nom. Action for Children's Television v. FCC, 852 F.2d 1332 (D.C. Cir. 1988) and Dial Information Service v. Thornburg, 938 F.2d 1535, 1540–41 (2d Cir. 1991).

6. Just recently, we issued a rulemaking notice to implement the Public Telecommunications Act of 1991, Pub. L. No. 102–356 (August 26, 1992), which, *inter alia*, requires the Commission to issue regulations that would prohibit the broadcast of indecent programming between 6 a.m. and 12 midnight on commercial broadcast stations (6 a.m. and 10 p.m. for certain public broadcast stations). *Notice of Proposed Rule Making in GC Docket No. 92–223 (Enforcement of Prohibitions Against Broadcast Indecency in 18 U.S.C. §1464)*, FCC 92–445, ___FCC Rcd ___ (released October 5, 1992).

7. *See* 138 CONG. REC. S646–49 (daily ed. January 30, 1992).

8. As described in section 624(d)(2), a "lockbox" or parental key is a device that enables subscribers to prohibit viewing of particular cable services within their homes during periods selected by them.

9. *See* para. 4, *supra*.

10. *See* section 612(c)(2) which, noted earlier, generally prohibits the cable operator from exercising editorial control over these channels.

11. The Senate drafters of this provision appear to have used the term programming involving "sexually explicit" conduct to mean the same types of indecent programming material that may be prohibited by cable operators on leased access channels. *See* 138 CONG. REC. S646 (daily ed. January 30, 1992). The Senate drafters also indicated that the provision relating to "material soliciting or promoting unlawful conduct" was intended to address programming that solicits prostitution. *Id.* at S649.

12. As noted para. 1, *supra*, section 611(e) of the Communications Act restricts the cable operator from exercising editorial control in other respects.

13. *See* para. 2, *supra*.

APPENDIX A
PROPOSED RULE

PART 76—CABLE TELEVISION SERVICE

1. The authority citation of Part 76 is amended to read as follows:

Authority: Secs. 2, 3, 4, 301, 303, 307, 308, 309, 48 Stat., as amended, 1064, 1065, 1066, 1081, 1082, 1083, 1084, 1085; 47 U.S.C. §§ 152, 153, 154, 301, 303, 307, 308, 309; Secs. 611, 612, ___ Stat. ___, 47 U.S.C. §§ 531, 532

2. Subpart ___ amended by adding the following new section:

§76.___ Restrictions on Indecent Programming on Leased Access Channels; Restrictions on Obscene Materials and and Other Types of Materials on Public, Educational, and Governmental Access.

(a) A cable operator may enforce prospectively a written and published policy of prohibiting on leased access channels programming that the cable operator reasonably believes describes or depicts sexual or excretory activities or organs in a patently offensive manner as measured by contemporary community standards for the cable medium.

(b) All programs intended for carriage on channels designated for commercial leased access use under this section and identified by the program provider as indecent shall be placed on a single channel, except for such programs prohibited by the cable operator pursuant to paragraph (a) above. A cable operator shall block such channel except for subscribers requesting access to such channel in writing.

(c) Program providers on leased access channels shall identify for cable operators no later than seven days prior to the requested carriage any programming that describes or depicts sexual or execretory activities or organs in a patently offensive manner as measured by contemporary community standards for the cable medium.

(d) A cable operator may prohibit the use of any channel capacity on the cable system of any public, educational, or governmental access facility for any programming that contains obscene material, sexually explicit conduct, or material soliciting or promoting unlawful conduct.

Reason for Action.
This proceeding is being initiated in order to seek comment on the best way to implement section 10 of the Cable Consumer Protection and Competition Act of 1992, Pub. L. 102-385, relating to indecent programs on leased access channels of a cable system and to cable operator restrictions on certain programs on public, educational, and governmental access channels.

Objectives.
The Commission's goal is to provide notice and opportunity to comment to members of the public regarding efficacious implementation of section 10 of the new Act.

Legal Basis.
Authority for this proposed rule making is contained in sections 4(i), 4(j) and 303(r) of the Communications Act of 1934, as amended, 47 U.S.C. §§ 154(i), 154(j), and 303(r) and section 10 of the Cable Consumer Protection and Cometition Act of 1992, Pub. L. 102-385 (1992).

Reporting, Recordkeeping and other Compliance Requirements.
The Commission is asking for comment on whether cable operators shall be required to retain any notifications made by program providers that the program they seek to present on the cable system's leased access channels is indecent.

Federal Rules that Overlap, Duplicate or Conflict with Proposed Rule.
None.

Description, Potential Impact, and Number of Small Entities Involved.
The rules proposed in this proceeding would impose new burdens on all cable operators, including smaller ones, by requiring them to channel indecent programs on leased access to a single channel but would also enable operators to exercise more control over the content of public, educational, and governmental access channels to the extent they involve programs which contain obscene material, sexually explicit conduct, or material soliciting or promoting unlawful conduct.

Any Significant Alternatives Minimizing the Impact on Small Entities Consistent with the Stated Objectives.
None.

APPENDIX E

COMPLAINT

UNITED STATES DISTRICT COURT
EASTERN DISTRICT OF PENNSYLVANIA

Civ. No. 96-963

AMERICAN CIVIL LIBERTIES UNION; HUMAN
RIGHTS WATCH; ELECTRONIC PRIVACY
INFORMATION CENTER; ELECTRONIC FRONTIER
FOUNDATION; JOURNALISM EDUCATION ASSOCIATION;
COMPUTER PROFESSIONALS FOR SOCIAL
RESPONSIBILITY; NATIONAL WRITERS UNION;
CLARINET COMMUNICATIONS CORP.; INSTITUTE
FOR GLOBAL COMMUNICATIONS; STOP PRISONER
RAPE; AIDS EDUCATION GLOBAL INFORMATION
SYSTEM; BIBLIOBYTES; QUEER RESOURCES
DIRECTORY; CRITICAL PATH AIDS PROJECT, INC.;
WILDCAT PRESS, INC.; DECLAN McCULLAGH dba
JUSTICE ON CAMPUS; BROCK MEEKS dba CYBERWIRE
DISPATCH; JOHN TROYER dba THE SAFER SEX
PAGE; JONATHAN WALLACE dba THE
ETHICAL SPECTACLE; and PLANNED PARENTHOOD
FEDERATION OF AMERICA, INC.,

Plaintiffs,

v.

JANET RENO, in her official capacity as
ATTORNEY GENERAL OF THE UNITED STATES,

Defendant.

PRELIMINARY STATEMENT

1. This is an action for declaratory and injunctive relief challenging provisions of the "Communications Decency Act of 1996" (the challenged provisions are referred to hereinafter as "the Act"). One provision imposes criminal penalties for "indecent" but constitutionally protected telecommunications to individuals under the age of 18; another criminalizes the use of any "interactive computer service" to "send" or "display in a manner available" to a person under 18 any communication that "depicts or describes, in terms patently offensive as measured by contemporary community standards, sexual or excretory activities or organs." The plaintiffs, providers of and users of computer communication systems, assert that the Act is unconstitutional on its face and as applied because it criminalizes expression that is protected by the First Amendment; it is also impermissibly overbroad and vague; and it is not the least restrictive means of accomplishing any compelling governmental purpose.
2. In addition, plaintiffs assert that the Act violates the constitutional right to privacy encompassed in the First, Fourth, Fifth, and Ninth Amendments because it criminalizes private "e-mail" computer correspondence to or among individuals under the age of 18 if the correspondence is deemed "patently offensive" or "indecent."
3. Plaintiffs further assert that the Act in effect prohibits the right to anonymous speech, guaranteed by the First Amendment, for vast portions of the computer networks.
4. Finally, plaintiffs American Civil Liberties Union, Planned Parenthood Federation of America, Inc., and others also assert that 18 U.S.C. Sec. 1462(c), both before and after amendment, is unconstitutional on its face because it violates the First Amendment by criminalizing the distribution or reception of any information via "any express company or other common carrier, or interactive computer service" of "information . . . where, how, or of whom, or by what means any" "drug, medicine, article, or thing designed, adapted, or intended for producing abortion . . . may be obtained or made."

JURISDICTION AND VENUE

5. This Court has jurisdiction pursuant to 28 U.S.C. Secs. 1331, 1361, and 2201. Venue is proper under 28 U.S.C. Sec. 1391(e).
6. Under Sec. 561 of the Act, this action must be adjudicated by a three-judge court convened pursuant to 28 U.S.C. Sec. 2284.

PARTIES
7. Plaintiff AMERICAN CIVIL LIBERTIES UNION (ACLU) is a nationwide, nonpartisan organization of nearly 300,000 members dedicated to defending the principles of liberty and equality embodied in the Bill of Rights. The ACLU is

incorporated in the District of Columbia and has its principal place of business in New York City. The ACLU sues on its own behalf, on behalf of others who use its online computer communications, and on behalf of its members who use online communications.

8. Plaintiff HUMAN RIGHTS WATCH, INC. (HRW) is a leading international human rights organization that monitors human rights abuses in over 70 countries. It is incorporated in New York and has its principal place of business in New York City. It sues on its own behalf, on behalf of others who use its online computer communications, and on behalf of its members who use online communications.

9. Plaintiff ELECTRONIC PRIVACY INFORMATION CENTER (EPIC) is a non-profit research organization that collects and distributes information concerning civil liberties and privacy issues arising in the new communications media. EPIC is a project of the Fund for Constitutional Government, a tax-exempt organization incorporated in the District of Columbia. Both EPIC and the Fund have their principal places of business in Washington, D.C. EPIC sues on its own behalf and on behalf of others who use its online computer communications.

10. Plaintiff ELECTRONIC FRONTIER FOUNDATION (EFF) is a nationwide, non-partisan organization of approximately 3,500 paying individual members that is committed to defending civil liberties in the world of computer communications, to developing a sound legal framework for that world, and to educating government, journalists, and the general public about the legal and social issues raised by this new medium. EFF is incorporated in California and has its principal place of business in San Francisco. EFF sues on its own behalf, on behalf of others who use its online computer communications, and on behalf of its members.

11. Plaintiff JOURNALISM EDUCATION ASSOCIATION (JEA) was formed in 1924. It is incorporated in Minnesota and has its headquarters in Manhattan, Kansas. Its purpose is to serve journalism educators through opposing censorship of student expression, creating aids for curriculum and instruction, facilitating the involvement of minority students, promoting the use of technology, and emphasizing professionalism through certification, workshops, conventions, and publications. It sues on its own behalf, on behalf of its members who use online communications, and on behalf of the students with whom the members work.

12. Plaintiff COMPUTER PROFESSIONALS FOR SOCIAL RESPONSIBILITY (CPSR) is a non-profit corporation incorporated in California with national offices in Palo Alto. CPSR has 22 chapters in 14 states and approximately 1,550 members. As technical experts, CPSR members provide the public and policymakers with realistic assessments of the power, promise, and limitations of computer technology. As concerned citizens, CPSR members direct public attention to critical choices concerning the application of computing and how those choices affect society. CPSR sues on its own behalf, on behalf of others who use its online computer communications, and on behalf of its members who use online communications.

13. Plaintiff NATIONAL WRITERS UNION (NWU) is a 4,000-member labor union for freelance writers founded in 1983. Its members include investigative journalists, trade book authors, technical writers, political cartoonists, poets, textbook authors, and multimedia contributors. NWU has its principal place of business in New York

City. NWU sues on its own behalf, on behalf of others who use its online computer communications, and on behalf of its members who use online communications.

14. Plaintiff CLARINET COMMUNICATIONS CORP. is incorporated in California and has headquarters in San Jose. ClariNet publishes an electronic newspaper in Usenet format with 1.2 million paying subscribers and a widely read humor newsgroup. ClariNet sues on its own behalf and on behalf of its subscribers and readers.

15. Plaintiff INSTITUTE FOR GLOBAL COMMUNICATIONS (IGC) is a national computer service provider that provides inexpensive access to the international computer network known as the Internet, as well as other online services, primarily to nonprofit organizations. It is a project of a California public charity; its principal place of business is in San Francisco, California. It sues on its own behalf and on behalf of others who use its online computer communications.

16. Plaintiff STOP PRISONER RAPE, INC. (SPR) is a nonprofit organization dedicated to combating the problem of prisoner rape. SPR is a non-profit corporation incorporated in New York and has its principal place of business in New York City. It sues on its own behalf and on behalf of those who use its online computer communications.

17. Plaintiff AIDS EDUCATION GLOBAL INFORMATION SYSTEM (AEGIS) is a nonprofit corporation incorporated in California that operates a free computer bulletin board system with one of the largest online archives of information on HIV and AIDS in the world. Its home computer is located in San Juan Capistrano, California. It sues on its own behalf and on behalf of those who use its online computer communications.

18. Plaintiff BIBLIOBYTES is a company that produces electronic books for sale via a "World Wide Web" site on the Internet. It is incorporated in New Jersey and its principal place of business is in Hoboken, New Jersey. It sues on its own behalf and on behalf of those who use its online computer communications.

19. Plaintiff QUEER RESOURCES DIRECTORY (QRD) is one of the largest online distributors of gay, lesbian, and bisexual resources on the Internet. It is an unincorporated association. Its system administrator resides in Reston, Virginia, its executive director resides in Los Angeles, California, and its home computer is located in Portland, Oregon. Other distribution point computer locations are in Maryland, California, New Zealand, the United Kingdom, Michigan, and Israel. QRD sues on its own behalf and on behalf of those who use its online computer communications.

20. Plaintiff CRITICAL PATH AIDS PROJECT, INC. is an AIDS treatment and prevention information project that offers AIDS treatment and safer sex information via a free computer bulletin board, electronic mailing lists, and a page on the World Wide Web. Critical Path is also an Internet Service Provider providing free access to the Internet for both organizations and individuals in the Philadelphia area. It is incorporated in Pennsylvania and its home computer is located in Philadelphia, Pennsylvania. It sues on its own behalf, on behalf of others who use its online computer communications, and on behalf of its members who use online communications.

21. Plaintiff WILDCAT PRESS, INC. is an independent publishing company that promotes its publications by providing free excerpts through a World Wide Web site on the Internet. It is a limited liability partnership and has its principal place of busi-

ness in Los Angeles, California. It sues on its own behalf and on behalf of those who use its online computer communications.

22. Plaintiff DECLAN McCULLAGH dba JUSTICE ON CAMPUS operates a non-profit online information clearinghouse on issues of student free speech. The home computer is located at the Massachusetts Institute of Technology in Cambridge, Massachusetts. McCullagh also maintains a list for people interested in censorship issues called "fight-censorship." McCullagh resides in Pittsburgh, Pennsylvania. He sues on his own behalf and on behalf of those who use JUSTICE ON CAMPUS and the fight-censorship list.

23. Plaintiff BROCK MEEKS dba CYBERWIRE DISPATCH (CWD), is the columnist and editor of CyberWire Dispatch, a popular and irreverent online political news column available on the World Wide Web and through a computer subscription program called a listserv. He also writes a column for HotWired, an online magazine. Meeks is a resident of Fredericksburg, Virginia. He sues on his own behalf and on behalf of those who use CYBERWIRE DISPATCH and read his column in HotWired.

24. Plaintiff JOHN TROYER dba THE SAFER SEX PAGE maintains a large archive of information about safer sex on the Internet's World Wide Web. Troyer is a resident of San Francisco, California. The home computer for the Safer Sex Page is located in San Francisco. Troyer sues on his own behalf and on behalf of those who use THE SAFER SEX PAGE.

25. Plaintiff JONATHAN WALLACE dba THE ETHICAL SPECTACLE, publishes an online magazine on the Internet's World Wide Web that examines controversial issues of ethics, law and politics in America. Wallace is a resident of New York City, and rents computer facilities in New Jersey for purposes of housing the magazine. He sues on his own behalf and on behalf of those who use THE ETHICAL SPECTACLE.

26. Plaintiff PLANNED PARENTHOOD FEDERATION OF AMERICA, INC. (PPFA) is the leading national voluntary health organization in the field of reproductive health care. PPFA and its 153 affiliates engage in public education and advocacy concerning safe and legal access to all reproductive health services, including abortion, and its affiliates provide these services. PPFA operates a site on the Internet's World Wide Web, through plaintiff IGC. PPFA is a New York State corporation with its headquarters in New York City.

27. Defendant ATTORNEY GENERAL JANET RENO heads the United States Department of Justice, which is the agency of the United States government responsible for enforcement of federal criminal laws, including the statute at issue in this case.

FACTS

Enactment of "Indecency" Standard for Cyberspace Communications
28. In February, 1996, Congress adopted and the President signed the Act. In relevant part, the Act provides:

"Section 502. Obscene or Harassing Use of Telecommunications Facilities Under the Communications Act of 1934.

Section 223 (47 U.S.C. 223) is amended—

(1) by striking subsection (a) and inserting in lieu thereof:

(a) Whoever—

"(1) in interstate or foreign communications . . .

"(B) by means of a telecommunications device knowingly—

"(I) makes, creates, or solicits, and

"(ii) initiates the transmission of,

any comment, request, suggestion, proposal, image, or other communication which is obscene or indecent knowing that the recipient of the communication is under 18 years of age regardless of whether the maker of such communication placed the call or initiated the communication; . . .

(2) knowingly permits any telecommunications facility under his control to be used for any activity prohibited by paragraph (1) with the intent that it be used for such activity, shall be fined under title 18, United States Code, or imprisoned not more than two years, or both."

(emphasis added) This provision appears in the United States Code as 47 U.S.C. Sec. 223(a)(1)(B) (hereinafter the "indecency" provision).

29. Subsection (h)(1) of Sec. 502(2) of the Act provides that

"the use of the term telecommunications device' in this section

(A) shall not impose new obligations on broadcasting station licensees and cable operators covered by obscenity and indecency provisions elsewhere in this Act; and

(B) does not include the use of an interactive computer service."

Because "interactive computer service" is defined broadly in the Act (see below), the definition of "telecommunications device" to exclude any "interactive computer service" leaves entirely uncertain the meaning and scope of the statutory prohibitions for computer communications.

30. Section 502(2) of the Act adds to 47 U.S.C. Sec. 223, in pertinent part:

"(d) Whoever—

(1) in interstate or foreign communications knowingly

(A) uses an interactive computer service to send to a specific person or persons under 18 years of age, or

(B) uses any interactive computer service to display in a manner available to a person under 18 years of age, any comment, request, suggestion, proposal, image, or other communication that, in context, depicts or describes, in terms patently offensive as measured by contemporary community standards, sexual or excretory activities or organs, regardless of whether the user of such service placed the call or initiated the communication; or

(2) knowingly permits any telecommunications facility under such person's control to be used for an activity prohibited by paragraph (1) with the intent that it be used for such activity,

shall be fined under title 18, United States Code, or imprisoned not more than two years, or both." (emphasis added).

This provision appears in the United States Code as 47 U.S.C. Sec. 223(d)(1) (hereinafter the "patently offensive" provision).

31. Subsection (h)(2) of Sec. 502(2) of the Act provides that "[t]he term 'interactive computer service' has the meaning provided in section 230(f)(2)." Section 230(f)(2) defines "interactive computer service" to mean "any information service, system, or access software provider that provides or enables computer access by multiple users to a computer server, including specifically a service or system that provides access to the Internet and such systems operated or service offered by libraries or educational institutions."

32. The provisions described in this section became effective immediately upon passage of the Act.

33. No definition is given in the Act for the term "indecent." The Federal Communications Commission, however, has interpreted the prohibition of "indecent" radio and television broadcasts under 18 U.S.C. Sec. 1464 to cover communications that "depict or describe, in terms patently offensive as measured by contemporary community standards for the broadcast medium, sexual or excretory activities or organs." The Commission has ruled that this definition includes the use of common Anglo-Saxon street terms for sexual or excretory functions, as well as sexual innuendos and double entendres. In addition, the Commission has ruled that communications with substantial literary, artistic, political, scientific, or other educational or social value, may be "patently offensive" or "indecent."

34. The Act contains two provisions that appear to establish partial defenses to criminal liability. Section 502 adds to 47 U.S.C. Sec. 223 a new subsection (e), which provides that "[i]n addition to any other defenses available by law: (1) No person shall be held to have violated subsection (a) or (d) solely for providing access or connection to or from a facility, system, or network not under that person's control, including transmission, downloading, intermediate storage, access software, or other related capabilities that are incidental to providing such access or connection that does not include the creation of the content of the communication." Various exceptions to this defense are set out in subsections (e)(2), (3), and (4), for conspiracies, co-ownership situations, and employer liability.

35. In addition, new 223 U.S.C. Sec. 223(e)(5) provides a defense for any person who "(A) has taken, in good faith, reasonable, effective, and appropriate actions under the circumstances to restrict or prevent access by minors to a communication specified in such subsections, which may involve any appropriate measures to restrict minors from such communications, including any method which is feasible under available technology; or

(B) has restricted access to such communication by requiring use of a verified credit card, debit account, adult access code, or adult personal identification number." New Sec. 223(e)(6) permits the Federal Communications Commission to "describe measures which are reasonable, effective, and appropriate to restrict access to prohibited communications under subsection (d)," but does not authorize the Commission to enforce the Act or approve such measures.

36. Section 509 of the Act may provide a different defense to liability. Section 509 adds a new section, Sec. 230, to Title 47 of the United States Code. Section 230(c)(1)

provides: "No provider or user of an interactive computer service shall be treated as the publisher or speaker of any information provided by another information content provider." This section appears to conflict with new 47 U.S.C. Sec. 223(e), which only provides a defense if a "facility, system, or network" on which "indecent" or "patently offensive" material appears is not under the "control" of the person who provides access.

37. Before passing this Act, Congress made no findings about alternative, less restrictive means of accomplishing the goals of the Act.

The Nature of the Online Medium

38. Online services use computers, phone lines, and modems to connect users to networks that allow them to communicate with thousands of other users throughout the world, and to access extensive information databases from a variety of sources. Most online services offer a package of services that can include: electronic mail to transmit private messages to one or a group of users or to an established mailing list on a particular topic; chat rooms that allow simultaneous online discussions; discussion groups in which users post messages and reply to online "bulletin boards"; informational databases; and access to the Internet.

39. Textual, audio, and video files can all be exchanged through computer communications networks if the user has the right computer hardware and software.

40. The Internet is the largest online network in the world. It links a large number of smaller networks set up by universities, industry, nonprofit organizations, and government. While estimates can only be approximations due to rapid growth, the Internet is believed to connect at least 59,000 computer networks, 2.2 million computers, 159 countries, and 40 million users. The Internet has no centralized distribution point.

41. Many users are connected to the Internet through an Internet Service Provider (ISP). ISPs provide connections, software, and tools for using the Internet. Like the large commercial online services, ISPs also often host online discussion groups and chat rooms that are housed and maintained through the ISP's computers.

42. Some businesses and institutions have a direct connection to the Internet, which means they are part of the vast network of computers that comprise the Internet. Many universities in the United States are directly connected to the Internet and provide accounts on their participating computer to students, faculty, and staff.

43. Some online services provide content as well as access to computer networks. That is, in addition to providing the technical ability to subscribers to send and receive information and messages, some online services create their own information databases.

44. Electronic mail, or e-mail, is the most basic online communication. Users are given a personal e-mail address that allows them to exchange messages or files with other persons and organizations that have Internet e-mail addresses.

45. "Gopher" is a popular way to create and access databased information on the Internet. Gopher is a menu-driven program that allows the user to "gopher" through multiple layers of menus to search for information on a particular topic. A "gopher

site" is a database that provides content associated with a particular person or organization. As a reference service, gopher sites often include links to related gopher sites that are associated with other organizations or persons.

46. The "World Wide Web" (Web) is a popular way to create and access databased information on the Internet. The World Wide Web contains sophisticated graphics and audio files in addition to text files. Web sites are databases that provide content associated with a particular person or organization; they allow users to link instantly to other documents and Web sites by clicking on highlighted words in the text of the document being viewed.

47. "Online discussion groups" are hosted by online services or by particular networks connected to the Internet. The host sets up a section on the network devoted to the discussion of a particular issue and any other online user with access to the host network can post messages on the topic by sending an e-mail message to the discussion group. Users can also post responses to particular messages.

48. "Online mailing lists," or "listservs" are e-mail distribution lists. Internet users subscribe to online mailing lists by sending messages from their own e-mail addresses. Any subscriber can then send a message that is distributed to all the other subscribers on the list.

49. "Chat rooms" are sections provided by online services and some computer bulletin board systems in which online users can engage in simultaneous live interactive online discussion.

50. Online discussion groups, chat rooms, and online mailing lists are sometimes moderated by someone not necessarily connected with the online service provider. Many of these "moderators" are volunteers who simply are interested in a particular topic. The moderators review incoming messages before they are posted to determine whether the messages are related to the subject matter of the group or conform to other standards set up by the moderator.

51. "Computer bulletin board systems" (BBSs) are online networks that are independent of the Internet and that usually cater to people interested in specialized subject matter or to people from a particular geographic region. Subscribers dial directly from their computers into the BBS host computer. BBSs often offer e-mail services among users, online discussion groups, and information databases.

52. A user with access to the Internet may use most gopher sites and Web sites without providing further identification or paying an additional fee. A user with access to newsgroups, online discussion groups, online mailing lists, and chat rooms may generally use particular services without providing further identification or paying an additional fee.

53. "Cyberspace" refers to the combination of all of the online communications systems described above.

54. Nobody owns cyberspace, and the ability of anyone to control what goes into or through online networks varies widely depending on the nature of the system. Anyone can purchase the necessary equipment to get online or to create her own web page.

55. Users of online systems are also content providers (that is, they are publishers), because they can transmit and distribute their own communications and can create

a permanent archive of information accessible by other users. There is no limit to the number of people on either side of the sending or receiving end of computer communications.

56. Online communications are interactive. This means, in part, that users of online systems must seek out with specificity the information they wish to retrieve and the kinds of communications they wish to engage in. It also means that users can easily respond to the material they receive or view online.

57. Online systems provide users with a multitude of options for controlling and limiting, if desired, the kinds of information they access through online networks. Commercial online services like American Online, Prodigy, and CompuServe provide features to prevent children from accessing chat rooms and to block access to some kinds of newsgroups based on keywords, subject matter, or specific newsgroup. They also offer screening software that automatically blocks messages containing certain words, and tracking and monitoring software to determine which resources a particular online user (e.g., a child) has accessed. They also offer children-only discussion groups that are closely monitored by adults.

58. Online users can also purchase special software applications to control access to online resources. These applications allow users to block access to certain resources, to prevent children from giving personal information to strangers by e-mail or in chat rooms, and to keep a log of all online activity that occurs on the home computer.

59. Once information is posted to an international online network like the Internet, it is not possible to allow only residents of a particular region or country to access that information; the information becomes available to anyone in the world who has access to the online network. There is currently no technological method for determining with specificity the geographic location from which users access or post to online systems.

60. Online users are given a password and user name which they must use in order to sign onto their online service. While some users use their full proper name as their online user name, many users have online names that are pseudonyms. These users therefore may send, view, and receive online communications anonymously.

61. There are forums for both "public" and "private" communications in cyberspace. E-mail and online mailing lists are private communications between specified persons or group of persons. Only the intended recipients of an e-mail message receive the message; in this sense e-mail is like regular mail. Similarly, only subscribers to an online mailing list should receive the messages posted to that mailing list. Web sites, gopher sites, online discussion groups, and chat rooms, by contrast, are public because anyone with online access can access them or participate in them at any time. These forums are the public libraries and public squares of cyberspace.

Relationship of the Plaintiffs To the Act

American Civil Liberties Union (ACLU)

62. In addition to its legal advocacy to uphold the Bill of Rights, plaintiff ACLU has long devoted considerable resources to public education about civil liberties. Since 1993, the ACLU's public education efforts have included extensive online resources that

offer electronic copies of ACLU publications, reports, court briefs, news releases, and other material related to the ACLU's legal, legislative, educational and advocacy work.

63. The ACLU maintains its extensive online resources through America Online and the Internet's World Wide Web. Many of the ACLU's online databases contain material of social value that contains sexual subject matter or vulgar language. Examples include copies of ACLU court briefs in cases involving obscenity, arts censorship, and discrimination against gays and lesbians. Indeed, the ACLU has posted the text of the "seven dirty words" comic monologue which the Supreme Court ruled "indecent" in the 1978 Pacifica case, and which the Court itself reproduced as an appendix to its opinion.

64. The ACLU also hosts unmoderated online discussion groups that allow citizens to discuss and debate a variety of civil liberties issues. These services allow online users to express their uncensored views on civil liberties issues and to interact with ACLU staff or featured speakers. Many of the communications in the ACLU's discussion groups have sexual content or vulgar language; for example, a discussion of masturbation in the context of the firing of former Surgeon General Jocelyn Elders; the content of Howard Stern's best-selling book, Private Parts; a discussion of why the word "fuck" has such expressive power; and a discussion of the defense of pornography and other erotic expression under the First Amendment.

65. The ACLU does not moderate its interactive services because such editing or censorship would be antithetical to the ACLU's belief in freedom of speech. Furthermore, the ACLU considers minors to be an important audience for its online resources. The ability of minors to participate in chat rooms or discussion groups with other minors and with adults is a vital part of their education. It is particularly important that minors be able to access information about their rights and to learn about and debate controversial issues. Thus, for the reasons discussed in this Complaint, the ACLU does not currently intend to self-censor any of its online communications as a result of the Act.

66. The ACLU's web site is hosted by a private company that has expressed concern about the material on the ACLU's site for fear that it would be held liable under the Act. The company has not yet decided what action, if any, to take as a result of this concern.

67. In addition to its own online resources, ACLU staff and members use other online services such as e-mail, outside discussion groups, and online mailing lists as an important low-cost method of communicating and sharing documents and information with each other and with those outside of the ACLU. Some of this material is also sexually explicit or contains vulgar language or descriptions of the human body or human reproduction.

68. Through its online resources, the ACLU distributes information to and receives information from its affiliates, clients, members, and the public, regarding how women can obtain abortions or abortifacient drugs or devices, and when doctors can perform abortions, including how to contact specific abortion providers, who performs specific abortion procedures, where to obtain specific abortifacient drugs and devices, when specific abortion procedures may be used, and the legal restrictions on obtaining and performing abortions in different states.

69. The ACLU also mails out information to and receives information through the mails from its affiliates, clients, members, and the public, regarding how women can obtain abortions or abortifacient drugs and devices, and when doctors can perform abortions, including how to contact specific abortion providers, who performs specific abortion procedures, where to obtain specific abortifacient drugs and devices, when specific abortion procedures may be used, and the legal restrictions on obtaining and performing abortions in different states.

70. The ACLU also gives out and receives information over the telephone and via FAX from its affiliates, clients, members, and the public, regarding how women can obtain abortions or abortifacient drugs and devices, and when doctors can perform abortions, including how to contact specific abortion providers, who performs specific abortion procedures, where to obtain specific abortifacient drugs and devices, when specific abortion procedures may be used, and the legal restrictions on obtaining and performing abortions in different states.

Human Rights Watch (HRW)

71. Plaintiff HRW uses online services to communicate with human rights activists and others in the field and to distribute its human rights reports worldwide through a gopher site on the Internet. HRW's online resources include testimony from victims of forced trafficking in prostitution in Thailand and India, reports on systematic rape in Bosnia, and reports of sexual abuse of female prisoners in the United States. These and other reports contain graphic language and subject matter. In the view of HRW, online communication is a powerful new way for human rights activists, dissidents and others to communicate and organize away from the watchful eyes of oppressive governments.

72. For example, a July 1995 report on slavery in Pakistan detailed tortures that are used to intimidate bonded laborers. That report discusses tortures that include beating of the genitals and rape.

73. HRW believes that the use of graphic language and descriptions is necessary to convey the true horror of human rights abuse. Removal of material considered "indecent" or "patently offensive" from direct victim testimony in HRW's human rights reports would greatly diminish its effectiveness in advocating for an end to human rights abuses.

74. HRW believes that minors as well as adults are interested in its online information, and that it is important for the success of the human rights movement that minors have access to this information. Thus, for the reasons discussed in this Complaint, HRW currently does not intend to self-censor any of its online communications as a result of the Act.

Electronic Privacy Information Center (EPIC)

75. EPIC maintains its public online resources through a site on the web and through an online mailing list to which any person with an Internet electronic mail address may subscribe. On average, 500 people visit the Web site each day.

76. EPIC's electronic resources include materials concerning free speech, censorship, and privacy issues. Because of the nature of these issues, some of the materials necessarily use sexually explicit speech or vulgar language. For example, the EPIC web site contains the text of the Supreme Court's opinions in FCC v. Pacifica Foundation, 438 U.S. 726 (1978), and Cohen v. California, 403 U.S. 15 (1971), both of which contain common four letter words.

77. EPIC's web site also contains the text of poems written by subscribers of America Online and removed from that system by America Online management on the grounds that they contain "vulgar or sexually oriented language." EPIC makes such information available in order to illustrate the potential effects of attempts to regulate online speech and expression.

78. EPIC believes minors to be an important audience for its online resources. EPIC staff frequently receive inquiries from high school students seeking information for research projects. EPIC staff refer these students to EPIC's web site as a potential source of relevant information.

79. Thus, for the reasons discussed in this Complaint, EPIC does not currently intend to self-censor its online communications as a result of the Act.

Electronic Frontier Foundation (EFF)

80. Since its inception in 1990, EFF has devoted considerable resources to educating the public about civil liberties and legal issues as they arise in cyberspace. Throughout EFF's existence, it has initiated and/or moderated several online forums, including a forum on the WELL (a California-based conferencing system and Internet Service Provider), on Usenet (two online discussion groups or "newsgroups") and on America OnLine. EFF also has its own computer site on the Internet.

81. EFF's public education efforts include the maintaining of extensive online resources both on forums it runs with online service providers, and on its own Internet site. These resources include articles, court cases, legal papers, news releases, newsletters, and excerpts from public discussions related to the EFF's legal, legislative, educational, and advocacy work. EFF also publishes a "home page" on the web which is accessible to anyone with a user account on another site on the global Internet, as well as anyone who uses an online service provider that includes a "Web browser" among its services.

82. EFF also maintains eight online mailing lists, both for specific civil-liberties and activist activities, and for informing the public about its activities. The primary mailing list has a subscriber base of approximately 7,500 individuals.

83. EFF's web page normally receives between 70,000 to 80,000 hits per day (a hit is an instance of individual access). The site normally transmits the equivalent of 120 million to 140 million words per day.

84. Since virtually all interactions on the Internet or other computer networks have a significant communicative element to them, EFF's policy positions and the discussion forums it sponsors strongly emphasize freedom-of-speech concerns, including concerns about the contours of obscenity law and liability and about the scope of

the Federal Communications Commission's jurisdiction to regulate so-called "indecency." In discussing what the Supreme Court, in the absence of a definition of indecency, might consider to be indecent, EFF must refer in detail to such texts as the George Carlin comedy monologue that was the subject of the litigation in FCC v. Pacifica, to the transcripts of Howard Stern broadcasts, and to literary works such as those of Allen Ginsberg and James Joyce. EFF's web site also provides "links" that enable users to visit other sites that contain discussions and examples of "indecent" material.

85. EFF believes it is important for minors to be able to educate themselves about the legal and constitutional structures that frame freedom of speech online. Some EFF members are minors. This Act would radically restrict access by EFF members who are minors to constitutionally protected material that they could legally be given in a library or bookstore.

86. Thus, for the reasons discussed in this Complaint, EFF does not currently intend to self-censor its online communications as a result of the Act.

87. Nearly all of EFF's approximately 3,500 members use online communications. EFF members both receive and transmit information through a variety of online communications. EFF members do not wish to be required to self-censor "indecent" speech in order to avoid prosecution.

Journalism Education Association (JEA)

88. JEA is one of the largest national organizations of high school journalism teachers and publication advisors. It has almost 1,600 members. JEA members increasingly use online communications as part of instruction in high school journalism classes or as part of teaching research methods for students who write for school publications.

89. JEA believes that access to online communications is essential for the education of high school students.

90. JEA members attempt to give students the skills to enable them to engage in independent online research. When students do online research directed or supervised by JEA members, but on computers that are not at the school or that are at the school but not being operated by a teacher, it is not possible for JEA members to ensure that students do not access material that might come within the definition of the Act.

91. Many high school students are sufficiently mature to be able to handle material that some might consider "indecent" or "patently offensive." Thus, it might not only be acceptable but also important for some students, under the supervision of JEA members, to access information about, for example, war crimes in Bosnia which might include graphic descriptions of rape.

92. If the Act goes into effect, JEA members fear they will be prosecuted if they fail to censor material that some people believe should be censored under the Act.

93. Section 223(f)(1) provides that "[n]o cause of action may be brought in any court or administrative agency against any person on account of activity that is not in vio-

lation of any law punishable by criminal or civil penalty, and that the person has taken in good faith to implement a defense authorized under this section or otherwise to restrict or prevent the transmission of, or access to, a communication specified in this section."

94. JEA members do not know if this section would protect them from liability for violation of First Amendment rights if they unnecessarily restricted access to important protected speech not covered by the Act.

95. JEA also sues on behalf of their minor students. The students wish to retain their right to access constitutionally protected information and ideas.

Computer Professionals for Social Responsibility (CPSR)

96. CPSR, a nonprofit organization of computer professionals, maintains a site on the World Wide Web. CPSR also maintains several listservs and hosts several online discussion groups. Board of Director discussions take part online and board votes are sometimes taken online. CPSR also maintains two newsgroups which are not moderated.

97. CPSR's web site is linked to a number of other Web sites, gophers and other computer networks. Many of the sites with which CPSR's site is linked appear to contain information that is of medical or health value but that might be considered indecent or patently offensive. Other linked sites contain other information that might also be considered indecent or patently offensive.

98. One of the listservs, which is also a CPSR working group, is called "Cyber Rights." People who participate in Cyber Rights often discuss issues of censorship and the application of indecency rules to cyberspace. Some of this discussion is frank and uses strong language and/or quotes matters that have been censored. Other listservs and discussion groups also discuss issues of censorship and contain strong language.

99. Minors have access to the computer communications of CPSR. CPSR believes that it is important that social responsibility be promoted among young people who are learning to use online resources and that access to the CPSR resources would advance this goal. CPSR does not wish to restrict its online resources to adults only.

100. Thus, for the reasons discussed in this Complaint, CPSR does not currently intend to censor its online communications as a result of the Act.

101. As computer professionals, CPSR members engage in a great deal of interaction through various computer networks. This includes e-mail, participation in listservs, participation in discussion groups, and use of various sites on computer networks. CPSR members fear prosecution as a result of their use of computer online communications.

National Writers Union (NWU)

102. Plaintiff NWU maintains a site on the World Wide Web, as do several of its leaders. It also maintains an online archive of NWU-related documents, and offers two online mailing lists to which any person, whether or not an NWU member, may

subscribe. Some of the material on the NWU's various web sites and mailing lists contains sexually explicit subject matter or vulgar words—for example, heated debates about homosexuality, and back issues of the NWU's newsletter, which include explicit articles about censorship, obscenity and indecency law, and gay rights.

103. Many NWU members use computers to communicate with each other via private e-mail, to exchange information, and to post literary work. Some of this material is sexually explicit or contains vulgar words. Human sexuality and the human body have always been important subjects of literature and journalism and, as writers, NWU members naturally address these subjects.

104. For example, one NWU member, Robert B. Chatelle, maintains a web page that contains links to erotic fiction that he has written.

105. The NWU and its members and leaders believe that minors should continue to have access to the NWU web site and other online resources. Thus, for the reasons discussed in this Complaint, NWU and some of its members do not currently intend to self-censor any of their online communications as a result of the Act. Other members would self-censor in order to avoid the risk of prosecution.

ClariNet Communications Corp. (ClariNet)

106. Plaintiff ClariNet Communications Corp. publishes an electronic newspaper known as the "ClariNet e.News" in Usenet format, which includes news articles, columns, and financial information. The news articles are taken from the same wire services from which print newspapers obtain their stories but, unlike some print newspapers, ClariNet does not censor the articles. ClariNet has published articles that use common Anglo-Saxon four letter words. It has also published articles that explicitly describe rapes and sexual assaults. Some of these descriptions are more explicit than the same stories in most print newspapers.

107. ClariNet also publishes a humor newsgroup in Usenet format at rec.humor.funny and on the Web. Some of the jokes include vulgar language or sexually explicit material. For instance, some of the jokes discuss sexual acts including oral sex. Some jokes also use strong and explicit language.

108. ClariNet believes that many minors have an interest in reading the articles and jokes it publishes and that minors do read the material published by ClariNet.

109. With regard to its newspaper, which is available primarily through educational institutions, corporations, and Internet service providers, ClariNet depends on the providers to institute a method to obtain access. Because of the vagueness of the statutory defenses, ClariNet does not know if the access systems used by the providers would constitute a defense to liability.

110. For the reasons discussed in this Complaint, ClariNet does not currently intend to censor its news articles as a result of the Act. With regard to its humor newsgroup, ClariNet is unsure what it will do to avoid liability.

Institute for Global Communications (IGC)

111. Plaintiff IGC provides Internet web sites, access to the Internet, and other online services primarily to nonprofit organizations. It serves approximately 400 nonprofit

groups, including SIECUS (the Sex Information and Education Council of the United States), the Family Violence Prevention Fund, Stop Prisoner Rape, Human Rights Watch, Pacifica Radio (disseminator of the original "dirty words" comic monologue), and numerous women's rights groups whose online communications deal with sexual subject matter, reproduction, rape, and domestic violence. It also serves approximately 15,000 other groups, including approximately 500–600 schools, providing access to online services.

112. IGC also sponsors online discussion groups. IGC does not moderate these groups but is aware that topics have included gay and lesbian sex and erotica, AIDS and HIV treatment, women's health, and violence against women; many of the participants are minors.

113. IGC does not have the resources to monitor the vast amount of information that is published and communicated through its networks. Nor would it be consistent with IGC's function to monitor and censor the content of communications that it facilitates. IGC has no way to determine whether or not minors have gained access to specific sites on its network, nor does it wish to restrict access to adults.

114. IGC does not understand whether the defenses provided by the statute would protect it from criminal prosecution.

Stop Prisoner Rape (SPR)

115. Plaintiff SPR maintains an extensive World Wide Web site on the Internet that contains, among other things, graphic and uncensored accounts of actual rapes, written by the victims themselves. The purpose of SPR is to provide education, information, and advocacy regarding sexual assaults in the nation's prisons, jails, juvenile facilities, and other detention sites. It provides encouragement and advice to survivors, as well as counseling and legal support. In 1995, "Impact Online," which gives awards for outstanding non-profit Internet sites, named the SPR site the best on the web for prison issues and one of the 30 best non-profit sites.

116. SPR believes that the graphic and uncensored nature of the information on its web site is essential to its goal of educating the public and combating the persistent problem of prisoner rape.

117. SPR believes that minors do access its web site, and believes it is essential to allow this access to continue. Minors are among the victims of prisoner rape and are in fact well-known and abundantly described in published literature on the subject to be particularly singled out as targets for sexual assault precisely because of their youth. Status as a minor is one of the surest demographic indicators of likely targeting for sexual assault of a prisoner in a facility which also includes adults. A significant portion of the SPR site contains recollections of individuals who were raped as minors while incarcerated with adults or in juvenile detention centers. The sharing of these experiences is invaluable to the many minors who have been imprisoned or who may be imprisoned and fear prison rape.

118. Thus, for the reasons discussed in this Complaint, SPR does not currently intend to self-censor its online communications as a result of the Act.

119. Plaintiff AEGIS, through its free computer bulletin board system, offers vital information about HIV and AIDS to people in many parts of the world who have no other access to educational material about the disease. Much of the information in AEGIS is necessarily sexually explicit because HIV/AIDS is a sexually transmitted disease. Documents available from the AEGIS bulletin board include but are not limited to materials from the Center for Disease Control, Gay Men's Health Crisis, AIDS Treatment News, and Body Positive Online Magazine.

120. In addition to its archived material, AEGIS sponsors many online discussion groups for people with AIDS or HIV. Discussion groups are offered in Dutch, French, Spanish, and German, in addition to English. Persons with HIV/AIDS use these online forums to share experiences with other victims of the disease. Medical, social welfare, and other public interest professionals also use the online forums to distribute information about the disease and to answer questions posed by users. Discussions in these groups are often sexually explicit.

121. AEGIS believes that it is essential to be able to use explicit language and pictures in its online communications and discussion groups. The information literally saves lives and must be communicated in terms that are not ambiguous or overly scientific and that all audiences can understand. Teenagers as well as adults need to have access to the archived information and online forums sponsored by AEGIS. Many teenagers are sexually active. They are entitled to information that could save their lives, presented in a factual and descriptive form that is easily comprehended.

122. Many people, including people who fear that they may be infected with HIV/AIDS, use AEGIS to get information about the disease because they can do so anonymously. AEGIS does not want to screen to prevent minors from gaining access to its resources because such screening would infringe upon the privacy and anonymity of all users of the system. Moreover, AEGIS does not have the resources to monitor its online resources to screen out content that is "indecent" or "patently offensive," and any such screening process would undermine the educational and health goals of AEGIS's online services. Thus, for the reasons discussed in this Complaint, AEGIS has not yet decided what changes to make, if any, as a result of the Act.

BiblioBytes

123. Plaintiff BiblioBytes produces electronic books for sale over the World Wide Web, including romance novels, erotica, classics, adventure, and horror stories. Some of these electronic publications contain language that is sexually explicit or vulgar or describes sexual or excretory activities or organs. One example of a current title in this category is Harlan Ellison's collection of short stories, Love Ain't Nothing But Sex Misspelled. Several of the stories in that collection include sexually explicit language and deal with events such as abortion and prostitution. Another example of a

current title that contains sexually explicit language is John Anderson's book, Panaflex X, which is a fictional account of a woman trying to get out of the pornography industry.

124. BiblioBytes believes that many minors have an interest in reading the books that BiblioBytes makes available online.

125. BiblioBytes now requires a credit card for purchase of its electronic books. BiblioBytes is unsure if this process, which probably screens out most but not all minors, is sufficient to avoid liability under the Act. For the reasons discussed in this Complaint, BiblioBytes does not currently intend to take any additional steps to self-censor its online communications as a result of the Act.

Queer Resources Directory

126. Plaintiff Queer Resources Directory (QRD) is one of the largest online distributors of gay, lesbian, and bisexual resources on the Internet. QRD is accessed approximately one million times a month and is distributed through several co-servers around the world. QRD contains links to online media; events; cultural information; business, legal, political and workplace issues; and gay, lesbian, and bisexual organizations. The topics covered include parenting, families, marriage, youth organizations, religion, and HIV/AIDS. Some of the material is sexually explicit; for example, discussions of safer sex and human sexuality, and publications such as Hothead Paisan (a satiric comic book about the adventures of a homicidal lesbian terrorist) and Cuir Underground (a magazine covering events and people in the leather and fetish community).

127. QRD does not wish to restrict minors from having access to its system. In fact, much of the material in QRD would be valuable to gay and lesbian teenagers who are struggling with feelings of confusion or isolation, as well as to straight youth who want information about homosexuality. In addition, QRD believes that it is essential that people be able to access its system anonymously.

128. QRD has not made a decision on what procedures to institute, if any, should this statute not be enjoined. QRD supports the use of voluntary Internet blocking software as an alternative to government regulation.

Critical Path AIDS Project, Inc.

129. Plaintiff Critical Path AIDS Project, Inc. provides free Internet access to individuals in the Philadelphia area and also operates a bulletin board, electronic mailing lists and a Web site devoted to providing HIV/AIDS treatment information for persons with AIDS and safer sex information for those at risk of contracting AIDS. Critical Path's online resources include AIDS prevention and treatment information in eight different Asian languages, which reach youths and adults at risk for AIDS in some of the most underserved communities in the nation. Critical Path also offers web subsites to such nonprofit groups as We the People (a large multiracial organi-

zation of HIV-positive individuals), Prevention Point (a needle exchange program), Fight the Right (a political action network), and will soon be providing a subsite to the Youth Health Education Project, a safer sex outreach organization specifically targeted to teenagers. In the fall of 1995 Critical Path was receiving about 10,000 access requests per day for information on its system from all over the world.

130. The Critical Path AIDS Project web page links directly or indirectly to thousands of databases in all 50 states and many countries, thereby permitting users to access communications and retrieve documents from the far reaches of the world, without leaving the Critical Path web site.

131. Much of the material on Critical Path's web site and bulletin board is necessarily sexually explicit. It is critically important as a matter of physical as well as emotional health that teenagers have access to the information that Critical Path provides.

132. Thus, for the reasons discussed in this Complaint, Critical Path does not currently intend to self-censor its online communications as a result of the Act.

133. Because of the vagueness of the defenses provided in the statute, Critical Path is unsure if it would be criminally liable for some of the communications posted by others for which it provides access.

Wildcat Press, Inc.

134. Plaintiff Wildcat Press, Inc. is a small independent publishing company specializing in classic gay and lesbian literature that promotes its publications by providing free excerpts through its World Wide Web site. Wildcat Press maintains high literary standards and has exhibited at the American Booksellers Association Convention.

135. Some of the material in Wildcat Press's publications is sexually explicit or contains vulgar language. For example, the 1974 novel The Frontrunner tells the story of a loving relationship between a young athlete and his coach during the days after the Stonewall Rebellion and before the AIDS crisis. The sequel to that book, Harlan's Race, published in 1990, follows one of the characters from The Frontrunner as he reflects on the changes in the sexual behavior of the gay community brought on by AIDS.

136. Wildcat Press sponsors the YouthArts Project which publishes two online youth magazines, "YouthArts East" and "YouthArts West," with support from students at the University of Pennsylvania and University of Southern California. The online magazines publish poetry, fiction, essays, fine art, and photography by teenagers and are targeted to an audience of teenagers. Some of the material is sexually explicit. Teenagers can obtain the magazine over the Web.

137. Wildcat Press wishes to continue communicating with all interested readers, regardless of age. Wildcat Press believes that teenagers, especially gay and lesbian youth, are not harmed by but benefit from providing content to and obtaining access to the YouthArts Project.

138. Thus, for the reasons discussed in this Complaint, Wildcat Press does not currently intend to self censor its online communications as a result of the Act.

139. Plaintiff Declan McCullagh began Justice on Campus, a World Wide Web archive of information on student free speech issues, in the fall of 1995. Justice on Campus receives about 150 visits to its web site daily. Although the site is housed on a private computer in Cambridge, Massachusetts attached to the Massachusetts Institute of Technology network, McCullagh maintains editorial control over communications posted on the site. Since many students, including college students, are under the age of 18, McCullagh believes that a substantial number of minors visit the web site. Justice on Campus has been recognized as serving an important educational purpose, and its materials are assigned reading in one course at the Massachusetts Institute of Technology.

140. Some of the communications on the Justice on Campus site are sexually explicit or contain vulgar language. For example, in the context of its free speech discussion, Justice on Campus reproduced the texts of communications by students at Cornell University which were alleged to constitute sexual harassment. The actual language was necessary in order to focus on the issue of whether college administrators overreacted to the material.

141. McCullagh also maintains a list entitled "fight-censorship" to which people can subscribe to receive information on censorship issues. The information includes explicit material that has been subject to censorship by others.

142. For the reasons discussed in this Complaint, Justice on Campus and McCullagh do not currently intend to self-censor their online communications as a result of the Act.

Brock Meeks dba CyberWire Dispatch

143. As publisher and editor of CyberWire Dispatch (CWD), plaintiff Brock Meeks addresses many political and cyberspace issues, including Congressional attempts to regulate and to censor the Internet. CWD often employs vulgar and graphic language to make a point about government censorship efforts. CWD has also published sexually explicit material.

144. Meeks also writes regularly as a columnist for the print magazine Wired and the online magazine HotWired. Meeks sometimes uses vulgar and graphic speech in his columns to satirize or make political points.

145. Meeks does not want to prevent minors, who are an important part of his audience, from reading the material in CWD and Hotwired.

146. Thus, for the reasons discussed in this Complaint, Meeks does not currently intend to self-censor his online communications as a result of the Act.

John Troyer, dba The Safer Sex Page

147. Plaintiff John Troyer maintains the Safer Sex Page, a large site on the Internet's World Wide Web that offers educational information on safer sex. The Safer Sex Page is accessed by more than 35,000 people around the world every week.

148. The Safer Sex Page includes a wide array of sex education materials from dozens of sources; brochures include graphics, audio, and video. The resources are both written specifically for the Safer Sex Page and based on information received from other groups including the Center for Disease Control, the United States Department of Health and Human Services, and the Los Angeles Gay and Lesbian Community Services Center.

149. By their very nature, information and discussions about safer sex include explicit language and pictures. Postings include guidelines about the risks associated with different sexual acts. Explicitness is necessary to make safer sex materials comprehensible. The public health threat of unsafe sex demands that people know with specificity how to protect themselves.

150. The Safer Sex Page includes an online discussion group called "Safer Sex Forum" that allows participants to add their own comments to a monthly discussion topic. Users of the Safer Sex Forum often post comments on sexual subjects; past topics have included masturbation, condom brands, and how to talk to a partner about safer sex.

151. Teenagers are an important audience for the resources offered through the Safer Sex Page and the Safer Sex Forum. Many teenagers are sexually active, or consider becoming sexually active before they reach adulthood. These minors are entitled to information that could save their lives.

152. Troyer is currently unsure whether he will self-censor his online communications as a result of the Act.

Jonathan Wallace dba The Ethical Spectacle

153. Plaintiff Jonathan Wallace publishes an online monthly newsletter entitled The Ethical Spectacle under the pen name Jonathan Blumen. The newsletter examines the intersection of ethics, law and politics in society. Past issues have included articles on human experimentation by the Nazis at Auschwitz, and the morality of pornography. An upcoming issue will excerpt the writings of James Joyce, Henry Miller, William Burroughs, and other authors whose works include explicit sexual content and vulgar language.

154. Wallace does not wish to prevent minors from gaining access to The Ethical Spectacle Web page or to lose any teenage readers who may find instruction in the newsletter.

155. Thus, for the reasons discussed in this Complaint, Wallace does not currently intend to self-censor his online communications as a result of the Act.

Planned Parenthood Federation of America, Inc. (PPFA)

156. PPFA's site on the World Wide Web provides a broad range of information relating to reproductive health. PPFA's site also provides educational and graphic information about all facets of reproductive health, from contraception to prevention of

sexually transmitted infections, to finding an abortion provider, to information about which Planned Parenthood affiliates have been providing abortions through use of the drug mifepristone. The educational information includes illustrations of how to place a condom on a penis, and of male and female genitalia. The information PPFA presents is intended to be accessible to minors who seek it; and therefore frequently employs vernacular terminology, such as "cum" when referring to semen or ejaculation.

157. PPFA's site also provides an e-mail service. Through this service, users can address questions to PPFA on subjects such as abortion, contraception, prevention of sexually transmitted infections, and sexuality, and PPFA responds with complete information. PPFA also receives information by e-mail regarding performing and obtaining abortions, practices necessary to reduce unintended pregnancies and sexually transmitted infections, and sexuality information generally.

158. PPFA's site is accessible to any user seeking access. PPFA believes limitations on access to its site would significantly diminish its effectiveness as a source of information, and PPFA does not currently intend to self-censor access.

159. In addition to communicating via interactive computer services, PPFA sends and receives information about performing and obtaining abortions through the mail and telephone and FAX.

Allegations Common to All Plaintiffs

160. The effect of this statute, if implemented, would be to reduce adults to obtaining access by computer to only that information that is fit for children.

161. Given that American society is comprised of people from an endless variety of religious, ethnic, cultural, political, and moral backgrounds, each with his or her own view of what constitutes "indecent" or "patently offensive" expression, these terms are completely vague and do not put any reasonable person on notice of what communications are prohibited.

162. Plaintiffs and their members do not know how to define the terms "indecent" and "patently offensive." All are forced as a consequence to guess at what communications will be prosecuted. Because of its vagueness, the statute invites arbitrary and discriminatory enforcement, and chills constitutionally protected expression by the plaintiffs, their members, and other users of interactive computer services.

163. The defenses provided under the statute are vague and contradictory. It is not clear what 47 U.S.C. Sec. 223(e)(1) means by a "facility, system, or network" not being "under [the] control" of a person since even online providers who do not themselves create the content of communications over their systems can technologically exercise "control" over the communications for which they are conduits. It is also not clear whether 47 U.S.C. Sec. 230(c)(1) provides a defense for anyone who is not a "publisher or speaker." Thus, those who act in part as access providers or hosts for interactive communications cannot know to what extent they will be held liable for "indecent" or "patently offensive" communications to minors.

APPENDIX E

164. Even if it may be technically feasible to devise a method to block access to computer communications by some or most minors, as a practical matter it is economically infeasible. All of the plaintiffs would suffer serious economic hardship if they were required to write separate versions of online communications: one for adults, and one for minors. Thus, the defense provided by section 223(e)(5) is not practically available.

165. Moreover, any blocking system would require advance identification of those seeking access to a web site, chat room, discussion group, or other online forum. Initiating age ID and blocking systems would undermine the essential purpose of the plaintiffs' communications—to be disseminated as easily, widely, and quickly as possible, with a minimum of burden and expense.

166. Any attempt to guarantee that minors could not access information that requires advance identification of those seeking access would also make it impossible for users to engage in constitutionally protected anonymous speech on matters of public and private importance.

167. For those plaintiffs who have members who are minors, blocking access to online communications would deny minors access to materials that they could legally receive in printed form or that they could legally given in a library or bookstore. It would deny them access to materials that they have a constitutional right to receive.

168. Section 223(e)(5) provides a defense for "good faith, reasonable, effective, and appropriate actions" to "restrict or prevent access by minors . . . including any method which is feasible." This defense is so vague that it is not possible for those plaintiffs who seek to fall within its provisions to know if they have taken the actions necessary to avoid liability.

169. The plaintiffs fear prosecution or other enforcement under the statute for communicating, sending, or displaying "indecent" or "patently offensive" material in a manner available to persons under age 18. They also fear liability for material posted by others to their online discussion groups, chat rooms, bulletin boards, listservs, or web sites. Plaintiffs ACLU, PPFA, and others fear prosecution for distributing and receiving information about abortions and abortifacient drugs and devices in violation of 18 U.S.C. Sec. 1462(c).

170. Moreover, plaintiffs fear that if the statute goes into effect, online services and other access providers such as educational institutions will ban communications that they consider potentially "indecent" or "patently offensive," thereby depriving the plaintiffs, their members, and those who use their online services of the ability to communicate about important issues.

171. The plaintiffs' web sites are linked to other web sites on the Internet in a virtually endless chain. There is no way for plaintiffs to screen the material on all of those linked sites or to prevent minors from accessing those sites.

CAUSES OF ACTION

172. Plaintiffs repeat and reallege Secs. 1–171.

173. 47 U.S.C. Secs. 223(a)(1)(B) and (a)(2)(the "indecency" provision) and 223(d)(the "patently offensive" provision) violate the First Amendment to the United States

Constitution on their face and as applied because they effect a total ban on constitutionally protected communications in many parts of cyberspace. Even in those portions of cyberspace where it is technologically and economically feasible to deny access to minors, Secs. 223(a)(1)(B) and (a)(2) and 223(d), are not the least restrictive means of accomplishing any compelling governmental purpose, and thus violate the First Amendment.

174. 47 U.S.C. Secs. 223(a)(1)(B) and (a)(2) and 223(d) are vague, in violation of the First and Fifth Amendments to the United States Constitution.

175. Even if the government could criminalize some constitutionally protected online communications to minors, 47 U.S.C. Secs. 223(a)(1)(B) and (a)(2) and 223(d) are unconstitutionally overbroad, in violation of the First Amendment, because they ban far more constitutionally protected expression to minors than possibly could be justified by any governmental interest.

176. 47 U.S.C. Secs. 223(a)(1)(B) and (a)(2) and 223(d) violate the First, Fourth, Fifth, and Ninth Amendment privacy rights of members and officers of the plaintiff organizations who use private e-mail.

177. 47 U.S.C. Secs. 223(a)(1)(B) and (a)(2) and 223(d) violate the First Amendment rights of members of the plaintiff organizations and other users of computer resources to engage in anonymous speech.

178. 18 U.S.C. Sec. 1462(c) on its face violates the First Amendment rights of members and officers of plaintiff ACLU, PPFA, and others who disseminate and receive information through express companies or other common carriers, or through interactive computer services, regarding women's access to abortions and abortifacient drugs and doctors' abilities to perform abortions.

WHEREFORE, plaintiffs respectfully request the Court to:

(1) Declare that 47 U.S.C. Secs. 223(a)(1)(B) and (a)(2), 223(d), and 18 U.S.C. Sec. 1462(c) violate the First, Fourth, Fifth, and Ninth Amendments to the U.S. Constitution and enjoin their enforcement.

(2) Award plaintiffs reasonable attorneys' fees and costs.

(3) Award such further relief as the Court deems just and appropriate.

Respectfully submitted,

Christopher A. Hansen
Marjorie Heins
Ann Beeson
Steven R. Shapiro
American Civil Liberties Union Fdn.
132 West 43rd St.
New York, NY 10036
212-944-9800

Laura K. Abel
Catherine Weiss
Reproductive Freedom Project
American Civil Liberties Union Fdn.

132 West 43 St.
New York, NY 10036
212-944-9800

Stefan Presser
Attorney ID No. 43067
ACLU of Pennsylvania
125 South Ninth St., Suite 701
Philadelphia, PA 19107
215-923-4357

David L. Sobel
Marc Rotenberg
Electronic Privacy Information Center
666 Pennsylvania Ave. SE, Suite 301
Washington, D.C. 20003
202-544-9240

Michael Godwin
Electronic Frontier Foundation
1550 Bryant St., Suite 725
San Francisco, CA 94103
415-436-9333

Attorneys for all plaintiffs

Roger Evans
Legal Action for Reproductive Rights
Planned Parenthood Federation Of America
810 Seventh Avenue
New York, New York 10019
(212) 261-4708

Attorney for Planned Parenthood Federation of America

Dated: February 8, 1996

APPENDIX F

FEDERAL COMMUNICATIONS COMMISSION   FCC 94-121
WASHINGTON, D.C. 20554
IN REPLY REFER TO:
Released: May 20, 1994

CERTIFIED MAIL. RETURN RECEIPT REQUESTED

Mr. Mel Karmazin, President
Infinity Broadcasting Corporation

> Licensee of Radio Station WJFK(AM)
> Baltimore, Maryland

> Controlling parent of:

> Sagittarius Broadcasting Corporation
> > Licensee of Radio Station WXRK(FM)
> > New York, New York

> Infinity Broadcasting Corporation of Pennsylvania
> > Licensee of Radio Station WYSP(FM)
> > Philadelphia, Pennsylvania

> Infinity Broadcasting Corporation of Washington, D.C.
> > Licensee of Radio Station W JFK(FM)
> > Manassas, Virginia

600 Madison Avenue, Fourth Floor
New York, New York 10022
Dear Mr. Karmazin:
This letter constitutes a NOTICE OF APPARENT LIABILITY FOR A FORFEITURE
to the four above-named licensees (collectively referred to as "Infinity") in the aggre-

gate amount of Two Hundred Thousand Dollars ($200,000), pursuant to Section 503(b) of the Communications Act of 1934, as amended.

The Commission has received a complaint alleging that indecent material was aired during the "Howard Stem Show," as broadcast by WWKB(AM), Buffalo, New York, on December 6, 1993 and January 19, 1994. Based on our experience and your acknowledgements in prior similar circumstances, we presume that the material aired by WWKB(AM) was also aired by the four above-named stations on the same dates as noted above and at a time of day between 6:00 a.m. and 10:00 a.m.FN1 Transcripts of portions of the allegedly indecent broadcasts, taken from tapes submitted by the complainant in the WWKB(AM) case. are attached.

Pursuant to 47 U.S.C. Sections 312(a)(6) and 503(b)(1)(D), the Commission has statutory authority to take appropriate administrative action when licensees broadcast material in violation of 18 U.S.C. Section 1464, which provides criminal penalties for anyone who "utters any obscene, indecent or profane language by means of radio communication."

The Commission has defined indecency as language or material that, in context, depicts or describes in terms patently offensive as measured by contemporary community standards for the broadcast medium, sexual or excretory activities or organs. *See Infinity Broadcasting Corporation of Pennsylvania*, 2 FCC Rcd 2705 (1987). The United States Court of Appeals for the District of Columbia Circuit has upheld the Commission's authority to restrict the broadcast of indecent material at times when there is a reasonable risk that children may be in the audience. *Action for Children's Television v. FCC*, 852 F.2d 1332 (D.C. Cir. 1988).

The excerpts from the "Howard Stem Show" reflected in the attached transcripts appear to be indecent in that they contain language that describes sexual activities and organs in patently offensive terms. Because the material aired at times when there was a reasonable risk that children may have been in the audience, it is legally actionable. Thus, it appears that on December 6, 1993 and January 19, 1994. Infinity violated 18 U.S.C. Section 1464 by airing indecent programming on each of the four above-named stations.

Accordingly, pursuant to Section 5O3(b) of the Communications Act, Sagittarius Broadcasting Corporation, Infinity Broadcasting Corporation of Pennsylvania, Infinity Broadcasting Corporation of Washington, D.C., and Infinity Broadcasting Corporation, licensees of Stations WXRK(FM), New York, New York; WYSP(FM), Philadelphia, Pennsylvania; WJFK(FM), Manassas, Virginia; and WJFK(AM), Baltimore, MD, respectively, are hereby each notified of their separate apparent liability for a forfeiture of Fifty Thousand Dollars ($50,000) for their apparent willful and repeated violations of 18 U.S.C. Section 1464 on the dates set forth above.

In determining the amount of these forfeitures, we find that the same exacerbating considerations concerning Infinity's history of apparent misconduct reviewed in assessing prior forfeitures against Infinity are applicable here. *See Infinity Broadcasting Corporation*, 8 FCC Rcd 2688, 2689-90 and n.3. (1992); *Infinity Broadcasting Corpora-*

tion, 8 FCC Rcd 6740, 6741 (1993); *Infinity Broadcasting Corporation*, FCC 94-26, adopted January 31, 1994. As in the earlier actions, we have continued to take account here of the various relevant factors set forth in Section 503(b) of the Communications Act of 1934, as amended, and reflected in our *Policy Statement on Standards for Assessing Forfeitures*, 8 FCC Rcd 6215 (1993), *appeal pending sub nom.*

USTA v. FCC. Case No.92-1321 (D.C. Cir. filed July 30, 1992).

In regard to this forfeiture proceeding, you are afforded a period of thirty (30) days from the date of this letter "to show, in writing, why a forfeiture penalty should not be imposed or should be reduced, or to pay the forfeiture. Any showing as to why the forfeiture should not be imposed or should be reduced shall include a detailed factual statement and such documentation and affidavits as may be pertinent." 47 C.F.R. Section 1.80(f)(3). Other relevant provisions of Section 1.80 of the Commission's Rules are summarized in the attachment to this letter.
This letter was adopted by the Commission on May 20, 1994.

BY DIRECTION OF THE COMMISSION
William F. Caton

NOTE

1. *See, e.g., Infinity Broadcasting Corporation*, 8 FCC Rcd 6740 (1993) (in responding to a letter of inquiry from the Commission as to whether Infinity's stations had aired the same Howard Stern Show material that had been aired by KFBI(FM), Infinity stated "it can be assumed that the substance of these shows was also broadcast by WXRK(FM), WYSP(FM) and WJFK(AM and FM) on those dates . . . [and] would have been aired by the aforementioned Infinity stations from approximately 6:00 a.m. to approximately 10:00 a.m." *Id.*).

APPENDIX G

Show Name: Eargazm   **DJ Name:** B and T.O.
Show Time: Saturday, 5–9 PM   **Date:** 11/18/00 "Profanity"
PLAYLIST   **Requests:** requests@eargazm.com
    Office: business@eargazm.com

Song Title	Band Name	Album
Offensive Language	George Carlin	Parental Advisory
Add It Up	Violent Femes	Add It Up
Dance Motherfucker Dance	Violent Femmes	
Precious	Pretenders	Pretenders II
Freaky Styley	Red Hot Chili Peppers	Freaky Styley
Love So Fine	Nick Lowe	Labour Of Lust
You're Breakin' My Heart	Nillson	Nillson Schmillson
Not Now John	Pink Floyd	Final Cut
Call It Democracy	Bruce Cockburn	World Of Wonder
Fuckin' Up	Neil Young	Faded Glory
White Punks On Dope	Tubes	The Tubes
The Elephant Is Dead	Bill Hicks	Arizona Bay
Properties Of Propaganda	Fishbone	Give A Monkey A Brain
Babelouge/R&R Nigger	Patti Smith	Easter
Lament	Doors	American Prayer
Mofo's Are After Me	Zoogs Rift	Island Of Living Puke
Miss America	David Byrne	Feelings
Break		
Drugs	Dennis Leary	No Cure For Cancer
Fuckin Ada	Ian Dury	Laughter
A Queer Revolution	Jerri Allyn	Experimental Theatre
Jesus Christ You're Tall	Nillson	Sandman

245

Abortion	George Carlin	Back In Town
Let Talk Dirty To The Animals	Gilda Radner	Live
nake Bit, Can't Shit	Root Boy Slim	Left For Dead
Drinking Fathers	Eddie Murphy	Comedian
Think Of Punk Rock When You Shit	Bloody Mess And The Skabs	6th Grade Field Trip
A Message From The Mayor	Marshall Efrom	Neutrino News Network
Rock Against Drugs	Sam Kinneson	You Should See Me Now
War On Drugs	Bill Hicks	Dangerous
Talking Asshole	Frank Zappa	You're A Hook
Broken Hearts Are For Assholes	Frank Zappa	Sheik Yerbouti
Stick It Out	Frank Zappa	Joe's Garage
Harry As A Boy	Frank Zappa	Thingfish
Outside Now	Frank Zappa	Joe's Garage
Briefcase Boogie	FrankZappa	Thingfish
Bobby Brown	Frank Zappa	SheikYerbouti
What Kind Of Girls / Bwana Dik / Latex Solar Beef	Frank Zappa	Live At The Filmore
Dickie's Such An Asshole	Frank Zappa	Broadway The Hardway

Break

Peaches And Regalia	Dixie Dregs	California Screamin'
Red Baron	Jazz Is Dead	Blue Light Rain
Sleeveless In Seattle	Dregs	California Screamin
Ionized	Dregs	California Screamin
Cab	Macalpine / Brunel / Chambers	Cab
Downstreatch	Tommy Bolin	The Energy Radio Broadcasts
Loop Garoo	Tommy Bolin	The Energy Radio Broadcasts

(Reprinted with permission; http://www.eargazm.com)

APPENDIX H

Before the
Federal Communications Commission
Washington, D.C. 20554

In the Matter of

The KBOO Foundation

Licensee of Noncommercial Educational
Station KBOO-FM, Portland, OR

File No. EB-00-IHD-0079
NAL/Acct. No. 200132080056
Facility ID # 65755

NOTICE OF APPARENT LIABILITY FOR FORFEITURE

Adopted: May 14, 2001   Released: May 17, 2001

By the Chief, Enforcement Bureau:

I. INTRODUCTION

1. In this Notice of Apparent Liability for Forfeiture ("NAL"), we find that The KBOO Foundation, licensee of noncommercial Station KBOO-FM, Portland, Oregon, apparently violated 18 U.S.C. § 1464 and 47 C.F.R. § 73.3999, by willfully broadcasting indecent language. Based on our review of the facts and circumstances in this case, we conclude that The KBOO Foundation is apparently liable for a forfeiture in the amount of seven thousand dollars ($7,000).

II. BACKGROUND

2. The Commission received a complaint alleging that KBOO-FM broadcast indecent material on October 20, 1999 between 7:00 p.m. and 9:00 p.m. during the

"Soundbox." The complainant submitted a tape containing allegedly indecent material that aired on the "Soundbox" on this date. After reviewing the complainant's tape, we issued a letter of inquiry to the licensee.

3.   In its response, The KBOO Foundation argues that the material is not indecent, and that no sanction is warranted. In this regard, The KBOO Foundation states that the "Soundbox" program features contemporary rap and hip hop music often structured around themes that provide a larger social or cultural context, to explore, for example, topics such as "violence, racial oppression or the judicial system." The KBOO Foundation asserts that it "broadcasts rap and hip hop music not to achieve commercial success, but to fulfill its mission of 'providing a forum for unpopular, controversial neglected perspective on important local, national, and international issues,'" and to "reflect the diverse cultures we serve." The KBOO Foundation also has supplemented its response by submitting declarations of the author of the lyrics of the allegedly indecent song cited in the complaint and of a professor at a local university. These declarations are offered in support of The KBOO Foundation's argument that, in context, the material allegedly broadcast on KBOO-FM is not indecent. In addition, The KBOO Foundation states that it provides training to its local programmers, most of whom are unpaid volunteers, concerning the Commission's rules and the station's policies, including its prohibitions against the broadcast of indecent material. The KBOO Foundation supplement also includes a petition signed by listeners who support the "Soundbox."

4.   The KBOO Foundation asserts, in the alternative, that the complaint should be dismissed based on the amount of time that has elapsed since the allegedly indecent material was broadcast. The KBOO Foundation states that it cannot determine with certainty whether it aired the allegedly indecent material cited in our letter of inquiry. However, The KBOO Foundation has determined that its music library contains the song "Your Revolution" that was excerpted in our letter of inquiry.

III. DISCUSSION

5.   Section 503(b)(1) of the Communications Act (the "Act"), 47 U.S.C. § 503(b)(1), provides in pertinent part:

> Any person who is determined by the Commission, in accordance with paragraph (3) or (4) of this subsection to have —
>
> . . .
>
> (D) violated any provision of section 1304, 1343, or 1464 of title 18, United States Code; shall be liable to the United States for a forfeiture penalty.

18 U.S.C. § 1464 provides criminal penalties for anyone who "utters any obscene, indecent or profane language by means of radio communication." As explained below, we believe that "Your Revolution" contains indecent material and that the licensee's broadcast thereof was willful.

6.   The Commission has defined indecent speech as language that, in context, depicts or describes, in terms patently offensive as measured by contemporary com-

munity standards for the broadcast medium, sexual or excretory activities or organs. *Infinity Broadcasting Corporation of Pennsylvania*, 2 FCC Rcd 2705 (1987) (subsequent history omitted) (*citing Pacifica Foundation*, 56 FCC 2d 94, 98 (1975), *aff'd sub nom. FCC v. Pacifica Foundation*, 438 U.S. 726 (1978). The Commission's authority to restrict the broadcast of indecent material extends to times when there is a reasonable risk that children may be in the audience. *Action for Children's Television v. FCC*, 852 F.2d 1332 (D.C. Cir. 1988). Current law holds that such times begin at 6 a.m. and conclude at 10 p.m. *Action for Children's Television v. FCC*, 58 F.3d 654 (D.C. Cir. 1995), *cert. denied*, 116 S.Ct. 701 (1996). Thus, to be actionably indecent, the material in question must not only meet the standard referenced above but also air after 6 a.m. and before 10 p.m. *See* 47 C.F.R. § 73.3999.

7. After carefully considering the record before us, it appears that KBOO-FM has willfully violated our indecency rule with respect to the broadcast of "Your Revolution." The KBOO Foundation points to the length of time that has elapsed since the broadcast that is the subject of the complaint, and argues that it cannot determine whether the song aired on the date and time alleged, or whether it might have aired an edited version of the song. In this regard, the station does not possess tapes or transcripts of the "Soundbox" for the date in question. However, the KBOO Foundation does not claim that tapes or transcripts are generated and retained, or that this material would have been available earlier. The KBOO Foundation acknowledges that the station's music library contains the song, and has provided a transcript of the lyrics of "Your Revolution." Although the KBOO Foundation asserts that an edited version of the song may have been broadcast, it does not indicate that the station possesses such an edited version of "Your Revolution." Moreover, the tape of the October 20, 1999 "Soundbox" submitted by the complainant contains the unedited version of "Your Revolution," which corresponds to the transcription included in The KBOO Foundation's response.

8. The rap song "Your Revolution" contains unmistakable patently offensive sexual references. We have considered The KBOO Foundation's arguments concerning the context of this material. Specifically, the KBOO Foundation asserts that the rap song "Your Revolution" cannot be separated from its contemporary cultural context. In the alternative, The KBOO Foundation argues that even if context is limited to the song's lyrics, "Your Revolution" is "a feminist attack on male attempts to equate political 'revolution' with promiscuous sex" and as such, is not indecent. However, considering the entire song, the sexual references appear to be designed to pander and shock and are patently offensive. In this regard, we reject The KBOO Foundation's argument that it is erroneous, as a matter of law, to find that the song is indecent without considering the artistic merit of the rap music genre. Merit is one of the variables that are part of the material's context, and the Commission has rejected an approach to indecency that would hold that material is not *per se* indecent if the material has merit.FN1 The contemporary social commentary in "Your Revolution" is a relevant contextual consideration, but is not in itself dispositive.FN2 The Commission previously has found similar material to be indecent, and we see no basis for finding otherwise in this case.FN3 In addition, although The KBOO Foundation has submitted a petition signed by listeners who support the "Soundbox," we have pre-

viously ruled that neither the statute nor our case law permits a broadcaster to air indecent material merely because it is popular.FN4

9.   Section 503(b) of the Act and 47 C.F.R. § 1.80 both state that any person who willfully or repeatedly fails to comply with the Act or the Commission's rules shall be liable for a forfeiture penalty. For purposes of 47 U.S.C. § 503(b), the term "willful" means that the violator knew that it was taking the action in question, irrespective of any intent to violate the Commission's rules.FN5 In assessing a forfeiture, we take into account the nature, circumstances, extent and gravity of the violation, and, with respect to the violator, the degree of culpability, any history of prior offenses, ability to pay, and such other matters as justice may require.FN6

10.   The Commission's *Forfeiture Guidelines* set a base forfeiture amount of $7,000 for transmission of indecent material.FN7 After considering all the facts and circumstances, we believe the base forfeiture amount is the appropriate sanction for the violation described above and that neither an upward nor downward adjustment should be made.

IV. ORDERING CLAUSES

11.   Accordingly, IT IS ORDERED THAT, pursuant to 47 U.S.C. § 503(b), and 47 C.F.R. §§ 0.111, 0.311 and 1.80, The KBOO Foundation is hereby NOTIFIED of its APPARENT LIABILITY FOR A FORFEITURE in the amount of seven thousand dollars ($7,000) for willfully violating 18 U.S.C. § 1464 and 47 C.F.R. § 73.3999.

12.   IT IS FURTHER ORDERED THAT, pursuant to 47 C.F.R. § 1.80, within thirty days of this NOTICE OF APPARENT LIABILITY, The KBOO Foundation SHALL PAY the full amount of the proposed forfeiture or SHALL FILE a written statement seeking reduction or cancellation of the proposed forfeiture.

13.   Payment of the forfeiture may be made by mailing a check or similar instrument, payable to the order of the Federal Communications Commission, to the Forfeiture Collection Section, Finance Branch, Federal Communications Commission, P.O. Box 73482, Chicago, Illinois 60673-7482. The payment should note the NAL/Acct. No. referenced above.

14.   The response, if any, must be mailed to Charles W. Kelley, Chief, Investigations and Hearings Division, Enforcement Bureau, Federal Communications Commission, 445 12th Street, S.W., Room 3-B443, Washington, D.C. 20554 and MUST INCLUDE THE NAL/Acct. No. referenced above.

15.   The Commission will not consider reducing or canceling a forfeiture in response to a claim of inability to pay unless the respondent submits: (1) federal tax returns for the most recent three-year period; (2) financial statements prepared according to generally accepted accounting practices ("GAAP"); or (3) some other reliable and objective documentation that accurately reflects the respondent's current financial status. Any claim of inability to pay must specifically identify the basis for the claim by reference to the financial documentation submitted.

16.   Requests for payment of the full amount of this Notice of Apparent Liability under an installment plan should be sent to: Chief, Revenue and Receivables Operations Group, 445 12th Street, S.W., Washington, D.C. 20554.FN8

17. IT IS FURTHER ORDERED THAT a copy of this NOTICE OF APPARENT LIABILITY shall be sent by Certified Mail Return Receipt Requested to: The KBOO Foundation, 20 S.E. 8th Ave., Portland, Oregon 97214; with a copy to its counsel, John Crigler, Esq., Garvey, Schubert & Barer, 1000 Potomac Street, N.W., Washington, DC 20007.

FEDERAL COMMUNICATIONS COMMISSION
David H. Solomon
Chief, Enforcement Bureau

ATTACHMENT

Radio Station: KBOO-FM, Portland, Oregon
Date/Time Broadcast: October 20, 1999, on the "Soundbox," between 7:00 p.m.
                         and 9:00 p.m.
Material Broadcast: "Your Revolution"
(Various female voices)

Your revolution will not happen between these thighs
Your revolution will not happen between these thighs
Your revolution will not happen between these thighs
Will not happen between these thighs
Will not happen between these thighs
The real revolution ain't about bootie size
The Versaces you buys
Or the Lexus you drives
And though we've lost Biggie Smalls
Maybe your notorious revolution
Will never allow you to lace no lyrical douche in my bush
Your revolution will not be you killing me softly with fujees
Your revolution ain't gonna knock me up without no ring
And produce little future M.C.'s
Because that revolution will not happen between these thighs
Your revolution will not find me in the back seat of a jeep
With L.L. hard as hell, you know
Doing it and doing and doing it well, you know
Doing it and doing it and doing it well
Your revolution will not be you smacking it up, flipping it or rubbing it down
Nor will it take you downtown, or humping around
Because that revolution will not happen between these thighs
Your revolution will not have me singing
Ain't no nigger like the one I got
Your revolution will not be you sending me for no drip drip V.D. shot
Your revolution will not involve me or feeling your nature rise
Or having you fantasize
Because that revolution will not happen between these thighs

No no not between these thighs
Uh-uh
My Jamaican brother
Your revolution will not make you feel bombastic, and really fantastic
And have you groping in the dark for that rubber wrapped in plastic
Uh-uh
You will not be touching your lips to my triple dip of
French vanilla, butter pecan, chocolate deluxe
Or having Akinyele's dream, um hum
A six foot blow job machine, um hum
You wanna subjugate your Queen, uh-huh
Think I'm gonna put it in my mouth just because you
Made a few bucks,
Please brother please
Your revolution will not be me tossing my weave
And making me believe I'm some caviar eating ghetto
Mafia clown
Or me giving up my behind
Just so I can get signed
And maybe have somebody else write my rhymes
I'm Sarah Jones
Not Foxy Brown
You know I'm Sarah Jones
Not Foxy Brown
Your revolution makes me wonder
Where could we go
If we could drop the empty pursuit of props and the ego
We'd revolt back to our roots
Use a little common sense on a quest to make love
De la soul, no pretense, but
Your revolution will not be you flexing your little sex and status
To express what you feel
Your revolution will not happen between these thighs
Will not happen between these thighs
Will not be you shaking
And me, [sigh] faking between these thighs
Because the real revolution
That's right, I said the real revolution
You know, I'm talking about the revolution
When it comes,
It's gonna be real
It's gonna be real
It's gonna be real
When it finally comes
It's gonna be real

NOTES

1. *See Infinity Broadcasting Corporation of Pennsylvania, Memorandum Opinion and Order on Reconsideration,* 3 FCC Rcd 930, 932 (1987).

2. *Id* at 932-33. The KBOO Foundation cites a case decided under Florida's criminal obscenity statute as support for its argument that material with artistic merit is not indecent. *Luke Records, Inc. v. Navarro,* 960 F.2d 134 (11ᵗʰ Cir. 1992), *cert. denied, Navarro v. Luke Records, Inc.,* 506 U.S. 1022 (1992). The court's determination that a lower court had not properly applied the tripartite obscenity standard of *Miller v. California,* 413 U.S. 15 (1973), does not control our indecency analysis here.

3. *See Capstar TX Limited Partnership (WZEE(FM)),* 16 FCC Rcd 901 (EB 2001); *CBS Radio License, Inc. (WLLD(FM)),* 15 FCC Rcd 23881(EB 2000)(Notice of Apparent Liability for Forfeiture), DA 01-537 (EB Mar. 2, 2001)(Forfeiture Order).

4. *See, e.g., CBS Radio License, Inc. (WLLD(FM)), supra.*

5. *See Jerry Szoka,* 14 FCC Rcd 9857, 9865 (1999); *Southern California Broadcasting Co.,* 6 FCC Rcd 4387 (1991).

6. 47 U.S.C. § 503(b)(2)(D). *See also The Commission's Forfeiture Policy Statement and Amendment of Section 1.80 of the Rules to Incorporate the Forfeiture Guidelines,* 12 FCC Rcd 17087, 17100-01 (1997), *recon. denied,* 15 FCC Rcd 303 (1999) ("*Forfeiture Guidelines*").

7. *Forfeiture Guidelines,* 12 FCC Rcd at 17113.

8. *See* 47 C.F.R. § 1.1914.

APPENDIX I

Before the
Federal Communications Commission
Washington, D.C. 20554

In the Matter of	File No. EB-00-IH-0293
Capstar TX Limited Partnership	NAL/Acct. No. 200132080014
	Facility ID #41980
Licensee of Station WZEE(FM),	JWS
Madison, Wisconsin	

NOTICE OF APPARENT LIABILITY FOR FORFEITURE
Adopted: January 16, 2001
Released: January 18, 2001
By the Chief, Enforcement Bureau:

I. INTRODUCTION

1. In this Notice of Apparent Liability for Forfeiture ("NAL"), we find that Capstar TX Limited Partnership ("Capstar"), licensee of Station WZEE(FM), Madison, Wisconsin, has apparently violated 18 U.S.C. § 1464 and section 73.3999 of the Commission's rules, 47 C.F.R. § 73.3999, by willfully broadcasting indecent language. Based on our review of the facts and circumstances in this case, we conclude that Capstar is apparently liable for a forfeiture in the amount of seven thousand dollars ($7,000).

II. BACKGROUND

2. The Commission received a complaint concerning a September 8, 2000, broadcast on WZEE(FM), called "The Real Slim Shady," which aired at approximately 3:30

p.m. on August 24, 2000. The complaint included an excerpt of that part of the broadcast the complainant found most offensive. After reviewing the excerpt, we issued a letter of inquiry to the licensee.

3.   In its response, Capstar FN1 states that it inadvertently broadcast an unedited version of "The Real Slim Shady." Capstar explains that the station received a compact disc ("CD") that contained several versions of the song. On all other occasions, according to Capstar, the station played an edited version. However, on the occasion complained of, a part-time disc jockey cued up the edited version but due to static electricity, the CD player skipped to the unedited version and it was aired. Capstar allows that the airing of the unedited version may have been in bad taste but argues that it "involves the isolated use of offensive words, but does not contain language that clearly and inescapably describes sexual or excretory activities and organs in patently offensive terms."FN2 In Capstar's view, the "The Real Slim Shady" does not come within the definition of broadcast indecency.

III. DISCUSSION

4.   Section 503(b)(1) of the Communications Act (the "Act") provides in pertinent part:

> Any person who is determined by the Commission, in accordance with paragraph (3) or (4) of this subsection to have —
>
> . . .
>
> (D) violated any provision of section 1304, 1343, or 1464 of title 18, United States Code; shall be liable to the United States for a forfeiture penalty.

18 U.S.C. § 1464 provides criminal penalties for anyone who "utters any obscene, indecent or profane language by means of radio communication." As explained below, we believe that "The Real Slim Shady" contains indecent material and that the licensee's broadcast thereof was willful, not inadvertent.

5.   The Commission has defined indecent speech as language that, in context, depicts or describes, in terms patently offensive as measured by contemporary community standards for the broadcast medium, sexual or excretory activities or organs. *Infinity Broadcasting Corporation of Pennsylvania*, 2 FCC Rcd 2705 (1987) (subsequent history omitted) (citing *Pacifica Foundation*, 56 FCC 2d 94, 98 (1975), *aff'd sub nom. FCC v. Pacifica Foundation*, 438 U.S. 726 (1978). The Commission's authority to restrict the broadcast of indecent material extends to times when there is a reasonable risk that children may be in the audience. *Action for Children's Television v. FCC*, 852 F.2d 1332 (D.C. Cir. 1988). Current law holds that such times begin at 6 a.m. and conclude at 10 p.m. *Action for Children's Television v. FCC*, 58 F.3d 654 (D.C. Cir. 1995), *cert. denied*, 116 S.Ct. 701 (1996).

6.   After carefully considering the record before us, it appears that Capstar violated our indecency rule with respect to the broadcast of the unedited version of "The Real Slim Shady." Capstar acknowledges that it broadcast the song at approximately 3:30 p.m. The four minute forty-four second rap song contains unmistakable offen-

sive sexual references. Considering the entire song, the sexual references in conjunction with the sexual expletives appear designed to pander and shock. Thus, we disagree with Capstar that we are precluded from finding the material indecent because the Commission has not taken action against "far more graphic references to sex" than "The Real Slim Shady." As we have previously explained, "the context in which material is offered is essential to making a determination as to whether material is indecent." *Capstar TX Limited Partnership (KTXQ(FM), Fort Worth, Texas)*, DA 00-2287 (Enf. Bureau, released October 6, 2000). In this regard, unlike the news story concerning organized crime boss, John Gotti, there is nothing about the context of "The Real Slim Shady" which removes the material from the realm of indecency.FN3 In sum, such a song is inappropriate for broadcast during times when children may be in the audience. The Commission previously has found similar material to be indecent,FN4 and we see no basis for finding otherwise in this case.

7.   We also disagree with Capstar that the broadcast of the unedited version of "The Real Slim Shady" was inadvertent. Capstar accepted the CD with the multiple versions of "The Real Slim Shady" and did not take sufficient care to ensure that the unedited version would not be played. We thus believe that the airing of the unedited version of the song, however unintentional, was still willful.

8.   Section 503(b) of the Act, 47 U.S.C. § 503(b), and section 1.80 of the Commission's rules, 47 C.F.R. § 1.80, both state that any person who willfully or repeatedly fails to comply with the Act or the Commission's rules shall be liable for a forfeiture penalty. For purposes of section 503(b) of the Act, the term "willful" means that the violator knew that it was taking the action in question, irrespective of any intent to violate the Commission's rules.FN5 As explained above, Capstar knew that it was broadcasting "The Real Slim Shady." In assessing a forfeiture, we take into account the statutory factors set forth in section 503(b)(2)(D) of the Act. Those factors include the nature, circumstances, extent and gravity of the violation, and, with respect to the violator, the degree of culpability, any history of prior offenses, ability to pay, and such other matters as justice may require.FN6

9.   The Commission's *Forfeiture Guidelines* set a base forfeiture amount of $7,000 for transmission of indecent/obscene materials.FN7 After considering all the facts and circumstances, we believe the base forfeiture amount is the appropriate sanction and that neither an upward nor downward adjustment should be made. In this regard, we reject Capstar's contention that its record at WZEE(FM) alone demonstrates that it has a history of overall compliance warranting a downward adjustment. On the contrary, we believe that Capstar's record must be viewed in conjunction with the broadcast record of its corporate parent, Clear Channel Communications, Inc., which has been found to have violated the Commission's rules on numerous occasions. See *Citicasters Co.*, DA 00-1640 (released July 26, 2000) ($6,000 NAL for violation of Section 73.1206 of the Commission's rules, forfeiture paid), *Citicasters Co.*, DA 00-1435 (released June 28, 2000), ($7,000 forfeiture order for violation of 18 U.S.C. § 1464, forfeiture paid), *Citicasters Co.*, 15 FCC Rcd 11906 (2000) ($23,000 forfeiture order for violation of 18 U.S.C. § 1464, forfeiture paid), *Citicasters Co.*, DA 00-1016 (released May 9, 2000) ($4,000 NAL for violation of Section 73.1216 of the Commission's rules, for-

feiture paid), *Clear Channel Broadcasting Licenses, Inc.*, 15 FCC Rcd 2734 (EB 2000) ($4,000 NAL for violation of Section 73.1216 of the Commission's rules, forfeiture paid).

IV. ORDERING CLAUSES

10. Accordingly, IT IS ORDERED THAT, pursuant to section 503(b) of the Act,FN8 and sections 0.111, 0.311 and 1.80 of the Commission's rules,FN9 Capstar TX Limited Partnership is hereby NOTIFIED of its APPARENT LIABILITY FOR A FORFEI-TURE in the amount of seven thousand dollars ($7,000) for willfully violating the 18 U.S.C. § 1464 and section 73.3999 of the Commission's rules.

11. IT IS FURTHER ORDERED THAT, pursuant to section 1.80 of the Commission's rules,FN10 within thirty days of this NOTICE OF APPARENT LIABILITY, Capstar TX Limited Partnership SHALL PAY the full amount of the proposed forfeiture or SHALL FILE a written statement seeking reduction or cancellation of the proposed forfeiture.

12. Payment of the forfeiture may be made by mailing a check or similar instrument, payable to the order of the Federal Communications Commission, to the Forfeiture Collection Section, Finance Branch, Federal Communications Commission, P.O. Box 73482, Chicago, Illinois 60673-7482. The payment should note the NAL/Acct. No. referenced above.

13. The response, if any, must be mailed to the Charles W. Kelley, Chief, Investigations and Hearings Division, Enforcement Bureau, Federal Communications Commission, 445 12th Street, S.W., Room 3-B443, Washington, D.C. 20554 and MUST INCLUDE THE NAL/Acct. No. referenced above.

14. The Commission will not consider reducing or canceling a forfeiture in response to a claim of inability to pay unless the respondent submits: (1) federal tax returns for the most recent three-year period; (2) financial statements prepared according to generally accepted accounting practices ("GAAP"); or (3) some other reliable and objective documentation that accurately reflects the respondent's current financial status. Any claim of inability to pay must specifically identify the basis for the claim by reference to the financial documentation submitted.

15. Requests for payment of the full amount of this Notice of Apparent Liability under an installment plan should be sent to: Chief, Credit and Debt Management Center, 445 12th Street, S.W., Washington, D.C. 20554.FN11

16. IT IS FURTHER ORDERED THAT a copy of this NOTICE OF APPARENT LIABILITY shall be sent by Certified Mail Return Receipt Requested to Capstar TX Limited Partnership, c/o Clear Channel Communications, Inc., 200 East Basse Road, San Antonio, Texas 78209-8328, attention: Rick Wolf, Corporate Counsel.

FEDERAL COMMUNICATIONS COMMISSION
David H. Solomon
Chief, Enforcement Bureau

Radio Station: WZEE(FM), Madison, Wisconsin
Date/Time Broadcast: August 24, 2000, approximately 3:30 p.m.
Material Broadcast:"The Real Slim Shady" (Rap lyrics)

Various voices, including the rap artist, Eminem
May I have your attention, please.
May I have your attention, please.
Will the real Slim Shady please stand up.
I repeat, will the real Slim Shady please stand up.

We're going to have a problem here.

Y'all act like you've never seen a white person before.
Jaws all on the floor
Like Pam and Tommy just burst in the door
And started whooping her ass worse than before
They were first divorced
Throwin' her over furniture

Aaaah!

It's the return of the . . .

Oh wait, no wait, you're kidding
He didn't just say what I think he did, did he?
And Dr. Dre said . . .

Nothing, you idiots!
Dr. Dre's dead, he's locked in my basement

Ha, ha.

Feminist women love Eminem
Sicka, sicka, sicka Slim Shady, I'm sick of him
Look at him
Walking around grabbin' his you know what, flippin' the you know who

Yeah, but he's so cute, though

Yeah, probably got a couple of screws up in my head loose
But no worse than what's goin' on in your parents' bedrooms
Sometimes I want to get on TV and just let loose
But can't, but it's cool for Tom Green to hump a dead moose

My bum is on your lips
My bum is on your lips
And if I'm lucky you might just give it a little kiss
And that's the message we deliver to little kids

And expect them not to know what a woman's clitoris is
Of course, they're gonna know when in their courses by the time they hit fourth grade
They got the Discovery Channel, don't they?

We ain't nothin' but mammals
Well, some of us cannibals who cut other people open like cantaloupes (eating sound)
But if we can hump dead animals and antelopes, then there's no reason
That a man and another man can't elope.
But if you feel like I feel like I got the antidote
Women, wear your pantyhose
Sing the chorus and it goes

I'm Slim Shady, yes, I'm the real Shady
All you other Slim Shadys are just imitating
So won't the real Slim Shady please stand up
Please stand up
Please stand up.

Cause I'm Slim Shady, yes, I'm the real Shady
All you other Slim Shadys are just imitating
So won't the real Slim Shady please stand up
Please stand up
Please stand up.

Will Smith don't gotta cuss in his raps to sell records
Well, I do, so fuck him and fuck you, too
You think I give a damn about a Grammy (flatulence sound)
Half you critics can't even stomach me, let alone stand me

But Slim, what if you win, wouldn't it be weird?

Why? So you guys can just lie to get me here?
So you can sit me here next to Britney Spears?
Shit, Christina Aguilera better switch me chairs
So I can sit next to Carson Daly and Fred Durst
And hear 'em argue over who she gave head to first
Little bitch put me up last on MTV

Yeah, he's cute, but I think he's married to Kim
Hee, hee

I sit down low to audio and MP3
And showed the whole world how you gave Eminem VD

Ahhh!

I'm sick of you little girl and boy groups
All you do is annoy me, so I have been sent here to destroy you

And there's a million of us just like me
Who cuss like me
Who just don't give a fuck like me
Who dress like me, walk, talk and act like me
And just might be the next best thing, but not quite me

Cause I'm Slim Shady, yes, I'm the real Shady
All you other Slim Shadys are just imitating
So won't the real Slim Shady please stand up
Please stand up
Please stand up.

Cause I'm Slim Shady, yes, I'm the real Shady
All you other Slim Shadys are just imitating
So won't the real Slim Shady please stand up
Please stand up
Please stand up.

I'm like a head trip to listen to
Cause I'm only givin' you things you joke about with your friends inside your
living room
The only difference is I got the balls to say it in front of y'all
And I don't gotta be false or sugar-coatin it at all
I just get on the mike and spit it
And whether you like to admit it
I just shit it better than ninety percent of you rappers out there
And you wonder how can kids eat up these albums like Valiums

It's funny cause at the rate I'm goin'
When I'm 30 I'll be the only person in the nursing home flirting
Pinching nurses asses when I'm jackin' off an' jerkin'
And I'm jerkin' but this whole bag of Viagra isn't workin'

And every single person is a Slim Shady lurkin'
He could be workin' at Burger King, spitting on your onion rings
Or in the parking lot, circling
Screaming I don't give a fuck!
With his windows down and his system up

So will the real Shady please stand up
And put one of those fingers on each hand up
And be proud to be out of your mind and out of control
And one more time loud as you can
How does it go?

I'm Slim Shady, yes, I'm the real Shady
All you other Slim Shadys are just imitating
So won't the real Slim Shady please stand up
Please stand up
Please stand up.

Cause I'm Slim Shady, yes, I'm the real Shady
All you other Slim Shadys are just imitating
So won't the real Slim Shady please stand up
Please stand up
Please stand up.

Cause I'm Slim Shady, yes, I'm the real Shady
All you other Slim Shadys are just imitating
So won't the real Slim Shady please stand up
Please stand up
Please stand up.

Cause I'm Slim Shady, yes, I'm the real Shady
All you other Slim Shadys are just imitating
So won't the real Slim Shady please stand up
Please stand up
Please stand up.

Ha, ha
Guess there's a Slim Shady in all of us

Fuck it, let's all stand up.

NOTES

1. Clear Channel Communications, Inc., the ultimate parent of Capstar, actually submitted the response. To avoid confusion, however, we will refer to the respondent as Capstar.
2. Letter from Rick Wolf, Corporate Counsel, Clear Channel Communications, Inc., to Charles W. Kelley, Chief, Investigations and Hearings Division, Enforcement Bureau, dated October 10, 2000, at p. 3.
3. *See Peter Branton*, 6 FCC Rcd 610 (1991) (subsequent history omitted).
4. *See, e.g., WQAM License Limited Partnership*, 15 FCC Rcd 2518, *recon. denied*, 15 FCC Rcd 15349 (2000) ("The Girl from Ipanema" parody).
5. *See Jerry Szoka*, 14 FCC Rcd 9857, 9865 (1999); *Southern California Broadcasting Co.*, 6 FCC Rcd 4387 (1991).
6. 47 U.S.C. § 503(b)(2)(D). *See also The Commission's Forfeiture Policy Statement and Amendment of Section 1.80 of the Rules to Incorporate the Forfeiture Guidelines*, 12 FCC Rcd 17087, 17100-01 (1997), *recon. denied*, 15 FCC Rcd 303 (1999) ("*Forfeiture Guidelines*").
7. *Forfeiture Guidelines*, *supra* note 3, 12 FCC Rcd at 17113.
8. 47 U.S.C. § 503(b).
9. 47 C.F.R. §§ 0.111, 0.311, 1.80.
10. 47 C.F.R. § 1.80.
11. See 47 C.F.R. § 1.1914.

APPENDIX J

Before the
Federal Communications Commission
Washington, D.C. 20554

In the Matter of	File No. EB-00-IH-0261
Citicasters Co.	NAL/Acct. No. 200132080027
	Facility ID #18114
Licensee of Station KEGL(FM),	
Fort Worth, Texas	

NOTICE OF APPARENT LIABILITY FOR FORFEITURE

Adopted: March 30, 2001   Released: April 3, 2001
By the Chief, Enforcement Bureau:

I. INTRODUCTION

1. In this Notice of Apparent Liability for Forfeiture ("NAL"), we find that Citicasters Co. ("Citicasters"), licensee of Station KEGL(FM), Fort Worth, Texas, has apparently violated 18 U.S.C. § 1464 and 47 C.F.R. § 73.3999, by willfully and repeatedly broadcasting indecent language. Based on our review of the facts and circumstances in this case, we conclude that Citicasters is apparently liable for a forfeiture in the amount of fourteen thousand dollars ($14,000).

II. BACKGROUND

2. The Commission received a complaint dated August 6, 2000, concerning broadcasts that aired on KEGL on May 30, May 31, August 1 and August 3, 2000. The com-

plaint included transcripts and pictures taken from the station's website. Review of the complaint revealed that the May 30 broadcast occurred at 11 p.m., while the August 1 broadcast did not appear to raise a *prima facie* question of actionable indecency. However, because the May 31 and August 3 broadcasts contained apparently indecent material and aired between 7 p.m. and 10 p.m., we issued a letter of inquiry to the licensee.

3. In its response, Citicasters asserts that it cannot verify whether the material aired. However, the licensee does acknowledge that it admonished "Kramer and Twitch," the hosts of the programs in question, following one of their shows in late May or early June because management believed that certain material may have been inappropriate for the station's audience. With respect to the August 3 broadcast, Citicasters argues that the material allegedly aired was not indecent. Citicasters submits that, at worst, the material includes a "few scattered and vague references of a sexual nature, . . . [which] are neither explicitly graphic nor pandering." Citicasters claims that it has a formal policy prohibiting the broadcast of indecent material; that KEGL's management routinely advises the station's on-air staff of the policy; and that it "vigilantly" monitors the station's broadcasts for compliance. Citicasters also notes that, beginning in December 2000, KEGL began airing the "Kramer and Twitch" program on a 12-hour delayed basis. Citicasters explains that, currently, the program is taped in San Jose, California, and then reviewed and edited by KEGL personnel prior to being broadcast by the station. In addition, KEGL regularly airs a message both before and after the "Kramer and Twitch" show, which notifies listeners that the program may contain material "more suitable for adults."

III. DISCUSSION

4. Section 503(b)(1) of the Communications Act (the "Act"), 47 U.S.C. § 503(b)(1), provides in pertinent part:

> Any person who is determined by the Commission, in accordance with paragraph (3) or (4) of this subsection to have —
>
> . . .
>
> (D) violated any provision of section 1304, 1343, or 1464 of title 18, United States Code; shall be liable to the United States for a forfeiture penalty.

18 U.S.C. § 1464 provides criminal penalties for anyone who "utters any obscene, indecent or profane language by means of radio communication." As explained below, we believe that language broadcast during the May 31 and August 3 programs of "Kramer and Twitch" was indecent and that the licensee's broadcast of that material was willful.

5. The Commission has defined indecent speech as language that, in context, depicts or describes, in terms patently offensive as measured by contemporary community standards for the broadcast medium, sexual or excretory activities or organs. *Infinity Broadcasting Corporation of Pennsylvania*, 2 FCC Rcd 2705 (1987) (subsequent

history omitted) (*citing Pacifica Foundation*, 56 FCC 2d 94, 98 (1975), *aff'd sub nom. FCC v. Pacifica Foundation*, 438 U.S. 726 (1978). The Commission's authority to restrict the broadcast of indecent material extends to times when there is a reasonable risk that children may be in the audience. *Action for Children's Television v. FCC*, 852 F.2d 1332 (D.C. Cir. 1988). Current law holds that such times begin at 6 a.m. and conclude at 10 p.m. *Action for Children's Television v. FCC*, 58 F.3d 654 (D.C. Cir. 1995), *cert. denied*, 116 S.Ct. 701 (1996). Thus, to be actionably indecent, the material in question must not only meet the standard referenced above but also air after 6 a.m. and before 10 p.m. *See* 47 C.F.R. § 73.3999.

6. After carefully considering the record before us, it appears that Citicasters has willfully and repeatedly violated our indecency rule. Citicasters does not deny that it broadcast the language in question before 10 p.m. The May 31 broadcast contains dialogue between the hosts and a teenage female caller, wherein, among other things, the hosts and the caller discuss bisexuality and masturbation, and the hosts attempt to have the caller masturbate during the course of the conversation. The tone of the conversation is pandering and titillating in that the hosts persistently inquire about the caller's frequency and methods of masturbation, and they assert that the caller's father masturbates despite his apparent disapproval of her doing so. As for the August 3 broadcast, we disagree with Citicasters' contention that indecent language was not aired. That broadcast features a conversation between the hosts and an adult film actor and actress. Among other things, they discuss whether the actor's girl friend is bisexual, whether the actress enjoys anal sex, and whether the actress will perform a sexual act on one of the hosts whose penis is "uncut." Once again, the tone of the conversation is pandering and titillating. It appears that both broadcasts were indecent in that they contain patently offensive descriptions of various sexual activities.FN1 The licensee's stated policy against the broadcast of indecent material apparently had no impact on the airing of the cited material, and its current procedures for editing "Kramer and Twitch" and advising audiences about its content have no bearing on whether a forfeiture should be imposed. *See Station KGVL, Inc.*, 42 FCC 2d 258, 259 (1973).

7. Section 503(b) of the Act and 47 C.F.R. § 1.80 both state that any person who willfully or repeatedly fails to comply with the Act or the Commission's rules shall be liable for a forfeiture penalty. For purposes of 47 U.S.C. § 503(b), the term "willful" means that the violator knew that it was taking the action in question, irrespective of any intent to violate the Commission's rules.FN2 As explained above, Citicasters knew that it was broadcasting "Kramer and Twitch" and each of the cited segments. In assessing a forfeiture, we take into account the nature, circumstances, extent and gravity of the violation, and, with respect to the violator, the degree of culpability, any history of prior offenses, ability to pay, and such other matters as justice may require.FN3

8. The Commission's *Forfeiture Guidelines* set a base forfeiture amount of $7,000 for transmission of indecent/obscene materials.FN4 After considering all the facts and circumstances, we believe the base forfeiture amount is the appropriate sanction for each of the two violations described above and that neither an upward nor downward adjustment should be made.

IV. ORDERING CLAUSES

9.   Accordingly, IT IS ORDERED THAT, pursuant to 47 U.S.C. § 503(b), and 47 C.F.R. §§ 0.111, 0.311 and 1.80, Citicasters Co. is hereby NOTIFIED of its APPARENT LIABILITY FOR A FORFEITURE in the amount of fourteen thousand dollars ($14,000) for willfully and repeatedly violating 18 U.S.C. § 1464 and 47 C.F.R. § 73.3999.

10.   IT IS FURTHER ORDERED THAT, pursuant to 47 C.F.R. § 1.80, within thirty days of this NOTICE OF APPARENT LIABILITY, Citicasters Co. SHALL PAY the full amount of the proposed forfeiture or SHALL FILE a written statement seeking reduction or cancellation of the proposed forfeiture.

11.   Payment of the forfeiture may be made by mailing a check or similar instrument, payable to the order of the Federal Communications Commission, to the Forfeiture Collection Section, Finance Branch, Federal Communications Commission, P.O. Box 73482, Chicago, Illinois 60673-7482. The payment should note the NAL/Acct. No. referenced above.

12.   The response, if any, must be mailed to the Charles W. Kelley, Chief, Investigations and Hearings Division, Enforcement Bureau, Federal Communications Commission, 445 12th Street, S.W., Room 3-B443, Washington, D.C. 20554 and MUST INCLUDE THE NAL/Acct. No. referenced above.

13.   The Commission will not consider reducing or canceling a forfeiture in response to a claim of inability to pay unless the respondent submits: (1) federal tax returns for the most recent three-year period; (2) financial statements prepared according to generally accepted accounting practices ("GAAP"); or (3) some other reliable and objective documentation that accurately reflects the respondent's current financial status. Any claim of inability to pay must specifically identify the basis for the claim by reference to the financial documentation submitted.

14.   Requests for payment of the full amount of this Notice of Apparent Liability under an installment plan should be sent to: Chief, Revenue and Receivables Operations Group, 445 12th Street, S.W., Washington, D.C. 20554.FN5

15.   IT IS FURTHER ORDERED THAT a copy of this NOTICE OF APPARENT LIABILITY shall be sent by Certified Mail Return Receipt Requested to Citicasters Co., c/o Kenneth E. Wyker, General Counsel, Clear Channel Communications, Inc., 200 East Basse Road, San Antonio, Texas 78209-8328; with a copy to Elizabeth E. Goldin, Esq., Wiley, Rein & Fielding, 1776 K Street, N.W., Washington, D.C. 20006.

FEDERAL COMMUNICATIONS COMMISSION
David H. Solomon
Chief, Enforcement Bureau

ATTACHMENT

Radio Station: KEGL(FM), Fort Worth, Texas
Date/Time Broadcast: (1) May 31, 2000 at 9 p.m.; (2) August 3, 2000 between 7:45 p.m.–9:15 p.m.

Material Broadcast: (1) Telephone conversation; (2) Interview and commentary
(1) May 31, 2000 (9 p.m.)

MV:	Male Voice(s) (Hosts)
FV:	Caller
Boy:	Caller's brother

MV: So you say you're 17 and your parents won't let you listen to us? Huh?

FV: Yeah, because my dad is like a bishop in my church, and so he thinks you guys are evil.

MV: Are you really 17? What year were you born?

FV: 1983.

MV: I guess that's right. Well, 17, technically, is the legal age of consent. So you really don't need his permission to listen to a radio show.

FV: True. But I still live under his house and so he could kick me out.

MV: What does he say about the show that he doesn't like?

FV: He says it will put evil thoughts in my head and stuff.

MV: What kind of evil thoughts do we put in your head? Have you been thinking about sex?

FV: Well, you guys had that girl on who like wanted to get off on another girl.

MV: Did that turn you on? Any of that?

FV: Yeah.

MV: Do you think you're bi-sexual in any way?

FV: Maybe. And that's why he doesn't like it.

MV: Are you a virgin? Yes?

FV: Yeah.

MV: So your dad blames us. And you may be bi-sexual, right?

FV: He doesn't say that, but he says that the whole pre-marital sex thing is evil.

MV: Of course. Of course, he thinks that. You should be able to make your own decisions. You're 17 years old, and if you wanted to have sex with one of us you could do that legally. We could have sex with you. And I think we should just because of her father.

How many times a week do you masturbate? How many times?

FV: Probably about four or five.

MV: How do you do it?

FV: It's private.

MV: Do you put your finger in or do you move it around? Do you use a vibrator? Where do you masturbate? In the shower?

FV:	In my room, usually.
MV:	How do you do it?
FV:	I get on my back and start touching myself.
MV:	How? It's okay. Really, you can tell us. Do you ever touch yourself through your panties? You know, just on the outside to get yourself revved up. Describe the whole thing. I want to hear it. Just tell me little details. First of all, tell me, do you shave?
FV:	Yes, but that's because my cousin taught me how to.
MV:	Who taught you how? Is it a female or a guy?
FV:	Well, she told me you kind'a have to because when guys are down there they don't want to . . . so.
MV:	So it's shaved and bald. What do you do when you masturbate? Ah, this is turning me so on. Who do you think about?
FV:	I do it like under the water thing.
MV:	In the bathtub? Do you do that?
FV:	It was really . . .
MV:	Nice? What do you sound like when you have an orgasm? Moan?
FV:	Hmm. Well, actually quiet so that my parents don't hear.
MV:	Your father would get mad if he thought you were masturbating?
FV:	He walked in on me one time.
MV:	Oh, God! What I would do to walk in on you masturbating, no doubt! What did he do to you?
FV:	He made me read every single Scripture that. . . .
MV:	What do you look like, sweetie?
FV:	Tall, thin.
MV:	How much do you weigh?
FV:	Probably 145.
MV:	So what do the Scriptures say about masturbating?
FV:	He gave me the one about David and Bathsheba. He had unclean thoughts about her bathing. And then he goes into the book of Romans.
MV:	Can I tell you something about your dad real quick, honey? And I am going to be painfully honest. He's been whacking off since he was 12 years old. Yes he has. He does it every single night whether he has sex with your mom or not. He thinks about other women besides your mom.
FV:	I know that my father and mom still do because she's been pregnant recently.
MV:	So he still masturbates. A guy always masturbates. So how do you feel when we tell you your dad masturbates? Is that gross?
FV:	I don't want to think about that.
MV:	He's probably twisting them off in the bathroom right now.

Have you ever kissed a girl?

FV:	No.
MV:	Have you ever wanted to?
FV:	Yeah.
MV:	When you are hanging out with your girlfriends, have you ever fantasized about going back to their house and having a sleep-over?
FV:	My freshman year in high school there was a girl who told me she liked me, and we were going to have a sleepover but my dad met her. . . .
MV:	That son-of-a-bitch! That bastard! That a-hole!

Do you have a car?

FV:	On the weekends.
MV:	Tell you what. We'll let you come up here, and we'll find a really attractive woman that you can sleep with.

Would you masturbate in front of us?

FV:	Uhm, I don't know.
MV:	Why not? You're 17. That's not crazy! You're totally legal. I think we could get you up here. I think we can get you to buzz your beaver in front of us.
FV:	I've never even like French-kissed a guy.
MV:	Oh well, of course, we'll take care of that! We'll do that for the first time here. We will corrupt you, baby! Hmmm. You won't even want to go home after this. You know what? You will be tearing pages out of your daddy's Bible. You're 17. You'll be smoking them! You're 17. You're legal. You can do whatever you want.

Are you a little turned on right now?

FV:	Well, yeah.
MV:	Would you masturbate on the phone for us?
FV:	I don't know.
MV:	Just do it a little bit. Now, we are going to turn off the microphone and be real quiet. We want to hear you moan. Go ahead. Go ahead.
FV:	I'm going to be embarrassed.
MV:	Go ahead, baby. Don't worry. It's kind of erotic. The mikes are off.
FV:	I like quietly whimper.
MV:	That's cool. Just do it, and we're turning the mikes off right now.
FV:	Okay. Bye-bye.

Colt, are you on the phone?

Boy:	Hello. Yeah.
FV:	Get off the phone!
MV:	Oh my God! Hey, Kenneth, are you the brother?
Boy:	Uh-huh.
MV:	Do you ever watch her at night while she's masturbating?
FV:	Don't say that!
Boy:	Do what?
FV:	Don't say that! Don't say that!
MV:	God [bleep] son-of-a-bitch! Whore! [Beep] sucker! She's dogging her vagina every single night with your dad's flashlight!
FV:	Hang up the phone!
MV:	God [beep]! God [beep]! You're going to hell! You're a sinner! I can't believe you're pregnant, you bitch! You're a whore!
FV:	Hang up the phone!
Boy:	What kind of [unintelligible] is this?
MV:	[Laughter]
Announcer:	Extreme night-time radio with Kramer and Twitch on 97.1, the Eagle.

(2) August 3, 2000 (7:45 p.m. to 9:15 p.m.)

MV:	Male Voice(s) (Hosts)
MV2:	Adult-film actor (Carlos)
FV:	Adult-film actress (Gina)
MV3:	Hosts' assistant (Frat)
MV:	Carlos is on the way and porno chicks.
. . .	
MV:	We also have Gina Rider. She's a porn star. She's going to be performing at the Clubhouse.

9:30 your first show, right?

FV:	Yes, and midnight.
MV:	You've done a couple hundred adult films, almost 200. You're from San Antonio. You've got a boyfriend?
FV:	Noooooooooo.
MV:	Are you having sex with us?
FV:	Who?
MV:	If she says no, it's a joke. If she says yes, let's do it!
MV:	So, Carlos, you're on the road all the time, especially with this tour. How's your sex life?
MV2:	Great! It really is, dude.
MV:	Carlos, I know you, and you're so business-minded. You don't drink. I bet you don't bang chicks on the road.

MV2:	No, I don't.
MV:	Do you have a girlfriend?
MV2:	Remember that tall blonde, thin chick?
MV:	Is she hot?
MV2:	Unbelievable, dude!
MV:	Is she Mexican?
MV2:	No. She's a white girl from Oregon.
MV:	Traitor!
MV2:	Traitor? What are you talking about, dude?
MV:	It's still pink in the middle.
MV2:	Exactly!
MV:	You are faithful to her?
MV2:	Yeah. I may talk a lot of smack, dude, but you know.
MV:	Is she faithful to you?
MV2:	I have no idea, dude.
MV:	Wait. Now is a blow [beep] cheating?
MV2:	I tell her this. If you cheat on me, and it's a mistake, just don't tell me.
MV:	A mistake? I fell on a penis. It slipped and fell in. . . .
MV2:	If she slips and falls into a pair of hairy [beep]. Just ignore it. I don't need that phone call.
MV:	Is she in town now? Is she touring with you?
MV2:	She usually comes. She took this week off.
MV:	Are you coming with us tonight? We're going to the Clubhouse tonight.
MV2:	Of course. I'm getting in trouble. She has friends here who are listening in to the show, and I am going to get a phone call.
MV:	Does she get angry when you go to a boob bar?
MV2:	I don't know. Sometimes.
MV:	Is she jealous?
MV2:	Sometimes. But she's freaky, though. She fulfills those, like, you know. . . .
MV:	Threesomes?
MV2:	She does some crazy stuff, dude.
MV:	Is she bi? Does she monge?
MV2:	No, no, no. She don't do that. It's hard enough to please one chick to do it well. Am I right? Hard enough to really please you and make you feel like. . . . I'm talking about in real life.
MV:	You've even said it on your tape before. Why is it when a woman doesn't have an orgasm, why is it my fault? It's not your fault! It's not your fault, Carlos. Come on!
MV2:	I know it's not my fault. But what I'm saying is it's hard to please one woman.
MV:	That's what the other bitch is for, Carlos!

MV2:	Yeah, but then the talk after. It's like bitch in stereo! Oh my God, you didn't do it right! And what about my left boob? I would just kill myself, dude.
MV:	We're going to talk to Gina Rider. Keep it on the Eagle.

[Music]

MV:	What do you look like, girl? You are gorgeous, girl! Oh my God! She sneezed and her boobs popped out. She just said, "I'm going to get naked." You can take off that dress if you want.
MV2:	Very nice booty, man. And she says she enjoys the back door action.
MV:	Oh, you do?
FV:	I love it!
MV:	For the first time? You just had your first back door?
FV:	No. I've been doing it in my personal life for about a year now. But I just did my first scene on camera like two months ago. It was great!
MV:	We're going to come back and see what happens here in the studio. Mmm, mmm, mmm, delicious!

. . .

MV:	Who give a crap! Frat boy is in his boxers right now. I have a feeling something is going to go down in here. Are you willing to get naked, Frat? Take them off.
MV3:	I am not getting all the way butt naked. I can't do that.
MV:	None of us guys want to see your peepee. And she's seen tons of them. I've got one, man. Come on!
MV2:	I'll pull it out just so you feel comfortable.
MV:	Frat, you'll go and whip it out in a bar and go and talk to people with your peepee out.
MV3:	But I am usually like lit, dude, when I am doing that.
MV:	Puss, puss, puss!
MV2:	I'll pull it out, and mine's got a hood on it. How bad could yours be?
MV:	[To FV] Cut or uncut, how do you like them?
FV:	I've been playing with cut, uncut, lately. I've always had cut, and my [beep] buddy's uncut.
MV3:	I'm uncut, baby! I've got a chance!
MV:	I want to ask her to have sex with me, but I'm not in front of you because you're going to mess it up. She might say, "Yeah." But you, my friend, would screw it up!

O.K., so get naked, Gina.

MV2:	Dude! What is wrong with you, bro?

MV:	I just don't want someone that looks like you to sleep with her. Look at her. She is phenomenally gorgeous. It would hurt my feelings.
MV2:	Ah, poor fatso!
FV:	We're all hanging out tonight, right?
MV:	All right, Gina. Your new flick is "Skin Tight," and you are 23, and you've been doing porno since you were how old?
FV:	21.
MV:	So, will you demonstrate on Frat? You know, wrestlers have moves and stuff. Porno stars have got to have something that they do that makes them special. Frat, get naked!

Do you have some kind of signature move that is yours like . . .

[To Frat] Grab your ankles and like take off your pants. Don't be a pud! Get naked!

MV3:	Who's going hold the mike?
MV2:	That's not your problem, dude. You're a big fat puss!
MV:	You're going to get naked in front of a porn star.
MV2:	What are you afraid of? She's like a doctor. She's seen it.
MV:	Gina, how far would you go with Frat in here? He's a pretty good looking guy. Nothing he's got is going to compare to anything you've seen before. Nothing. We've seen it.
FV:	I've got to see what he looks like.
MV:	Take it off, Frat! Take it off!
MV2:	Did you see that look of horror?

NOTES

1. See, e.g., Citicasters Co. (WXTB(FM)), 13 FCC Rcd 15381 (Mass Media Bureau 1998). See also Regent Licensee of Flagstaff, Inc. (KZGL(FM)), 15 FCC Rcd 17286 (Enforcement Bureau 2000).

2. See Jerry Szoka, 14 FCC Rcd 9857, 9865 (1999); Southern California Broadcasting Co., 6 FCC Rcd 4387 (1991).

3. 47 U.S.C. § 503(b)(2)(D). See also The Commission's Forfeiture Policy Statement and Amendment of Section 1.80 of the Rules to Incorporate the Forfeiture Guidelines, 12 FCC Rcd 17087, 17100-01 (1997), recon. denied, 15 FCC Rcd 303 (1999) ("Forfeiture Guidelines").

4. Forfeiture Guidelines, 12 FCC Rcd at 17113.

5. See 47 C.F.R. § 1.1914.

FURTHER READING

Allen, Steve. *Vulgarians at the Gate: Trash TV and Raunch Radio.* New York: Prometheus Books, 2001.

Barker, David. *Rushed to Judgment: Talk Radio, Persuasion, and American Political Behavior.* New York: Columbia University Press, 2002.

Benjamin, Louise. *Freedom of the Air and the Public Interest: First Amendment in Broadcasting to 1935.* Carbondale: Southern Illinois University Press, 2001.

Bruce, Tammy. *The New Thought Police.* New York: Prima Publishing, 2001.

Carter, T. Barton, Marc A. Franklin and Jay B. Wright. *The First Amendment and the Fifth Estate: Regulation of Electronic Mass Media,* 5th ed. New York: Foundation Press, 1999.

Colford, Paul D. *Howard Stern: King of All Media.* New York: Diane Publishing, 1996.

Douglas, Susan J. *Listening In.* New York: Times Books, 1996.

Fish, Stanley. *There's No Such Thing as Free Speech.* New York: Oxford University Press, 1994.

Foerstel, Herbert N. *Banned in the Media.* Westport, Conn.: Greenwood Publishing, 1998.

Greenberg, B. S., J. D. Brown and N. L. Buerkel-Rothfuss. *Media, Sex and the Adolescent.* Cresskill, N.J.: Hampton Press, 1993.

Gunter, Barrie. *Media Sex: What Are the Issues?* Mahwah, N.J.: Lawrence Erlbaum Associates, 2002.

Hamilton, Maureen, ed. *Obscenity and Pornography Decisions of the United States Supreme Court.* New York: Excellent Books, 2000.

Harrison, Maureen and Steve Gilbert, eds. *Obscenity and Pornography Decisions of the United States Supreme Court.* New York: Excellent Books, 2000.

Harvey, Philip D. *The Government vs. Erotica.* New York: Prometheus Books, 2001.

Heins, Marjorie. *Not in Front of the Children: Indecency, Censorship, and the Innocence of Youth.* New York: Hill and Wang Publishing, 2001.

Hilliard, Robert L. and Michael C. Keith. *The Broadcast Century and Beyond: A History of American Radio and Television.* Boston: Butterworth–Heinemann/Focal Press, 2001.

————. *The Quieted Voice: The Rise and Demise of Local Radio.* Carbondale, IL: Southern Illinois Press, 2005.

Jones, Derek, ed. *Censorship: A World Encyclopedia.* Chicago: Fitzroy Dearborn, 2001.

Keith, Michael C. *Sounds in the Dark: All Night Radio in American Life.* Ames: Iowa State University Press, 2001.

————. *Talking Radio: An Oral History of Radio in the Television Age.* Armonk, N.Y.: M. E. Sharpe, 2000.

Legal Guide to Broadcast Law and Regulation. Washington: NAB, 1998.

Lipschultz, Jeremy H. *Broadcast Indecency: F.C.C. Regulations and the First Amendment.* Boston: Focal Press, 1996. Millwood-Hargrave, A. *Sex and Sexuality in Broadcasting.* London: John Libbey, 1992.

Overbeck, Wayne. *Major Principles of Media Law.* Fort Worth, TX: Harcourt Brace, 2003.

Pease, Allison. *Modernism, Mass Culture, and the Aesthetics of Obscenity.* London: Cambridge University Press, 2000.

Roussomano, Joseph. *Speaking Our Minds: Conversations with the People Behind Landmark First Amendment Cases.* Mahwah, N.J.: Lawrence Erlbaum Associates, 2002.

Sterling, Christopher H. and John Michael Kittross. *Stay Tuned: A History of American Broadcasting.* Mahwah, NJ: Lawrence Erlbaum, 2002.

Tedford, Thomas L. and Dale A. Herbeck. *Freedom of Speech in the United States*, 4th ed. State College, Pa.: Strata Publishing Company, 2001.

Teeter, Dwight L. and Bill Loving. *Law of Mass Communications: Freedom and Control of Print and Broadcast Media.* New York: Foundation Press, 2001.

Tillinghast, Charles H. *American Broadcast Regulation and the First Amendment.* Ames: Iowa State University Press, 2000.

Wright, George. *Selling Words: Free Speech in a Communication Culture.* New York: New York University Press, 1997.

INDEX

letter to Infinity Broadcasting from,
242–3
and Mae West incident, 10
Notice of Apparent Liability against
Capstar TX Partnership by,
254–67
Notice of Apparent Liability against
Citicasters Co. by, 262–72
Notice of Apparent Liability filed
against Infinity Broadcasting by,
242–3
Notice of Apparent Liability filed
against KBOO Foundation by,
247–53
Notice of Apparent Liability filed
against WGLD by, 61
reaction of, to topless radio, 60
regulation of obscenity by, 61–2
"safe harbor" standards established
by, 34–5, 37
Sarah Jones files suit against, 94
and "Seven Dirty Words" case, 26
stance on enforcement of prohibition
against obscene and indecent
broadcasts, 200–2
station call letters screened by, 124
strong stance taken by on
enforcement of prohibition of
indecent broadcasts, 200–2
television and indecency
determinations by, 36
and topless radio, 17
2001 Policy Statement on statutory
basis for actions by, 114–16
web site of, 122
Federal Communications Committee
Commissioners, 149, 150, 151
indecency rules and cable and
satellite, 149–50
invalid complaints, 147
petition filed against, 149
Federal Council of Churches of Christ
in America, 120
Federal Radio Act of 1927, 6
Federal Radio Commission, 2, 6, 85

Felling, Matthew, 124
Female shock jocks, 78–9
Feminine Forum, 53, 57, 58, 60
Femme Forum, 58, 61–3
as FCC test case, 61–3
and Notice of Apparent Liability,
61
Ferris, Charles, 27
Fifth Amendment, 43
"Filthy Words" monologue. *See* "Seven
Dirty Words" case
Fines, 35, 37, 38, 40, 43, 47, 66, 102,
105, 108, 109, 112, 203–6. *See
also* Notices of Apparent
Liability
and child pornography over Internet,
43
of college radio stations, 93
and early talk shows, 53
against Emmis Communications,
146
increase in levels, 146
against Infinity Broadcasting, 35,
146
against *Johnson and Tofte* morning
show, 79–80
movie, 123
refusal to pay, 115
against Sonderling Broadcasting,
62–3
and topless radio, 63
against Viacom, 145
webcast, 136
Finland, concern with indecency in the
media in, 137–8
First Amendment, 25, 26, 28, 34, 36,
40, 41, 43, 46, 126–7, 150,
159
and Children's Internet Protection
Act, 44
guarantees by, 10–12
and indecent speech, 45
protections under and *Federal
Communications Commission v.
Pacifica Foundation*, 164, 173

Hemingway, Ernest, 7
Herb v. Pitcairn, 168
"Here Comes the Missus" (song), 84
Heresy, 3
Heritage Foundation, 125
Hess v. Indiana, 173, 178
Hicklin, Benjamin, 4
Hicklin rule, 4, 5
Hiram College, 121
HMV, 97
Holiday, Billie, 87
Hollywood blacklists, 159
Holmes, Justice Oliver Wendell, opinion
    in *Schenck v. United States*, 172
Holmes, Peter, 4
Home Dish Satellite Network, 123
"Homosapien," 97
Homosexuality, talk radio and emotions
    around, 52
"Honey Love," 96
"Honky Tonk Angel," 97
Hooks, Benjamin, 27
"Hot talk" format, 79
HotWired (magazine), 220
House Subcommittee on
    Communications, 61
Howard Stern Show, 103–4
  complaints in Canada about, 119
  and FCC fines, 66–7, 70
  FCC indecency rules implementation
    and, 32
  FCC Notices of Apparent Liability
    filed against Infinity
    Broadcasting and, 37, 67–70,
    242–4
  right-wing calls for monitoring of, 29,
    30
HRW. *See* Human Rights Watch
Hudson, Al, 89
Hughes, Gregg, 75
Human Rights Watch, 232
  Communications Decency Act of
    1996 provisions challenged by,
    218, 227
Hutton, Rose, 57

I Ain't Never (song), 12
"I Am the Walrus," 97
"I Can't Control Myself," 97
"I Can't Get No Satisfaction," 88
Idaho Microwave, Inc. v. FCC, 192n.11
IGC, *See* Institute for Global
    Communications
*Illinois Citizens Committee for
    Broadcasting v. FCC*, 185,
    193n.16
"I'm Not Your Puppet" (song), 93
Imus, Don, 29, 65, 73, 74, 135
Indecency, 2, 23
  amount of fines, 145, 146
  difference between political satire
    and, 94
  FCC primer on, 203
  FCC 1987 statement of its authority
    regarding, and definition of,
    91
  FCC 2001 Policy Statement on,
    93
  historical concepts of, 3
  lack of clear definitions on,
    11
  and noncommercial radio stations,
    121
  objections to subject matter
    differentiated from, 114
  number of complaints, 145, 150–1
  regulations, 150
  violations, 146
Indecent broadcasts, FCC takes strong
    stance on enforcement of
    prohibition of, 200–2
"Indecency clause," early violations of,
    6
Indecent language, obscene language
    versus, 17
Indecent programming, FCC 24-hour
    ban on, 33
Indecent speech
  and First Amendment protection,
    45
  radio stations fined for, 14

MacDonald, Torbert, 61
Madison School District v. Wisconsin Employment Relations Comm'n., 194n.21
Madonna, 91, 97
Magazines, 12, 13, 14
Mail
and criminalization of obscene materials sent through, 4–5
"Makin' Bacon," 31–2
Malthus, Thomas Robert, 119
"Mambo Italiano" (song), 87
Manual Enterprises, Inc. v. Day, 170, 190
Mapplethorpe, Robert, 92
Market transformations, and broadcast industry, 115
Marks v. United States, 190
Marshall, Justice Thurgood, opinion in *Federal Communications Commission v. Pacifica Foundation*, 165, 181, 189
Martin, Dean, 87
Martin, Kevin, 147, 150, 151
Martin, Ron, 57
Massachusetts, publishing activities criminalized by colonial legislature in, 3
Mass Communication (Barnouw), 159
Mass media, 2
Maurstad, Tom, 124–5
MCA, 89, 90
McCarthy, Charlie (Edgar Bergen's dummy), 8
McCarthy period, 159
McCullagh, Declan, 220, 236
McGeady, Paul J., 133
McKinney, James, 30
McNinch, Frank R., 10, 142
Media marketplace, and programming decisions, 117. *See also* Ratings
Meeks, Brock, 220, 236
Meier, Gary, 73
Meir-Weil, Dr. Yaakov, 138
Memoirs v. Massachusetts, 184
Metromedia, 55, 60

Meyer Music Markets, 90
Miami Herald, editorial on FCC in, 48
Miami Herald Publishing Co. v. Tornillo, 174
Michael, George, 90
Middle Ages, censorship in Europe during, 3
Midnighters, 96
Miller, Henry, 247
Miller, Marvin, 15
Miller v. California, 15, 16, 127, 170, 173, 179, 189, 190, 194n.19, 197n.2, 200
MIM. *See* Morality in Media
Minow, Newton, 27
Monday Night Football, 147
Monetary forfeitures, 102. *See also* Fines
Moore, Morgan, 58
Moore v. East Cleveland, 189
Moorman Mfg. Co. v. Bair, 198n.2
Morality in Media, 29, 126, 155
"clarifications" by, 126
open letter to Congress members from, 131–3
Morals argument, and obscenity laws, 155
Morrison, Van, 88
Motion picture industry rating system, 40
Movement to Restore Democracy, 88
Movies, and FCC fines, 123
MSO. *See* Multiple-systems owner
MTV, 90, 91
Mt. Wilson FM Broadcasters, 150
Mueller, Erich "Mancow," 74, 76, 153
Multimedia dirty discourse, 121–4
Multiple-system owners, 91
Multnomah County Library v. United States, 44
Music
censorship of, 85–99
changing perceptions and censoring of, 87–99
FCC indecency classifications and, 107–10

indecency complaints against, 85
labeling of, 96
Music Plus, 99

NAB. *See* National Association of
Broadcasters
NAB Board, 150
Nader, Ralph, 27
NALs. *See* Notices of Apparent Liability
National Association of Broadcasters,
28, 36, 59, 90, 119, 124
*National Association of Theatre Owners v.
FCC*, 192n.11
National Endowment for the Arts, 92,
93
National Federation of Community
Broadcasters, 149
National Federation for Decency, 29
National Hispanic Media Coalition,
123
National Parents-Teachers Association,
28
National Writers Union
Communications Decency Act of
1996 provisions challenged by,
216, 218, 230
Navarro, Mireya, 124
NBC, 41, 118, 120
broadcasting of *Beyond the Horizon*
on, 121
Chase and Sanborn Hour on, 1, 8, 9
song censors at, 9
Ness, Ralph, 149
Ness, Susan, 115
Newspapers, 14
complaints sent to, 134–5
Newsweek, 74
Newton John, Olivia, 90
New York Times Co. v. Sullivan, 194
New York v. Ferber, 29
NFD. *See* National Federation for
Decency
Nixon, Richard, 88, 89
Notices of Apparent Liability, 13, 37,
114–15, 131. *See also* Fines

against Capstar TX Limited
Partnership, 254–61
against Citicasters Co., 262–72
against Infinity Broadcasting, 35, 37,
61–4, 251–2
against KBOO Foundation, 247–53
protests against, 112
and State University of New York
FM station, 93
and University of Pennsylvania, 26
against WGLD and *Femme Forum*, 61
Nuzum, Eric, 87, 99
NWU. *See* National Writers Union
NYPD Blue (television program), 37

Oboler, Arch, 1
Obscene material, definition of, by
Supreme Court, 2
*Obscene Profits: The Entrepreneurs of
Pornography in the Cyber Age*, 122
Obscene Publications Act (or Lord
Campbell's Act), influence of, 4
Obscene speech, and Congressional
initiatives, 33
Obscenity
FCC regulation of, 61–3
first convictions for, 3
influence of Hicklin rule and
judgments on, 64
lack of clear definitions on, 13
Potter Stewart on, 2
roots behind defining and controlling
of, 3
and *Roth v. United States*, 11–12
Supreme Court's definition of, 14
"Obscenity: The Case for a Free Market
in Free Speech," 156
*Office of Communication of United Church
of Christ v. FCC*, 169
Ohralik v. Ohio State Bar Ass'n., 196n.3
Once and Again (drama series), 156
O'Neill, Eugene, 10, 121
"One Toke over the Line," 96
On Golden Pond (play), 125
Online discussion groups, 223

INDEX